Creating and Governing an Integrated Market for Retail Banking Services in Europe

Corporate Finance and Governance

Herausgegeben von Dirk Schiereck

Band 5

PETER LANG

Frankfurt am Main · Berlin · Bern · Bruxelles · New York · Oxford · Wien

Matthäus Markus Sielecki

Creating and Governing an Integrated Market for Retail Banking Services in Europe

A Conceptual-Empirical Study of the Role of Regulation in Promoting a Single Euro Payments Area

PETER LANG
Internationaler Verlag der Wissenschaften

Bibliographic Information published by the Deutsche Nationalbibliothek
The Deutsche Nationalbibliothek lists this publication in the Deutsche Nationalbibliografie; detailed bibliographic data is available in the internet at http://dnb.d-nb.de.

Zugl.: European Business School, Diss., 2010

Cover Design:
Olaf Glöckler, Atelier Platen, Friedberg

D 1540
ISSN 1869-537X
ISBN 978-3-631-60834-0

Preface

Regulation of banking markets is a large and exiting field of research that has increasingly gained importance with the creation of the single economic area and the introduction of the euro currency. Over the past decades, EU market regulation has enforced the political desire to make the integrated European market more tangible and beneficial for its more than 350 million citizens. From my work in a European bank, I experienced how much of the banking industry's operations and business is affected by regulation: deposit protection rules, capital requirements and credit regulation are only few to mention. While most of these policies aim to achieve greater stability in the banking sector and to minimize economic damage, new EU legislation has started to intervene directly in the industry's sovereignty of setting prices for selective banking products and services. Studying the implementation process of an EU price-regulation on cross-border payments prompted me to look beyond the obvious motives of EU regulation from both a theoretical and an empirical point of view.

Writing this thesis as an external Ph.D. student at the EBS University and in parallel to my full-time employment allowed me to combine the inspiring exchange of ideas with my fellow researchers and professors and the practical views of professionals in the banking industry. It was exciting and instructive to look for answers to my research question in both the academic as well as in the business and political areas of regulation.

My greatest professional debt in writing this book is to my two supervisors: Professor Dr. Joachim Ahrens and Professor Dr. Dirk Schiereck. Joachim Ahrens, my first supervisor, has wholeheartedly believed in a successful completion of this book and spent many hours inspiring, encouraging and providing me with detailed comments on the ideas developed in this book. I also greatly appreciate Dirk Schiereck's continuous support, his valuable professional input on the banking focus of this study and his offer to include this book in his series *Corporate Finance and Governance*. Both supervisors' faith in this study was instrumental in moving it forward.

While writing this book, I was fortunate to benefit from a particularly favorable and flexible study environment at the EBS University. I owe a special thanks to Eliane Zapp-Roussel for all the help and good advice during my Ph.D. studies.

More than most, this study would have been impossible without the exceptional encouragement, support and faith from numerous persons.

I am extremely grateful to my best friend Dr. Joachim Vogt, who wrote his dissertation at the same time as me and was a constant source of support and motivation for this book. Joachim read several versions of this manuscript, and every time provided me with insightful comments, made corrections and pointed out omissions. Our intellectual discussions have always been a source of inspiration for me – for this book, but also during our long-term friendship.

I also owe special thanks to my great friends: Dr. Patrick Heinecke, Dr. Patrick Heinemann and Dr. Björn Schmidt, who have been my supportive and motivating companions on this challenging academic journey and have always pushed me in moving this study forward. I also found great personal recognition and encouragement for my dissertation project in parallel to my work from Dr. Burkhard Ziegenhorn and Dr. Daniel Zapf.

The deepest debts are the most personal. I thank my family, in particular my parents, who have enthusiastically supported and motivated me since I started this research project. I devote a significant part of this dissertation to my grandparents and Dr. Witold Kowalenko. My grandfather has always been interested in the results of my work and I have enjoyed our intensive intellectual discussions about all kinds of areas of life.

Finally, I dedicate this book to my beloved wife, Anna, in gratitude for her patience, support and gentle encouragement. Anna has stood by me throughout the writing of my dissertation, and has always been my constant source of strength, joy and inspiration. Without her, I would have not been able to complete this book.

Schwalbach am Taunus, January 2011 Matthäus Sielecki

Foreword

Since the Treaty of Lisbon came into force in 2009, extensive amendments to the Treaty have been made to reform many areas of European law, empowering the European Commission and the European Parliament to implement orders for EU legislative acts. At the same time, the economic impact of the credit crisis and the threat of sovereign default of EU member states have demonstrated the pressing need for a debate on principles about the institutional design of an integrated financial area in Europe. In this respect, political and academic discussions have centered either on the up- and downsides of a European policy-driven versus a market-driven integration process, or on the territorial distribution of political powers and competencies between the EU- and the member state level.

This book is a valuable contribution to the academic discussion about the role of regulation in facilitating the creation of a single financial market in Europe in general, and the banking market in particular. The author presents a comprehensive analysis of different regulation theories and explains why traditional approaches fall short in justifying regulatory intervention by the EU to create a single market. The conceptual framework developed in this book provides theoretical insights into the interconnection of the functional and the territorial dimensions of regulation research and into methods to ex-ante evaluate the effectiveness and efficiency of regulatory measures in a structured way. Matthäus Sielecki illustrates the practical application of this framework to the European retail payments market and examines the impact of the cross-border payments directive and the Single Euro Payments Area (SEPA) project to deliver on this directive in a detailed case study to answer his research question on the role of regulation in market integration.

The case of European integration shows that institutions matter. However, appropriate rules require an effective enforcement, which is not always the case when applying EU directives to harmonize the financial market. The theoretical implications derived in this book stress the importance of effective governance to implement and enforce public policies and to improve private sector coordination. For market practitioners and EU policy makers, the overall findings will be relevant for their decision-making. The fact that a single market in retail banking has not yet evolved is less a sign for market or coordination failure than of government failure: artificial and regulatory barriers need to be removed in a first instance to provide a level playing field for banks and payment service providers on the one hand and a safe and trustworthy legal environment for consumers on the other. Here, the legislative bodies of the EU should focus on their core competency as regulators to achieve harmonization in these areas first, even if political resistance from the EU member states will be very high.

In the aftermath of the worldwide banking crisis and the need for the EU to develop harmonized rules to ensure financial market stability (and to avoid a regulatory 'race to the bottom' or an arbitrage among member states), a centrally led supervisory agency is deemed necessary. However, this may be implemented only at the expense of national supervisory agencies that will have to hand over responsibility and sovereignty to the EU level. A strong political determination, supported by all heads of government and inspired by the European idea is critical to establish a single market with a central supervisory agency.

This balanced, theoretically and conceptually well grounded analysis will benefit a wide range of readers in the academic as well as in the business and policy-making communities. The book significantly contributes to a better understanding of harmonization processes and regulation needs in financial and banking markets.

Göttingen, January 2011 Prof. Dr. Joachim Ahrens

Table of content

List of tables

List of figures

List of abbreviations

ACH	Automated Clearing House
AT	Austria
ATM	Automated Teller Machine
BACS	Bankers Automated Clearing System
BCG	Boston Consulting Group
BE	Belgium
BEUC	Bureau Européen des Union Consommateurs
BIC	Bank Identifier Code
BIS	Bank for International Settlements
bn	Billion
BNB/ NBB	Banque Nationale de Belgique/ Nationale Bank van België
BSC	Banking Supervisory Committee
CBF	Commission Bancaire et Financière/Commissie voor het Bank- en Financiewezen (Banking and Finance Commission)
CEBS	Committee of European Banking Supervisors
CEIOPS	Committee of European Insurance and Occupational Pensions Supervisors
CESR	Committee of European Securities Regulators
CESR	Committee of European Securities Regulators
CIS	Conference of Insurance Supervisory Authorities
cp.	Compare
CSM	Clearing and Settlement Mechanisms
CY	Cyprus
DE	Germany
DEA	Data Envelopment Analysis
DMUs	Decision-Making Units

DTA	Datenträgeraustausch - Data exchange
EACB	European Association of Co-operative Banks
EACHA	European ACH Association
EACT	European Associations of Corporate Treasurers
EAPB	The European Association of Public Banks
EBA	Euro Banking Association
EBF	European Banking Federation
EC	European Committee
ECB	European Central Bank
ECOFIN	EU Council on Economic and Financial Affairs
ECON	Committee on Economic and Monetary Affairs
EEA	European Economic Area
EFMA	European Financial Management & Marketing Association
EFR	European Financial Services Roundtable
EFSA	EU regulatory and supervisory authority
EMU	Economic and Monetary Union
EMZ/ RPS	Elektronischer Massenzahlungsverkehr/ Retail Payment System
EPC	European Payments Council
ES	Spain
ESBG	European Savings Banks Group
ESCB	European System of Central Banks
ESFSA	European System of Financial Supervisory Authorities
et al.	et alii
EU	European Union
FI	Finland
FISIM	Financial Intermediation Services Indirectly Measured
FR	France
FSA	Financial Services Authority

FSAP	Financial Services Action Plan
GDP	Gross Domestic Product
GR	Greece
HICP	Harmonized Indices of Consumer Prices
ibid.	ibidem
i.e.	id est
IAS	International Accounting Standards
IBAN	International Bank Account Number
IE	Ireland
IFRS	International Financial Reporting Standards
IGC	Inter-Governmental Conference
IIMG	Inter-Institutional Monitoring Group
IPI	International Payment Instruction
ISO	International Organization for Standardization
IT	Information Technology
IT	Italy
KWG	Kreditwesengesetz
LLR	Lender of Last Resort
LOOP	Law Of One Price
LP	Lamfalussy Process
LU	Luxembourg
M&A	Mergers and Acquisitions
MEP	Members of the European Parliament
MoU	Memoranda of Understanding
MT	Malta
NCBs	National Central Banks
NIE	New Institutional Economics
NL	Netherlands

OCA/CDV	Office de Contrôle des Assurances/ Centrale dienst voor verzekeringen (Insurance Control Office)
OECD	Organisation for Economic Co-operation and Development
PE-ACH	Pan-European Automated Clearing Houses
PR	Property Rights
PSD	Payment Services Directive
PT	Portugal
RPE	Regulation (EC) 2560/2001 on Cross-border payments in Euro
SCT	SEPA Credit Transfer
SDD	SEPA Direct Debit
SEC	Securities and Exchange Commission
SECA	SEPA Euro Cash Area Framework
SEM	Single European Market
SEPA	Single Euro Payments Area
SI	Slovenia
SIT	Système Interbancaire de Télécompensation
SK	Slovakia
SMEs	Medium-size enterprises
STEP2	Straight-Through Euro Payments
STET	Systèmes Technologiques d'Echange et de Traitement
STP	Straight-Through Processing
SWIFT	Society for Worldwide Interbank Financial Telecommunication
TARGET	Trans-European Automated Real-time Gross Settlement Express Transfer System
TC	Transaction Costs
TCE	Transaction Costs Economics
U.K.	United Kingdom

UCITS	Undertakings for Collective Investments in Transferable Securities
US	United States
XCT	Cross-border credit transfers

A Introduction

1. Research problem and relevance

1.1 Financial market integration and economic development in Europe

> "This policy [for a supranational union], which is far removed from all emotionalism and passions, does not require us to forget the past or be careless about the future. It must be and must always be based on both reason and on experience."
>
> Robert Schuman, 16th May 1949, at the Festival Hall in Strasbourg.

To answer the question on the driving force for an integrated market in Europe, it is worth recalling that this endeavor has always been politically motivated. Known as one of the fathers of modern Europe, Jean Monnet (1943) advocated the formation of the *United States of Europe* as a guarantee of prosperity and social development. However, the means have always been of an economic nature. The Treaty of Rome constituted the creation of a unified economic area with a common market as the mission of the Community (European Community, 1957). Therefore, the pursuit of a single European banking market could be understood as a fundamental part of the European integration project, motivated by benefits for the financial sector as well as for firms and consumers.

Since the late 1990s, the European Union (EU) has been working specifically towards creating a single European market for financial services. Despite the substantial progress that has been made, it is still far from being complete. Major steps have been accomplished in particular with the implementation of various measures of the Financial Services Action Plan (FSAP) since its adoption in 1999. These measures enabled the emergence of largely integrated interbank and wholesale markets (which have actively been pushed forward by the major corporate and investment banks). However, integration of the retail banking sector is far from complete since country-specific differences in banking services[1], infrastructure and legal provisions still exist. With regard to the size and importance of this segment, the untapped potential to reap the benefits of continued market integration is considerably high. Retail banking represents more than 50% of the total banking activity in Western Europe,[2] generating a gross income of approximately EUR 250–275 billion, equivalent to 2% of total EU GDP.

1 Retail banks offer savings and loans products as well as other services of financial intermediation, predominantly provided through local distribution channels.

2 In terms of gross income, see "*Report on retail banking sector inquiry*", European Commission (2007b).

More than three million jobs are provided by this sector today (European Commission, 2007b, p. 7).

There is a widespread consensus among academics, the banking industry and political observers, including the European Commission (EC), that "an efficient and integrated European financial market will help to support growth and job creation within a competitive economy",[3] as envisioned in the Lisbon Agenda. These assumptions are mainly based on the reductions in the cost of equity, bond, and bank finance and an increase in the intensity of competition in previously fragmented markets. Corporate clients would primarily benefit from lower costs of capital, while the advantages for retail clients would arise from both cheaper financial services and a greater product variety. In 1988, the European Commission published the findings of its studies on the economics of integration in the widely known "Cecchini Report" (European Commission, 1988). It intended to derive quantitative estimates of the benefits of the single market and suggested a price reduction of financial services in many European countries by 25% by converging to the prices of the lowest-cost supplier. At that time, the potential Europe-wide gains of financial liberalization and capital market integration were estimated at approximately 1.5% of GDP over a 6-year period. The respective welfare gains of a more recent study (London Economics, 2002, p. 6) amount to as much as a one-time increase of 1.1% in the EU's GDP, or EUR 130bn, in total. In addition, employment has been forecasted to be 0.5% higher – amounting to about one million new jobs – upon the completion of the single market for financial services.

In this respect, retail banking integration can hence be viewed as a *means to improve efficiency* through economies of scale and an extended market area of financial service sectors. Consumers can benefit from saving opportunities and a broader product offering, while small and medium-size enterprises (SMEs) will have the choice to raise capital in various markets. Financial integration is therefore an *important means to increase economic growth* in the European Union (Kleimeier & Sander, 2007, p. 1) and an *instrument* to increase competition, innovation, growth, efficiency in production and consumer welfare.[4]

The EU Commission is consequently pressing ahead with new legislation focusing in particular on retail market issues (even though there is also more to do with respect to the structure of financial supervision in the EU, the alignment of consumer protection and contract law, and tax issues, among other things).

---

3 See European Commission (2001b).

4 Recent empirical studies on financial development and growth find a positive relationship between the level of development of financial intermediaries, stock market liquidity and the depth of financial markets, and aggregated economic growth or the determinants of growth, such as private saving rates, physical capital accumulation and total factor productivity growth (see, for example, Demirgüc-Kunt & Maksimovic, 1998; Jayaratne & Strahan, 1996; Rajan & Zingales, 1995).

1.2 Reasons for fragmented retail banking markets in the EU

Many academic observers attribute this disappointing situation to two factors. On the one hand, it is more difficult to create a level playing field in nationally fragmented retail banking than it is in other financial markets (fragmentation along the supply and demand-side and with regard to regulation). On the other hand, there are *economic*, *regulatory,* and *social* obstacles that impede full integration. *Economic* obstacles comprise all the market characteristics that hinder integration and free competition from a market point of view – explainable by the nature of the retail banking business and country differences across the EU. *Regulatory* obstacles include different national regulatory regimes that have evolved through decades of national regulatory activity in formerly purely domestic markets. Finally, *social* obstacles represent *natural* barriers to integration such as local language and consumer preferences and a vital part of the cultural diversity in Europe. While social barriers limit the scope of economic integration in a natural way – at least in the short and medium term – and policy-makers can address regulatory barriers, economic barriers need to be approached with alternative means.

Table 1 provides an overview of the areas of fragmentation and the associated classes of integration obstacles mentioned above. This overview highlights the difficulties in defining an integration strategy, which must be developed on a case-by-case basis and requires careful assessment of the extent to which obstacles can and should be removed (cp. Heinemann, Schröder, Schüler, Stirböck, & Westerheide, 2003). It is therefore important to understand that integration should not be maximized at any cost, and to identify the economic, regulatory, and social limits of integration. Integration is not an objective in itself but rather an instrument to increase competition, innovation, growth and consumer welfare. Not every instance of increased integration is necessarily helpful in achieving those final objectives. A detailed assessment of each characteristic follows in Chapter C.

Table 1: Market characteristics and obstacles to integration

Areas of fragmentation	Classes of integration obstacles: Economic	Regulatory	Social
Supply-side	• Localized services and distribution channels • Traditionally high level of cooperation (network effects) • Multi-market contacts • Varying market structures and concentration • Varying degrees of price transparency • Significant barriers to market entry	• High degree of international and national regulation • Restrictions of market entry • Product specification	
Demand-side	• Information asymmetry • Inelastic demand for certain products and services • High switching costs	• Consumer protection • Civil law	• Cultural preferences, habits and historical reasons • Language
Regulatory framework		• Significant differences of prudential rules and regulation • Domestic ownership and supervision structures	• National belief structures

Source: Author's illustration.

1.3 Financial market integration and banking regulation

In view of the rising governmental attention to the European level and policy interventions towards financial market integration, it becomes obvious that banking regulation has extended its traditional field of activity into a new functional and territorial dimension. Besides the regulatory function of preserving system stability and free competition, financial market integration has become an equivalent policy objective to EU policy-makers. This goal of creating a single market has given leeway to regulatory interventions as the steering instruments of choice. Instead of a "retreat of state" (Müller & Wright, 1994), these policies have resulted in efforts to meet the public expectations of a single market – by means of regulation (Grande, 1994a, 1997c, 2005; König & Benz, 1997b; Majone, 1990; Vogel, 1996).

In addition to the change in its function, banking regulation is also undergoing changes in its territorial dimension, as more and more regulatory responsibility is being transferred from a national to the EU level, empowering European agencies such as the EC and the ESCB. This development has not always been compatible with national regulatory sovereignty, which has evolved through decades of regulatory activity aimed at providing rules for what was perceived as purely national financial markets.[5] Given this biased constellation of interests, it is explainable that today's status of completion of a single financial market has largely been driven by EU regulations that aimed at opening domestic markets and partially harmonizing national financial systems and product offers.

It was evident in the Treaty of Rome that the objectives of economic development and integration are inseparable. Since 1957, a lot of regulatory progress has been made with respect to the creation of a single market for financial services. Beside the Treaty of Rome, key regulatory milestones include the 1977 First Banking Directive, the 1985 Second Banking Directive, the 1992 Maastrich Treaty, and the 1999 Financial Services Action Plan (Kleimeier & Sander, 2007, p. 2). According to Dermine (2002, p. 3), each of these five regulatory milestones characterized a new phase in Europe's legal environment. Actions taken by the European Commission and the Council of Ministers can be divided into five periods: the deregulation of market entry (1957–1973), the harmonization of banking regulations (1973–1983), the completion of the internal market (1983–1992), the creation of the single currency (1992–1999), and finally the Financial Services Action Plan[6] (2001–2005). The latter has been a great step forward in this direction. Some 39 measures out of 42 have been adopted within the relatively brief period of six years (European Commission, 2005d, p. 3).

Despite many years of continuous regulatory efforts and the substantial progress that has been made in equity, bond and wholesale banking markets,[7] a truly single market for all financial services – including retail banking – is lagging behind expectations and remains a severe detriment to Europe's competitiveness and growth prospects (Diekmann, 2006; Kleimeier & Sander, 2007; Speyer, 2005). Being aware of the inefficiencies the EC has given top priority to overcoming these impediments to integration and attaches great importance to the problem-solving capacity of regulation. These priorities were unveiled in a Green Paper published on 3 May 2005 (European Commission, 2005e, pp. 3-5),

---

5 The Commission is considering the idea of creating a 26th regime to grant specific financial products a European status (e.g. mortgages). Despite the slow progress in the integration of the retail banking market, partly caused by the fragmentation of national regulation in the 27 EU member states, such an approach has received widespread scepticism and a lack of national promoters (Eurofi, 2006, p. 1).

6 The Commission adopted the Financial Services Action Plan (FSAP) in May 1999 with the goal of creating an adequate framework for a single European market in financial services by adhering to three overarching objectives: a single wholesale market, an open and secure retail market, and adequate prudential rules and supervision.

7 Recent research includes, for example, Diekmann (2006), European Banking Federation (2007), European Central Bank (2003b; European Central Bank, 2004a, 2006b), Kemppainen (2004a), Kleimeier & Sander (2007), Noyer (2006) and World Savings Bank Institute & European Savings Bank Group (2006).

which analyzed the current state of European financial market integration and provided an assessment of priorities for the post-FSAP period. Five main areas were identified where action was necessary to facilitate further the construction of a single market for financial services. These were: an improved legislative apparatus, elimination of capital market fragmentation, consumer protection within a single market, supervisory coordination and an integrated infrastructure to underpin financial transactions (Howell, 2004a). It was also made clear that the focus lies in implementing existing rules rather than creating new ones and in enhancing the transposition on a member state level.

1.4 Research questions and objectives

As mentioned above, the economic relevance of an integrated retail banking market in Europe is undisputed among academics and EU policy-makers. Furthermore, consensus prevails that the current market fragmentation is highly inefficient from a macro-economic point of view prevails. The poor progress towards a single market is mainly justified with the existence of various economic and regulatory obstacles, and EU regulations aiming at overcoming the symptoms of the fragmented market appear to be politically rather than economically motivated. A frequently used argument to justify policy interventions, such as the pricing regulation for retail payments,[8] claims that market forces on their own have failed to create an integrated market. Whether this argument proves to be valid from a theoretical and empirical perspective remains largely unsettled in academic literature. Therefore, the hypothesis derived from current observations of the European retail market can be formulated as follows: *in highly fragmented, heterogeneous markets, market forces on their own may fail develop a single market, so that the intervention of regulation is required.* With respect to the role of EU-regulation in promoting market integration this study raises the research question about *the key decision factors influencing the choice for regulation compared to a market solution and how can policy interventions be measured with regard to their effectiveness and efficiency.*

The research objective resulting from the preceding considerations is threefold:

(i) *Theoretical contribution* – Refining economic theories on banking regulation and European integration by developing a conceptual model to assess the efficiency and effectiveness of regulation, encompassing a comparative institutional approach to regulation and combining the functional and territorial view on regulation.

8 See the Regulation (EC) No 2560/2001 of the European Parliament and of the Council of 19 December 2001 on cross-border payments in euro (2003).

(ii) *Practical contribution* – Using the example of the European retail payment market and SEPA to assess the catalytic character of regulation to facilitate the creation of a single market. Thereby, normative means of overcoming the impediments to integration persistent in the European retail banking market should be developed, followed by recommended courses of action for European integration policy.

(iii) *Future research* – Provide an initial study base for subsequent research on regulation and European integration in other industry.

2. Research scope and definitions

2.1 Definition of retail banking services

Client segments are a commonly applied differentiation criteria in banking. Accordingly, one can distinguish between *wholesale banking* and *retail banking* (see Achleitner, 2001, p. 12). Wholesale banking serves primarily legal persons, such as corporations, credit institutions or institutional investors with both products from the primary market (loans and deposits) and the secondary market (securities). In contrast, retail banking concentrates on the mass business, serving a large number of natural persons or small and medium enterprises (SME) with all banking products (loans, deposits and securities). From a product provision viewpoint, one can further distinguish between banks that focus on the primary market (*commercial banks*) and those banks that provide secondary market products and services (*investment banks*). Figure 1 illustrates the comparison of wholesale banking and retail banking to the categories commercial and investment banking.

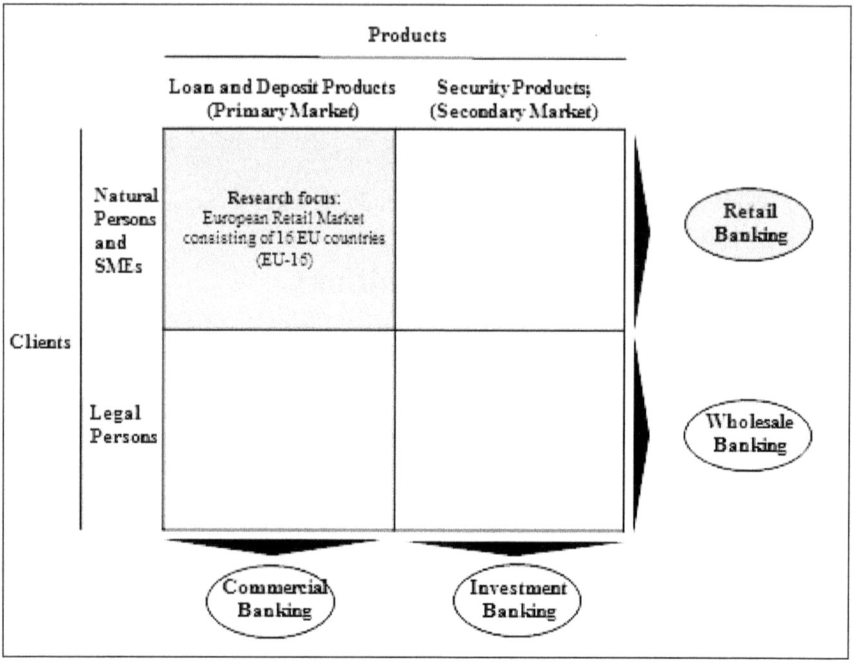

Figure 1: Classification of bank types
Source: Brinker (1998, p. 14).

Retail banking activity is commonly understood to comprise banking services for

(i) consumers (individuals/private households); and
(ii) small and medium-sized enterprises (SME).

One should be careful with the delineation of each of these two segments, since it is not standardized by, for instance, a taxonomy for central banks' statistics or other official databases. To a large extent, cultural habits, market developments, or the individual business strategies decide upon the inclusion or exclusion of customer categories from these segments (European Commission, 2006b, p. 13). For example, some specialized banks classify services for wealthy individuals or households as private banking while others see them as a separate client segment. In SMEs, the definition of the size category is even more discretionary. Whether a certain size category of SME belongs to the segment of retail banking or the segment of corporate banking varies from bank to bank and is even inconsistent across EU member states.[9] Finally, some retail banks have specialized in mortgage or online business, offering only a limited range of banking products and services. In order to reduce this complexity, this study will follow the less rigid definition of retail banking services put forward by the European Commission (see Table 2). This study focuses on account-related services, which include accounts and payment services. Particular mention should be made of the latter, as payment services have undergone a major change process since the introduction of the euro currency.

Retail banking services that can be securitized and traded in secondary markets (loans including credit lines and leasing) are excluded as they form part of the investment banking products that are out of the scope of this analysis.

Table 2: Definition of retail banking services and products

	Consumers	**Small and medium-sized enterprises**
Products	Personal banking as banking products and services for consumers	Business banking as banking services for enterprises up to a maximum turnover of EUR 10 million annually[10]
Current accounts	The bank account that individuals use for most of their household transactions such as receiving wages or paying bills	The bank account that SMEs use for the bulk of the payments they make and receive
Deposit accounts	An account that individuals use for saving. The accounts provide instant ("sight deposits") or time-limited ("time deposits") access to funds.	
Term loans	A loan account operating for a specified time period, which is used to fund personal or household consumption	A loan account operating for a specified time period, which an SME uses to finance its business expenditure
Credit lines	–	An open-ended facility that incorporates the credit element of a loan – enabling SMEs to draw down finance – and the flexibility of a current account for making and receiving payments
Leasing	–	Involves a bank's paying for part or all of the cost of a capital asset for an SME, and the SME then hiring this asset from the bank
Payments	• Payments comprise the payer's transfer of a monetary claim on a party acceptable to the payee (beneficiary) • Payment systems form the core of money transmission services in personal and SME banking, and are significant structures within the retail banking sector as a whole	

Source: Author's illustration based on European Commission (2006b, pp. 13-15).

9 Normally, banks classify companies with an annual turnover of below EUR 5m or even EUR 2m as customers of retail banking. In most cases, enterprises with an annual turnover higher than EUR 10m require different operational requirements and thus are classified as *corporate* or *commercial* clients (European Commission, 2006b, p. 14).

10 The EC defines these size categories as micro and small enterprises, and not as medium sized enterprises. However, the author will follow industry and literature habits and also use the term "SME banking" or "SME customers" for this sub-segment (European Commission, 2003b).

Financial markets in Europe comprise several sub-markets, with retail banking being one among many (others are e.g. equity and bond markets, money markets, asset management etc.), which show different levels of integration.[11] The European Commission's studies on financial market integration show that retail markets are the most fragmented segment of EU financial services (European Commission, 2006b). The average EU customer's possibility to purchase retail financial services from companies that are based in other member states have so far been quite limited. While wholesale and money markets are almost fully integrated, retail financial services are predominantly provided through local distribution channels – with the exception of investment funds. This is the sole area where financial market integration has advanced in recent years, as illustrated in Table 3.

Table 3: Financial market integration summarized

	Interbank markets	**Wholesale markets**	**Retail market**
Prices	■■■	■■■	■□□
Cross-border services	■■■	■■■	□□□
Establishment	■■■	■■■	□□□
Pan-European infrastructure	■■■	■■■	■□□
Product availability	■■■	■■■	■□□

Source: Diekmann (2006, p. 3) and Shirreff (2007).
Note: shading indicates the level of integration.

If looking at other industries, retail financial services in Europe are not leading but rather following the spread of other consumer services, such as the sale of merchandise, entertainment, or communications. Shirreff (2007, p. 2) identified

11 For a more detailed discussion on the current state of financial market integration and the remaining barriers to full integration, see for example Adam et al. (2002), Calcagnini et al. (2002), Galati and Tsatsaronis (2001), Kleimeier (2003) or Mendizabal and Quiros (2001).

three main reasons why the integration of financial services is a "different kettle of fish". Firstly, financial services require a solid legal framework, since they do not involve tangible goods, such as a car or washing machine, but an abstract equivalent. Secondly, most national banking systems are characterized by oligopoly structures, mainly historically grown from government interventions after (financial) crisis. Unlike other consumer services, retail financial services comprise high switching costs. This is reflected in the reluctance of customers to switch their main bank account from one provider to another even when they are unhappy with the service. Finally, governments have been protective of their national banking systems, supporting them in times of crisis and relying on them at times when the government itself is short of cash – an uneasy mutual dependence (Shirreff, 2007).

Furthermore, critics of market integration claim that retail financial services are intrinsically unsuited to cross-border activity due to their very nature and that regulatory obstacles will always stand in the way of commercially viable structures. While these could be valuable arguments, four major driving forces for medium-term market transformation indicate that pan-European retail banking market strategies could emerge, which would help a single market to evolve: the increasingly international preferences of customers, the growing role of direct distribution channels, regulatory trends, and limited domestic market opportunities for EU retail banks (Diekmann, 2006).

2.2 Definition of banking regulation and supervision

Regulation is a popular subject of study in several disciplines across and beyond the social sciences. The various definitions of regulation are oriented towards different research methods and reflect specific disciplinary concerns.

From an economic perspective, the term regulation represents part of the broad field of economic policy. Following the classification of economic policy instruments into *public regulation* and *process regulation*, the underlying definition of regulation adopted in this research refers to *public regulation* as termed by American regulation policy research (Apolte et al., 2003; Breyer, 1982; Kahn, 1971; Noll, 1985, 1989; Selznick, 1985). Accordingly, regulation is considered to be a specific form of state supervision and control of private economic organizations. Here, regulation goes beyond the pure regulatory policy and legal framework setting (competition and anti-trust law). Rather, it can be characterized as an external, long-term, individual, case-dependent control of market development through governmental actors, who define and apply rules through a formalized, administrative process *for the public benefit* through direct state intervention in the economic and contractual freedom of a specific sector (Brander, 2005; Noll, 1985; Selznick, 1985). These activities include among others the control of market entries, investments, capacities, production and sales quantities, prices, quality and terms of conditions (Eickhof, 1997, p. 563).

The definition of regulation deployed in this study is therewith distinguished from other approaches. Some comprise the whole magnitude of governmental activities and relationship patterns respectively between governmental and non-governmental actors under the term of regulation, which is particularly the case in British literature. Others, such as French regulation theory, use the term regulation to analyze the relationship between governments and the economy in capitalistic societies (see Bieling & Deppe, 1996).

Similar to any other industry, banking is also subject to tax, anti-trust, environment, or any other type of regulation, which will be disregarded in this work. Banking regulation is therefore defined as any public intervention that restricts the activities of banks in the above-mentioned manner. Furthermore, it traditionally includes limitations of interest rates, bank risks and deposit insurances for investor protection (Steden, 2002, p. 5).

While regulation typically refers to the rules that govern the behavior of banks, supervision is the oversight that takes place to ensure that banks comply with those rules (Barth, Caprio, & Levine, 2006, p. 1.B). This function is executed by independent supervisory agencies, in order to insulate regulators from political pressure from bankers and to ensure the stability of the financial system. Academics and representatives of supervisory agencies have aimed at formally distinguishing between the two terms: *regulation* was understood as the formulation and design of rules and laws while *supervision* described the process of monitoring and enforcement of regulation. This definition will also be applied in this work.

The justification for any regulation usually stems from a market failure such as externalities, concentration of market power, or asymmetry of information between buyers and sellers (Santos, 2001, p. 9). With regard to the banking industry, there is still no consensus in the literature on whether banks need to be regulated at all and, if so, how regulation should be adapted. This partly reflects the lack of consensus on the nature of market failure that characterizes the current discussion on the role of regulation in financial market integration. Nonetheless, academic research primarily refers to two rationales for regulating banks: the risk of systemic crisis and the inability of depositors to monitor banks (Goodhart, Hartmann, Llewellyn, & Rojas-Suarez, 1998). The extent to which regulation is an adequate approach to facilitate the integration of fragmented markets such as the retail banking market and provides a third, functional justification for public intervention will be investigated at a later stage of this work.

2.3 Defining integration and single market for the purpose of the study

Despite being the key element of European integration, there is still no clear-cut definition of a *single market* in general, not to mention for retail banking services. The terms *market integration* and *single market creation* are used synonymously in this thesis, taking the scope of the single market to encompass the integration of financial markets and the associated regulatory arrangements. Given the fact that national financial systems have historically been segmented, financial integration is part of the currently emerging process of financial internationalization with the ultimate goal of establishing a single financial area in Europe within the context of a common economic area (Gortsos, 2007, p. 3). Financial markets *inter alia* include money markets, equity markets, bond markets and the wholesale and retail banking sector. The focus of the current study, however, will be retail banking markets and the author will thus abstract from the integration developments in equity and bond markets and in the wholesale sector.

The European Central Bank defines financial integration in the following terms: "the ECB (…) considers the market for a given set of financial instruments or services to be fully integrated when all potential market participants in such a market (i) are subject to a single set of rules when they decide to deal with those financial instruments or services, (ii) have equal access to this set of financial instruments or services, and (iii) are treated equally when they operate in the market"[12] (European Central Bank, 2007, p. 5).

Financial integration is not necessarily synonymous with "frictionless financial markets" (London Economics, 2002, p. 13), though greater integration may lead to reduced frictions in some areas. Frictions in financial markets (and in retail banking in particular) that are inherent to the industry structure and may not disappear with financial integration. The presence of economies of scale due to the large fixed costs of setting up a clearing and settlement infrastructure, the existence of network externalities and the nature of the incentive problems may represent examples in retail banking. These frictions will affect the functioning of financial markets even if financial integration is fully achieved (ibid.).

Since the Treaty of Rome and the earliest studies of regional economic integration, differing views on the policy approach to integration, *negative* vs. *positive* integration, have given rise to controversial discussion among academics and EU policy-makers. While *negative* integration included the abolition of ob-

12 The term *market* is used in a broad sense, covering all possible exchanges of financial instruments or services, be these via an organized market, such as a stock exchange, or via an over-the-counter market created by a financial institution supplying a financial instrument or service (European Central Bank, 2007, p. 5).

stacles to market integration, *positive* integration was defined as the development and implementation of effective supranational policies (Majone, 2005, p. 143). The Rome Treaty itself did not attach any normative connotation to the distinction. While the common market was to be achieved by both methods, for a long time greater reliance was placed upon negative law.[13] More recently the demand for EU interventions has changed: positive integration has increasingly been identified with positive values like social protection and the correction of market failures, and negative integration with deregulation and the narrow interests of traders. In fact, economic and other special interests may find it convenient to support measures of positive integration, while fundamental rights and the diffuse interests of consumers are often better protected by measures of negative integration (Majone, 2005, p. 144). With regard to achieving financial integration in and scrutinizing the role of regulation, this work views negative integration as the *necessary conditions* for a single financial area (for retail banking services), which comprises the abolition of obstacles to the carrying out of cross-border financial transactions and the establishment of financial firms on the territory of other EU member states. Positive integration however is seen as the *sufficient condition* for achieving a single financial market, presupposing the adoption and implementation of policies. Such policies will ensure policy objectives are realized and equal terms of competition between banks in the single area are preserved, provided that they offer services of the same nature and are exposed to similar risk (Gortsos, 2007, p. 4).

Against this background, *a single market in retail banking services among the EU member states is defined as the result of financial integration and holds when regulatory and economic obstacles to integration are overcome and banks and end-consumers start viewing the EU as their home market.* Different approaches can be taken to achieve this goal: by market forces (market-led process of integration), by self-regulation or agreed principles, or by binding rules arising from inter-governmental or supranational institutions. To facilitate an evaluation of the effectiveness of different integration approaches, the desirable characteristics of a single market for retail banking services are defined by the following features: (i) positive welfare effects, (ii) the existence of a consistent and flexible legal and regulatory framework and (iii) harmonized banking supervision and oversight on a European level. These characteristics will be explained in more detail below.

Positive welfare effects of a single market should be beneficial for EU retail banking clients (i.e., through increased choice, lower prices, lower risk), and

13 See Articles 12–17 (elimination of customs duties); 30–7 (elimination of quantitative restrictions to intra-Community trade); 48–73 (free movement of persons, services, and capital); and 85–94 (rules against distortion of competition) (European Community, 1957).

provide attractive growth opportunities for retail banks with cross-border market expansion plans (i.e., access to new markets).[14] The existence of a *consistent and flexible legal and regulatory framework* for the European retail banking market avoids any unnecessary or excessive regulatory and legislative stickiness, which limits innovation and competitiveness. For instance, consumer protection standards should differ according to the sophistication of customers with rules for institutional business being more liberal than those for retail business are (Heinemann et al., 2003). Finally, *harmonized banking supervision and oversight on a European level* should avoid that national authorities hamper the consolidation of the national and European banking industries through measures that affect their financial institutions. These measures include, for example, state ownership, state guarantees implicit protectionism via tax advantages for local products or simply the unwillingness to swiftly and consistently transpose EU directives into national law.

Although European financial integration has advanced considerably in recent years, many barriers prevent the emergence of a full single financial market. This study focuses on the identification and analysis of obstacles to full integration of the retail banking market, deriving the appropriate regulatory responses and measures.

2.4 Institutions and governance

At present, the integration of financial markets is a central policy objective of the EU, which relates to setting incentives for market participants in the financial service industry. Retail banking in Europe is particularly characterized by a multitude of differing interests on the national and EU government levels and between consumers, corporations and financial intermediaries. To encompass behavior aspects of incentive setting into the analysis of retail banking integration, this dissertation takes the research perspective of New Institutional Economics (NIE) into consideration.[15] The NIE is a necessary theoretical building

---

14 Positive welfare effects for retail banking clients associated with a higher level of market integration include, among others, the following: (i) guaranteed *direct access* to the capital market and financial services of other EU member states, (ii) *distribution (*a significant bias towards homemade financial products in distribution channels is not compatible with a true single market in an industry where transport costs are practically irrelevant, (iii) *price and performance transparency* and low-cost access to information on pan-European products, (iv) *same conditions* prevailing for domestic and cross-border payments, and (v) a *unified, functionally interlinked market infrastructure* as a pre-condition for a single market (Heinemann et al., 2003).

15 Institutions represent "a set of persistent and connected formal or informal rules including means of enforcement" (Richter & Furubotn, 1996, p. 7). Economic and political institutions structure incentives towards a joint goal and facilitate exchange, whether poli-

block to scrutinize the role of the market behavior-shaping capabilities of banking regulation in the context of market integration. The core assumption of this framework is that *institutions matter* (Bulmer, 1998).

In this study, banking regulation represents the relevant institution under investigation (i.e., the rule including means of enforcement). In this context, *governance* refers to the capacity of the EU's institutional matrix (i.e., of the legislative bodies, such as national and supranational supervisory or regulatory agencies, member state governments, and so forth) to implement and enforce EU public policies and to improve private sector coordination towards market integration" (Ahrens, 2002, p. 129).

As the EU does not resemble, or have, a government, this governance approach offers some descriptive framework on the character of the polity. Moreover, within Europe, the integration process has been inextricably bound up with the transformation of the traditional system of nation states. Kohler-Koch (1996) has seen the transformation of governance as affecting the role of the state, the rules of behavior of market participants and politicians, the pattern of interaction, and the level of action. Kohler-Koch further describes that the state's role has having moved from "authoritative allocation and regulation 'from above' to the role of a partner and mediator" (ibid., p. 371). From this perspective, EU governance is meant to find joint solutions through multileveled partnerships and through mediating the claims of affected interests (Bulmer, 1998). Whether such a mediating role of institutions, as defined according to NIE research, may also facilitate overcoming obstacles to integration of the European retail banking market will be examined in this work.

3. Research status and planned approach

For quite some time now, the field of European integration studies has witnessed a marked shift in focus away from theorizing about the *why* of integration to detailed analysis of *how* to facilitate integration and with what consequences for political and economic order in Europe. With regard to the integration retail banking markets, there a no studies known to the author that investigate the current research problem explicitly or that has this problem as a subject of research. Unlike the case of the common currency or the European economic area, a coherent economic theory that may explain the creation of one common market out of multiple, heterogeneous retail banking markets does not exist. Furthermore, systematic analyses of policy options in this context and theoretical or empirical assessments of the various potential policy channels for improving market out-

tical, economic, or social. This framework of research maintains the basic principles of neoclassical economics but modifies this framework by focusing on institutions and including positive transaction costs (TC) and the constraints of property rights (PR).

comes and enhancing welfare is largely missing (G. Schaefer, 2008, p. 3).[16] Therefore, in order to answer the initial research question of the role of regulation in facilitating market integration, and to fill the identified research gap in regulation theory, this study develops a theoretical-conceptual framework that would allow both theorists and practitioners to systematically examine the barriers to integration in a market;

(i) to identify the underlying market, government or coordination failures justifying policy intervention; and
(ii) to derive efficient and effective policy measures.

In order to achieve this research objective, three associated areas of research identified in academic literature need to be examined and eventually combined into a coherent theoretical framework: studies on traditional banking regulation theory, studies on European integration and studies on the measurement of costs and benefits of regulation.

In a first conceptual step, the author differentiates between a *functional* and a *territorial* dimension of regulation to classify existing academic literature as proposed by Majone (1994b). The functional dimension includes the theoretical frameworks of NIE and regulation theory to assess the functional necessity for regulation and to derive key decision factors for the choice of regulatory intervention. Subsequently, the author will look into these results from a *territorial* perspective. By taking the argumentative frameworks of the different strands of European integration theories into account, the multi-level policy-making process and governance structure of a single retail banking market in Europe is discussed. Special academic interest has been aroused in this view since the distribution of competencies between the national and the European level and the relation between national sovereignty and European integration has been increasingly shifting to a European level. Such hierarchical principal-agent relationships, with multiple principles with different, possibly conflicting objectives, may influence the effectiveness and influence of various instruments and strategies of control (Majone, 1996, p. 37). Applied to the banking market, the author differentiates the current scope of banking regulation research of this study from traditional explanations for banking regulation as analyzed in a multitude of banking research.[17]

The third area of research consists of methodologies to measure the costs and benefits of regulation that are applied in both academic literature and practi-

16 While some analytical papers have been prepared by the European Commission (2002; 2005a) no theoretical or empirical investigation has been conducted in this context. To the author's knowledge, no theoretical or formal paper analyzing retail banking market integration with regard to obstacles to integration exists.

17 See Steden (2002) for a comprehensive overview of traditional banking regulation research.

cal assessment frameworks. While various different measurement approaches exist, in order to properly assess the effectiveness and efficiency in removing barriers to integration, a framework is required that compares actual market outcomes in a regulated world with outcomes that would have evolved without regulation (both ex-post and ex-ante analysis) (Oxera, 2006).

The practical application of the developed conceptual model, testing the underlying research hypothesis and deriving policy recommendation, will be carried out in a case study of the European retail payment market and the creation of a Single Euro Payments Area (SEPA).

4. Research strategy and design

4.1 Research strategy

In order to test the research hypothesis and to achieve the research objective, this study follows a two-step conceptual-empirical research strategy as defined by Grochla and Wittmann (1976):

(i) In the analytical-conceptual step, relevant regulation theories are scrutinized with the aim of developing a conceptual model to assess the effectiveness and efficiency of regulation in overcoming barriers to integration. The model aims to identify the key decision-making factors determining the choice of regulatory intervention.

(ii) In the empirical step, an explanatory single-case study is conducted. It concretizes the conceptual model and adds to the conceptual findings of the analytical investigation to eventually recommend courses of action.

Referring to Yin's (2002) case study research methodology and proved in several examples of case study research in academic literature,[18] there are valid reasons for applying an *explanatory* method and a *single-case study* design in the empirical part of this study. The rational for choosing an *explanatory* method is founded on two conditions. First, the research question on *how* to facilitate integration through regulation posed in this study deals with the operational links of regulation and market behavior needing to be traced back over the period of time (i.e., after the regulation coming into force). Rather than mere frequencies or incidences, this study seeks to understand how the banking market and EU regulators have managed the situation. Second, case studies are preferred in examining contemporary events, as they can deal with a full variety of evidence –

18 See Gross et al. (1971) in Yn (2002) for the single-case study as the critical case or Allison's original study of a single case, the 1962 Cuban missile crisis. Both case studies forcefully demonstrate how a single-case study can be the basis for significant explanations and generalizations.

documents, interviews and observations – beyond on what might be available in surveys, experiments or econometric models.

A *single-case study* design is selected as there are no comparable cases known in the financial services industry to date that would better reflect the co-ordination problem in retail banking markets. Furthermore, price directives have been a popular regulatory instrument applied by the EC in the past and are likely to continue playing an important role in European policy-making. Finally, the European retail payment market and the SEPA initiative are a unique and extreme case and a critical test of regulation theory. It determines whether regulation theory's propositions are correct or whether some alternative explanations might be more relevant. A direct comparison and interpretation of patterns found in this case with the theoretical proposition made at the beginning will finally validate the findings.

4.2 Research design

This dissertation seeks to answer the initial research question on how regulation may resolve the collective action dilemma persistent in retail banking market integration. The theoretical proposition is reflected in the hypothesis, which assumes that fragmented markets by themselves will fail to create a single market in Europe unless some kind of regulatory intervention is applied (i.e., as a catalyst) to overcome barriers to integration.

While the theoretical proposition derived from the analytical-conceptual step deals with the overall European retail banking market as the unit of analysis, the retail payment market (as a relevant sub-unit of the retail banking market) and the Single Euro Payments Area (SEPA) project represent the unit of analysis investigated in the single-case study. Linking data to the theoretical proposition is done in two ways. On the one hand changes that occurred after the price regulation are analyzed (i.e., price and transaction volume changes, investment activity, changes in market structure, etc.). On the other hand an analytical generalization to the theoretical proposition is performed. Similar to experiments, case studies do not represent samples that, when enumerating their frequency, can be statistically generalized (Yin, 2002, pp. 10-11). Since the goal of this case study is to expand and generalize regulation theory, the patterns found in the payment market and in the SEPA case are compared and interpreted with criteria derived from the theoretical proposition.

To meet the test of construct validity, this study uses multiple sources of evidence to establish a chain of evidence. Each barrier to integration identified in the retail payment market is linked to a type of market, government or coordination failure. They, in turn, are made measurable through different quantity- and quality-based indicators. To ensure reliability of results so that later investigators arrive at the same findings and conclusions when following the procedures as described in this study, all procedures and sources of evidence will be documented properly.

This dissertation draws on multiple sources of research, such as:

- Analysis of relevant academic publications on regulation theory, European market integration and regulation impact assessments.
- Analysis of official documents and reports (e.g. activity reports of national public authorities, publications of the European Commission and the European Central banks).
- Analysis of reports, studies and surveys publicly available of regulated corporations.
- Selective interviews with experts from banks and their research departments and from bank associations.
- Analysis of quantitative data on consumer price indices.
- Company research including annual reports and websites
- Analysis of national and international technical press and literature.

In addition to the analysis of the relevant technical and academic literature, the application of quantity- and quality-based indicators is favorable for many reasons. The small number of comparable cases and historical examples sets boundaries to a quantitative aggregated data analysis. Ex-post quantitative effects induced by regulation can be assessed only over time when long enough time series have been gathered i.e. by the means of comprehensive EU-wide pricing surveys. Furthermore, the disclosure of private information on firms' cost structure would be a useful proxy for such an assessment. Even then, there is the potential caveat to assess the effects of the regulatory intervention reliably. It may prove to be cumbersome to detect "the pure regulation effects" on price and production cost developments because other factors, like different pricing conventions (i.e. bundling of banking services) and technological developments (i.e. Internet banking) also have an influence on prices and costs over time. Representative empirical data for both prices and costs are only selectively comprehensively available to date.

5. Methodology and structure

In this study, the research question about the role of regulation in promoting the integration of fragmented market as persistent in European retail banking is answered in the following course:

First, Chapter B provides a theoretical basis for the analysis of regulation by critically reviewing the American and European literature on banking regulation policy and EU market integration efforts. This research project draws, amongst others, on the institutional economics approach to regulation to examine its behavioral implications in the banking sector. Although regulation represents a prominent theme in NIE,[19] the avant-gardes of this school of thought have left their application to the banking sector unconsidered for a long time. While the regulation of banking markets has been a popular research topic for the last three decades, to date, only a selective number of academic works on NIE and banking regulation reflect a deeper investigation.[20] In this regard, Chapter B provides a theoretical overview of NIE with reference to banking and subsequently takes stock of the existing, modern theories of regulation. The author will hereby distinguish between the *functional* and *territorial* dimensions of regulation and will illustrate this differentiation in the EU market. While both dimensions of regulation already represent a complex field of research when examined in isolation, this works seeks to combine both dimensions and to examine their reciprocal dependencies in European regulation policy. With regard to the functional dimension, the American regulation policy research represents one of the most comprehensive areas of research on regulation and examines the market conditions that justify regulatory intervention. In the context of an "Comparative Institution Approach" (Demsetz, 1969, p. 1), three types of failure are scrutinized in the functional dimension of banking regulation and specified in detail with the respective economic theories: *market failure* and the Normative (Public Interest) Theory; *government failure* and the Positive (Private Interest) Theory; and *coordination failure*, which has been described in the NIE literature and also in Keynes' model of business cycles.

The territorial dimension on banking regulation complements the functional view and depicts the additional complexity of regulation in a multilevel European Union where conflicts of interest do not only occur between market and state but also between states and between different national financial markets. The territorial aspect of regulation claims that in the course of European market integration, public regulation has shifted to the European level. This chapter restricts itself to the essential aspects of the current state of research on European Integration Theory and describes the territorial dimension only at a high level. At a later stage of the analysis, this subject is taken up again in more detail, when critically reviewing the research findings from the functional analysis of regulation. The research questions that guide the territorial aspects comprise the locus of banking regulation, the distribution of competencies within the European multilevel governance structure and the self-concept of supra-national regulators.

---

19 See Goldberg (1976) and Williamson (1975).

20 Prominent examples of institutional-economic research in the Anglo-Saxon literature are Goldberg (1976) and Williamson (1975). However, neither have analysed the banking sector in detail. In the German-speaking region, Richter (1996), Zimmer (1993) and Steden (2002) have analysed banking regulation from an institutional-economic point of view with a focus on deposit insurance schemes.

Based on the preliminary theoretical considerations on the complex issues of regulation, this chapter will scrutinize the shift of paradigms in the EU banking regulation and will contrast the scope of traditional banking regulation with the scope of regulation currently observable in the EU banking market. As indicated in "Research Objectives and Hypothesis", banking regulation has experienced significant changes in its functional and territorial dimensions in the course of European integration. Although the banking sector represents a popular research subject in the field of regulation policy, most of its analysis has concentrated on the role of banking regulation in maintaining economic and system stability and free competition. With the creation of a single market and the increase of policy intervention on the EU level, new questions regarding the function of regulation in influencing market development have arisen. Traditionally, assessments of the necessity for regulation have concentrated on the question of market or government failure (Grande, 2000). While the assessment of market or government failure presents an economic explanation for regulation and deriving the consequences of regulation, behavioral aspects such as the principal-agent problem also need to be considered. Coordination failure as a third type of failure refers to a situation where (i) a misalignment of incentives of market participants results in market coordination problems and (ii) missing markets result in information asymmetries. The economics of coordination failure pertains to the research area of comparative institutional studies and has increasingly gained prominence in policy research.[21] The current situation in the European retail banking market, where a diffuse set of agents is involved in an activity characterized by increasing returns to scale and asymmetric information, depicts the detrimental outcome of coordination failure. This chapter concludes that the function of regulation in market integration should comprise the elimination of market, government and coordination failure. The evaluation of all three is reflected in the key decision factors determining the choice of regulatory instruments in the conceptual model in Chapter D.

As mentioned in above, the role of regulation as a catalyst for financial market integration in Europe requires a detailed analysis of banking regulation to contrast traditional, economic efficiency-oriented regulation with the political elements of regulation that are observable in reality. In this respect, Chapter C deals with the analysis of traditional banking regulation, its justification, design and shortcoming when it comes to regulating market structures or facilitating the development of a single market in Europe. This chapter will briefly discuss the causes of banking crisis and bank insolvencies from an NIE perspective to examine whether state intervention is justifiable and necessary. Subsequently, traditional regulatory measures and instruments are described, followed by an

21 See, for example, Aoki, Murdock, and Okuno-Fujiwara (1998).

overview of the main regulatory organizations in the banking sector. A critical review of traditional banking regulation and concludes this chapter.

Following this critique of traditional banking regulation and the theoretical foundation of functional and territorial dimensions of regulation, Chapter D outlines the conceptual-empirical investigation to assess the benefits of regulation in the process of market integration. In order to achieve the research objectives, this work follows an analytical and empirical research strategy (Grochla & Wittmann, 1976, p. 634). It appears that only a conceptual-empirical approach is able to explain the largely unknown role of regulation (as will be seen) in an explorative manner, to answer the research questions and eventually to reach the research objective. In the first step, an analytical investigation is performed with the aim of developing a conceptual framework of analysis for banking regulation that caters for the different dimensions of regulation and that compares market outcomes with and without regulation. The model builds upon a well-proven conceptual framework effectively used by United Kingdom (U.K.) regulators[22] and includes the functional and the territorial dimension of regulation in the key decision factors for and drivers of the choice for regulatory intervention, such as price directives, as a type of regulatory intervention with potential catalytic market effects. Furthermore the conceptual framework seeks to measure (i) the effectiveness of regulation in terms of removing obstacles to integration and (ii) the efficiency of regulation in terms of its costs and benefits, including the respective measurement techniques. This cost-benefit analysis will set out the relevant dimensions of benefits, the mechanisms through which regulation may deliver these benefits, and the approaches that can be adopted to measure the relevant dimensions, both quantitatively and qualitatively.

Next, Chapter E applies this generic conceptual framework to the current situation in the European retail banking market and illustratively applies the conceptual framework to the retail payment service industry. The explanatory case study on the effects of EU Regulation 2560/2001 and the emerging Single Euro Payment Area (SEPA) initiative seeks to illustrate how EU policy intervened in the market based on politically motivated assumptions and vague causalities. By applying the conceptual framework, this chapter looks into the actual obstacles to integration and assesses the extent to which the regulation eventually removed these obstacles. Furthermore, this analysis examines the indirect positive welfare effects in terms of initializing a partly self-regulated development by the banking industry by acting as a catalyst to overcome coordination failure. By analyzing the changes that occurred after the price regulation (i.e.

---

22 Oxera (2006) developed a framework for assessing the benefits of financial regulation for the U.K. Financial Services Authority (FSA). This report stands out due to its practical applicability and can be seen in the broader context of the debate on the costs and benefits of financial regulation.

price development, investment activity), the case study provides an analytical generalization relying on the theoretical proposition of Chapter B. Finally, this chapter interprets the results from the SEPA initiative and concludes with practical implications for regulatory policy-making in creating a single European market for retail payments.

Policy recommendations, which have resulted from analysis and discussions throughout the study, are summarized in the final chapter (Chapter F) to formulate an overall normative proposition for the new functional and territorial scope of banking regulation in the course of market integration in Europe. It discusses the role of strong European regulatory agency that takes an active role in the market integration process, provided that it is endowed with the respective mandate and competency to remove regulatory barriers to integration in the first place. This concept gives special attention to the specific problems of European retail banking markets and seeks to offer valuable policy recommendations on how the right incentives can overcome coordination problems and facilitate the creation of a single market in other industries as well.

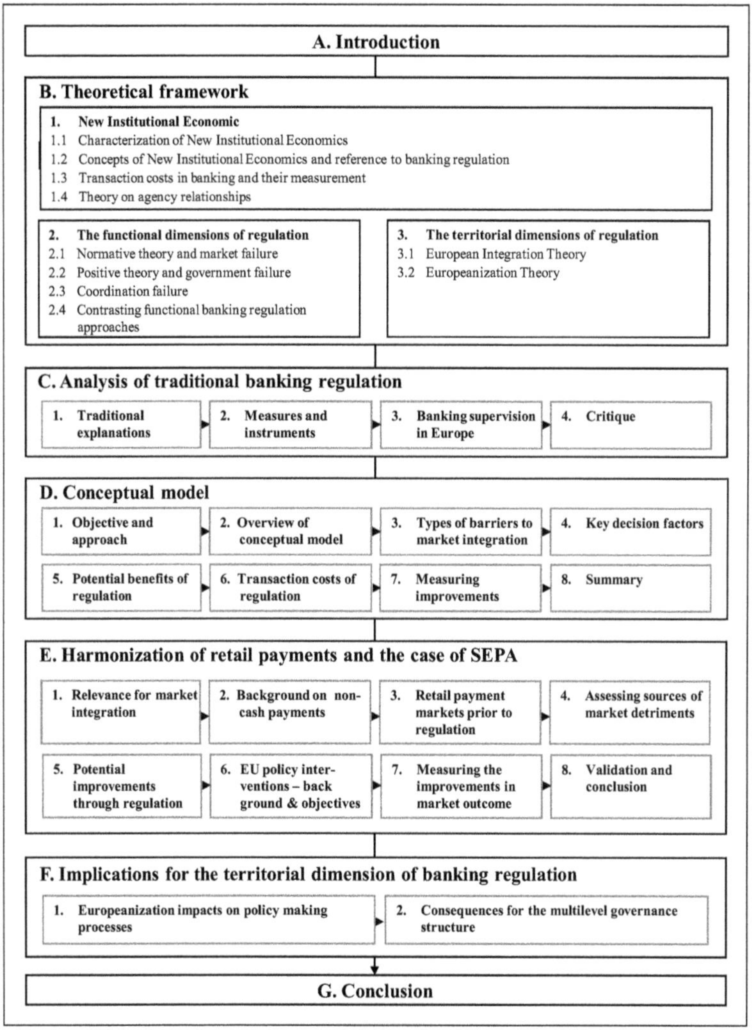

Figure 2: Structure of work
Source: Author's illustration.

Table 4: Summary Chapter A

Summary Chapter A – Introduction
• The retail banking market in Europe is composed of consumer clients (personal banking as banking products and services) and small and medium enterprises (business banking as banking services for enterprises with a maximum turnover of EUR 10m p.a.). The market is characterized by a high degree of national regulation, significant fragmentation and differences regarding market structures and entry barriers. Furthermore, the demand-side is characterized by information asymmetries, customer immobility and very limited bargaining power.
• There is no integrated market for retail banking products and services in Europe to date. From a macro-economic perspective, such market fragmentation is inefficient and leads to high transaction costs. Numerous economic, regulatory and natural obstacles hinder harmonization. Therefore, EU regulation seeks to overcome these obstacles and to abolish differences in current prices, instruments and infrastructures, arguing that market forces have failed to drive convergences. To find theoretical or empirical proof for this argument, the research hypothesis derived from observations assumes *that in highly fragmented, heterogeneous markets, market forces on their own may fail to develop a single market, so that the intervention of regulation is required.* With respect to the role of EU-regulation in promoting market integration this study raises the research question about *the key decision factors influencing the choice for regulation compared to a market solution and how can policy interventions be measured with regard to their effectiveness and efficiency.*
• Traditional explanations for banking regulation fall short in explaining the need for governments to intervene to create a single market. Furthermore, there is no economic theory that would model the transformation of multiple heterogonous markets, each with their differing sets of habits, preferences and governance structures. In this respect, the research objective of this study is to refine relevant economic theories and to develop a conceptual framework that would allow both theorists and practitioners to systematically examine the barriers to integration in a market, to identify the underlying market, government or coordination failures justifying policy intervention, and to derive efficient and effective policy measures.
• In order to achieve the research objectives, this dissertation follows an analytical-empirical research strategy. An explanatory single-case study design on the European retail banking industry and the case of SEPA is applied to link the empirical research step with the theoretical transposition.

Source: Author's illustration.

B Theoretical framework

This chapter provides an overview of the theoretical fundamentals required to analyze systematically banking regulation and market integration. Three theoretical components will be presented in detail: New Institutional Economics (NIE), the functional dimension of regulation including the Public and Private Interest Theory, and the territorial dimension of regulation comprising the Europeanization Theory.

The broad field of banking regulation can be considered a problem of institutional arrangements in the banking sector (Krahnen, 1993, p. 804). The objective is to conduct the behavior of banks, bank employees and customers in a way that an optimally functioning banking system can be created. In this respect, the behavior-shaping effect of institutional arrangements on individuals and firms is the subject of NIE. Theoretical instruments such as the Principal Agent Theory facilitate a systematic analysis of the operating principles of institutions by including the interaction of different actors and interest groups. Hence, NIE is an essential theory component for an analysis of banking regulation and a number of preliminary institutional-economic considerations will be outlined in this chapter.

Regulation theory in general deals with governmental interventions in individual economic sectors and has advanced considerably over the last three decades. Given the specific conditions in a European multilevel system, this book takes a differentiated view on banking regulation by distinguishing between a functional and a territorial dimension to analyze policy implications for the integration of retail banking markets in Europe.

The functional aspect means that governmental supervision and control by means of banking regulation are not transient phenomena but necessary and long-term governmental assignments. Two reasons can be found in the relevant literature (Grande, 1993a, 1997c; Schuppert, 1997). Firstly, the *economic efficiency* of regulatory control and intervention (in terms of Pareto optimum) is required to create and maintain competition and free markets. Secondly, the social consequences of competition are a reason for the intensifying public regulation. Establishing *social efficiency*[23] beyond the Pareto optimum is also recognized as the state's responsibility and cannot be politically neglected by decision-makers. Practically, undesirable results or consequences of functioning markets are being corrected or compensated for in accordance with a politically defined understanding of welfare. This trade-off between economic and social efficiency of regulation is characteristic of the functional dimension of regula-

23 In banking markets, ensuring system stability, confidence, and a sound operation of the financial system are traditional arguments put forward to intensify public regulation.

tion. Hence, this dimension will be examined in an application-oriented way: instead of providing an abstract of the history of economic theories on regulation, this research project concentrates on three types of system failure that have been described in academic literature: market failure, government failure (including political aspects of regulation), and coordination failure.

The second, territorial dimension of regulation focuses on actors, organizations, and processes of banking regulation between EU nation states and the EU, observing a major shift of public regulation to the EU level in the course of European market integration. Majone (1990) and Howell (2004a) assume that regulation policy is particularly susceptible to Europeanization and that it is clearly grounded in a functional delegation perspective. While *negative integration* (i.e. the opening up of national markets) has a certain momentum of its own and can be promoted "to a certain extent behind the back of the EC and the European Court of Justice, measures of *positive integration* require an explicit political legitimacy" (Scharpf, 1996, p. 114). Hence, positive regulation on the European level also has its limits as the need for consensus for measures of positive integration (i.e. market corrections) remains very high (even under the new EU voting rules of a qualified majority) and as the interests of member states usually strongly diverge. These elements of Europeanization Theory will be discussed in more detail in this last section of this chapter.

Figure 3 summarizes the theoretical models applied to the problem of banking regulation and integration. While a one-dimensional consideration of banking regulation would be short-sighted, this chapter further elaborates on merging these two viewpoints and illustrates the resulting shift of banking regulation paradigms: from a traditional focus on eliminating primarily market failure and maintaining stability in national markets towards a market-shaping function aimed at eliminating coordination failure and incentive misalignment on a supranational, European level to create a single market. This theoretical proposition will be transferred into a conceptual framework to assess the benefits of certain government interventions (Chapter D). In the following chapters, the theoretical proposition is tested and discussed in the European retail banking market and applied to the retail payment market in the SEPA case study in Chapter E.

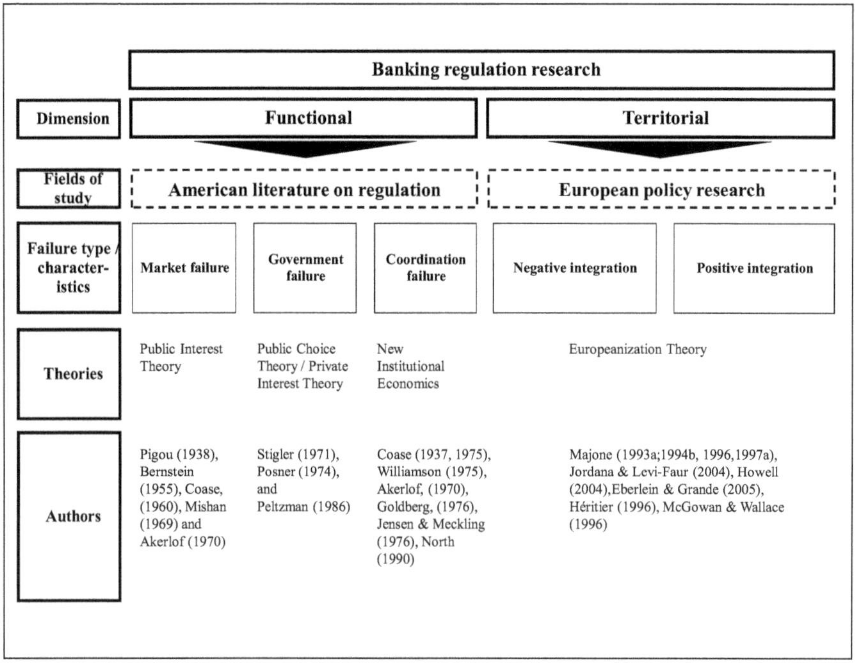

Figure 3: Overview of theoretical framework
Source: Author's illustration

1. New Institutional Economics

This section examines banking regulation mainly from an institutional-economic viewpoint. The following theoretical overview of New Institutional Economics briefly elaborates on characteristics and delineations from other theories, on its terminology, its approach, and its reference to the function of banking regulation.

1.1 Characterization of New Institutional Economics

New Institutional Economics (NIE) as a unified research paradigm took shape in the 1980s, evolving as a critical reaction to the behaviorist and system-theoretical approaches of the 1960s and 1970s.[24] NIE does not consist of a single theoretical framework. Instead, it comprises various different directions, the public choice approach, the economics of law approach, and the Neo-Austrian

24 Important pacemakers of this theory were the research directions of Coase (1937; 1960), Williamson (1975), Alchian and Demsetz (1972) and Jensen and Meckling (1976).

School, which share the common attribute of emphasizing the behavior-shaping effect of economic and political institutions (Erlei, Leschke, & Sauerland, 1999, pp. 42-44). Hence, NIE delineates a branch of economic theory, which focuses on institutions and organizations while maintaining the principles of neo-classical economics such as the utility maximization assumption, the marginal benefit principle, the efficiency assumption, and the rational-choice model, or the *homo economicus* with bounded rationality (Richter & Furubotn, 1996, pp. 33-37). Nevertheless, the NIE adapts the protective belt of neo-classical economics by including positive transaction costs (TC) and the constraints of property rights (PR), as illustrated in Figure 4.

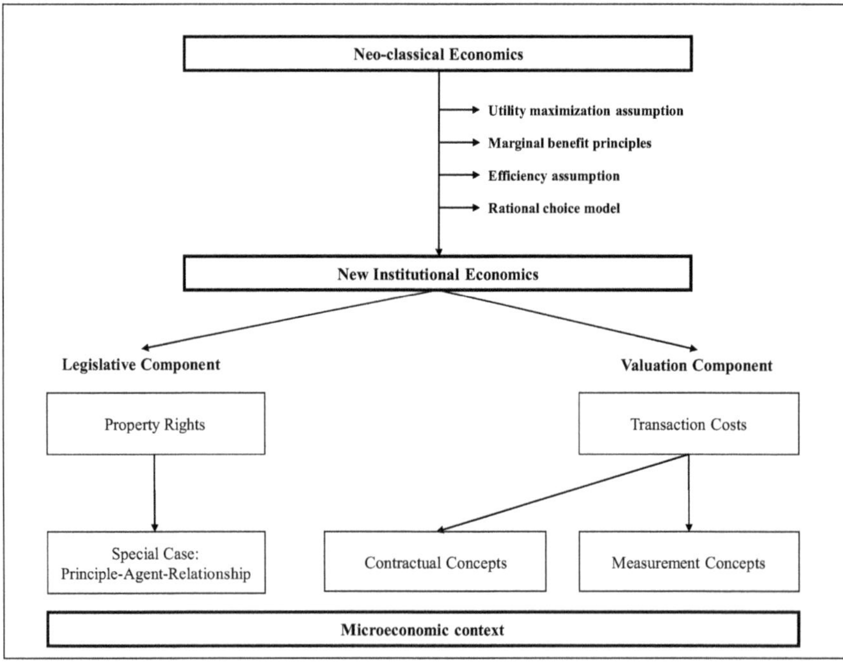

Figure 4: Neo-classical economics and the New Institutional Economics
Source: Adapted from Buchenrieder (2002).

The strands of NIE deal with the examination of situations with information asymmetries in exchange relationships (transaction or principal agent relationships). Such situations are usually characterized by opportunistic behavior, i.e. the exploitation of information advantages on the cost and disadvantage of others.

Another attribute of NIE is that the behavior of individuals or organizations is not considered completely determined, but provides a certain leeway of action for respective actors. NIE differs from other theoretical frameworks in the following ways.

(i) Institutions are not a neutral element within the economic functional system but have a major impact on economic behavior. By limiting the behavioral options of actors, institutions may enable a transaction in many cases (Krahnen, 1993, p. 794).
(ii) Frictions are inherent to economic systems. In exchange transactions, costs occur, whose level impacts on the modality in which economic activities are organized and carried out.

In this context, the notion of institutions is taking a central role. For the purpose of this study, institutions can be generally characterized as "[...] the rules of the game in a society or, more formally, the humanly devised constraints that shape human interaction. In consequence they structure incentive in human exchange, whether political, social or economic." (North, 1990, p. 3). North further elaborates that these rules of the game comprise formal rules and informal constraints, including their enforcement characteristics (ibid., p. 4).[25] The term "formal rules" includes political (and judicial) rules, economic rules, and contracts. Political rules broadly define the hierarchy of the polity, its basic decision-making structure, and the explicit characteristics of agenda control (Buchenrieder, 2002, p. 12). Contracts contain the provisions specific to a particular agreement in exchange. Informal constraints are extensions and qualifications of rules that "solve" innumerable exchange problems not completely covered by formal rules. They, as a consequence, have a tenacious survival ability even when societies and economies transform dramatically. Informal constraints include conventions (i.e. rules of the road), norms of behavior (recognized rules of conduct that define interpersonal relationships in family, school, or business), and self-imposed codes of conduct (i.e. standards of integrity and honesty) (North, 1990).

Economic rules define property rights (PR) and comprise the exclusive authority of a particular individual to select the uses of economic goods (Alchian, 1977, p. 128). In a similar way, Furubotn and Pejovich (1972, p. 1139) characterize PRs as the "sanctioned behavioral relations among men that arise from the

25 North's definition of an institution was further refined by Ostrom (1990, p. 51), who describes institutions as "[...] the sets of working rules that are used to determine who is eligible to make decisions in some arena, what actions are allowed or constrained, what aggregation rules will be used, what procedure must be followed, what information must or must not be provided, and what payoffs will be assigned to individuals dependent on their actions... All rules contain prescriptions that forbid, permit, or require some action or outcome. Working rules are those actually used, monitored, and enforced when individuals make choices about the action that they will take."

existence of things and pertain to their use". Neither definition implies that PR's are derived from ownership in a legal sense.[26]

At present, there is no standard definition of the notion of institutions. If institutions are conceived as being constructivist, an intended result of individual or collective decisions, then the term institution represents structures such as firms, associations, property rights, or constitutions. Even though in evolutionistic terms institutions are also conceived as results of human interaction, these results are less subject to intention and planning and are rather created through spontaneous and repetitive experience. Examples are markets (as abstract), property rights, land, tree and animal tenure, inheritance systems and other systems of exchange that are determined by implicit contracts, rules or social norms. Institutions are the guide to human interaction and reduce uncertainty by providing a stable, although not necessarily efficient structure to everyday life. In contrast, organizations develop as a consequence of the institutional environment. Furthermore, they are instrumental concretizations for fulfilling the func-

---

26 In the NIE, the term PR is often used in a wider sense, namely in the sense of *entitlements*. The term *entitlements* was coined and popularized by Sen (in Devereux, 2001, p. 246) and comprises the "set of different commodity bundles that a person can acquire through the use of the various legal channels of acquirement open to someone in his position" (Sen, 1984, p. 484). Drawing on Furubotn and Pejovich (1974, p. 4) and Eggertsson (1990, pp. 83-84), the following types of private PRs can be distinguished and summarized in two characteristic aspects: exclusivity and transferability.
The enforcement of PRs means excluding others from the use of scarce resources. Exclusive ownership requires costly measurement and delineation of assets and enforcement of property rights, that is, excluding others, which depends on coercion. Typically, both individual owners and the state undertake the enforcement of PRs. State enforcement increases the value of privately owned assets and constitutes one of the cornerstones of market exchange (Buchenrieder, 2002, p. 17). Scrutinizing the banking industry from the NIE point of view requires a distinguished understanding of the four types of property that are established in the NIE literature (Pejovich, 1974):

- *Private ownership*: the PRs outlined above are assigned to an individual person or organization
- *Common ownership*: rules that govern the joint use of social or ethnic groups have been established and neither individuals, organization nor the state hold exclusive rights
- *State ownership*: the PRs are assigned to the state
- *Open access*: the PRs are not fully assigned

Both open access and common ownership can be due to prohibitive TCs of establishing and enforcing exclusive rights over a resource relative to its value or to a refusal by the state to legitimize and enforce contracts in particular areas (Eggertsson, 1990).
To a certain extent, PRs are always restricted or partitioned. When the state imposes some limits on exclusive rights, literature usually refers to these restrictions as the attenuation of PRs. Attenuations are reflected in laws and regulations such as price controls for goods and services, production quotas, or licensing (Pejovich, 1974). In the course of analysis, this research project will follow up on this aspect when scrutinizing the role of regulation in the European payment market.

tions postulated by the institutions. They comprise of groups of individuals bound together by a common objective function. Firms, trade unions and co-operatives are examples of economic organizations, whereas political organizations include parties and legislative bodies. A real family is an example of a social organization (North, 1990, p. 5; Wolz, Blass, Namerova, & Buchta, 1998).

The European banking system represents in this respect a set of institutions, whereas banks, associations and client lobby groups correspond to economic or political organizations.

When applying NIE concepts to banking regulation with the ultimate goal of providing policy recommendations, it is important to take into account that institutions in the finance sector do not exist on their own but to perform a certain function. The underlying so-called functional approach does not solely deal with what currently is but with what should be done (Merton, 1993; Merton & Bodie, 1993). NIE is such a functional approach. It does not emanate from a given institutional structure but from the economic function of the banking sector, raising the question of the optimal institutional structure with regard to banking regulation or economic integration. Hence, this study distinguishes itself from a purely institutional approach of traditional banking management, which describes and systemizes financial and banking markets and which seeks to provide recommendations for an enhanced provision to financial services in retail banking.

1.2 Concepts of New Institutional Economics and reference to banking regulation

Questions on banking regulation raise specific epistemological problems. Like other social sciences (and in contrast to natural sciences), economics and fields of banking regulation research are confronted with the problem that their objects of research are individuals and their behavior. Inherently, social phenomena usually show a high level of complexity (Hayek, 1972, p. 286). Because of this complexity, and as time elapses, it is impossible to repeat an experiment with economic systems. Hence, theoretical statements on banking regulation can only be empirically tested or falsified to a very limited extent (Zimmer, 1993, p. 21). Instead of a direct falsification of ordo-theoretical statements on banking regulation, an indirect testing, based on logical linkages of tested economic hypotheses, can deliver promising results. The conceptual structure of NIE qualifies as such a system of statements.

Usually, NIE comprises several theories, which share one of the two principal lines of argumentation: (i) highlighting the incentive mechanisms of institutional arrangements or (ii) emphasizing the transaction costs associated with the exchange activities. The incentive-related theoretical strands of NIE comprise the Principal Agent Theory, the Property-Rights Theory, and the Public-Choice Theory, also referred to as the "New Political Economy" (Erlei et al., 1999;

Stiglitz, 1988). The most relevant theoretical concepts of the second research direction of NIE are Transaction Cost Theory (Coase, 1937; Williamson, 1975), the Theory of the Firm (Coase, 1937; Jensen & Meckling, 1976), the Theory of Incomplete Contracts (Goldberg, 1976; Williamson, 1975), and Information Economics (Akerlof, 1970).

This study seeks to build a conceptual link between the two principle lines of argumentation – *incentive mechanisms* and *transaction costs* – and to develop concrete ideas of institutional arrangements that provide incentives for the European retail banking industry to overcome economic barriers to integration by lowering the costs and increasing the benefits of integration. Hence, the description of the Principal Agent Theory, the Transaction Cost Theory and Information Economics is taking a central stage while factoring out the other aforementioned theoretical concepts. The latter two approaches are "theories of contracts" and are of significant importance to the financial sector and banking regulation, as they explicitly consider the multitude of often-contradictory motivations, interest, and incentives that result in the behavior of actors in the financial sector (Cezanne & Mayer, 1998, p. 1348). Especially information asymmetries as a market failure play a decisive role in banking regulation and in the integration process of the European retail banking market. In this specific situation with a multitude of special interests involved, the Principal Agent-Theory provides a valuable concept to describe the problem of effectively controlling the administrative agent through the political principal, i.e. the EC or national governments(Ahrens, 2002, p. 130; Shepsle & Weingast, 1987; Weingast, 1984, 1995). Similarly, the relationship between the regulator and regulated industries can be analyzed analogously as a problem of control.

1.3 Transaction costs in banking regulation and their measurement

Economic transactions, namely the exchange and enforcement of property rights, involve costs that are referred to as transaction costs (TC). The economics of TC is mainly derived from the seminal works of Coase (1937; 1960) and Williamson (1975). In the meantime it has grown far beyond the firm-theoretical perspective pursued by Coase (in Cezanne & Mayer, 1998, p. 1348) and the emphasis on the costs and benefits of a transaction. TCs occur in all kind of social and economic activity and include in particular the (coordination) cost of designing, enforcing and utilizing an institutional framework (Richter & Furubotn, 1996, p. 46).

The NIE plays an important role in the field of banking. By drawing on the existence of information deficits, transaction costs and the reduction of the principal agent problem, NIE effectively seeks to explain the existence of banks.[27] Furthermore, if, from NIE point of view, TC emerge as an outcome of coordination problems, institutions may contribute to solving these problems, and, as a consequence, reduce TC (Richter, 1996, p. 330). Transaction Cost Theory explains the evolution of banks as an attempt to reduce transaction costs (Coase, 1984; Williamson, 1985), which cannot be explained in the neo-classical condition of perfect competition. Accordingly, only direct financial relationships between savers and borrowers without the involvement of intermediaries would occur.

Costs of banking regulation can also be considered transaction costs. When scrutinizing banking regulation with Transaction Cost Theory potential benefits of regulation also need to be opposed to the cost of regulation and supervision. According to Dixit (1996, p. 148) economic policy should strive for at least an avoidance of new or additional transaction costs when creating a new regulation, which means that it should strive for a stable arrangement that reduces the uncertainty of interactions.

There is a mutual relationship between transaction cost and Information Economics, (also referred to as the Theory of Information Asymmetries). TCs originate in activities comprising the search for information regarding potential contracting parties and the price and quality of economic assets. If the costs for obtaining information are high, information deficits occur. On the other hand, the existence of information deficits leads to transaction costs, which arise from monitoring and enforcing a contract. Hence NIE argues that market failure that would justify regulatory intervention can occur as a result of information deficits (or asymmetries) (Akerlof, 1970).

A financial system, where banks act as financial intermediaries, is traditionally characterized by information asymmetries and multiple principal agent relationships. These include for example the relationship between retail clients and banks, banks and corporate clients, or regulators and banks. Regulators usually have an information disadvantage on the strategy, cost and income structure of banks and on the willingness of management to comply with the general policy framework to accelerate e.g. the EU's programme of developing a single market for retail banking. The agency problem and the problem of information asymmetries play an important role in all areas of regulation as all directly or indirectly involved parties, such as banks, regulatory agencies, clients and the public, have conflicting interests. Hence, cooperation problems in financial contracting result from the potential opportunism of financial market participants. In contrast to the neo-classical interpretation, such opportunism equates with egoism and aims

27 The fact that the "Theory of the Firm" is meanwhile regarded as equally important as Management Theory, traditional Institution Theory, and Capital Market Theory reflects the increased importance of NIE (Schierenbeck, 2006, p. 244).

at harming others. Williamson (1985, p. 47) sees opportunism as "[...] self-interest seeking with guile. This includes but is scarcely limited to more blatant forms, such as lying, stealing and cheating. Opportunism often involves subtle forms of deceit [...] both ex ante and ex post types are included."

By taking conflicting interests into consideration (i.e. between bank managers, shareholders or creditors), the principal agent approach provides a valuable and constructive contribution to the refinements of Capital Market Theory (Hummel, 1999, p. 206).

Prior to closing a contract (i.e. the provision of a loan, the placement of a deposit or transferring a payment), uncertainties on the quality of the contract partners prevail (*hidden information* or *hidden characteristics*), which could lead to problems of adverse selection. Furthermore, there is a behavioral uncertainty about the contract partner's intention (*hidden intentions*) throughout the lifetime of a contract (*moral hazard*, *hold up*). These kinds of agency problems can be reduced or solved by giving ex-ante incentives. The reduction of information asymmetries, *self-selection* and credible *signalling of quality* are means of incentive-compatible contract design and are crucial for agency relationships (Richter, 1996, p. 330). This means that well-defined contracts lower transaction costs and incentivize contract partners to avoid adverse behavior for the sake of their own interest.

As mentioned earlier, analyzing banking regulation from an NIE perspective is an analysis of institutional arrangements of the banking sector. Transactional efficiency and the diligent consideration of costs and benefits are measurement criteria of institutional arrangements. Deriving recommendations from theory implies that, dependent on the initial situation, the institution or form of organization such as market or hierarchy with or without regulation should be chosen that best protects against opportunistic behavior (Richter, 1996). Since the 1990s, the theoretical and empirical refinements of financial contracts of NIE have increasingly lead to a stronger focus of banking and finance theory on the reality of market relationships (Hummel, 1999, p. 207).

The New Institutional Economics has often been criticized for falling short in integrating these different approaches and for neglecting production costs. Most importantly however, the transaction cost concept has been subject to considerable debate. Sydow (1999, p. 168) argues that transaction costs are difficult to define and even more difficult to measure. One criticism is that the concept is overly general and does not lend itself to meaningful operationalization. Further criticism points out the difficulty of quantifying some transaction costs or that transformation and transaction activities frequently overlap such that it is difficult to distinguish one type of cost from the other (Polski, 2000). In addition, the assumption of opportunism being a source of transaction costs has been criticized many times as it presupposes an extremely rational human ideal.

However, this type of debate is not unique to transaction cost economics. Similar to other intuitively appealing concepts in social sciences, conceptual development depends upon being precise about the question being asked, as well as the context in which it is likely to arise (North, 1990). North (1986), Wallis and North (1986) and Williamson (Williamson, 1985) have all argued that transaction costs are embedded within layers of *governance structures*[28] and that one must operationalize the transaction cost concept in particular economic environments.

1.4 Theory on agency relationships

The theory of agency relationships is a branch of transaction cost economics. Eggertsson (1990, p. 40) differentiates between two distinct but almost separate agency literatures: the "principal-agent literature" and the "positive theory of agency". While the former is generally more mathematical and non-empirical, the latter shows the opposite characteristics. Whereas the NIE is primarily concerned with the positive agency literature, the term "principal-agent" is now being used interchangeably (Eggertsson, 1990, p. 42). Today, the theory of agency relationships is most commonly used to analyze hierarchical relationships but has also general applications to all forms of exchange (Williamson, 1996, p. 173).

The availability and tradability of information is limited. It can be communicated from one person to another, but it may be difficult to verify whether it is strictly true. Hence, incomplete or distorted disclosure of information to hide the true facts provides the basis for *opportunism* (Richter & Furubotn, 1996, pp. 163-164). In agency relationships are characterized by uncertainty and asymmetric information (Eggertsson, 1990). In such circumstances, decision-making is represented by the agency relationship in which two parties interact in a presumably mutually beneficial hierarchical relationship, where one party is better informed than the other. In this situation the uniformed party is referred to as the *principal* while the other, who has the information is called the *agent*. Determining which party is the principal and which the agent strongly depends on the circumstances. Each individual in a hierarchical structure (except at the ultimate level) is a principal and an agent at the same time when rights are cascaded down the organizational tree (Buchenrieder, 2002, p. 30).

In agency relationships, the principal delegates property rights to an agent, who is subject to formal or informal contracts and conventions, to act in the principal's interest in return of some kind (Jensen & Meckling, 1976, p. 5).

28 Williamson (1985) defines governance as a function of specific assets and governance mode costs. In his model, governance structures are distributed in three different ways, two extreme ones, hierarchy and market, and an intermediary one, the hybrid mode.

Hence, agency problems are traditionally characterized by the fact that an agent's decision does not only impact on his own but also on the principal's utility (Buchenrieder, 2002, p. 30). Conflicting interests between principal and agent as well as asymmetric information may cause behavioral risk, as the principal usually does not observe the agent's actions but rather the results of his actions. In order to evaluate and measure an agent's behavior and attributes, proxies such as a university degree or numbers of hours worked can be applied. If these proxies disclose the quality of the agent only to a limited extent, asymmetric information is the result, which may give rise to opportunistic behavior on the part of the agent (Eggertsson, 1990). Hence, agents are likely to make suboptimal decisions from a principal's point of view unless they are effectively constrained. However, market competition can reduce the agency cost to principals in various ways and raise the costs of opportunistic behavior to agents (Richter & Furubotn, 1996, pp. 268-272). Jensen and Meckling (1976, pp. 310-311) differentiate between three types of agency costs:

(i) monitoring costs, which include efforts on the part of the principal to control the behavior of the agent through budget restrictions, compensation policies, operating rules, and so forth;
(ii) bonding costs to guarantee that the agent will not take certain actions that would harm the principal or to ensure that the principal will be compensated if the agent does take such actions; and
(iii) residual costs, which are also costs of the agency relationship and which comprise the monetary equivalent of the reduction in welfare experienced by the principal.

There are two sorts of opportunism that a principal must guard against in any transaction: *moral hazard* or *ex-post opportunism* and *adverse selection* or *ex-ante opportunism*. Moral hazard applies after a contract has been agreed and the agent tries to obtain an advantage at the expense of the principal (Buchenrieder, 2002, p. 31). When trying to enforce contracts, it becomes apparent that it is very costly to monitor the overall performance of an agent and that only one or two measurement indicators are practicable. If the agent knows the measured dimensions of a contract, he is inclined to neglect tasks and to concentrate on performing well on these measured dimensions (Alchian & Demsetz, 1972, p. 311; Jensen & Meckling, 1976). Adverse selection can be illustrated by considering a case where specific measurement proxies are applied prior to entering into an employment contract. The issue of agent opportunism could only be overcome if watertight, solemn, and binding contractual agreements are established. Here, governments can largely assist by providing a clear legal framework for the formation and enforcement of contracts, as (i) the design of watertight contracts is difficult and expensive, and (ii) opportunistic behavior of agents remains present in equilibrium contracts of hierarchical relationships. Residual costs, however, stay even after the principal has taken advantage of all profitable opportunities to limit opportunism.

In sum, the total costs of agency that occur to the principal include the investments made in limiting shirking plus the costs associated with remaining or residual shirking (Jensen & Meckling, 1976, p. 310). In particular in relational contracts, in employment as well as credit or insurance contracts, principal agent relations occur. Figure 5 illustrates a broader framework in which to view bank regulation and supervision that involves a sequence of agency problems surrounded by the entire apparatus of political, legal, cultural, and technological forces influencing the operation of banks.

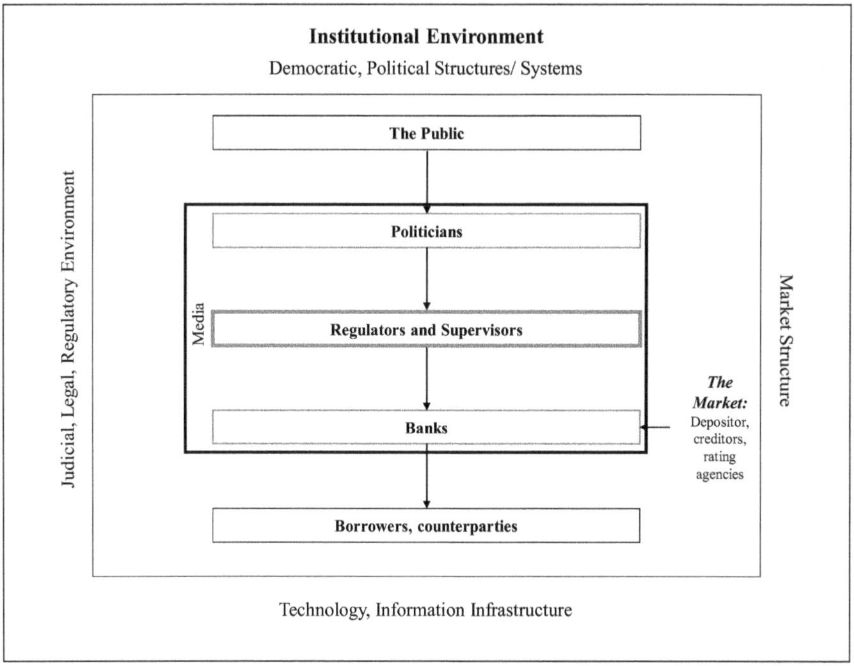

Figure 5: Framework for agency problems in the banking sector
Source: Author's illustration, modified version of the figures in Barth et al (2006, p. 6) and Buchenrieder (2002, p. 32).

At each of the five levels in this exhibit, principal agent problems and agency costs occur. For example, in the lending relationship, the financial intermediary or the bank is the principal offering loans and the borrower is the agent. The lender lacks complete knowledge of the true capability and willingness of the borrower to repay the loan and to behave in a responsible way, servicing the debt. Information asymmetries – the borrower having better information about issues such as their own business activities, behaviors, and effort than the bank – make this problem difficult, and lead to a variety of loan characteristics, such as the demand for collateral and short maturities (Buchenrieder, 2002, pp. 32-33). The borrower may not inform the lender about the true risks of the investment to secure the most advantageous borrowing conditions.

Similar agency problems continue at the next level as bank regulators and supervisors with imperfect information about banks and financial intermediaries seek to design rules and enforcement procedures that induce banks to behave in desirable ways (Barth et al., 2006). In most cases, such decisions made by the regulator result in higher transaction costs for the regulator to enforce these rules and on the part of banks to comply with these rules. At this same level, traditional corporate governance problems complicate the oversight of banks: informational asymmetries make it difficult for the market – depositors, equity holders, other creditors, and rating agencies – to monitor and control bank managers (ibid.). The series of agency problems continues at the next level, where politicians, including officials from all branches of government (European and member-state level), seek to influence bank regulators. While regulators face agency problems in controlling and monitoring banks, politicians face similar problems in controlling the regulators (ibid.). Regulators have much more information about bank activities, regulatory policies, and enforcement procedures than politicians, which may make it difficult for politicians to control regulators throughout the EU or in each single member state.

At the top level of the sequence of agency problems lies the most difficult problem: how does the public induce politicians to act in the best interests of society to increase welfare (Barth et al., 2006)? As explained in the following two chapters, occasionally politicians are motivated to behave with society's best interests in mind (the *public interest* view) and at other times, politicians promote their own private well-being to the detriment of society (the *private interest* view). The ability of the public to monitor and control politicians has key implications for the selection and operation of bank regulations and supervisory practices, and hence for bank performance and economic prosperity (ibid., 2006, p. 1.B).

Figure 5 frames the sequence of principal agent relationships and political connections within a broader institutional setting. Banks are inextricable parts of a nation's social framework where, for example, the presence and quality of checks and balances in government influence the degree to which politicians behave in a public or private interest manner (Barth et al., 2006, p. 1.B). The power and independence of the judiciary as well as legal statutes shape the extent to which rules and regulations are followed, and the ability of private market participants to exert corporate control over banks. An independent and active media can play a key role in monitoring corruption and investigating each of the relationships in the sequence of agency problems depicted in Figure 5. Finally, the level of information technology affects the flow of information about banks, which can influence both the official and private oversight of banks. This framework suggests that an array of institutional factors influences the effect of banking policies on welfare and provides important insights to counteract agency problems as explanations for market or coordination failure (ibid., 2006, p. 1.B).

2. The functional dimension of regulation

Banking regulations' primary functional focus lies on prevention or protection. Protective regulation comprises measures aimed at protecting the depositors and shareholders with the ultimate objective of creating confidence in the market. Among the protective regulations, state-regulated deposit insurance is the most prominent. Preventive regulation however comprises regulation with licensing and the sound operation of banking institutes. While protective regulation has to cope particularly with moral hazard issues, preventive regulations have to deal with issues of adverse selection (Buchenrieder, 2002, p. 95). Numerous rationales for regulation have been mentioned in academic literature, including overcoming market failures with regard to competition, institutional safety and soundness, consumer protection, credit allocation, and monetary control. Foremost, regulation and supervision of the financial system is necessary to reduce banks' incentives to engage in *moral hazard* due to the *safety net*, such as the loan-loss reserve facilities, deposit insurance, or protection of the payment systems. All of these create moral hazard problems that shift the costs and risks from private banks to the public and therefore elicit restrictions on bank behavior that need to be designed to limit such exploitations.

This chapter provides an overview of the most prominent areas of regulation research, focusing on the functional dimension of banking regulation to correct undesirable results or consequences of functioning markets. In particular, banking regulation is parameterized by describing the three types of failure appearance: market failure, government failure and coordination failure.

2.1 Normative theory and market failure

The public interest view is one of the two broad conceptual foundations for banking regulation in literature. It dominates the thinking on regulation during much of the twentieth century and has dominated the scientific discussions on regulation by the normative assumption that public regulation is determined by the public's interest in eliminating market failure or the control of market power respectively (Public-Interest School). Delegating this responsibility to politically independent experts was considered a guarantee of the protection of public interest (Bernstein, 1955).

2.1.1 Traditional reasons for market failure

The theory of allocative market failure is geared to the ideal of perfect competition. Market failure holds if the optimal welfare cannot be achieved and derives from a four-part taxonomy consisting of (i) external effects, (ii) the indivisibility (including natural monopolies and cutthroat competition), (iii) information asymmetries and (iv) adaptation inefficiencies. Other theorists draw on a more dynamic definition of market failure (Eickhof, 1997, p. 564) and argue that market failure holds when the coordination capability of a market is missing (i.e. in the case of public goods or external effects). On the contrary, competition failure can be observed where the competition process is disrupted, which is the case with natural monopolies, cutthroat competition, and information deficiencies (Eickhof, 1993, p. 210, 1997, p. 564).

This section seeks to explain the different elements of market failure and to examine briefly the applicability of concepts such as natural monopolies, cutthroat competition, public goods, external effects, and information asymmetries to the banking sector.

The threat of a *natural monopoly* and the need for government intervention exists in a particular market, where a single firm can serve that market at a lower cost than any combination of two or more firms. Until the 1970s, a natural monopoly was considered to occur in cases of scale economies, with average costs declining when output increases throughout the entire range of market demand. In this literature, economies of scale were attributed to high fixed costs and low or zero variable costs; and also considered a barrier to entry (Mosca, 2006, pp. 2-3; Samuelson & Nordhaus, 1987, p. 157). Based on the monopoly power derived from such a situation, a natural monopoly was seen as a market failure, and regulatory intervention was required (i.e. in the forms of nationalization, regulation, or antitrust) (Khemani & Shapiro, 1993).

The criticism from the Austrian Monopolist Theory and from the theory of *contestable markets*[29] caused a radical change in the definition of natural monopoly. Nowadays, it means a situation is characterized by the sub-additivity of cost functions (production costs less if it is carried out by one firm only), and by sustainability (entry is not profitable).[30] This new theory demonstrates that scale economies neither define natural monopoly properly nor do they alone constitute a barrier to entry. Instead, this theory implies that "if there is a free entry, this will prevent the monopolist from setting high prices, as they would trigger entry" (Motta, 2004, p. 70).

29 The idea of contestability and a detailed exposition of a consistent theory of market structure and its determinants is provided by Baumol (1982).

30 See Mosca (2006) for a detailed historical review of the concept of natural monopoly and of its policy implications.

Natural monopolies can also be the result of network effects when positive economies of scale occur on the demand-side. In these cases, two scenarios are likely: (i) there will be no entry of new competitors and the formation of a monopoly will lead to higher prices and a decreasing output; or (ii) the market entry of new competitors will deteriorate the market result due to the aforementioned sub-additivity of cost functions (Steden, 2002, p. 21).

It is often assumed that banks can exploit economies of scale with regard to gathering and processing information about firms, managing different types of risks for customers, advertising and distributing financial services, enforcing contracts and building reputation capital with clients (Barth et al., 2006, p. 2.B.1). Even if such an argumentation would imply tendencies towards the formation of a monopoly, a significant increase of economies of scale is only empirically supported for selective areas of the banking business, i.e. the payment and clearing services. While the threat of natural monopoly based on overall increased economies of scale in the banking industry as a whole has not yet been empirically tested, the efficiency gains based on economies of scale in a bank's value chain are considerable (both for universal and for specialized banks). In particular, the transaction-driven product areas in banking, which encompass production and support functions (back office), are strongly scale- and efficiency-driven (Canalis, 1999, p. 3).

Another element of market failure is *cutthroat competition.* Such a situation is characterized by an excess of competition next to the sub-additivity of cost functions, leading to a market failure in terms of overcapacities and increasingly tough pricing competition. In this case, market participants immediately request governmental restrictions of market entry and price competition (in banking, for example, by limiting the maximum interest rate paid on deposits) (Apolte et al., 2003, p. 88). Today, the majority view, however, is that regulation does not achieve the desired effects when applied to cut-throat competition. At least, market restrictions of any kind should be viewed skeptically: natural, inherent tendencies towards a monopoly often serve as an argument for transferring market supply to public organizations or to introduce governmental price regulations. In most cases, the justification for a public monopoly appears foreshortened: fixed costs are high in an optimum production level of a natural monopoly. From this high level of fixed costs the need to move the production of certain goods under public administration is deduced. This conclusion is not necessarily required, as high fixed costs are compatible with the fact that long-term average costs increase before market saturation is achieved (Fritsch, Wein, & Ewers, 1999, p. 209). As mentioned earlier, the existence of sub-additative costs is a pre-condition for cut-throat competition. Since this pre-condition seems not to be met in the banking sector, in particular in the retail services business, there are no indications for tendencies towards cutthroat competition.

The reference to *public goods* is an old, traditional argument in any discussion on regulatory intervention in the banking area. Compared with private goods, public goods are characterized by non-exclusiveness of interested parties in utilizing the goods (e.g. street lighting, judicial systems) and by the non-rivalry in their consumption (Apolte et al., 2003). If a consumer of a good or service cannot be excluded, it is impossible to charge for their utilization. Furthermore, the free-rider problem will also prevent firms from any investments or production. However, if the provision of certain goods or services was desired from a macroeconomic perspective, the state itself would have to engage in their production or provision. To some extent, the public good rationale is also put forward to justify governmental intervention in the banking industry (e.g. savings banks in Germany), where the opinion of banking services being a public good still prevails (Steden, 2002, p. 23). In general, the criteria of non-exclusiveness and non-rivalry are not ascertainable for all banking goods and services and hence government intervention with a reference to the public good argument can only be justified on a case-by-case basis. Whether the services provided in the European retail banking market can be included in this argumentation will be subject to further analysis.

Negative external effects exist in situations where disadvantages from the production or the consumption of goods and services occur to a third party without being compensated for. Market failure is in effect when firms produce a higher output and are neither made liable for any damages caused nor pay the costs of these damages. In this case, government regulation seeks to heal market failure by internalizing external effects by e.g. levying taxes on environmental pollution or by enforcing rules. In the banking industry, a collapse of a bank will have negative external effects on the overall economy. The bankruptcy of Lehman Brothers in September 2008, for example, has resulted in deep repercussions in the banking industry and has caused further distrust of investors and clients. It is foreseeable that the resulting bank crisis will cause a major threat to the global real economy. Hence, the statement that external effects exist cannot be dismissed a priori out of hand and will be catered to at a later stage of this study.

Information asymmetries occur when a market participant has better information than his contractual counterpart or when both lack complete information (Apolte et al., 2003, p. 204). Information asymmetries can lead to market failure or even to a situation where a market cannot develop (i.e., the *lemon problem*, see Chapter B). In traditional banking regulation, information asymmetries are in effect an expense of the depositors and the financial regulator. As will be shown in the course of this analysis, asymmetric information as a market failure plays a pivotal role in banking regulation.

In conclusion, we can assume that regulation is justifiable when market or competition failures are in effect. By means of regulation, the government can seek to correct negative macro-economic effects resulting from market failure. From a traditional point of view on banking regulation, the explanatory concepts of *external effects* and *information asymmetries apply*. Whether economies of scale or the reference to public goods provide a sound normative argument for the EU government to intervene in the European retail banking market will be further examined in Chapter E.

2.1.2 The public interest view

The public interest view holds that governments regulate banks to facilitate their efficient functioning by reducing market failures, for the benefit of a broader segment of society (Barth et al., 2006, p. 2.A). In banking, the public interest would be served if the banking system allocated resources in a socially efficient manner[31] and performed well the other functions of banking ell. According to Levine(1997, p. 691), these functions comprise among others facilitating payments, mobilizing savings and allocating capital. In this context, socially efficient implies that the banking system allocates resources in a way that it (i) maximizes output (i.e. supporting economic while facilitating risk amelioration), (ii) minimizes variance, and (iii) is "distributionally preferred"[32] (Mishan, 1969). The degree to which the specific focus is on output maximization, variance minimization, or broadening access to capital is dependent on national preferences. However, when applied to banking, the public interest view clearly involves adopting bank regulatory practices that expand output and opportunities while minimizing unnecessary risks to large segments of society, regardless of individual national weights on these objectives.

Pigou's (1938) classic treatment of regulation argues that where the market is imperfect, Adam Smith's invisible hand will not work. Monopoly power, externalities, and informational asymmetries create a constructive role for governments to help offset market failures and to enhance social welfare. This public interest or *helping-hand* view (Shleifer and Vishny, 1998) takes as given that (i) there are significant market failures and (ii) governments have the incentives and capabilities to ameliorate these market failures. In the banking environment, this view of governments considers the official supervision of banks, limits on

---

31 In a socially efficient condition undesired result or consequence of functioning markets are corrected or compensated for according to a politically defined understanding of welfare (Barth, Caprio, & Levine, 2004, p. 2).

32 Mishan (1969) emphasizes that economic policy performance should be assessed in two dimensions. Optimal strategies produce outcomes that are simultaneously Pareto-efficient and "distributionally preferred" (i.e., they help the representative citizen and avoid anti-egalitarian effects on the distribution of income). In this regard, cross-country arrangements to detect, prevent, and resolve bank insolvencies must not result in increased loss exposures that disadvantage the citizens of any partner country.

bank activities, restrictions on bank entry, and a deposit insurance scheme as appropriate policies to ease market failures and to improve resource allocation (Barth et al., 2004, p. 2).

According to Coase (1960), in a world with no information or transaction costs, with governments that maximize social welfare, and with well-defined and enforceable property rights, markets will achieve efficient outcomes. However, if the prerequisites for this laissez-faire *invisible hand* theory hold,[33] government regulation of banks would be at best irrelevant and at worst potentially harmful to social welfare. In other words, the public interest in this case would be best served by a passive role for government because the prerequisites for active government interventions – significant market failures – do not exist.

An extensive literature attests to information problems in banking, and most discussions of market failure in this area relate to imperfect information.[34] While acknowledging the function of regulation to overcome information asymmetries, governments may be well intentioned but inept. This *ineffective-hand* view of regulation does not question the existence of market failures, or the incentives of the government. According to the ineffective-hand view, even if there are market failures and even if governments demonstrate exemplary integrity, official regulation might be generally ineffective at actually easing market failures (Barth et al., 2004, 2006). This ineffectiveness results mainly for two reasons. Firstly, the mandates assigned to the regulatory agency are ambitious and difficult to fulfill in practice, which the best regulatory agency in the world could not satisfy. Secondly, weak skills, and meager resources could result in a regulatory environment that does not achieve its goals. Contrary to the public interest view, which predicts that stronger official supervision will enhance bank performance and stability, the ineffective-hand view expects no improvement at all, even in the absence of any undermining of regulation by private interests. The latter will be the view to which this chapter turns now.

2.2 Positive theory and government failure

A fundamental problem of the market failure approach is that it takes a *perfect market*[35] as a reference point for judgment. As these kinds of ideal conditions hardly ever exist in reality, any market will fail to hold up to a perfect market as a reference point, implying the necessity of regulation in almost any case. Markets fail such a comparison not because there are actual problems in these mar-

33 According to the *invisible-hand* view, the market produces an efficient outcome in which government regulations are likely to be ineffective at best and perhaps harmful to financial sector performance (Barth et al., 2004, p. 2).

34 See also Akerlof (1970), Stiglitz (1988) and Colomiris and Kahn (1991).

35 The economic term of a perfect market implies a long-term equilibrium under perfect competition, perfect information transparency, and the absence of transaction costs.

kets but because they are evaluated against an unreachable, idealistic reference point. Argumentations that build on the reasoning of allocative market failure tend to call immediately for government intervention.

However, before considering every imperfect market condition a potential market failure and thus a ubiquitous threat, more dynamic and efficient approaches to regulation should be examined that acknowledge the self-healing process of markets. This can be observed in contestable markets, where markets in which there are only a few companies that, because of the threat of new entrants, behave in a competitive manner, or, for example, in *lemon markets*, where building-up a reputation overcomes the asymmetric information problems. Hence, market failure matters less in practice than is often supposed.[36]

Just because banking regulation can be observed in a certain market, does not necessarily mean that it is justified. In fact, in most cases the regulation of an industry does not comply with the requirements of normative theory. The positive theory of regulation, representing an area of the Public-Choice Theory, seeks to clarify this discrepancy (Stiglitz, 1988). In contrast to the normative theory, the positive theory does not deal with the question of what should be but it seeks to explain the as-is situation. Part of this theory is reflected in Bernstein's life-cycle approach; it assumes that, at the beginning, governments serve the interest of the public welfare but turn to serve the interests of individual groups over time. The private interest view of regulation, also called the *private interest theory* of regulation or *regulatory capture view*, characterizes a regulatory process that is primarily shaped by the private interests of the regulator or the regulatees, rather than by the public interest (Peltzman, 1976; Stigler, 1971). The private interest view accepts the presence of market failures but conceives regulation as a product, with various suppliers and demanders interacting to determine the exact shape and purpose it serves (Barth et al., 2006, p. C.2).

Stigler (1971) and Peltzman (1976) have been the principal theorists of the private-interest view of economic regulation. Both draw their reasoning from the demand-side of regulation, the special interest pressure from producers and electoral pressure from consumers. Stigler's (1971, p. 4) main argument comprises two primary premises:

(i) The fundamental asset controlled by the state is the power to coerce. Any group that can control how this power is used can profit.
(ii) Since individuals or organizations are self-interested actors, they will seek to obtain the state's coercive power to support their interests. Efforts to do so, however, are costly.

The implication is that special-interest pressure of large firms or producers is always more persuasive than that of consumers so producers always win. These

36 The Economist (1996, p. 66).

compact, well-organized interest groups are able to use the coercive power of the state to capture rents for themselves at the expense of more dispersed groups: "as a rule, regulation is acquired by the industry and is designed and operated primarily for its benefit"(Stigler, 1971, p. 3). Stigler's logic can be summarized as follows:

- Large firms have high benefits from mobilizing, since they are a small group and since they are homogeneous. Hence, they have less difficulty with collective action problems.
- Small firms do not organize for political reasons because of collective action problems and low potential benefits.
- Consumers do not self-organize as the costs of doing so are high compared with the benefits.

Stigler's reasoning is mainly criticized for looking only at the demand for regulation and largely ignoring the supply-side view, ignoring the regulator's motivations. Stigler does touch on the supply-side slightly, pointing out that legislatures want political support, campaign contributions, future employment, bribes, and so on. By underemphasizing the supply-side, he ends with an unrealistic conclusion that consumers always lose. Peltzman's (1976) modification of Stigler's model corrects this problem, resulting in far more realistic predictions. Peltzman seeks to give equal attention to supply-side factors – that is, factors that might motivate regulators to produce regulations that benefit consumers even though producers lobby better. Peltzman replaced Stigler's vague concept of a *regulator* with the more concrete idea of a *legislator*, with all the electoral motivations that implies. In this context, Peltzman's theory presents a balanced theory of both supply and demand of regulation, which specifies a political equilibrium for a regulator. As regulators want to be re-elected, they base their decision about a proposed regulation on marginal political costs and marginal political gains. Governments and legislators are usually the main suppliers, and although consumers may demand regulation, industry itself is an important influence on the demand-side both for and against certain types of regulation.

Applied to banking, the private interest view on regulation would expect to see regulations that enhance the power or well-being of bankers and those producer interest groups that are politically well connected. Actually, the central role of banks in allocating resources makes them subject to and attracts the attention of every interest group seeking money. These are, among others, bankers themselves, politicians, unions, or other stakeholders in the banking system. Hence, these groups in society compete in attempting to influence national or subnational policies toward banks in ways that favour themselves even if these policies do not maximize social welfare (Barth et al., 2006, p. C.2). Accordingly, the private interest school supports greater reliance on market discipline, information disclosure, a light hand by the regulatory authorities, and significant oversight of the regulatory process itself (Shleifer, 2005). At the same time, the interest group approach emphasizes how the costs and benefits of regulations can have a differential impact on various interest groups, viewing them as a good that is sold by politicians and bureaucrats to the addressees of regulation (Demsetz, 1968).

Although the public interest view of regulation assumes the government has the incentives and capabilities to reduce market failures, this condition may not always hold. Since the work of Stigler (1971) and Peltzman (1976), regulation has been viewed as a product and is therefore analyzed by focusing on supply and demand forces. This view could be described as the case of *regulatory capture*, i.e., the creeping gain of control of a regulation agency through the interests of regulated industries, or *political capture*, i.e., the *grabbing hand* of Shleifer and Vishny (1998), depending on where one sees the division of gains going. In both phenomena, regulators may thereby lose sight of the ultimate objective of regulation, which is to ameliorate market failures. In fact, regulatory capture is particularly serious in industries such as banking where there is a conflict of interest between the firms' objectives (to maximize profits) and the objectives of the regulation (to provide consumer protection and maintain systemic stability) (Wilson, 1980). The regulatory capture view holds that governments regulate banks to facilitate the financing of government expenditures, to funnel credit to politically attractive ends, and, more generally, to maximize the welfare and influence of politicians and bureaucrats, even when loftier, public-interest objectives are the ostensible goal. A proponent of regulatory capture might describe the same situation as one in which bankers enjoy large rents, in return for which they are willing to finance government expenditures, within certain constraints, and to do other favors for government officials (Barth et al., 2006).

Finally, the extent to which market failure can be corrected by the government at all remains an open question. From the viewpoint of Positive Regulation Theory, regulation is not always sensible nor required to cure imperfect markets. Often, regulated markets comprise inefficiently operating industries and a high cost of regulation, which exceed the cost of negative externalities. Such a situation will lead to even more inefficient results than without government intervention and ultimately involves the danger of government failure. Even if market failure exists, a "comparative institutional approach" (Demsetz, 1969, p. 1) can provide an adequate framework to weigh market failures against government failure and to question the purpose of state intervention. Until the 1980s, there was mostly consensus on the rationale of regulation and the economic sectors in need of regulation. Since then, a global tendency towards liberalization, privatization, and deregulation resulting in an increased scepticism towards the government's ability to cure market failure could be observed. In this regard, government failure is making a good case for submitting markets again to the mechanisms of market economy and free competition. Furthermore, technological innovation has overcome assumed market failure in many industry sectors over time, i.e. the evolved mobile phone industry in the telecommunication sector. The latter has therefore also significantly benefited from deregulation over the last two decades. In contrast, the banking sector has not benefited as much from technological development but has witnessed instead an increase in regulation density.

2.3 Coordination failure

As described in the previous sections, market failure is the strongest reason for defending an active role for the state in the economy. In addition to economic research on market-imperfections and government failure, development economists widely use the theory of coordination failure to define a new case for industrial policy (Aoki et al., 1998; Matsuyama, 1997; Rodrik, 1996). Unlike market failure, which unconditionally justifies the immediate substitution of state-led coordination for market coordination, coordination failures, coordination failure in the economy can be more general: it occurs, for example, when price signals fail to achieve efficient allocation (Aoki et al., 1998, p. xvii). The focus of publications on coordination failure lies in the idea that the economy may fail to achieve coordination among complementary activities. In terms of developmental economics, some investment projects are not undertaken because complementary investments do not exist, and these latter investments do not occur precisely because the former are absent (Glavan, 2008, p. 225). Hence, coordination failure leads the market to an (equilibrium) outcome inferior to a potential situation where resources would be allocated in an optimal way.

According to the coordination-externality argument, the economy works like an ecosystem, where

> [a] key factor determining how any individual will behave is his environment. One of the most important aspects of that environment is the behavior of others. Under some conditions, ecosystems have multiple equilibria, and individuals may fail to "coordinate" on the equilibrium that is preferred by everyone […]. The basic mechanics of coordination failure are simple: an individual's behavior—for example, to produce or to prey on the production of others—creates externalities. The externalities affect not only the welfare of others, but also their decisions. The interaction of the slightly distorted behaviors of many different agents may produce very large distortions and can lead to the existence of multiple equilibria, some very good for every member of the economy, and some very undesirable" (Samuel Bowles, Durlauf, & Hoff., 2006, emphasis in original, cited in Glavan (2008, p. 225)).

Matsuyama compares this coordination problem with "the problem of hundreds of people, scattered in a dense, foggy forest, trying to locate one another—is of such fundamental difficulty that no algorithm can solve it. What the economics of coordination tries to show is that *even* the market mechanism cannot solve the problem" (1997, pp. 134-135). For Rodriguez-Clare (2005, p. 5), "[a] firm's productivity depends not only on its own efforts and abilities and general economic conditions (e.g. the macroeconomic environment and the legal system), but also on the actions of other firms, infrastructure, regulation, and other public goods. The problem is that, due to economies of scale, thick market effects, knowledge spillovers, and other problems of non-excludability, the provision of these inputs and services is plagued by market failures."

The literature on coordination problems has a long tradition and a vast literature explores these market failures, which often give rise to a multiplicity of equilibria. Paul Rosenstein-Rodan argued in his seminal 1943 article "Problems of industrialization of Eastern and Southeastern Europe"[37] that an investment made by one firm could have a positive effect on the profitability of investment by other firms. In this respect, higher investments give rise to an increase in aggregated demand. Under economies of scale, this increases the profitability of investments made elsewhere in the economy (i.e. through positive spillover effects).[38] Murphy et al. (1989) identified multiple equilibria in these circumstances: a low-investment and a high-investment equilibrium. Every market participant would be better off at the high-investment equilibrium, but there are no market forces taking an economy from the low-investment to the high-investment equilibrium. Hence, some kind of state coordination is required to move from the bad to the good equilibrium (Rodriguez-Clare, 2005, p. 6). Thus, when an economy is in the bad equilibrium, there is a coordination failure.

There are many other economic activities that involve joint decisions and where the interdependence among multiple agents leads to coordination failure. When the investment or effort choice of each agent affects the other, the coordination of input decisions is necessary to achieve economic efficiency. In this context, Rodrik (2004) notes that "many projects require simultaneous, large-scale investments to be made in order to become profitable" (ibid., p. 12). Furthermore, Rodrik illustrates the classical coordination problem using the proverbial chicken-and-egg dilemma, where a producer will only invest in a greenhouse if he can be assured that there will be enough supplier services nearby. In reverse, all of these services have high fixed costs, and are unlikely to be provided by private entities unless they have an assurance that there will be enough greenhouses to demand their services in the first place. Rodrik concludes that "coordination failures can arise whenever new industries exhibit scale economies and some of the inputs are non-tradable (or require geographic proximity)" (2004, p. 13).[39]

37 See Rosenstein-Rodan (1943, p. 205).

38 See Murphy, Shleifer, and Vishny (1989, pp. 1004-1005).

39 In an earlier publication, Rodrik (1996, p. 2) is more precise about what the two necessary conditions for these types of coordination failure are: the existence of some scale economies, and imperfect tradability across national borders of some of the goods, services, or technologies associated with skill-intensive manufacturing.

Considering, for example, the case of the SEPA initiative in the European retail payment market, where the private banking sector must make considerable fixed investments that would benefit all the banks in Europe. If each bank invests without considering the benefits that accrue to other market participants, the investment choice is assumed to be lower than that which maximizes the joint return from the investment. If all banks could commit to cooperating, then they could all choose efficient levels of investment. By cooperation, all banks are able to generate a high pay-off for all agents involved. If they do not cooperate, pay-offs will be lower for all.

Throughout the years, transition and development economics have mainly contributed to the research on coordination failure. Economists developed the idea that interdependencies among market participants prevent an optimal allocation of resources and the policy recommendation based on it should be considered carefully (Glavan, 2008, p. 230). The current discussion in the relevant literature centers on the role of governments in overcoming this *hold-up problem* and in ensuring optimal resource allocation. It characterizes the distinction between a market-friendly view and the developmental-state view as one where market and government were substitutes. The market-friendly view emphasizes that coordination problems should be resolved by market-based institutions while the developmental-state view underlines that important coordination problems should be resolved by governments. Generally speaking, these two views consider markets and government as rival institutions for determining the locus of coordination in the economy (Aoki et al., 1998, pp. 18-19). A third view has emerged that does not see the government and the private sector as rivals, competing for control over economic activity. Instead, this "market-enhancing view" as Aoki, Kim and Okuno-Fujiwara (1998) call it, emphasizes the role of government action in promoting private-sector coordination. This perspective recognizes the ability of the private sector to coordinate a large fraction of economic activity (whether across markets, within firms, through intermediaries, or jointly with government), while also recognizing the potential for governments to facilitate the development of private-sector institutions (i.e. price mechanism with state intervention). Various policy instruments induce coordination and cooperation in private sector institutions and aim at increasing their capabilities to resolve market failures. The market-enhancing view recognizes the ability of governments to complement private institutions rather than being a substitute for the market mechanism.

While this view derives from the economic development process in East Asia (Aoki et al., 1998, p. 24), this research project seeks to illustrate that, even within highly developed Western-European economies, coordination failure will be pervasive and may even become more difficult to resolve as technological and market opportunities become more uncertain and complex. This is the case with the development of the European retail banking market, where EU authorities are increasingly accompanying a market-led integration process. In this new approach, EU authorities are mostly alert to potential coordination failures where market forces alone may not be able to achieve a positive outcome. In the European multilevel system, the interests of various private actors and national governments are even more diffuse and difficult to coordinate. Together with industrial associations, public organizations therefore play an important role as facilitators, helping the industry to overcome such coordination problems.

A an example from the banking sector, which will be examined in more detail in this book's case study, is the establishment of the Single Euro Payments Area (SEPA). In this case, there is some evidence of a substantial *first-mover disadvantage* – first movers bear high costs by complying with specific standards, but do not necessarily reap the highest rewards (Tumpel-Gugerell, 2005a).

2.4 Contrasting functional banking regulation approaches

Over the course of time and across countries, approaches to bank regulation have varied from extremely light to all encompassing, from highly interventionist regulations and even outright government ownership to episodes of *free* banking. In this regard, the three types of economic failure described in the functional dimension of banking regulation and the theoretical reasoning supporting the explanations are historically interlinked. While all three agree upon the ultimate objective of regulation, which is to ensure economic and social efficiency while enabling free competition, they strongly differ regarding the degree of governmental intervention and the instruments to be deployed to correct market detriments (see Table 5).

While the government and coordination failure views consider social efficiency as a function of regulation and incentive problems to explain coordination failure, the market failure view and the Public Interest Theory focus on economic efficiency as a principal objective of regulation. The latter provides a sound starting point for assessing the necessity for regulation to eliminate market failure but obliviously has become less convincing as it naively holds that politicians and others involved in the promulgation of legislation by and large pursue what they think is the *public interest* (Ogus, 2004, p. 35). Therefore, the explanatory power of the NIE and the Private Interest Theory provides a comprehensive explanation for the behavioral and political aspect of regulation to describe and eliminate government and coordination failure. Both views are critical for analyzing economic and political obstacles to the integration of European retail markets, to derive policy implications.

In this respect, a certain tension between economic and social efficiency cannot be dismissed out of hand. Public regulation is, by this fact itself, permanently confronted with a trade-off between public welfare and competition, even if it is organized through independent regulatory organizations. Decision-makers will hardly politically reject social requirements beyond a Pareto-optimal level. The protection of labor, environment, or consumers is only one example of such a social regulation, which has experienced a significant amount of quantitative and qualitative regulation both on the national and in particular on the European level. The latter strongly suggest a more detailed view on the theoretical concepts of the territorial dimension of regulation – European regulation and integration policy – that will be addressed in the following chapter.

Table 5: Comparing functional banking regulation approaches

	Market failure	Government failure	Coordination failure
Approach	Normative Theory – investigating which type of regulation is the most efficient under which conditions	Positive Theory – providing an economic explanation for regulation and deriving the consequences of regulation	
Principal objective of regulation	Economic efficiency	Economic and social efficiency	
Diagnosis	Market mechanism fails to ensure an optimal allocation of resources	Regulated markets comprise often inefficiently operating industries and a high cost of regulation, which exceed the cost of negative externalities	Coordination failures can arise whenever new industries exhibit scale economies and some of the inputs are non-tradable or require geographic proximity
Reasons for state intervention	• Reference to public goods • Negative external effects • Indivisibility (including natural monopolies and cutthroat competition) • Information asymmetries	• Market failures are accepted • Regulation as a political product, with various suppliers and demanders (private interests) interacting to determine the exact shape and purpose it serves	• Overcoming "hold-up" problem and ensuring optimal resource allocation • Emphasizing the role of government action in promoting private-sector coordination • Incentive setting
Explanatory theory	Public Interest Theory New Institutional Economics	Private Interest Theory Regulatory Capture Theory	New Institutional Economics Theory of Coordination Failure
Role of government	• Facilitate, maintain or imitate market operations • Allocation and assertion of individual property rights • Assertion of freedom of contract and enforcement of contract compliance	• Regulation as a good that is sold by politicians and bureaucrats to the addressees of regulation • Decisions about a proposed regulation are based on a comparison of marginal political costs and marginal political gains.	• Government policy to facilitate or complement private-sector coordination using private-sector institutions to resolve coordination problems whenever feasible • A market-enhancing view on regulation is proposed (the government framing the market mechanism)
Relevance for banking regulation	• Achieves greater stability in the banking sector and minimizing crisis costs	• Supports greater reliance on market discipline, information disclosure, a light hand by the regulatory authorities, and significant oversight of the regulatory process itself	• Check whether this method can be adapted to banking regulation, in particular to examine the mechanism of coordination to promote market integration
Example	• Deposit insurances • Minimum economic capital reserves for loan provision and other financial products	• Banks to facilitate the financing of government expenditures • Funneling credit to politically attractive ends	• Building an airport in a region that has no hotels would not lead to any traffic, but hotels without a regional airport may not be profitable either
Relevance to research question	Medium: • Individual national retail banking markets are functioning and efficient • Any market failures in the industry are eliminated on national levels	Medium: • The banking industry is one of the most regulated industries • The lack of market integration is only partially caused by the private-sector resistance – regulatory obstacles are more important detriments	High • Examine the capacity of government policy to facilitate or complement private-sector coordination, i.e. through a target government frame with price-mechanisms
Critiques	• "Ineffective hand view": official regulation might be generally ineffective at actually easing market failures	• Creeping gain of control of a regulation agency through the interests of regulated industries, or "political capture", i.e. the "grabbing hand" • Regulators may lose sight of the ultimate objective of regulation – to ameliorate market failures	• Little empirical research performed to date on the adaptability to highly developed, mature Western-European economies • Generic proposition difficult in *ex-ante* considerations

Source: Author's illustration.

3. The territorial dimension of regulation

This dimension of research focuses on the territorial view of regulation. It combines the thesis of a changing function of government with the argument that, in the course of market integration, public regulation is shifting from a national to a European level. Majone (1997b; 1994b), for example, assumed that regulation policy is particularly susceptible to Europeanization, which is mainly driven by two factors. Firstly, in a number of risk-associated policy areas, protective norms and standards have taken on greater importance.[40] Secondly, with the privatization of public enterprises, the liberalization of markets in the 1980s and 1990s, and the process of integration, the regulatory monitoring of market power has become more prominent across all industries (Eberlein & Grande, 2000, p. 84).

The European banking and financial service industry has gone through this process of integration, which reached its peak with the adoption of the single currency in 1999. The completion of the single market for banking has involved the implementation of EU regulations aimed at opening domestic markets and partially harmonizing national banking systems. In particular, a strong regulatory thrust came from the pressure exercised by special interest groups representing firms, consumers, and EU politicians who aimed at centralizing regulatory decision-making on an EU level, strongly encouraged by the *negative integration*.[41] This triggered off the production of additional banking directives without leading market liberalization into a *retreat of state* (Eichner, 2000, pp. 66-67). Rather, these policies have created a "regulatory paradox": the "liberalization" of the EU banking market has resulted in efforts to meet the public expectations of a single market – by means of regulation (Grande, 1994a, 1997c, 2005; König & Benz, 1997b; Majone, 1990; Vogel, 1996). While many expected that the introduction of the euro would foster the establishment of branches across borders, trigger international consolidation in the banking sector, and increase the volume of cross-border sales, an integrated market for EU retail banking has largely failed to materialize (Kleimeier & Sander, 2007, p. 5).

In the context of the new, policy-oriented European research, a number of studies on regulation policy in the European multilevel governance system have emerged. The focus of these investigations is the territorial dimension of regulation. Here, academic research has focused on the distribution of competencies between the national and the European level, and the relation between national sovereignty and European integration. The liberalization of different infrastructure sectors (e.g. telecommunication or energy) raises questions on the condi-

40 Among these are, in particular, labour and health policy and consumer and environmental protection (Eberlein & Grande, 2005, p. 95).

41 See Chapter A for the definitions of *positive* and *negative* integration.

tions for enforcing European policy (market opening and integration) against national resistance (Schmidt, 1997). The vertical perspective also dominates the analysis of regulation issues: how can different national regulation traditions and policy approaches be arranged to suit the uniform requirements of a single market (Héritier, et al., 1994)?

Against this backdrop, this study follows up on two particular research findings. In the area of environment regulation, Héritier (1996) showed that no enduring, dominant regulation approach has yet evolved on the European level. Instead, a patchwork of regulation solutions is assessed on the supranational level and also considered to exist in the future (Héritier, 1996). With regard to the distribution of competencies between the EU and its member states, McGowan and Wallace (1996) observed an increase in regulation activity at the European level. At the same time, they also noticed a division of labor between national and European regulation (two-tier regulation). In this regulatory setup, the framework is formulated on the European level, whereas the responsibility for implementation remains with national regulatory agencies. Such a regulatory regime also provides room for maneuver for national authorities in Europeanized policy areas. National agencies and authorities deal with firms and citizens as addressees of regulation whereas European agencies regulate national regulatory agencies. Here, European regulation can hardly fall back on any vertical controls. European regulatory agencies seem to strive for the objective of a Europe-wide uniform regulation by becoming network coordinators focusing on instruments of information exchange, shared policy knowledge, and administrative coordination (Dehousse, 1997, p. 259). Such repercussions of European policy on national regulation environments have recently been discussed under the central issue of the Europeanization of national policy (Caporaso, Cowles, & Risse, 1998).

Despite the appreciation of existing research findings, European policy studies still lack a deeper understanding of the complex interaction between national and European regulation policy, i.e. of the patterns and consequences of "parallel operation and incidence of supranational, national and subnational regulation" (Begg, 1996, p. 529) in the European multilevel system. With regard to the initial research question of this work, another problem supervenes. So far, the functional dimension of regulation, i.e. the question on the demarcation between economy and policy, between market and government, in the European multilevel system has mostly been disregarded by policy-oriented EU studies (Genschel, 1998). For this reason, this research project seeks to contribute to the further development of the studies of EU policy-making by establishing a link between the territorial and functional dimensions of regulation.

This chapter provides an overview of the main theories on European integration to put the findings from the functional analysis of regulation into the context of the intergovernmental structure of the EU. In particular, the Europeanization Theory, which evolved from the grand theories, provides valuable insights into the process of EU policy-making. A top-down integration approach driven by the EU through coordinating directives has characterized the European banking process since the 1980s. In order to evaluate better the process alternatives such as a bottom-up or a market-driven approach, an assessment of the function of regulation (i.e., banking services as referred to as public goods) has to preface the discussion on the locus of regulation. Here, constructing a single European market for financial services and reaching a compromise in the areas of member state sovereignty, belief, and preference structures will be difficult and coordination problems will challenge government authority on all levels.

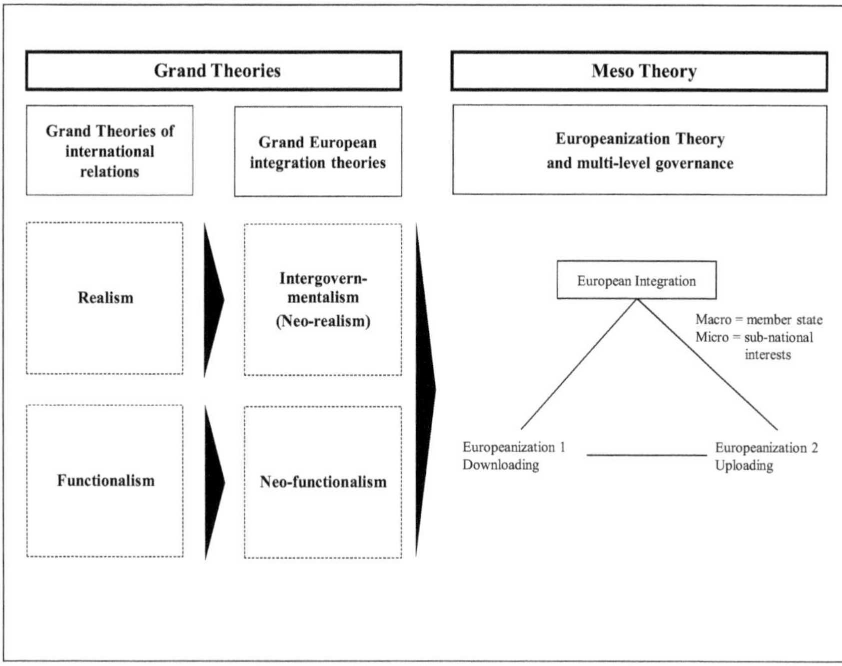

Figure 6: Theoretical concepts of European integration
Source: Author's illustration, including a modified version of the figure in Howell (2004a, p. 49).

3.1 European Integration Theory

This section aims to provide an overview of the contemporary theoretical work on European integration. This involves revisiting the classical *pre-theories* of international relations and the grand European integration theories, chartering their development and their engagement with one another. This overview includes a short discussion of their explanatory power of integration with respect to the policy-making at all levels – supranational, national and sub-national. This is in particular important to understand in order to allocate regulatory power that facilitates and coordinates banking market integration to an adequate, competent authority. In this regard, this section starts by reviewing the grand theories before continuing to the meso theory of Europeanization.

While realism and functionalism attempted to explain the international level, intergovernmentalism and neo-functionalism sought to provide positivist explanations in terms of predictions and cause and effect on the European level.

The realist theory is based on Thomas Hobbes' concept of international relations as forming the basis for what he calls "international skepticism", where "certain structural features of an anarchical world order make international morality impossible" (Beitz, 1979, p. 13). It emphasizes the importance of the nation state in the process of international politics and provides a positivist methodological approach used by realists, which could also fail to identify important variables when explaining integration (Howell, 2004a, p. 33).

Based on the realist critique, intergovernmentalists (or neo-realists) consider that the member states of the EU were self–interested and sovereign, incapable of and unwilling to act in a collective manner. The main emphasis of intergovernmentalism is that the interstate bargaining and national preferences provide the main thrust and rationales for European integration (Moravcsik, 1993, 1997, 1998). Moravcsik proved that the primary source of integration resided with member states and in this context takes an intergovernmental position. In this regard, integration is driven by interstate bargaining, states are unitary actors with economic interests and compete for these interests to be promoted by national governments in EU decision-making, while supranational organizations seem to have a limited impact on outcomes. Moravcsik further argues that "European integration resulted from a series of rational choices made by national leaders who consistently pursued economic interests – primarily the interests of powerful economic producers and secondarily the macroeconomic preferences of ruling government coalitions – that evolve slowly in response to structural incentives in the global economy" (1998, p. 3). However, Richardson (1996) argued that the European integration is "not simply the outcome of inter-state bargaining" (p. 5), but a complex process that involves numerous actors and rules, federal, functional and neo-functional variables as well as realist or intergovernmental processes.

The modern understanding of functionalism in the realms of international relations is commonly attributed to David Mitrany. Functionalist theory asserts a positive relationship between functional need and structural adaptation. If needs (or functions) were satisfied, the creation of complementary structures realized through organizations with specific tasks would follow (Mitrany, 1970, 1975b, 1975c). Because structures pattern behavior, states will tend to cooperate peacefully. In a narrower sense, a functional outcome may produce a "pluralist international community where national control is marginalized through functional linkages", or, in a broader sense, "a situation where the nation state disappears and is replaced by international functional rationality" (Howell, 2004a, p. 35). Effectively, functionalism is the internationalization of politics, with decision-making being carried out at the most rational or functional level. Mitrany considered that functionalism does not pursue some form of end result in the context of a political community as human beings have no concept of what the end result of integration should encompass (Mitrany, 1975a). Compared with federalism, which provides for the establishment of some form of federal state as an end result, functionalism identifies the process towards this goal.

Unlike functionalism, neo-functionalism suggests that integration is more easily achieved in a regional setting with an incremental approach. In this respect, Haas (1958) and Lindberg (1963) provided an explanation of the process and progression of European integration through the analysis of supranationality, sub-national interests, and spillover. In both theorists' views, we can identify a shift of loyalties by sub-national actors towards a new centre, whose institutions possess or demand jurisdiction over the pre-existing national states (Haas, 1958, p. 60; Lindberg, 1963, p. 6). Sub-national interests shift their allegiance to a supranational body and in doing so further develop supranational institutions and provide a stimulus for spillover. Haas (1976) differentiated between three types of spillover: [42]

(i) *Functional* spillover, which indicated that integration in one industry created its own momentum and necessitated further integration both in the same, and in other industries
(ii) *Cultivated* spillover, which assumed that the EC would be pro-active in the management of European integration
(iii) *Institutional/ political* spillover, which describes the build-up of new powers and tasks to a central institutional structure

Tranholme-Mikkelson (1991, p. 4) observed an interaction between spillover and supranationality in that the "establishment of supranational institutions designed to deal with functionality specific tasks will trigger economic, social and political processes which generate pressures towards further integration". Whether cultivated and institutional/political spillover still affect the formation and continuation of a common market in Europe, the functional linkage of tasks and the "expansive logic of sector integration" (Haas, 1958, p. 243) has been a point of contention for neo-functionalists.

A further interpretation of neo-functionalism sees European integration as the process of transferring exclusive expectations of benefits from the nation

42 Cited in Howell (Howell, 2004a, p. 37).

state to some larger entity. Schmitter (1971, p. 238) further outlines that "[it] encompasses the process by virtue of which national actors of all sorts (government officials, interest group spokesmen, politicians as well as ordinary people) cease to identify themselves in their future welfare entirely with their own national government and its policies". This view of neo-functionalism was revisited and criticized for being insufficient and obsolete, as European integration had created a policy-making system that was partially integrated but that political integration was unlikely (Pedersen, 1992; Webb, 1983). Furthermore, Keohane and Hoffman (1990) considered a pooling of sovereignty rather than a transfer from the member states to supranational institutions and Corbey (1995) amended neo-functionalism by arguing that dialectic functionalism provided the forward motion for European integration. In fact, European integration was "a process of action (decision to act) and reaction (response to integration). Progress is generated by mutual interaction of the institutions of the EU, member states and interest groups. Since integration proceeds in stages, the dialectics of the process has to be given more attention" (Corbey, 1995, pp. 62-63).

Sandholtz (1993) argued that membership of the EU defined preference parameters and decisions, and that intergovernmentalism alone failed to explain the impact that membership of the EU has on member-state preferences, interests and demands. In fact, if European integration was to be fully understood, a combination of approaches and a lower level of abstraction than the grand theories was necessary.

A detailed assessment of European Integration Theory as performed by Howell (2004a, pp. 32-40) implies that there can be an "amalgamation" of international relations and European integration theories in advancing the understanding of the European integration process. Through multilevel governance and Europeanization, this area of research can be extended again: recent research on European integration has moved away from grand scale theories about the causes and directions of this phenomenon to meso or middle-range theories about precise terms of change and the impact of EU involvement on the policy-making process (Adshead, 2002, p. 25). In order to deal with the limitations and problems of the grand theories, the Europeanization can be perceived as a meso theory in particular in relation to neo-functionalism and intergovernmentalism, which includes certain aspects of both theoretical models. The next chapter concentrates on providing a brief overview of Europeanization and its relationships with European integration and regulation.

3.2 Europeanization Theory

This section builds on the previous section in developing an understanding of European Integration Theory and how this may be applied to the European integration process, or being more specific with regard to the research topic, how this may be applied to retail banking market integration.

Many meso theories have included historical institutionalism and state-centric and multilevel governance to deal with the limitations of the grand theories. However, there have been criticisms of multilevel governance as a theory that only provides descriptions of what is happening in the EU. In this respect, Europeanization attempts to deal with these perceived deficiencies through a synthesis of multilevel governance and elements of the grand theories.

Over the last decade, Europeanization has been a fashionable term with many definitions. Dyson and Goetz (2004) acknowledge the difficulties of clearly defining the concept and indicated how the notion differs from a very narrow to a very broad sense:

> "(I)t is sometimes used narrowly to refer to implementation of EU legislation or more broadly to capture policy transfer and learning with the EU. It is sometimes used to identify the shift of national paradigm and instruments to the EU level." (ibid., p. 2)

The academic work of Howell (2004a, pp. 42-46) represents the most ambitious attempt to overcome some of the criticisms leveled by the grand theories of integration. Howell discusses the problem of the "conceptual stretching" of Europeanization and outlines the difference between Europeanization and European integration. His attempt to draw boundaries around this concept leads to a definition of Europeanization as a continual, interactive, or dialectic process between the uniformity of the EU and the diversity of the individual member states. By breaking up the theory into constituent parts, Howell proposes two categories of Europeanization and their possible variations:

(i) top-down (policy downloading, EN1), or
(ii) bottom-up (policy uploading, EN2)

In its most explicit form, Europeanization is conceptualized as the process of downloading (EN1) EU directives, regulations and institutional structures to the domestic, member-state level (Howell, 2004b, p. 53). For instance, two coordination directives primarily affected the European banking sector in the earlier times of the European Union. The First Banking Directive[43] cleared many impediments to the freedom of establishment for banks and other financial organizations and introduced home country supervision and a common position for the granting of banking licenses. The Second Banking Directive[44] aimed at removing authorization problems, e.g. 12 different supervisors, a definition of banking activities and cross-border trade. It enabled a single banking license, a list of banking activities, and minimum capital levels. The directive also provided su-

43 The European Parliament and the Council of the European Union (1997).
44 The European Parliament and the Council of the European Union (2000).

pervisory rules in terms of internal management, audit systems, and control levels of major shareholders. Furthermore, once banks could trade cross-border, other credit institutions lobbied for a level playing field in financial services (Howell, 2004b).

This conceptualization of Europeanization, however, has been extended in the literature in terms of uploading (EN2) to the EU, shared beliefs, informal and formal rules, discourse, identities, and vertical and horizontal policy transfer. Shared beliefs, for example, may be observed in the creation of the Single European Market (SEM), where diverse beliefs relating to the market are streamlined under one regulatory structure. Even though differing interpretations of regulation re-emerge at the domestic level, certain beliefs have been shared, e.g. liberal market structures in the SEM (Howell, 2004a, p. 80).

Europeanization as a meso theory provides the opportunity to break down intergovernmentalism and neo-functionalism in such a way as to allow a certain degree of empirical reliability. Aspects of Europeanization, such as downloading or uploading, for example, may be empirically investigated and verified or negated (Moravcsik, 1998, p. 33). Furthermore, Europeanization may be interpreted as a means of overcoming some of the criticisms leveled at grand theories. For instance, functional spillover (or task expansion) can be understood in terms of top-down Europeanization and the interpretation of the legislation downloaded from the EU as aspects of intergovernmentalism (Howell, 2004a, p. 55). The latter recognizes the distinction between integrative legislation provided by the EU and different national interpretations caused by Europeanization. European integration may be understood as both the outcome of domestic uploading to the EU level through Europeanization and the process of downloading once an accepted compromise is reached. By means of uploading and cultivated spillover, EU diversity is integrated through shared beliefs. However, when downloading comes into play, each EU member state will interpret policies and regulations based on their own cultural perspective and belief structure. This implies that integration does take place, but not to the extent that EU policy originally anticipated. Furthermore, uploading may be conceived in either macro or micro terms: national preferences may be uploaded by member-state governments through, for example, the Council of Ministers or Inter-Governmental Conferences (IGCs) (macro term), whereas, in micro terms, the uploading of industry and sector preferences mainly happens through economic interest groups. While macro uploading is closely linked with intergovernmental perspectives, micro uploading is related to neo-functionalism (Howell, 2004a, p. 57).

In conclusion, this chapter has provided an overview of the theoretical work on European integration and elaborated on the grand theories of integration. The gaps remain wide between these theoretical models, which seek to explain the broad patterns of European integration and the EU's policy-making process. In this respect, this chapter implies that there can a combination of international relations and European integration theories in furthering these explanations and understandings.[45]

45 As a meso theory that emerges from the grand theories, the concept of Europeanization is introduced. While still having numerous definitions and interpretations and while still having explanatory difficulties in relation to European integration, Howell's concept of Europeanization adds significant value to the study and analysis of the EU. In contrast to the grand theories, Europeanization incorporates elements of policy transfer, shared beliefs, discourse, identity, indirect impacts, diversity and uniformity, and fit and misfit. In his assessment of the impact of banking directives on UK financial services sector regulation, Howell (2004b) shows that in the context of financial services there is uploading and downloading as well as European integration in the formulation of directives and the marketplace. By providing empirical validity for this concept, Howell's work gives direction to the territorial dimension of regulation examined in this study.

Table 6: Summary Chapter B

Summary Chapter B – Theoretical framework
• Banking regulation can be examined from a functional and a territorial dimension. This study combines and examines both dimensions with regard to the research question. • From a functional point of view, banking regulation is a broad field of academic research as it refers to the classical dichotomy of market versus government. Therefore, a number of economic theories that deal with this topic, namely the Public Interest Theory, the Private Interest or Regulatory Capture Theory and New Institutional Economics are compared with regard to their relevance to the research question. • While these theories look at regulation as a function to change the way markets work, regulation within the multilevel government structure of the EU and the member states has increasingly received academic attention in European policy research. The outcome of this development is the idea of a territorial dimension of regulation, which can be applied to assess the theoretical implications for regulation to facilitate the creation of a single market. • The review of the grand and meso theories on European integration shows that Howell's concept of Europeanization as a process of policy uploading and downloading (Howell, 2004a) represents a promising theoretical framework to analyze and explain the formation of regulation in Europe. By including the Europeanization view into the conceptual model in Chapter D, the author seeks to elaborate the way uploading and downloading processes can be utilized to the benefits of the single market for retail banking services.

Source: Author's illustration.

C Analysis of traditional banking regulation

This chapter aims at analyzing traditional banking regulation and assessing whether the underlying justification for regulation is transferable to the role of regulation in promoting the integration of European retail markets. Initially, this chapter will seek to answer the question on the justification and objectives of banking regulation based on the theoretical foundation for understanding regulation as laid out in Chapter B. Apart from explaining regulation theory, the previous chapter already indicated that the concepts of external effects and information asymmetries provide some evidence and argument for diagnosing market failure and justifying regulatory intervention. In particular, this chapter will seek to shed light on the argument of proponents of regulation that the banking industry, compared with other industries, needs to be subject to particularly strict regulation. According to their view, this sector presents an exceptional target of economic policy as any disruption of the banking market's function will have negative external effects on the overall economy.[46]

Furthermore, this chapter investigates whether a cost-benefit analysis of regulation can contribute to the theoretical justification of regulation and seeks to determine the level of regulation density, taking Germany as an example. It briefly discusses the causes of banking crisis to determine the capacity of regulation to avoid bank insolvencies. Afterwards, the regulatory measures and instruments that seek to implement the regulatory objectives are evaluated, followed by a brief overview of the regulatory organizations. The final section discusses the deficits of current regulation and reviews the findings with regard to the research question of this study.

1. Traditional explanations for banking regulation

The justification for any regulation usually stems from a market failure such as externalities, market power, or asymmetry of information between buyers and sellers. In the case of banking, there is still no consensus on whether banks need to be regulated and, if so, how they should be regulated. This partly reflects the lack of consensus on the nature of the market failure that makes free banking not optimal. Nonetheless, there are two justifications that are often presented for regulating banks: the inability of depositors to monitor banks and the risk of a systemic crisis.

46 Other industries, such as the utility and the telecommunication sector, are also subject to increased regulation because of the high costs societies need to bear in the case of supply disruption.

1.1 The inability of depositors to monitor banks

Banking regulation is commonly explained with the argument for creditor protection. In the case of bank insolvency, depositors lose their deposits and most of their savings. For reasons of consumer and creditor protection, such an enormous loss of wealth is undesired and thus takes the centre stage of prudential regulation and supervision (Steden, 2002).

The information-economic viewpoint can provide a sound justification for regulation as some banking sector particularities exist that support the argument for creditor protection. Even though bank clients enter into long-term obligations with banks, most clients are in an inferior position compared with banks as they have less economic knowledge and information is distributed asymmetrically to their disadvantage. The average private saver simply trusts in the security of his savings and does not question the stability of banks, be it because he is incapable or unwilling due to the high cost of information to do so. In this regard, regulation can be justified by information asymmetries of bank clients and the agency problem with the bank. Due to low equity-to-asset ratios, the risk of depositor damnification is usually higher in banking than in other sectors. In particular, the existence of financially weak private savers, whose deposits and savings accounts comprise their only capital reserves, would be threatened with a loss of their savings. Banks are subject to moral hazard and incentivized to exploit information asymmetries that remain unnoticed by their clients to their own advantage, for example by engaging in highly profitable but also risky financial activities. This appears to be problematic in particular in situations where under complete information and transparency risk-averse private savers would consciously not have business relations with such a bank (Knorr, 1999, p. 359). Furthermore, information deficits could lead to a situation where depositors start to panic and withdraw their savings at the slightest doubt of their bank's solvency regardless of whether these doubts are reasonable or not. Such a run could also affect the majority of solvent banks. Therefore, special rules for the protection of creditors are necessary.

The lack of trust may also lead to a situation where depositors cease to put their money into bank accounts. Consequently, their capital would not yield productive investments and the financing of profitable investment projects could not materialize, hence lowering overall economic welfare.

Transaction Cost Theory also provides explanations for banking regulation. Williamson (1985, p. 32) virtually asks to "[o]rganize transactions so as to economize on bounded rationality while simultaneously safeguarding against the hazard of opportunism". Banking regulation and supervision is less of a classical contract than of an ongoing process, a kind of permanent business relationship, which Williamson (1985) conceptualized as a relational contract comprising ongoing rather than single-time negotiations. Information asymmetries are detrimental to the regulator or supervisor after (moral hazard) but also before the conclusion of the contract (adverse selection). Regulators and supervisors can hardly monitor the actions of banks (the principal-agent relationship) and anticipate future events.

From an institutional-economic perspective, regulation is sensible if it is the most cost-efficient contractual design for an ongoing business relationship between many principals and few agents (Richter, 1991, p. 46). A large number of private bank clients are in a long-term contractual relationship with a small number of banks and both have transaction-specific investments, which meet the condition stipulated above. Compared with other firms, bank debt is mainly held by simple depositors without the necessary information to perform efficient monitoring. In addition, because most of them hold only a small deposit, they have little incentive to perform any information-gathering functions that monitoring a bank would require. This free–riding problem creates a need for a private or public representative of depositors, which can be met by a regulation that imitates the control and monitoring that private savers would exert if they had the proper information and were sophisticated and fully coordinated (Santos, 2001, p. 86).

According to the school of thought of NIE, the institution of regulation continuously resumes the required negotiations with the agents (banks) on behalf of the principals and establishes a cost-optimal control and monitoring of the relational contract. However, such control and monitoring does not necessarily need to be provided by the state but can also be taken up by a private organizations. Furthermore, the rationale of regulation does not build on the existence of natural monopolies but on complex, continuous business relations between multiple principals and a small number of agents.

1.2 The risk of a systemic crisis

The most effective argument in support of regulation of the banking sector is system stability. It is based on the belief that a systematic and system-wise crisis could emanate from such an instability of the banking system (Santos, 2001, p. 10). Hence, the objective of banking regulation is to protect the banking system and to prevent damage to the overall economy as a negative external effect. Given the vitally important function of banks in an economy, it is unsurprising that any breakdown of this function and its disastrous consequences should be avoided through regulation. The relevant literature provides different reasons for the instability of the banking sector.

The inherent instability of a bank and its exposure to *runs* (massive withdrawals of client funds) is primarily attributed to clients' sensitivity to trusting in their bank's ability to provide liquidity services (Cohen & Crockett, 2001, p. 45). Secondly, a bank needs to operate with a balance sheet where the liquidation value of its assets is less than the value of liquid deposits in order to provide these liquidity services. Under these circumstances, given that depositors' expectations about the value of their deposits depend on their place in line at the time of withdrawal (*first come, first served rule*), a run can occur without the release of adverse information about the bank's assets (and even when there is perfect information about the bank's assets) (Santos, 2001, p. 10). For example, if depositors panic, they may try to withdraw their funds out of fear that other depositors will do so first, thus forcing an otherwise sound bank into bankruptcy. A further reason for the inherent instability of banks that also fuels the above-mentioned behavior of clients results from the nature of a bank's operating model: banks finance themselves with short-term deposits while their assets are invested in rather illiquid and long-term securities. Therefore, unregulated banks are latently threatened by illiquidity.

On the other hand, the insolvency of one bank can also have direct effects on other banks. The extent of such a *domino effect* depends on how closely banks are financially and operationally intertwined in the interbank market. In this activity, electronic large-value interbank clearing systems (also called netting or net settlement systems) have gained importance. In these systems, where banks exchange huge sums during a business day and settle net balances at the end, payments become irrevocable only if every participant is able to settle its end-of-day balance. Clearly, if one of these *daylight debtors* suddenly proves unable to meet its obligations, its direct creditors' ability to settle may be jeopardized as well, potentially setting off a chain reaction (P. Angelini, Maresca, & Russo, 1996, p. 854). Certainly, there are also other reasons for banks to file for bankruptcy or have liquidity problems. Even then, a crisis of an individual bank could negatively affect other banks through spillover effects and become a reason for a system crisis.

A further risk that might lead to a system crisis exists more on the macroeconomic development. A decline in prices in the real estate market or a reduction of the money supply by the central bank could give rise to many banks becoming illiquid or filing for bankruptcy at the same time, which again would lead to a broad banking crisis. A popular argument holds that, in this case, even a low probability of a systemic crisis would justify regulation. In this context, economic theorists and politicians refer to a government's responsibility to provide a framework for a sound operation of the overall economy, which includes a functioning banking system.

The negative spillover effects from a banking crisis on other industries arise typically from a tightened supply of credit (*credit crunch*), when banks cease to provide credit or even call in their money. When firms and other credit enquirers are confronted with a situation of restricted credit supply, all industry sectors will face a higher cost of capital and the real economy suffers damage. These negative effects include reduced economic growth or even a recession, losses on deposits and savings, which again leads to reduced demand and economic growth, increased real interest rates, unemployment, increased margins between deposit and credit interest rates, and ultimately a decreasing public trust in the financial system. The global financial market and credit crisis that had its beginning in September 2008 with the bankruptcy of Lehman Brothers is the most recent example of the chain of negative impacts. Hence, banking regulation can be justified with the negative external effect argument to the extent that the overall economic costs of bank insolvency exceed private costs and that the social costs of a bankruptcy are not considered in the internal decision-making of a bank.

Finally, and this was also observed in the aftermath of the collapse of Lehman Brothers, a looming crisis of the banking system also constitutes a social threat. In order to maintain a proper functioning and operation of the financial system, governments are forced to intervene and to rescue and restructure the individual banks or the overall system. The social costs thereby incurred are additionally in most cases, an incalculable burden on public budgets. From this point of view, governments are interested in intervening with regulatory measures to prevent banking crisis from happening. Hence, the next section deals with the cost-benefit consideration of traditional banking regulation.

1.3 Cost-benefit assessment of traditional banking regulation

Regulatory intervention can only be justified if it serves economic efficiency and if it passes a cost-benefit test. A cost-benefit analysis is defined as "an analytic procedure which estimates the net economic value of a given policy or project. It converts all costs and benefits into a monetary metric and then measures whether the benefits outweigh the costs" (Cowen, 1998, p. 1). Even if market failure, government failure or coordination failure exist in the banking sector, any regulation should have to pass a cost-benefit test or at least undergo some further process of scrutiny to justify the costs incurred through the regulatory burden. On the other hand, these costs must be weighed against the benefits of regulation, which traditionally are the costs avoided through system stability. This section will shed some light on the cost-benefit analysis of traditional banking regulation.

1.3.1 The benefits of regulation

Banking regulation aims at mitigating the risk of a banking crisis and system instability, lowering the economic costs of such negative effects. In this regard, these negative effects also directly affect the overall macroeconomic environment and lead to an economic crisis. The Asian crisis of 1997/98 or the most recent world economic crisis that started in 2008 notably reflect the direct correlation. The cost of a banking crisis comprises a decrease in economic growth due to credit tightening, increased interest margins, and the intervention of the state to help the troubled banking sector to re-capitalize or by providing risk umbrellas and guarantees. As regulation increases overall trust in the banking sector, it also restrains individuals from not saving money. A systemic banking crisis, resulting from the bankruptcy of a single bank or from other causes, could lead to enormous fiscal costs, in particular for rehabilitating troubled banks. The fiscal clean-up from Sweden's 1991 crisis was 6% of GDP and Norway's 1987 crisis was 8%. Spain's post-1977 clean-up cost over 16% of GDP and estimates for Japan's bill vary widely, with many in excess of 20% of GDP (Reinhart & Rogoff, 2008, p. 4). The total costs resulting from the most recent global financial crisis are hardly predictable[47] as the overall crisis costs are expected to be a lot higher and it is difficult to quantify the costs of a global economic crisis. However, the avoidance of most of these costs can be considered a benefit of banking regulation (Steden, 2002, p. 43).

1.3.2 The cost of regulation

The costs of regulation comprise direct costs on the one hand and indirect or compliance costs on the other hand. The former consist of the regulatory agencies' operating costs. In addition to the direct costs of running the regulatory agencies, there are internal costs, which banks bear in complying with the regulations. These include not only the costs of the personnel and systems required to provide information to regulators, to perform internal checks on compliance and to carry out *form filling*, but in addition the income from business lost as a result of the costs imposed by regulation (Franks, Schaefer, & Staunton, 1998, p. 1550).

Indirect or compliance costs of regulation include the overall loss of economic welfare resulting from the compliance with governmental ruling. In this context, regulation can even limit competition or prevent unprofitable banks from market exit. Furthermore, indirect costs occur if an optimal allocation of capital is restrained. For example, banks are held back from executing economically sensible transactions or services and have to retain more economic capital than considered optimal by the owners. The indirect costs of regulation are predicted to be substantially higher than the direct costs of regulation (Franks et al., 1998, p. 1564). Both types of cost are considered "social costs" (Fritsch et al., 1999, p. 94) and represent the so-called "regulatory burden" of banks. However, a view focusing on regulation costs only lacks an appraisal of the benefits of

47 Most recent examples of government intervention in the global financial crisis are, among others, the German Finanzmarktstabilisierungsfonds (FMSF) with a volume of more than EUR 100m or the bank rescue package of around GBP 500bn announced by the British Government in October 2008.

regulation: Llewellen (1995, p. 3) has argued that “Public debate is distorted by the almost exclusive emphasis on costs and it leads to simple assertions that the costs of regulation greatly exceed the benefits because the costs are allegedly high”. This is usually connected with the determinants of the costs firms would incur in the absence of regulation.

This measurement of incremental regulatory cost raises a difficult problem. Direct costs of regulation, for example, are hardly captured separately from other operating costs by any accounting system. In addition, compliance costs do not take account of the costs that would be incurred by the banking industry in the absence of regulation. Franks et al. (1998, p. 1551) illustrate this with an example of UK securities firms. Under the current regulations, these firms maintain minimum capital requirements, which are determined in relation to the size and riskiness of their positions. However, any firm with an effective risk management department would control the relation between the size of its positions and its capital, and so not all the costs associated with capital requirements should be regarded as incremental. In the same way, regulation may partially substitute a firm’s monitoring of counterparty risk that it would need to carry out in the absence of regulation. In their assessment, the total costs of regulation for securities firms were estimated at GBP 182-239m. (of which GBP 54m. took account of direct costs and costs of compliance accounted for GBP 128-185m.). Even if it is difficult to estimate the exact level of the social costs of regulation for the entire banking industry, this sample representing the securities and investment firms provides a good indication of the substantial cost impact of regulation in the banking sector.

1.3.3 The trade-off of regulation: cost of crisis vs. costs of regulation

Usually, it is supposed that an increase in regulation intensity will lead to an increase in the social utility of regulation as the risk of a crisis is mitigated and crisis costs are avoided. However, the social costs of regulation, resulting from comprehensive monitoring and from imposing restrictions on the economic activity of banks, will increase at the same time. Figure 7 visualizes both types of cost as two diametrically opposed curves and illustrates the total economic cost of regulation as the sum of these two types of cost (see dotted line).

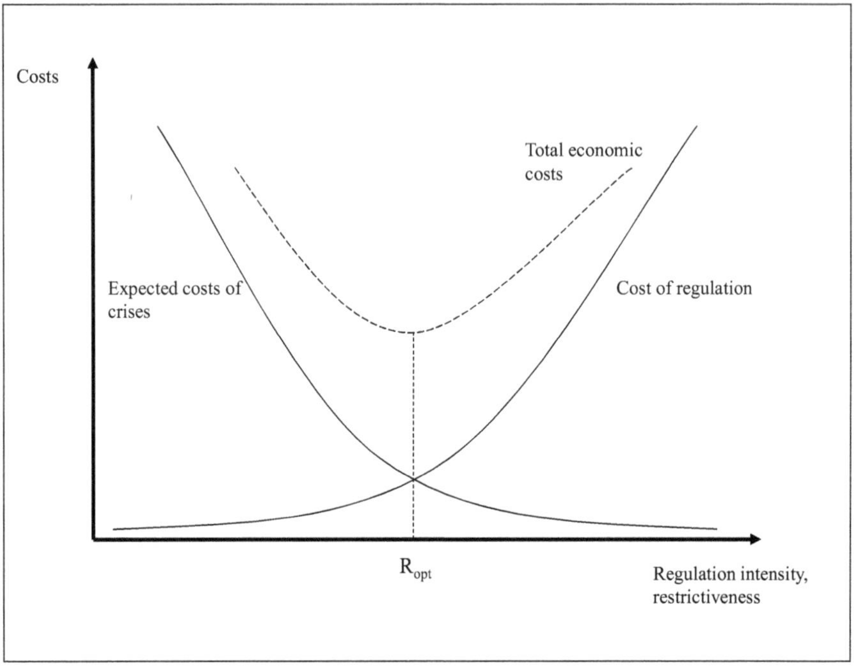

Figure 7: Social costs and benefits of regulation
Source: Author's illustration, adopted from Steden (2002, p. 47).

The illustration indicates that, when regulation intensity is low, i.e. lower regulation density and restrictiveness, the expected costs of crisis are high. The product of the potential cost of a crisis and the probability of a crisis represents a function of regulation density, as lower regulation intensity assumes a higher probability of a crisis. The costs of regulation, however, show a positive correlation with regulation intensity, as more intensive regulatory efforts and extensive monitoring imply higher management and administration costs, limiting the business activity of banks and thus increasing the indirect costs of regulation.

The exhibit above reveals that cost-benefit assessments are able to justify regulation. Increasing regulation intensity in an unregulated banking environment (lower-left corner in the exhibit) lowers the sum of all costs, including social costs. Hence, if banking regulation can lower the total economic cost (thus having a positive welfare effect), its application is justifiable.

Furthermore, the illustration shows that a maximum level of regulation intensity is not desirable either. Even though the likelihood of a banking crisis is reduced to almost zero in this case, a significant increase in the cost of regulation would also unnecessarily increase the total costs. A regulatory optimum, where the total economic costs are minimal and where the marginal costs of regulation equal the marginal costs of a crisis is theoretically imaginable.[48]

The question is now: has the optimal level of the costs of regulation been reached in Europe? As mentioned earlier, an assessment of costs is difficult. While there is a common notion for estimating the benefits of regulation as an avoidance of the costs of crisis, the increasing utility arising from creditor protection and the overall sense of security remains difficult to assess.

Already, before the financial crisis that started in 2008, the banking industry and market economy-friendly academic research had perceived that the intensity of regulation had also exceeded its optimal level. This observation has particularly been supported by the reversion of the external effect argument. Any implementation of regulation creates the problem of external effects, as the major part of regulation costs are not borne by the regulatory authorities or the government and hence not internalized in the decision-making process. The costs of regulation do not fall back onto those who regulate and consequently represent negative external effects. Under these circumstances, the intensity of regulation is assumed to be above its optimal level of efficiency. Figure 7 shows that the cost-optimal point moves to the right side if regulatory costs are only considered in parts. The depicted process explains why governmental banking regulation can overreach the optimal level from a cost-benefit point of view and result in overregulation.

Furthermore, it can be asserted that it is almost impossible to quantify the costs and benefits of banking regulation and the idea of determining an optimal level of regulation can hardly be parameterized. Nevertheless, one can confirm that. For any question on the utility of banking regulation for society, the efficiency of policies and rules needs to be considered. Any attempt to reduce the costs of crisis increases the costs of the regulated industry and eventually those borne by bank clients.

Summarizing the findings from Chapter C, banking regulation can be considered inevitable to correct market failure. In the banking industry, market failure is assumed where bank creditors are unable to assess the risk content of a bank due to information asymmetries and high transaction costs. The introduction of a supervisory authority representing the interest of banking clients is an inexpensive way from a transaction cost point of view to monitor banks. Hence, regulation is justified by the protection of creditors to safeguard depositors from the negative consequences of a banking collapse, which would also have negative external effects on other banks and on the overall economy. Regulation

48 The condition for a cost minimum is the equilibrium between a marginal increase in the cost of regulation and a marginal decrease in the expected cost of crisis. If IR represents the intensity of regulation, CR the cost of regulation, and CC the cost of crisis, the following equation must hold: $\partial CR/\partial IR = -(\partial CC/\partial IR)$ (Steden, 2002, p. 48).

seeks to avoid bank insolvencies occurring more often than necessary and to avoid overall financial system instability by lowering the social costs of such events. However, a cost-benefit assessment of banking regulation shows that high social costs occur through regulation, which give the impression that the banking sector in Europe tends to be overregulated.

These explanations for banking regulation have been parameterized for both the justification of a prescribed system of deposit protection and the adoption of numerous risk-mitigating policies. While the deployment of regulatory measures to maintain banking system and economic stability has been investigated thoroughly over the last decades, its role in facilitating market integration in Europe is still subject to further analysis. A problem resulting from regulation is that the rule-making on an EU level may sometimes lack adequate measures to enforce the transposition. This observation, which will be analyzed in detail in the next chapters, may lead to adverse behavior of market participants. For example, first-mover banks that obey the rules and take investment decisions at an early stage have a competitive disadvantage compared with countries or strong interest groups that defer their investments into the future. When approximating the target date for implementation, and regulatory authorities realize that an important part of the market is not yet prepared, target dates are eventually shifted or the directive is blocked from being implemented. By waiting, market participants or national government succeed in playing out their market strength and avoid making prescribed investments. While this phenomenon can be observed in all regulatory environments and industries, the transposition of regulatory directives from the EU into member states is in particular susceptible to adverse behavior, where the interest of the regulator, the demand, and the supply-side diverge for the most part.

This chapter assessed that regulatory intervention can be justified to overcome market failure and to mitigate risk. However, a cost-benefit assessment of regulation should be conducted to assure economic logic. The cost of regulation lies not only in the cost of preventing bank failure, but also in the opportunity costs of foregone innovation. Excessive or outmoded regulation results in loss of international competitiveness, thus imposing future adjustment costs on the economy. Hence, there is a need to review regulations constantly and to deregulate or re-regulate.[49]

---

49 A study of Japan's experience of financial deregulation since 1984 carried out by BIS (see Osugi, 1990) conducts an impact assessment of financial market liberalization measures on the internationalization of the Japan's economy in the 1980s. In the context of the global financial crisis in 2008-2009, more recent studies apply cost-benefit assessments to evaluate policy measures that aim to expand existing or introduce new guarantees for financial institutions to avoid a global systemic crisis (see, for example, the BIS Paper by Panetta et al., 2009; or the OECD article by Schich, 2009).

With regard to the question of whether the underlying justification for regulation is transferable to the role of regulation in promoting the integration of European retail markets, similar explanations can be given. Regulation is justifiable only if it is effective, i.e. it eliminates detrimental market outcomes (market or coordination failure), and if it is efficient, i.e. the economic (or social) benefits exceed the cost of regulation.

These findings now lead to the question on the measures and instruments regulators traditionally deploy in the banking sector to correct market failures and prevent system instability. The following section examines the basic instruments and their respective approaches.

2. Measures and instruments

Given the previously described traditional explanations of banking regulation, certain regulatory measures must be taken to avoid systemic banking crisis and to protect creditors. In this regard, in particular problems of individual bank insolvency that could spread throughout the banking sector must be avoided.

In this respect, different approaches to banking regulation exist, which comprise protective and preventive measures. In most countries, these so-called three columns of supervision include preventive measures such as risk limiting norms and restraints of competition, protective measures, i.e. deposit insurance and the central bank functioning as the *lender of last resort (LLR)*, who can supply liquidity to banks in case of a crisis.

Preventive regulatory measures comprise different types of risk limiting regulations Jackson (1999) classifies risk regulation into the following categories:

(i) admission and licensing provisions
(ii) reporting requirements
(iii) balance sheet structure rules
(iv) restriction on the functional organization of particular business areas

Regulation can be enacted on both the member state and the supranational level such as the recommendations on banking laws and regulations issued by the Basel Committee on Banking Supervision.[50]

Regulation that limits certain types of banking business activity or its geographic footprint such as the *dual banking system* or the prohibition of *interstate*

50 In 1974, the Basel Committee on Banking Supervision was created by the central bank Governors of the Group of Ten nations and meets regularly four times a year. Its membership is now composed of senior representatives of bank supervisory authorities and central banks from the G-10 countries (Belgium, Canada, France, Germany, Italy, Japan, the Netherlands, Sweden, Switzerland, the United Kingdom and the United States), including representatives from Luxembourg and Spain.

banking in the US[51] has become less important. Instead, most of today's international banking regulation focuses on the limitation of financial risk in proportion of the liable equity. Regulations that aim at mitigating financial risk include among other prescriptions on minimum liquidity requirements or on the diversification of bank assets. The latter implies for example that banks in Germany should not have single loss exposures of more than 25% of their equity.[52] The financial risks are assessed and put in relation to a bank's equity, i.e. depending on the risk volume of a bank, a capital cap is place as a risk buffer. The underlying justification of minimum equity requirements for banks is based on the assumption that a higher proportion of equity increases protection against insolvency risk.

The supervision and monitoring of financial firms through regulatory authorities refers to the column of preventative regulatory measures. These measures differ from country to country: while in the US, regular on-site examinations are being conducted, in Germany, annual financial statements are audited and controlled and different reports have to be published during the fiscal year. The on-site examination in the US focuses on five aspects of a bank: *Capital Adequacy*, *Asset Quality*, *Management Quality*, *Equity and Liquidity*. Just as savers appoint banks as *delegated monitors*, societies appoint supervisory authorities to monitor the behavior of banks. However, in Germany, supervisory authorities do not intervene into a bank's day-to-day business and does not control single client engagements, which would run contrary to the market-economy oriented economic system (Steden, 2002, p. 61).

3. Banking supervision in Europe

Many factors have affected the traditional regulatory model in Europe before the Economic and Monetary Union. The introduction of the euro currency and the creation of the ECB, the dominant appearance of financial conglomerates and complex financial products have proven that the prevailing structure of financial services supervision appears outdated.

The structure and operating framework of financial services supervision was traditionally divided into the sectors banking, insurance and securities (European Commission, 1985, Paragraphs 102-103). Due to its size and systemic risk in-

51 Both *dual banking* (co-existence of state banks and national banks) and the prohibition of *interstate banking* (expansion of banking activities across state lines through bank holding company acquisitions) represent examples for the wide variations in credit and lending regulation and permissible activities from one state to another in the U.S.

52 The so-called "Anlagebuch-Großkrediteinzelobergrenze" of 25% is defined in the §12 of the German credit and securities law (KWG). Hence, a bank that 8% equity funded is limit in the provision of a single credit to 2% of its balance sheet totals (25% * 8%) (Steden, 2002, p. 61).

volved, the emphasis of supervision was placed more on banking than on insurance regulation. Even though in many member states competent securities regulation and supervision bodies hardly existed, the securities market supervision was based on self-regulation (Andenas & Gebhardt, 2001, p. 152).

3.1 Regulatory and supervisory organizations in Europe

In Europe, the areas of regulation and supervision need to be clearly differentiated. Although the two spheres are inseparably linked, the essential function of each area of responsibility must be acknowledged with regard to the allocation of competencies. Against this background, the definitions given for each function are as follows: "supervision is the executive function (control), while regulation is the underlying legislative function (rule-making) (World Savings Bank Institute & European Savings Bank Group, 2006, p. 58). Since its inception, the EU has worked on the principle of establishing the most effective allocation of governing competencies (principle of subsidiarity) in this manner. Even though recent decades have seen a move towards rule-making at the European level, supervision continues to remain allocated to the member states. Furthermore, there is a significant difference in terms of their operating procedures: while the political element has always had a strong role in regulation, it has been largely non-existent in supervision.

3.1.1 The EU Level

With the foundation of the European System of Central banks (ESCB) in 1998, Stage Three of the European Economic and Monetary Union was entered and the participating Member States lost their monetary sovereignty and transferred it to the European Central Bank (ECB). According to the EC Treaty (Art. 107, 1) the ESCB is composed of the ECB and the national central banks and is view as its basic task the ownership of the Community's decisions of financial policy and their execution. The legal competencies for banking supervision mainly rest with the individual national supervision authorities (Andenas & Gebhardt, 2001, p. 152). The ECB can advise the Community organs and the competent authorities of the Member States and be consulted by them on questions regarding the range of organization and application of the Community's legal regulations in respect of prudential supervision of the financial institutions and the stability of the financial system (European Central Bank, 1992, Art. 3.1. and 12.1.). Furthermore, the ECB can execute special tasks concerning prudential supervision of financial institutions (except for insurances) as long as the Council authorizes the ECB in unanimous vote (European Central Bank, 2003a, p. 10)

Traditionally, there are two forms of cooperation between national authorities at the EU level; firstly memoranda of understanding (MoU) that are passed between supervisors on a bilateral or multilateral basis. Secondly, forums for the exchange of information and expertise and cooperation between different supervisors are established. The latter form of cooperation has been further developed with the adoption of the Lamfalussy Process (LP) in securities-market regulation area first, but subsequently extended to the areas of banking, insurance and asset management. The LP was intended "to speed up the legislative process and ensure more consistent application and enforcement of EU securities-market legislation" (Kern, 2003, p. 4). Endorsed by the EU Council in March 2002, and following the removal of number of political barriers, the LP has been operating for more than half a decade. It is characterized by the decomposition of new legislative acts into framework and implementing decisions through a well-defined four-stage process. At the first and second stage (level-1 and level-2), policy proposals are drafted and legislated through intensive consultation with market participants in various formal or informal expert forums, which provide an opportunity to gather information and opinions throughout the entire legislative and regulatory process at EU level. The consistent application of level-1 and level-2 measures is coordinated at level-3 committees (CESR, CEBS and CEIOPS)[53] and enforced at a level-4 by the EU Commission. Since its creation in 2001, CESR has published numerous guidelines, recommendations and standards with regard to coordinating the approaches in the EU. This includes both, the areas covered by EU legislation (i.e. recommendations for the consistent implementation of the EU legislation regarding the draft of proposals), and also the areas not covered by the EU legislation (i.e. standards for securities clearing and settlement in the European Union) (World Savings Bank Institute & European Savings Bank Group, 2006, p. 58). Although younger than CESR, the other two committees, CEBS and CEIOPS, have also been publishing standards aimed at national supervisors in view of coordinating national approaches.[54]

With the establishment of level-3 committees, all other previously established forums have continued to exist. In this regard, the following active forums need to be mentioned: the Banking Supervisory Committee (BSC), which was established by the ESCB to assist the ECB's role in prudential supervision; the "Groupe de Contact" and the Conference of Insurance Supervisory Authorities (CIS), both forums exchange views and practices between regulators.

---

53 CESR: Committee of European Securities Regulators; CEBS: Committee of European Banking Supervisors; CEIOPS: European Insurance and Occupational Pensions Supervisors.

54 In September 2005 for example, CEIOPS published "recommendations regarding the implications of the IAS/IFRS – Introduction for the prudential supervision of insurance undertakings". On December 21, 2004, CEBS released the "guidelines on prudential filters for regulatory capital."

3.1.2 Member state level

Today, the legal framework for the supervision of credit institutions (including insurance and securities firms) constitutes in one of the core principles of the internal market, that of home country control principle and delineated for the first time in the European Commission's White Paper of 1985: "[...] the principle of home country control [...] means attributing the primary task of supervising the financial institution to the competent authorities of its Member State of origin." (European Commission, 1985, paragraphs 102-103). It states that supervision is the responsibility of the national competent authorities and it allows a financial institution based in one country to be supervised by its national competent authority. This implies that a firm can provide services in another EU country while being supervised by its national supervisor.[55] However, this principle does not apply to firms that decide to open a subsidiary in another EU member state, where the subsidiary then becomes subject to the control of the host member state. At present, there is an emerging re-appreciation of the principle and its applicability to modern financial institutions and markets. The debate now focuses on the determination of the respective supervisory roles of EU institutions and member states on the one hand, and of home and host member states on the other (Andenas & Gebhardt, 2001, p. 169).

3.2 Harmonization developments of European banking supervision

The harmonization requirements of banking and financial market supervision within the EU are a lot more detailed than those requested by the Basel Committee on Banking Supervision. In the course of internal market creation, many directives on different banking-topics were issued and transposed into national supervision law. These directives comprise both, banking supervision as well as financial market supervision and pursue the principle of minimal harmonization. The alternative of a complex, joint supervision with respective organizational structures was abolished in the 1970s. The first measures for reaching harmonization in the banking sector go back to the first Banking Coordination Directive

55 Article 26 of the Consolidated Banking Directive (Directive 2000/12/EC) states: "the prudential supervision of a credit institution (...) shall be the responsibility of the competent authorities of the home Member State, without prejudice to those provisions of this Directive which give responsibility to the authorities of the host Member State". The Directive indicates that "competent authorities" shall mean the national authorities who are empowered by law or regulation to supervise credit institutions" (Article 1). However, there are exceptions to this general principle. For example, with respect to liquidity risk, the supervision of a branch is the responsibility of the competent authority of the Member State where that branch is located.

in 1977 on the coordination of laws, regulations and administrative provisions relating to the taking up and pursuit of the business of credit institutions (No. 77/780/EEC). The second Banking Co-ordination directive in 1989 (No. 89/646/EEC) followed the chosen political bearing with regard to the requirements of a single EU market. With these two core banking directives being adopted, the community achieved significant convergence in substantive regulatory standards. However, it did not attempt to effect the established organization of the banking supervisory authority by imposing on the member states a specific scheme for the organization of their national agencies. Instead, the organizational aspects of banking regulation and, in particular, the allocation of responsibilities for prudential supervision in a narrower sense, were left with the national discretion of the member states. The current European community regime only demands cooperation between the various *competent authorities* to which the member states delegate functions in the area of prudential supervision[56] and leaves the degree of their cooperation to their own discretion (Andenas & Gebhardt, 2001, p. 173).

Besides banking supervision, financial market supervision comprises the second area of EU supervision. Directives on financial markets activities in the EU mainly include admission to stock exchange trading, publication requirements and insider rules. These directives have triggered the adoption of several securities trading rules in most of the Member States and lead to a mostly harmonized legal framework across Europe.

3.2.1 Current developments in national supervisory structures

The organizational arrangements for the supervision of the banking and the financial sectors vary across the EU countries. This diversity also applies to the dynamics of the restructuring processes evidenced especially over the most recent years. While some countries have maintained a largely unchanged organizational setting and allocation of responsibilities, others (for example the UK) have undergone substantial reforms or are still being reshaped. Both the national supervisory structures and the mechanisms for cooperation among the authorities comprise part of these reform processes. They represent a response to the rapid developments in the financial sector, also with a view to national peculiarities. Furthermore, they aim at enhancing the effectiveness and efficiency of supervision.

---

56 For general harmonisation attempts, see First Banking Directive, Art. 7(1), as amended by Art. 14(1) of the Second Banking Directive, Arts. 7 and 15(2); for the harmonization of risk limiting standards, see EU Directive on the Monitoring and Control of Large Exposures of Credit Institutions (92/121/EEC of 21 December, 1992), the Second Consolidated Supervision Directive, Art. 7(2)-(4), (7), the Investment Services Directive, Art. 23, and the Capital Adequacy Directive, Art. 7(3).

This section briefly summarizes the main recent changes in national supervisory structures for the financial sector in the EU countries and the resulting setting. A number of elements may be drawn from an analysis of the ECB (2003a) of recent reforms of supervisory structures and from the resulting setting in the EU member states. These findings will provide a better understanding of the regulatory obstacles that still impede the harmonization of particularly fragmented banking markets such as the retail banking market.

First, recurrent reforms have materialized in the consolidation of supervisory structures (i.e. the reduction of the number of competent authorities). While the degree of consolidation and the resulting number of supervisory authorities differs across countries, three models of supervisory structures continue to coexist in the EU. The first model is based on a separation of competencies along the borderlines of financial sectors. The second model relies on the full consolidation of supervisory responsibilities across financial sectors into a single supervisory agency. A third model currently evolving envisages the consolidation of supervisory responsibilities by objectives across sectors. It assigns supervisory tasks to two distinct agencies, with one aiming at safeguarding the soundness of financial institutions and the other focusing on the conduct of business tasks with a view to ensuring transparency. Furthermore, while central banks in general remain extensively involved in the prudential supervision of the banking sector, the degree of supervisory competency allocated to national central banks still differs heavily. This observation can be followed in Table 7, which provides a comprehensive overview of the involvement of national central banks in supervisory tasks. Except for the direct responsibility, three forms of national central bank involvement are not mutually exclusive. Firstly, central banks perform specific supervisory tasks, which mainly include the monitoring of risk categories incurred by financial institutions and the carrying out of audits. Secondly, central banks participate in the decision making of supervisory agencies as representatives in supervisory boards and/ or management committees. Finally, central banks may cooperate closely the supervisory agency in the operative areas, sharing resources such as statistical information, staff and administration functions (European Central Bank, 2003a, p. 2; Kern, 2003, p. 3).

While in one two-thirds of the euro-zone member states the functions of banking and market supervision are clearly separated from the conduct of monetary policy and its implementation, in the other third they are not (see Table 7). Compared to 2001 where the proportion equally balanced, there is a trend towards a separation of monetary (strict central banking) from regulatory functions, even though empirical evidence does not provide clear support either for a separation or a combination of these functions in a central bank. The question whether central banks in their function as lender of the last resort should be involved in supervision as well, has been intensively discussed in literature and in the politics of the EU. Andenas and Gebhardt (2001, p. 155) show in their analysis that the concept of banking supervision, central banking, monetary policy and payment systems – as used in the EC Treaty, in directives, indeed, in economic and legal theory – are less than precise and potentially even overlap. They also highlighted some constitutional concerns going against a delegation of broad and open-ended decision-making powers to the ESCB in the area of prudential supervision.[57]

A third element drawn from the reform process of supervisory authorities in the EU is the increasingly formalized reinforcement of cooperation among institutions. With regard to cooperation in the area of supervision, in some countries[58] arrangements for supervisory co-operation have developed mainly in the form of special cross-sector committees, which comprise of competent authorities such as the central bank. On the other hand, an increasing number of cooperative arrangements in the field of financial stability have recently emerged. These specific financial stability committees include all authorities contributing to financial stability, notably ministries of finance, central banks and supervisory authorities[59]. Besides financial stability, also distinct topics such as macro-prudential issues are gaining importance for cooperation among competent authorities (European Central Bank, 2003a, p. 4). Finally, and this is considered one of the most promising recent developments of regulatory decision-making in the EU, the increasing interest of the private sector in regulatory and supervisory issues, and of supervisors in conferring with the private sector, has led to the establishment of consultative forums. Such an approach of cooperation and consultation on regulatory topics has so far worked only in some cases. Further efforts are required to facilitate an effective coordination of the banking industry's expertise and the decision making power of supervisory authorities and the ESCB.

For the purpose of this study one can state that the organizational structures in the field of European financial supervision are changing in three ways:

(i) The number of supervisory authorities is being reduced and three basic models are emerging: agencies responsible for sectoral supervision, agencies responsible for different kinds of supervision, and a single supervisory agency. As of late, there seems to be a broad tendency towards the latter two models.

(ii) The involvement of national central banks in the supervisory process continues and takes three main forms, in particular the participation in the

57 In practice, in countries such as Belgium and Germany, where the two functions are separated, the central bank usually collaborates closely with the supervisory authorities in elaborating prudential policy and in the collection and analysis of banking statistical return to ensure efficient information sharing (European Central Bank, 2003a).

58 For example, Belgium, Netherlands and Portugal.

59 For example, Austria, Germany, France and UK.

oversight of the supervisory agency, the operational execution of specific supervisory tasks and the provision of resources.

(iii) While most cooperation among authorities used to take place informally or was mainly subject-driven, an increasing emphasis is placed on formal arrangements to develop supervisory cooperation.

While financial market regulation and supervision in Europe has made considerable progress in re-arranging the regulatory responsibilities between central banks and supervisory authorities, the case for a single European financial market supervisor has not moved forward the way it should. However, current political pressure for a single financial market requires a more effective coordination of prudential supervision for not only financial stability, bank safety and soundness, but also for financial market harmonization.

Table 7: Institutional setting for financial supervision in the EU

Country	Number of public institutions responsible of supervision	Central banks involved in banking supervision	Form of central bank involvement in banking supervision			
			Central bank is the banking supervisor[60]	Central bank is involved in the management of the banking supervision[61]	Central bank is allocated specific tasks in banking supervision[62]	Central bank and banking supervisor shares resources
BE	2[63]	Yes	No	Yes	No	No[64]
DK	1	No	No	No	No	No
DE	1	Yes	No	No	Yes	Yes
GR	3	Yes	Yes			
ES	3	Yes	Yes			
FR	66	Yes	No	Yes	No	Yes
IE	17	Yes	No	No	No	Yes
IT	3	Yes	Yes			
LU	2	No	No	No	No	No
NL	38	Yes	Yes			
AT	1	Yes	No	Yes	Yes	No
PT	3	Yes	Yes			
FI	2	Yes	No	Yes	No	Yes
SV	1	Yes	No	Yes	No	No9
UK	1	Yes	No	Yes	No	No10

Source: Author's illustration, adopted from the European Central Bank (2003a, p. 3)

60 The central bank is involved in banking supervision when it is the banking supervisor itself or, where this is not the case, involved in the management/oversight of the banking supervisor, contributes to supervisory policy-shaping, carries out tasks in line supervision, processes supervisory reporting or shares resources with the supervisory agency (European Central Bank, 2003a, p. 3).

61 The central bank is involved in the management of the banking supervisor if the former is represented in the management (e.g. management committee, secretary-general and chairman) or in the supervisory or oversight board of the latter (European Central Bank, 2003a, p. 3).

62 The central bank carries out off- and on-site monitoring in specific areas (European Central Bank, 2003a, p. 3).

63 The two existing supervisors will merge on 1 January 2004 in only one institution (European Central Bank, 2003a, p. 3).

64 The law foresees a pooling of resources between the Commission Bancaire et Financière/Commissie voor het Bank- en Financiewezen (Banking and Finance Commission - CBF), the Office de Contrôle des Assurances/Centrale dienst voor verzekeringen (Insurance Control Office - OCA/CDV) and the central bank, the Banque Nationale de Belgique/Nationale Bank van België (BNB/NBB) (European Central Bank, 2003a, p. 3).

3.2.2 Intermediary steps towards a harmonized EU financial market legislation

Given the fast pace of change in financial markets, the regulatory system existing at the time of the introduction of the euro was judged to be too slow, too rigid and ill-adapted to the needs of modern financial markets. The set-up produced bureaucracy, legal ambiguity and it lacked, above all, power of enforcement.

In order to create and maintain a competitive regulatory framework in the EU, efficient regulatory and supervisory structures must be established first. In July 2000, the EU Council on Economic and Financial Affairs (ECOFIN) appointed the Committee of Wise Men chaired by Alexandre Lamfalussy to identify administrative, regulatory and other types of obstacle that impede cross-border securities transactions and market integration, and to make suggestions as to how to remedy the shortcomings. The Council's objective was to identify measures to realize growth and competitiveness of European securities markets. Its mandate was limited to securities markets, leaving the regulation of banks, insurance companies and financial conglomerates outside its scope of action (Kern, 2003, p. 3).

In February 2001, the Wise Men Committee concluded in its final report that the EU's efforts to create a single market in financial services suffered from two severe shortcomings. First, there were gaps in the existing legislation and the conventional legislative process of the EU was far too cumbersome. Second, the Committee concluded that EU legislation governing financial markets lacked consistent implementation by the member states (European Commission, 2001a; Kern, 2003).

The Committee therefore recommended that the existing regulatory system in the area of securities-market regulation should be reformed with regard to speed, professionalism, consistency, transparency and close cooperation between regulators and market participants as guiding principles. The Committee proposed a number of detailed reform measures centered on the four-level Lamfalussy Process (LP) – that were intended to speed up the legislative process and ensure more consistent application and enforcement of EU securities-market legislation.

First assessments of the effectiveness of the LP confirm its functioning and acknowledge the LP being a valuable instrument (Lannoo, 2008, p. 4). This position is shared by the EU's Inter-Institutional Monitoring Group (IIMG), which published its first interim report on the LP in 2003[65]. In order to ensure that the full benefits of the LP can be realized, the IIMG rightly raises a number of is-

65 See the First Interim Report on the "*Monitoring the New Process for Regulating Securities Markets in Europe (The Lamfalussy Process)*" form the Inter-Institutional Monitoring Group (2003).

sues that will need to be addressed by all policymakers and stakeholders. These issues comprised among others:

- the need to cope effectively with the time pressure from political deadlines;
- the appropriate consultation of market participants;
- an adequate level of regulatory detail at the legislative levels of the LP; and
- the resolution of certain legal and organizational problems, primarily related to the choice of legal instrument for implementing measures, and to the influence of the European Parliament on their adoption.

The issues raised by the IIMG contain the criticism raised by a number of market participants. While being partially justified, most of the problems initially encountered were teething troubles that have largely eased in the meantime.

In this regard, the LP represents a significant intermediate step towards a harmonized banking regulation and supervision system. Eventually however, the single European financial market designed to establish a single EU regulatory and supervisory authority (EFSA). An enabling clause should thus be inserted into the new Treaty to provide for the establishment of an EFSA later on.

4. Critique

This section discusses the deficits of current regulation and assesses the capacity of traditional banking regulation to maintain financial market stability, bank safety and soundness. It starts with a preliminary consideration of adequate evaluation criteria before applying these to the traditional concept of banking regulation.

4.1 Evaluation criteria

There is a considerable body of literature on regulatory impact assessment and cost-benefit analysis.[66] From an economic perspective, every regulatory measure is assessed in the first place with regard to its effectiveness. While in general it represents the degree of regulatory objective achievement, in terms of traditional banking regulation, it is the pertinence to avoid banking crisis. In the second place, banking regulation can be assessed according to its efficiency. Fritsch et al. (1999, p. 71) further distinguish between static and dynamic efficiency. While banking regulation is considered statically efficient if the targeted outcome of regulation is achieved at a lowest cost and at a lowest possible negative impact on banks' activities. Dynamic efficiency refers to the incentive effects caused by a regulatory instrument and assesses the level negative economic results can be avoided by stimulating the efforts of market participants. Regulation

66 See Cowen (1998) for an comprehensive overview of the current literature on cost-benefit assessments of regulation.

can be assessed regarding its capabilities to set incentives for developing and implementing risk-mitigating opportunities and for facilitating technological progress.

Other evaluation criteria mentioned in the literature are the simplicity of rules and directives and the cost of regulation. Both can be aligned into the system of effectiveness and efficiency: cost-benefit assessments evaluate the static efficiency of regulation, while at the same time showing that effectiveness cannot be uncoupled from any efficiency considerations. The required simplicity of rules aims at the administrative practicability of regulation. Many times, questions on the design of regulation center on balancing simplicity and accurateness, which show that there is sometimes a trade-off between efficiency and effectiveness. Having evaluated the efficiency of banking regulation in the aforementioned cost-benefit assessment, the following section assess the effectiveness of tradition banking regulation by taking Germany as an example. It turns out that this aspect can be criticized in the current regulatory approach and that the transferability to other regulatory areas of responsibility, i.e. the creation of a single market, is limited.

4.2 Effectiveness

When assessing effectiveness, existing banking regulation seems to fail in avoiding system crisis, existence-threatening losses or bank insolvencies. Regulation has oftentimes been criticized for underestimating the complexity of risk and for applying rules that are excessively simplistic and inflexible. The 2007–2009 financial crisis evidences that bankruptcies of banks still happen (Lehman Brothers, September 2008) and that the crisis became systemic because of the generalized loss of confidence, leading to massive bail-out plans in the US and in Europe. The recent past has shown that risk was not assessed properly and increasing skepticism emerges on banking regulation's capability to avoid banking failures and banking crisis (European Central Bank, 2009a; Panetta et al., 2009).

It shows that banking regulation always has to adapt to the developments of financial markets and hence always lags their dynamic movements. Governments tend to react only when risks have materialized (i.e., Herstatt Bank, 1974) and seem to have difficulties in keeping pace with the dynamics of banking business. Economic development seems to progress faster than the ability of governments to respond with "command-control" regulation (OECD, 1997, p. 9). Within the current system of regulation, any additional rule produced in the hope that it may function which eventually fails to deliver on its intended targets will only further inflate regulation. Further, new regulation will lead to evasive reactions of the banking sector (supervision arbitrage) and to the development of innovative financial instruments to circumvent the new regulation. Credit derivatives and securitization is a good example; they allow banks to maintain their equity-to-asset ratio of 8% while increasing or decreasing their credit risk at will (The Economist, 2001, p. 16).

US banks in particular have developed measures and instrument to circumnavigate existing rules. Such behavior makes originally well-designed regulation ineffective and requires permanent revision by the regulators. Such a game of alternating rulemaking and subsequent bypassing activity will lead not only to failing regulatory objectives but also to a waste of resources. A further point of critique is directed at the effectiveness of traditional supervisory norms and their quantitative and financial ratio-oriented approach. Prudential regulation tends to lead to a crowding out of voluntary solutions and private, market-oriented arrangements (Blundell & Robinson, 1999, p. 14).

Furthermore, the fact that the prescription of financial ratios mainly aims at limiting financial risk is also subject to criticism, as most bank failures are eventually born on financial risk. Preliminary risk levels however, such as the indirect risks in a bank's management and governance system are hardly prosecuted. While single regulations place high demands on the professional requirements of the management board, management-related risks are usually neither captures nor confined. The experience of numerous bank failures shows that still severe deficits exist in capturing operational risks by the regulators. As both operational and strategic risk mainly comprise qualitative components, they are difficult to explain with quantitative norms. Financial ratio-oriented regulation implies that on certain reporting dates the adherence to defined financial (balance sheet) ratios is reviewed. Still, banks are able to change their balance sheet and risk exposure with their computer-based trading systems within a very short period. This raises general questions on the meaningfulness of balance sheet and financial statement analysis and asks for ways to effectively control the risk of a bank between two reporting dates (Federal Reserve Deposite Insurance Corporations, 1999, p. 83).

The equity prescription of the Basel Accord, which represents key element of traditional banking regulation, has been criticized for several reasons. Firstly, the minimum equity requirements cannot guarantee a bank's solvency. As the credit crisis in 2008-2009 shows, a high equity ratio does not necessarily safeguard the bank from insolvency as it deteriorates abruptly when problems occur and is hence not a good early indicator for a crisis (Peek & Rosengreen, 1997, p. 49). An advantage however is that the Basel Accord is easy to implement and allows for a plain and comparable measurement of a bank's solvency. Nevertheless, the Basel rules and standards are very roughly outlined, measuring risk with only four categories imprecisely and undifferentiated and thus requiring a disproportionate capital burden. The interest margin earned from firms with a good rating oftentimes does not compensate for the equity that needs to be held. This means that banks are incentivized to deal in more risky credits as they are more profitable. They tend to provide more credits to debtors with a higher risk, as latter have to pay higher interest rated and banks' net interest margin is higher (Steden, 2002, p. 67).

Finally, the equity requirement regulation also massively affects the resource disposition of banks and both, the regulation and the equity-to-asset ratio lack a profound theoretical and empirical foundations (Paul, 2000, p. 286). So far, there is no confirmed knowledge about the economic impact for regulatory capital requirements and the sole reference to the risk buffering function of equity does not legitimize regulatory minimum capital levels. Blum and Hellwig (1995, p. 47) have indicated that these requirements are pro-cyclical and even amplify economic fluctuations. The latest economic crisis illustrates this well: in an economic downturn when default rates increase, banks reduce credit provisions in order to meet regulatory requirements, which ultimately lead to a credit crunch and intensify a recession.

Against this background, the extreme view of "free-banking" as called for by Benston and Kaufmann (1996, p. 689) and Dowd (1996, p. 679) argues that all kinds of bank regulation is detrimental. As prudential banking regulation focuses more on rules and prescriptions than on incentives, impedes that markets themselves

Whereas the distinction of an integrated retail banking market as a means or an end is of course somewhat academic, it helps to clarify and categorize objectives and their measurement. If integration is an objective in itself, measures of cross-border activities provide the most appropriate indicators. In this sense, M&A or cross-border deposit-taking and lending would in themselves be welcomed signs of integration. If integration is considered a means to create a more efficient retail banking market, indicators of the efficiency of the retail banking systems come to force. If the retail banking market is considered a means to promote growth, even more broadly based analysis of financial system development may be called for. The author therefore regards banking market integration as one but not the only means to create an efficient, stable and growth-enhancing financial sector in Europe. This view allows to review the opportunities and the limits of retail banking market integration as well as to identify policy alternatives.

Table 8: Summary Chapter C

Summary Chapter C – Analysis of traditional banking regulation
• This chapter scrutinizes the traditional explanations for banking regulation, its measures and instruments and the current banking supervision structure in Europe. Compared to the previous theoretical discussion, this chapter focuses on the practical application of banking regulation theory in Europe. • Traditionally, two justifications for banking regulations are given: the inability of depositors to monitor banks (information asymmetries and principal-agent problems) and the risk of a systemic crisis (externalities). • Banking regulation is associated with costs and benefits. Ideally, prior to enacting a law, a cost-benefit assessment is performed. In terms of traditional regulation, costs of regulation consist of the direct cost of running a regulatory agency and the indirect cost of compliance for the regulated market. The benefits of regulation are the avoided costs of a banking crisis. • European banking regulation applies different measures to avoid systemic crisis and to protect creditors. Practically, one can differentiate between preventive and protective measures. • Regulatory and supervisory organizations in Europe have different responsibilities: banking regulation is the legislative function while supervision is the executive or control function. The latter is the responsibility of the national competent authority. While several forms of cooperation between national authorities and the EU level exist, most are subject-related. A more effective coordination of prudential supervision on the European level is required for not only financial stability and system soundness, but also for financial market harmonization. • Translating the findings of this chapter into the role of regulation to facilitate the creation of a single market reveals the explanatory shortcomings of this approach. To answer the research question appropriately, the starting point for an analysis of retail banking integration should be a thorough assessment of the underlying failure that requires EU regulators to intervene.

Source: Author's illustration.

D Conceptual model

1. Objective and approach

The previous chapters showed that there is a considerable body of literature on regulatory impact assessment in general and cost-benefit analysis in particular. The existing studies often fail to provide a comprehensive understanding of the elements of benefits that regulation may be delivering, or to discuss how different types of potential benefits can be measured. Empirical cost-benefit studies of regulation often concentrate on the quantification of costs, leaving the benefits assessment aside for a qualitative discussion. Measurement efforts or an explicit analysis of the mechanism through which regulation is expected to deliver the promised change, have been neglected in large part. Therefore, the conceptual model outlined in this chapter adopts a financial regulation impact assessment framework developed by Oxera (2006) for the U.K. Financial Services Agency (FSA). The theoretical consideration to assess market failure, government failure and coordination failures, as well as the implication of the territorial dimension of regulation in terms of policy uploading and downloading, are incorporates into the conceptual framework.

Based on the preceding review of existing literature, the research framework of this study aims to refine measurement of regulatory interventions. In order to test the research hypothesis and to investigate whether regulation can act as a catalyst to reach a certain market outcome that is superior to one without regulation, a two-step analysis is performed: First, the key decision factors that may be considered by regulators to choose a targeted regulatory intervention need to be identified. Second, the actual measurement of benefits is conducted. To assess the effectiveness (in terms of overcoming barriers to integration) and efficiency (in terms economic and social efficiency) of such a regulatory intervention, this conceptual model aims to identify the relevant elements of benefits, the mechanisms through which regulation may deliver these benefits and the approaches that can be adopted to measure the relevant elements of benefits (Oxera, 2006, p. 7). More specifically, the model seeks to establish the following:

(i) Identify the key decision factors for regulators to intervene – based on the findings from theories on banking regulation the rationale for selecting a specific type of regulation is described. This includes, in particular, the review of three different types of economic failures (market failure, government failure and coordination failure), risk considerations, and the territorial dimension on regulation requirements.
(ii) Identify the actual benefits that should be measured (measurement subject) and how should they be measured (measurement modality) – the model is designed to identify the elements along which banking regulation delivers

benefits by improving market outcome (i.e., removing barriers to integration). Next, the types of benefits and how they can be measured are discussed.

A shortcoming of existing regulation assessments has been its static and quantitative focus, concentrating on financial ratios and risks. As shown in the previous chapter on the discussion of traditional banking regulation, adhering solely to regulatory-defined, quantitative thresholds does not necessarily achieve the intended purpose to stabilize the banking system. Other, qualitative aspects of regulation covering organizational, managerial or strategic risks can complement or even replace quantitative instruments of banking supervision for certain economic problems, i.e., the slow progress of retail banking market integration in Europe. In this regard, this model seeks to identify the key decision factors determining the type of regulatory intervention necessary to improve a certain detrimental market outcome.

In terms of measurement of benefits of regulation, economists and advisory organizations have developed numerous empirical tools and modeling techniques to perform statistical analysis, which have been recorded in detail in the relevant literature (see section 0.). Instead of discussing these different tools and techniques in detail, this study investigates at a conceptual level how benefits can be measured and refers to some tools and techniques and the relevant literature only where it is purpose- and goal-oriented.

While aiming at providing a generic methodology that can be applied to the whole spectrum of regulation, the limitation of scope in this study allows for a conceptual and empirical validation of integration issues in the retail banking market only. Furthermore, it is designed to assess both benefits and costs of regulation. The chosen methodology identifies the types of benefits of regulation first and then measures them ex-ante or ex-post. In the wider context of regulatory impact assessment and cost-benefit analysis, the benefits of regulation, which represent the research focus of this study, are set against costs of regulation in order to evaluate the cost efficiency of a type of regulatory intervention. The generic nature of this conceptual model allows for capturing costs imposed by regulation or occurred through the negative impact of regulation sufficiently.

This conceptual model should be seen in the wider context of "incentive-compatible self-regulation" (Alchian & Demsetz, 1972) and coordination failure theory, and of the debate on the costs and benefits of banking regulation in the context of Transaction Cost Economics. While the decision factors for a regulatory intervention are subject to a prior assessment of the current market outcome and interlinked incentives of participants in the banking industry as well as the related level of risks (financial, operational or systemic) involved, the following methodology assesses these factors in a first instance before defining the measurement process. Both parts eventually merge into a consolidated framework that compares market outcomes without regulation to ones with regulation.

Measuring the effectiveness and efficiency of regulatory intervention to facilitate the creation of a single market for retail banking services falls into the wider debate on the costs and benefits of regulation (Oxera, 2006, p. 8). A myriad amount of research can be found in relevant literature on this subject but can ultimately be split into theoretical studies suggesting abstract transaction cost approaches to regulation and practitioner studies conducted by politico-economic consultancies or advisors that seek to provide a practicable decision-making methodology for political decision makers. In this context, the present conceptual model has the ambition to bridge the two strains of research on measuring the effectiveness and cost-efficiency of regulation. A study conducted by Deloitte on behalf of the British Financial Services Authority, for example (Deloitte, 2006), has estimated the (direct) cost of compliance in three markets of the financial services sector for financial services firms only. However, the costs of regulation will eventually be borne by all the users of financial services as banks and insurance firms pass down most of their incremental costs through profit margins to private individuals and companies. To remain in this logic, the level of these costs should, therefore, also be considered from a private client perspective and should be outweighed by the benefits of the regulatory intervention.

Chapter D focuses on the description of the model and the explanation of different chains of causality through which a specific rule may deliver benefits. The following chapter will practically illustrate the conceptual process in the SEPA case study. The actual measurement of the costs and benefits is in scope of the case study.

The combination of the theoretical strains of the territorial and functional dimension of regulation into a recommendation for the key decision factors for regulatory process, and the framework for benefits evaluation has two practical implications: First, some of the measurement tools described here require further in-depth research from regulatory agencies, as the complexity of some of the tools and models greatly increases depending on the problem in such a way that a generic model can no longer be applied. Second, policy proposals must be developed on the basis of established and properly evidenced benefits. This implies, for example, that policy timelines should be set wisely, taking sufficient time into consideration to carry out the required analysis and to provide sound estimates of benefits.

This chapter starts with an overview of the framework of analysis and then defines the key decision factors that determine the ultimate structure of the regulatory intervention. The next section describes how benefits are identified within this model, and the following section summarizes the modality of benefits of regulation.

2. Overview of conceptual model

The conceptual model for the analysis of retail banking market integration and the role of regulation is summarized in Figure 8. The author adapts the impact assessment framework of Oxera (2006) with the results of the theoretical analysis derived from the functional and territorial dimension of regulation. Given the scope of this study and the research question on the role of regulation in integrating fragmented markets, such as the European retail banking market, benefits of regulation can, in principle, be measured as the improvements in market outcome (i.e., degree to which obstacles to integration are removed) that result from regulation (Oxera, 2006, p. 10). Here, an ex-ante analysis perspective is more difficult to conduct than an ex-post analysis. The latter analysis aims to evaluate the impact of regulation that already exists. Such an ex-post measurement requires a comparison of actual market outcomes in a regulated environment with outcomes that would have emerged in a non-regulated environment (ibid. p.10). An ex-ante assessment however requires the measurement of likely improvement of market outcomes, i.e., the removal of impediments to regulation, compared with the status quo.

The measurement of the effectiveness of removing obstacles to integration or overcoming market failures due to regulatory intervention turns out to be difficult in practice. In this regard, a systematic analysis and measurement of the mechanisms through which regulation delivers benefits and reduces transaction costs is required.

Market and government failures are two of the four key decision factors identified in this study that determine the level of regulatory intervention. This model includes the types of failures identified in Chapter B, namely *market failure* as defined by the Normative Regulation Theory and *government failure* for the Positive Regulation Theory. Where none of these failures exists, any regulatory intervention would cause net transaction costs to increase. To identify the potential benefits of regulation (e.g. the utmost benefits that regulation, in principle, could deliver), it is important to understand the types and severity of market failure that would affect a market without regulation. These failures would include aforementioned phenomena such as information asymmetries, market power or externalities, and regulatory capture by interest groups. Besides market and government failure, risks and incentives (used interchangeably with coordination failure) are two additional key decision factors that are critical to identify potential benefits or transaction costs. The misalignment of incentives between market participants builds on the theoretical framework of the coordination failure theory and NIE. High risks, such as systemic risk in the banking sector, can, in many cases, outweigh the market impact of severe market failures. The extent to which an individual factor determines the choice of regulatory intervention depends on the type of obstacle to integration and the economic costs that occur in a situation with no regulation. The single factors are defined in more detail in the next chapter.

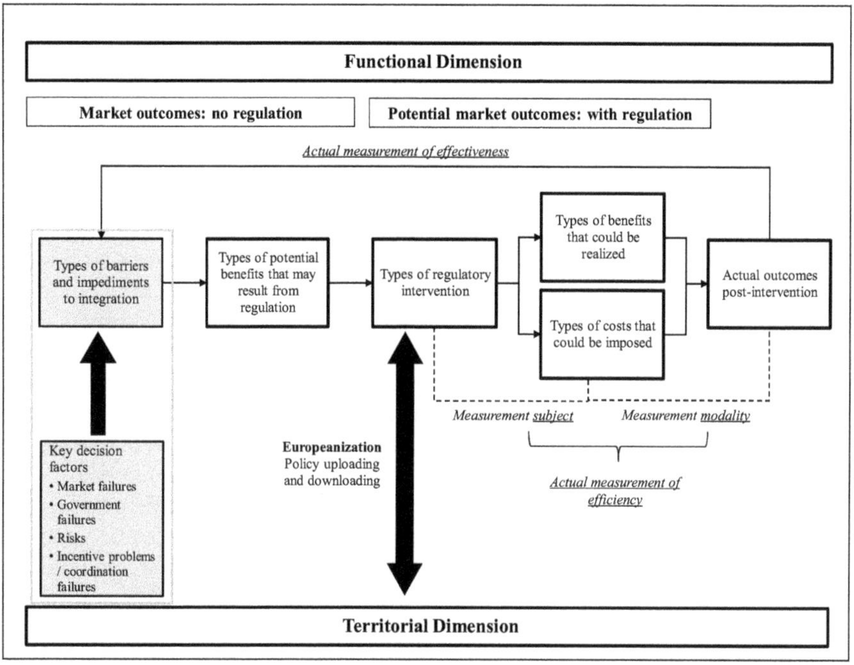

Figure 8: Overview of conceptual model
Source: Author's illustration, including a modified version of the figure in Oxera (2006).

As stated earlier, the approach of this model is generic in principle and can be applied to the measurement of any type of regulatory intervention such as an anti-trust ruling, the introduction of specific acts and roles and deregulation measures. However, given the specific focus on the European market integration and the hypothesis that regulation can act as a catalyst for an economic-efficient development, the territorial dimension of regulation impacts the decision factors in this specific case a lot stronger than in a one-dimensional context. From a methodological point of view, two thoughts need to be considered: sequencing of regulatory interventions and the interdependency of rules (overlap or mutual enhancement). Regarding sequencing, the introduction of a specific rule may lower transaction costs and deliver positive market impacts. However, removing it may have no effect at all if the market has permanently adjusted market practice to meet previous requirements.[67] The interdependency of rules exists, for

67 The sequencing and timing of rules and economic reforms is a promising theory strain of New Institutional Economics and was predominately coined for the introduction of

example, in cases where the benefits of a rule measured in isolation may be small but are large when measured as part of a complementary set of rules.

This model identifies potential benefits as improvements in market outcome, i.e., increased choice, lower transaction risk or prices. While taking a more practical approach, this work distances itself from the more statutory objectives for an internal market set by the European Commission (2005e, p. 3), which are defined at very high levels of abstractions (i.e., increasing Europe's competitiveness, growth prospects or market confidence). Nevertheless, these objectives are implicitly or explicitly linked to market outcomes, and falling short in achieving these objectives is reflected in the barriers and impediments to integration. The description of the current market outcome without regulation is used as a starting point of this analysis. The economic and political barriers to integration affect the market outcome along three categories of detriments: consumers, producers and the overall economy. The benefits will hence also be measured against these categories, which all relate to the market delivering economically efficient outcomes. Having defined the types of problems that determine negative market outcome without regulation, the set of potential benefits along the three categories that may result from regulation are defined consecutively.

A detailed analysis of the detrimental market outcomes and the potential benefits of regulation is performed in the next process step. To decide upon the most effective and efficient type of regulatory intervention requires an assessment from an economic (functional dimension of regulation) as well as from the political (territorial dimension of regulation) perspective. The decision factors elaborated earlier in this research (namely market failure, government failure, coordination failures and risks) provide a structured approach to refine the detrimental market outcomes and to define their potential mitigation through regulation (or the maximum benefits that could be attained by regulation under a market failure framework). This identifies the set of benefits that is realized by actual regulation, the subject of measurement (the *what to measure*) and indicates which regulatory measures can actually be applied in the given situation.

Regarding the modality of measuring the improvements in market outcomes relating to benefits and costs, available empirical methodologies are drawn upon. However, it turns out that in practice, a direct measurement of benefits and costs (efficiency of regulation) is not always possible, and predictions about the impact of certain regulatory interventions are rare. In these cases, alternative techniques have been developed, for example, by Oxera (2003), Benham (2004) and Polski (2000), which will not be further detailed in this work.[68]

---

politico-economic reforms in transformation countries (see, for example, Buchenrieder, 2002).

68 These include, for example, methodologies to measure the cost of exchange (Benham & Benham, 2004), analysis of data series on the impact of regulation on the operating

In the present model, regulatory intervention may deliver benefits by improving detrimental market outcome through one (or the combination of all) of the three mechanisms under consideration for a decision on the type of regulation: reducing market failures (and/or government and coordination failures), aligning incentives between producers, consumers and regulators, and reducing the frequency of risks or lessening their impact (Oxera, 2006, p. 5).

The measurement of benefits cannot proceed without considering the cost of a regulatory intervention. The imposed costs comprise direct cost of compliance for banks as well as indirect cost (i.e., negative market impacts) and must be netted against the inferred benefits of regulation (see Chapter C). When costs of regulation exceed the benefits, government or regulatory failure occurs, leading to deteriorated market outcomes as a result of regulation.

European retail banking market is the *relevant market* under investigation in this model. However, put more generically for the purpose of a broader application, in the relevant market providers of financial services, like banks, and their customers (other banks, corporate or private clients) transact with each other in the specified product(s). While the benefits and cost of regulation can be measured along the entire provider-customer relationship chain, the market outcome at end-consumer level is particularly important for policy makers (Oxera, 2006, p. 5). Hence, this conceptual model also focuses on the market outcomes of that specific market segment but aims at taking also the outcomes in the economic market (i.e., the market in which products compete) into consideration.

The following sections emphasize the direct impact improvements of regulatory intervention on market outcomes. The decision factors determining the type of intervention comprise the ultimate analysis of detrimental market outcomes in the absence of regulation (market failure, government failure, coordination failure or incentive misalignment and risks) and seek to provide a relevant conceptual contribution to policy formulation.

3. Types of barriers and impediments to market integration

The first step of analysis in the proposed methodology includes a description of the relevant problem and the current market outcome associated. The detrimental market outcome without regulation is closely being examined, and reference to potential regulation that would positively affect the situation is provided. In the context of market integration, retail banking – the market of services to banks' retail customers and small- and medium-sized business clients – is one of the least integrated markets in Europe. Both banks and consumers still concen-

costs of banks (Polski, 2000) or the assessment of financial services market profitability with regard to competition policy impact.

trate largely on their national domestic markets. This section describes the status quo of retail banking integration and elaborates on the impediments to regulation such as economic, political and social obstacles. It takes stock of the present degree of integration from a bank, consumer and overall economic perspectives, and identifies potential moves from the regulator to alter the situation to eventually create a single European retail banking market.

Recalling the definition of full integration stated in Chapter A, integration is achieved when banks and clients start viewing the EU as their home market and all regulatory obstacles are removed. The first part of the definition refers to market participants' behavior and their willingness to identify the whole EU as their domestic retail market. This implies that banks and end-consumers would interact across national borders in the same way that they do on a national basis even without further positive effect such as a broader product range at lower prices having materialized. This behavior is at least partly attributed to path dependency (long-term, steady adjustments in the behavior of banks and end-consumers) and the remaining differences that continue to exist between member states despite all attempts of integration in the past years.

The second part of the definition of integration, the removal of regulatory obstacles, simply refers to the situation in which banks and consumers are able to act across Europe. While natural barriers resulting from long-term structural differences between the member states, such as language and business customs, cannot be reduced or removed by regulation, regulatory obstacles stand in the way of Europe-wide activity and can be removed by European policy. In this regard, the European Central Bank made it clear that a market for a given financial product (which could be segment-specific products in practice) is fully integrated when all market participants (i) are bound by a single set of rules, (ii) have equal access to the financial product and (iii) are treated equally when they are active in that market (discussed in Baele, Ferrando, Hördahl, Krylova, & Monnet, 2004, p. 6). The way towards achieving this goal and creating a single market out of 30 individual markets in the EU member states is termed *integration process.* To this understanding of regulation, it is irrelevant whether market participants then actually take advantage of a single market and engage in cross-border activities or whether this integration process eventually triggers the positive welfare effects ascribed to it (S. Schaefer, 2009, p. 4).

The following sections compare the status quo of retail market integration against this definition to identify the detrimental market outcomes from an end-consumer, supplier and overall economic perspective. The conceptual model anticipates that the resulting list of detriments in the absence of regulation determines the potential benefits that regulation may achieve.

3.1 End-consumer perspective

Viewing Europe as a home market

Despite the introduction of the Euro currency, the large majority of retail customers purchase their financial products and services in their domestic home market. However, according to regular market studies and client surveys conducted by the European Commission, Europeans are increasingly developing international preferences, gradually changing their buying behavior, and slowly trending towards purchasing a financial product or service in another member state. While this emerging segment comprises only a negligible proportion of EU citizens and effectively only 5% of EU citizens bought a financial product from another member state, the proportion having an intention to purchase in the coming years is notably larger (European Commission, 2003d, 2005c). The main reason for today's low level of utilization of cross-border services is practically and largely related to migration and the movement of workers within the EU member states (OPTEM, 2003).

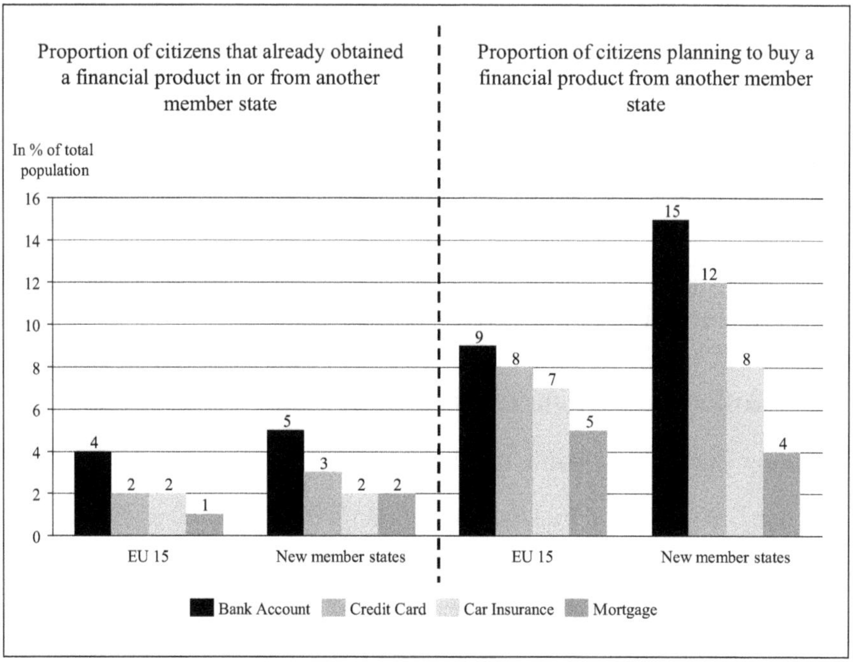

Figure 9: Consumers' actual and intended purchases of financial products
Source: Eurobarometer (2003d, No. 60.2).

Among the financial products EU citizens are planning to purchase, bank accounts (15%) and credit cards (12%) take a lead. Consumer loans (e.g., mortgages) and insurance, as well as payments are also expected to expand. However, these products still face material legislative harmonization barriers, and the demand for cross-border banking services is expected only to increase if regulatory frameworks across Europe are further coordinated. The sheer size of the potential market from 5% percent of EU citizens (around 23 million) in 2003 to 10% in 2010 (around 40 million) constitutes the potential benefit for the current market outcome in case these obstacles can be removed by regulation.

Removal of obstacles to integration

Regarding the obstacles to integration, the limiting factor for marketing cross-border banking services for retail clients is not a general reluctance to purchase financial services in another EU country because of different language or cultural preferences. It is, rather, the lack of confidence about the legal and regulatory framework applicable to these transactions. The major regulatory hindrances include discrepancies in consumer protection rules, national taxation, product specifications defined by national regulations and the civil law (Diekmann, 2006, pp. 4-5). For example, discrepancies in contract law hinder banks from standardizing processes, and specific national regulatory regimes require distinct forms and procedures, adding to end-consumers' uncertainties. Heterogeneous taxation prevents banks from designing pan-European products for retail clients, making it difficult for them to fully recognize the benefits of a single market in Europe. These artificial hindrances to market integration are by far more significant than the *economic* or *social* barriers. Their removal is subject to financial market policy, whereas banking service providers have to develop response strategies to manage natural obstacles. If prudential rules are largely harmonized at the international level, the shift to online banking, for example, as an alternative distribution channel, indicates that product innovation may be able to open new markets for end-consumers.

3.2 Banks' and financial service providers' perspective

Viewing Europe as a home market

The supply-side of retail banking markets shows common features that are typical for banking markets in general. The main characteristic differentiating this sub-sector from other banking fields is that its product offering targets the fragmented demand-side of end-consumers and small enterprises. Retail banking is composed of deposit and loan products, payments and other services of financial intermediation. Despite technological development of new distribution channels such as internet banking, local branch networks remain an important point of service delivery for banks (European Commission, 2006b, p. 19). Today, banks offer cross-border retail financial services by means of local entities such as subsidiaries (separate, local legal entity) or branches (affiliated to mother firm in home country), resulting from either mergers or acquisitions (M&A), joint ventures or greenfield investments (Diekmann, 2006). With the exception of investment funds (UCITS), which are sold to retail clients through some local distributors, direct cross-border distribution in the EU without local presence hardly exists currently.

Removal of obstacles to integration

Given the already high level of domestic retail bank consolidation in some countries,[69] cross-border engagements are required to achieve further economies of scale. From the several options for the means of market entry, significant emphasis is placed on cross-border M&A in the European retail market. By this means, large players are able to enter new markets and swiftly acquire the required scale in their operations to compete against established domestic banks. Furthermore, there is empirical evidence that in the banking industry, cross-border M&A tends to generate superior benefits for the consumer in the host country (Walkner & Raes, 2005, p. 22). However, there remain significant barriers to cross-border M&A in banking, in particular arising from the current regulatory banking supervisory framework. A survey undertaken by the European Commission in 2005[70] identified several barriers to cross-border M&A, which can be divided into two categories of obstacles: economic and regulatory. The survey pointed out that some economic barriers are, to a large extent, unavoidable when banks assess the case for making a cross-border acquisition. Cost savings, for example, will be relatively lower than in domestic M&A. Product mixes differ in member states and reduce economies of scope while little overlap in distribution and IT networks as well as back office functions reduces gains from realizing economies of scale. With regard to regulatory barriers to cross-border M&A, preferential or discriminatory tax regimes create significant barriers to small- and medium sized banks while supervisory requirements were seen as a barrier by all institutions. With regard to removing these detrimental market outcomes, regulation could potentially facilitate market integration through building a more supportive environment for cross-border M&A in the European banking sector (European Commission, 2006b, p. 34).

Besides regulatory obstacles to market integration, which limit ownership structures and the scope of activities for certain banks in certain countries, other entry barriers result from market structures and the behavior of participants, par-

---

69 In the U.K., The Netherlands and Belgium, the market share of the four largest retail banks exceeds 70% (Diekmann, 2006).

70 See: http://europa.eu.int/comm/internal_market/finances/docs/cross-sector/mergers/survey-results_en.pdf.

ticularly with respect to cooperation agreements and the functioning of networks such as payments systems or credit agencies (European Commission, 2006b, p. 21). With regard to networks, access for new market entrants is, in many cases, artificially hampered by regulatory provisions or the behavior of incumbents such as disadvantageous fee structures for smaller banks or newcomers (for further details see Chapter E).

4. Key decision factors for a functional assessment

4.1 Key decision factors

This section briefly outlines the key decision factors determining regulatory-policy making. The present conceptual model requires a thorough evaluation of these factors and the consideration of the territorial dimension of regulation for a given problem. Without considering this perspective, the model could not accommodate the complexity of multi-level decision making in the EU.

4.1.1 Market failure

Market failures, as defined in this model, comprise the problems explained in the Theory of Market Failure (Public Interest Theory) and the Theory of Government Failure (Public Choice Theory/Private Interest Theory). They state the rationale for regulation and are critical to understand the effectiveness and efficiency of market outcomes. They are commonly attributed to the existence of information asymmetries, externalities, market power and externalities. Based on the theoretical considerations of the previous chapter, it can be distinguished between the following reasons for market failures:

Table 9: Reasons for market failures and examples in retail banking

Reasons for market failure	Examples in retail banking
Information asymmetries	*Product offering related* Consumers and small enterprises cannot obtain relevant information from alternative banks or evaluate the characteristics of a financial product due to their limited capability to process information and the lack of information provided by banks. *Provider related* Consumers are imperfectly informed about the quality (i.e., solvency) of a bank. *Pricing related* For many consumers and SMEs, it is difficult to assess the effective price of a banking product (i.e., an bank account) and even more difficult to compare products across various domestic or cross-border suppliers with different products. *Consumer related* As banks learn about the credit quality over time, a longer banking relationship is beneficial for banks and customers. As most credit registers are national, switching to foreign bank lenders is more difficult than within domestic borders.
Market power	Banks tend to use their market position to charge excessively high prices.
Externalities	*Positive externalities* Information may be underprovided in an unregulated market: making information available is beneficial not only to the provider of information but also to other participants in

	the market. *Negative externalities* The behavior of one bank in the market may adversely affect the reputation of other banks and thus lower overall consumer confidence in the market. *Network externalities* Network goods such as payment systems exhibit network externalities, which mean that adding another customer increases value to the existing customers and to the providers of the network.

Source: Author's illustration including examples from the European Commission (2006b), Kleimeier & Sander (2007) and Oxera (2006)

4.1.2 Risks

Traditionally, risk and market failure are inextricably linked in the banking industry. The most relevant risks in this context are systemic risk, operational risks and financial (or credit default) risk. If risk were low, the potential detriment from a market failure would be low as well. For example, unless there was risk that the consumer could lose funds or else be affected in the event of bank default, the lack of information about a bank's financial position would not necessarily be associated with a consumer detriment (Oxera, 2006, p. 13). In the same way, the existence of externalities combined with risk of default raises concerns about systemic failures in the banking sector.

On the other hand, the presence of risk as such does not necessarily require regulatory intervention. For instance, if risk exposure of banks is made transparent to consumers and customers were able to anticipate that their savings were threatened by bank default, they would be able to consider this risk in their decision-making and adjust the charges that they would be willing to pay to their bank. Likewise, if risk characteristics of investment products or other types of financial services were transparent and understood by consumers, risks would be priced in terms of expected returns (Oxera, 2006, p. 6).

These examples show that it is the combination of both market failure and risks that needs to be assessed in order to determine a type of regulatory intervention that will improve market outcomes.

4.1.3 Incentive misalignment and coordination failure

Like risks, incentives of market participants in the banking industry and coordination problems are inextricably linked to market failure. While the coordination problem describes a situation where market participants are dependent on the actions of other participants and there would be a *first-mover disadvantage* in terms of initial investment efforts in large-scale infrastructure for example, an alignment of regulatory, supplier and consumer incentives may improve market outcome by solving the chicken-and-egg problem. Similarly, incentive alignment between consumers and banks by means of completely specified contracts would avoid a detrimental market outcome even if consumers were not able to fully monitor the activities of their bank. The problem of incentive misalignment gives rise to or intensifies a market failure and raises questions on regulation acting as trigger for activating self-regulatory forces.

4.2 Territorial considerations

Territorial considerations of regulatory interventions to improve market outcome raise questions on (i) what is the intrinsic political motivation and objective behind the decision-making, (ii) which regulatory agencies or interest groups on a supra-national, national or sub-national basis are involved in the coordination of regulation and (iii) how is the policy-making process shaped in terms of policy uploading and downloading?

Regulation of a specific market cannot be examined isolated from general European policy, in particular not when considering integration of a European project. In this context, this step of analysis aims at examining the impact of policy agenda on the EU and national level that, besides economic considerations, determine the type of regulatory intervention required to improve market outcome.

Furthermore, the territorial consideration in this model explicitly refers to the statutory objectives for the internal market in Europe set by the European Commission and the member states. These objectives are linked to the market outcome in the same way that they are linked to the underlying sources of detriments (Oxera, 2006, p. 11). Due to the high levels of generality of these objectives and the fact that they do not lend themselves easily to direct measures, this conceptual model has defined potential benefits as improvements to the market outcome that regulation may deliver.

While the market outcomes under investigation in the current model may not cover everything that is captured, for example, by the Commission's financial services policy objectives (European Commission, 2005e, p. 14), such as the establishment of effective levels of prudential control, it allows for identification and measurement of further detriments and the impacts of regulation beyond the remits of the Commission's objectives. For instance, *financial exclusion* is a market detriment for consumers and banks not explicitly captured the EC's objectives. The same applies to the reverse, *wider access*, which represents a potential benefit that regulation could realize and that should be captured in an impact assessment.

The relationship between detriments and the overall objectives of the Commission's financial services policy is provided below.

Table 10: Relationship between detriments and EC objectives

	Related market detriment			
Financial services policy objective 2005-2010 from the European Commission	**Market failure**	**Government failure**	**Risk**	**Incentive misalignment / coordination failure**
Removing remaining economically significant barriers	•			•
Free circulation of capital at the lowest possible costs	•		•	•
Adequate and effective levels of prudential control		•	•	•
Financial stability		•	•	•
Consumer protection	•	•	•	•

Source: Author's illustration including references to the European Commission Green Paper on Financial Services Policy 2005-2010 (2005e).

As outlined earlier, this step of analysis should also discuss the questions on the involvement of regulators and the characteristics of the underlying policy-making process on a case-by-case basis. With regard to the involvement of regulatory agencies in the rule- and decision-making process, once the problems determining the detrimental market outcomes are defined and examined, a correct mapping of responsibility to the respective national or supra-national level for competition policy and supervisory aspects is required.

While policy objectives are usually defined top-down (as is the case for the integration of the European retail banking markets), the concrete policy-making and decision-making process may involve various national regulators but also interest groups and industry experts. Their participation and contribution in the policy-making process may result in an uploading to the EU level.

5. Market detriments and potential benefits of regulation

Following the examination of the types of barriers to integration and the findings from the market failure, government failure, risk and incentive misalignment problems, the next step of analysis foresees a more detailed analysis. The objective is to generate a list of potential detriments and the potential benefits that regulation can deliver. Again, the methodology distinguishes between a consumer and a bank's perspective.

5.1 Consumer perspective

There are several detrimental market outcomes for consumers that relate to the broadly defined *consumer protection* objective for the Commission's financial services agenda. It stems from a consumer or any other user of banking services point of view, seven broad types of consumer detriments, split into economy and policy-related categories as outlined in Table 11.

These detriments emerge from the theoretical framework provided earlier and the identification of key decision factors such as market failure, associated risks and incentive problems. Furthermore, they draw on policy recommendations in various studies on retail banking regulation.[71]

With reference to Table 11, the following illustrates how the dimensions of outcome can be modeled with sources of detriment.

Higher Costs Detriment

All three types of risks outlined earlier – operational, financial and systemic risks – may involve higher costs for consumers. For example, operational failures and bank defaults can cause financial losses for consumers (Oxera, 2006, p. 15). They would have adjusted their decision if they were able to evaluate the full risk of these losses. However, as they are imperfectly informed about risks, market failure arises from the problem of asymmetric information. Conversely, banks may be induced to engage in behavior that is unfavorable to consumers, potentially increasing the risk of losses. Systemic risks, however, refer to negative externalities or spill-over effects where the insolvency of one bank can trigger further default in the overall banking system.

Furthermore, higher costs for consumers may also relate to increased transaction costs as defined in NIE. In situations of information problems, where consumers need to spend time and money to search for suitable products or suppliers and for monitoring performance afterwards, system inefficiencies may arise. Negative externalities represent another market failure that may lead to higher transaction costs. This could be the case in a situation where banks dedicate resources to a specific product or service to build or maintain their market reputation. The negative externality emerges when these additional costs are charged to end-consumers through higher prices and the enhanced market reputation would be adversely affected by the actions of other banks in the market.

71 The policy recommendations refer to Kleimeier & Sander (2007), Heinemann & Jopp (2007b), Diekmann (2003), Shirreff (2009), the European Commission (2008) and Schaefer (1999).

Reduced Choice Detriment

Informational problems may lead to sub-optimal consumer purchase decisions (*suboptimal choice*), or to a reduced variety of products offered by banks (*reduced choice*). Suboptimal choice is mainly driven by consumers' lack of access to, or knowledge of, their investment or the risk associated with products and by their inability to identify which products best serve their requirements. On the other hand, if consumers are imperfectly informed, unable to evaluate a product or the quality of services provided by banks or if there is system-wide lack of consumer confidence, banks may be inclined to cease investments in the development of innovative products. Furthermore, the variety of products offered may also be reduced in oligopolistic market structures where few firms have market power and entry barriers exist for new entrants.

Higher Price Detriment

Finally, the consumer detriment of higher prices in the absence of regulation is attributed to market power. It gives banks or any other provider of banking services the ability to restrict output and raise prices beyond the level that would apply in perfectly competitive markets.

Restricted Access Detriment

Another type of consumer detriment, summarized under the heading *financial exclusion* in Table 11 refers to public policy objectives rather than to market outcomes that have so far been described from an economic perspective. Markets may not generate an outcome considered adequate to meet financial needs of consumers even if there were no market failures or related problems (Oxera, 2006, p. 15). In some cases, consumers may not be able to purchase a banking product or service although the market is efficient and prices reflect marginal costs. Here, regulation could deliver benefits to those consumers suffering financial exclusion and improving their access to required products or services. Whether, as a side effect, subsidies were required and higher prices would have to be borne by other consumers, needs to be evaluated in detail.

In summary, Table 11 captures the market outcomes that are detrimental to consumers not necessarily from an efficiency point of view (broadly relating to the overall objective of "consumer protection") but also from a distributional point of view. The operational risk dimension, for example, may be able to capture a mixture of efficiency and distributional outcomes (Oxera, 2006, p. 16). Operational failures raise, on the one hand, efficiency concerns where the market by itself cannot correctly price the risk, and in many cases simply transfer the risk from the bank to the consumer, who needs to bear the risk of loss of funds eventually. The transfer of risk between the affected parties can be considered a potentially detrimental market outcome for consumers in this generic conceptual model. Even though this distributional objective is not explicitly in the EC objectives, it needs to be borne in mind in the following analysis of sub-markets such as the European payment market (Oxera, 2006, p. 9).

Table 11: Types of consumer detriments and potential benefits of regulation

Obstacle type	Types of consumer detriment in the absence of regulation		Example/explanation of detriment	Potential benefits of regulation
Economy-related	Higher Costs	Operational risks	Losses that arise to consumers as a result of an operational failure by a firm (e.g., "mis-selling" or other negligent advice, fraud, systems breakdown); higher prices if failure is compensated by the firm and cost passed on to consumers	Reduction of expected losses and other costs associated with operational failure
		Financial risks	Losses that arise to consumers as a result of the default of a firm (e.g., deposited funds cannot be returned, losses from operational failures cannot be compensated)	Reduction of expected losses and other costs associated with financial failure
		Systemic risks	Costs incurred by consumers due to widespread failures of the financial system	Reduction of expected losses and other costs associated with systemic failure
	Reduced Choice	Sub-optimal choice	"Mis-buying" of financial products (e.g., when poorly informed consumers decide to buy a product not suitable for them)	Value that consumers derive from better choice (i.e., more optimal fit between what they buy and what they need)
		Limited choice	Lack of consumer confidence may make it not worthwhile for firms to offer certain types of product, reducing the choice set available to consumers	Value that consumers derive from increased choice (i.e., reduction in opportunity cost of not being able to buy what could be available)
	Higher prices	From market power of firms	Consumers pay excessively high prices to a firm exercising its market power	Reduction of excessive prices
		From transaction/ system inefficiencies	Consumers incur higher transaction costs (e.g., due to the need to monitor financial intermediaries if there is no regulator to perform this function)	Reduction of transaction costs/prices arising from inefficiencies, including consumer search costs
Public policy-related	Restricted access	Financial exclusion	Even if markets were efficient, some consumers may not be able to gain adequate or affordable access to financial services	Value consumers derive from improved access to financial services

Source: Author's illustration, adopted from Oxera (2006, pp. 8,14).

5.2 Bank detriments and potential benefits of regulation

While banks can be both *consumers* and *producers* of financial services and the potential detriments summarized in Table 11 focus on capturing those characterizing the end-consumer level, most of them apply to intermediary consumers as well. In this regard, even wholesale banks are "consumers" somewhere along the vertical chain of the industry and are purchasers of financial market transactions that are affected by regulation. From a standpoint of a *producer* or *supplier* of banking services, the following detrimental market outcomes may arise in the absence of regulation.

Higher transaction costs

Banks may face high transaction costs in an unregulated market when they need to expand their efforts for monitoring their counterparties. If so, regulation would yield benefits to banks in terms of a reduction of transaction cost. Cost of capital (or funding costs), as another type of transaction costs for banks, is also higher in a market without regulation. Regulatory capital requirements testify banks' solvency and have a signal effect in the market of an approved financial position. This enables banks to obtain a better external rating and to reduce funding costs in the market.

Lower profits

Besides the fact that higher transaction costs reduce banks' profits, revenues made with end-consumers may also deteriorate in the absence of regulation. Demand-side effects such as the lack of consumer confidence in the market or towards certain financial products could make the provision of certain products unprofitable, hence squeezing these products off the market. Here, the existence of statutory regulation may create that confidence for consumers to engage in certain financial transactions and generate demand for consumers who would otherwise be too risk-averse to purchase these products.

In the logic of this conceptual model, the potential benefits of regulation are measured with regard to improvements in market outcomes. Under the proposition of competitive markets, the costs and benefits incurred by banks are passed on to end-consumers. Consequently, the potential benefits arising to banks are of an intermediate nature and should already be incorporated in the final benefits arising for end-consumers as reflected in Table 11. For example, increasing consumer confidence through regulation may allow banks to gain profits on products or services that would not be profitable in an unregulated environment, broadening choice for customers. Similarly, the reduction of transaction costs related to monitoring and funding would be passed on to end-consumers through lower prices.

In cases where markets are not competitive, benefits that arise for banks are eventually not or not fully passed on to the end-consumers of banking products or services. Transfers from banks to consumers or vice-versa constitute welfare-neutral redistributions of income, where the total surplus does not change even if one supply-side is better off and the consumer side is worse off (Oxera, 2006, p. 10). However, in uncompetitive markets, monopoly rents may be used in unproductive ways and may lead to an overall detrimental market outcome for the economy. Furthermore, policy makers tend to attach greater importance to end-consumer surplus than producer surplus (influence of industry interest group lobbying is factored out in this example), making the redistribution no longer neutral. Given the EC's consumer protection objective, a greater emphasis on end-consumer benefits is assumed and the benefits withheld by banks should, therefore, not be captured in this analysis and measurement of improvement in market outcomes for retail clients in the banking market. Regulation imposed on banks may be beneficial to the overall economy, even though these benefits are not passed on to end-consumers through lower prices. Bank profits result in benefits for tax authorities, dividends paid out to shareholders and high wages paid out to employees.

Nevertheless, the causes or drivers of benefits arising to banks need to be differentiated. If banks benefit because regulation reduces banks' costs of operations and increases their efficiency there is some benefit to the overall economy, even if it is not reflected in reduced consumer prices. If, by contrast, the benefits arise because regulation weakens competitive forces and allows banks to raise prices, any benefits received need to be offset with a detriment for end-consumers.

In the context of the European Union and the integration of different, heterogeneous markets, benefits may be arising to banks that do not necessarily translate into benefits for consumers in their domestic market and are thus not perceived as improvements to the market outcome. This may be the instance if European regulation delivers benefits to banks' international operations, for example, facilitating their business expansion into other member states, which would not be captured as improvement for consumers in the banks' home markets. Nevertheless, they would arise for the most part for banks and the European economy.

Against this backdrop, being specific about where exactly regulation is expected to improve outcomes for banks and deliver benefits that are not fully passed on to the end-consumer is particularly important when identifying and measuring the benefits at the level of banks (assuming these benefits do not come at the expense of end-consumers). Besides that, this is also important in cases where all benefits fully flow through to the end-consumers. It turns out that direct measurement of improvements in final market outcomes that result from regulation is often difficult and that intermediate benefits at a banks' level can serve as proxy for the eventual benefit. Oxera (2006, p. 11) illustrates a potential approximation taking the European wholesale banking market as an example: regulation in the wholesale banking market to reduce inefficiencies may provide benefits also for end-consumers in terms of lower prices. Where it is too difficult to obtain estimates on the final price reduction for end-consumers, measurement could include the quantification of wholesale transaction cost reduction provided by banks as an approximation. Under the assumption of competitive markets, the cost reduction at the bank level can then be used to estimate the reductions in the ultimate market price paid by the consumer.

6. Assessment of transaction cost of regulation

Regulatory intervention has a direct impact on market outcomes and is not without costs. To have a positive net welfare effect, the cost of regulation must be lower than the cost of a negative externality or a market detriment. An appropriate measurement of changes in market outcomes would allow an evaluation of both costs and benefits of regulation by comparing market outcomes (in other words, a European retail banking market with and without barriers to integration). As there is always a cost element set off against the benefits of regulation, regulatory cost in terms of increased transaction costs for market participants (not only the cost of preventing bank failure, but also the opportunity costs of foregone innovation) needs to be assessed as well (Sydow, 1999, p. 168). Excessive or outmoded regulation may impose future adjustment costs that are disproportionate to the economic problem it seeks to address in the market, such as reducing a type of market failure, mitigating risks and improving incentives. Regulation may also crowd out a market solution to the underlying problem when the existence of regulation makes end-consumers feel fully protected and unreasonably disregard the risk of loss in their decision-making. Too detailed rules instead of a principle-based judgment may likewise lead to regulatory arbitrage or distort incentives of banks, thereby increasing risk. All in all, regulatory failure occurs where costs exceed the benefits of regulation and the eventual market outcome is negative.

It is important to note that along and within the dimensions of regulation, the impact of the same regulation may have different effects, improving one dimension and having a negative impact on the other dimension of regulation. Within the functional dimension, product regulation may limit the scope for consumers to purchase the wrong product, at the same time having a negative impact on technological development and innovation, thus reducing consumer choice. Similarly, information transparency regulations on the territorial dimension may improve the choice for end-consumers, lowering the *hidden information* problem across European countries, but may adversely affect the market power if creating barriers to entry into the market. These examples re-emphasize the need to consider both dimensions of regulation and their effects on market outcomes, taking into account the benefits and the costs of regulation. The proposed conceptual model and the approaches for measurement aim at being applied to all effects of market outcome, negative (cost of regulation) and positive (benefits of regulation).

A related issue, which is not further elaborated in this model, is the consideration of distributional objectives of regulation. The improvement in market outcome for one type of end-consumer may be detrimental for another, depending on the policy preferences and the parties involved in the decision-making process. Some form of weighting method that includes policy and distributional preferences may be required, which would give greater weight on the benefits arising to end-consumers who are of a particular political concern than to other groups not destined as beneficiaries.

7. Measuring improvement of market outcome through regulation

The measurement of costs and benefits of regulation should aim at providing a quantitative assessment of impacts on market outcome. The deduction of the modality applied in this model is based on the preparatory conceptual framework of Oxera (2006) and builds on a review of empirical measurement instruments in the literature.

7.1 Review of direct empirical measurement instruments

7.1.1 Ex-post analysis

The quantification of costs and benefits of regulation requires, on the one hand, information about the relevant metric (i.e., transaction cost or market price) and about the perceived value of the change to consumers. In some cases, the change of market outcome is already quantifiable (for example, in the change of prices), and costs and benefits can be easily monetized. However, there are cases where the change in the metric may be not or to a lower extent expressible in monetary terms (such as mis-buying incidents), and a valuation for the change in this metric may be required. Relevant literature provides a broad range of well-developed instruments for the monetization of benefits, such as revealed preference services, including consumer willingness-to-pay surveys or the direct measurement of the financial loss for samples of transactions (Oxera, 2006, p. 14). Despite the importance of the financial quantification of costs and benefits, this conceptual model focuses on the methodological problems to identify and measure the change in the relevant metrics. In this regard, each type of consumer detriment identified earlier in this chapter should be examined in the measurement exercise individually with regard to the applicability of the three empirical analyses from an ex-post and ex-ante perspective: before-and-after comparisons (ex-post only), surveys to collect subjective improvements and international comparisons or benchmarking.

The direct measurement of costs and benefits is most promising in ex-post analysis, when the relevant metric defining a market outcome can be compared before and after a regulatory intervention. In this regard, relevant literature proposes the event-study methodology to measure the performance improvements around a specific event action (i.e., a regulatory action). Aldridge (2005), for example, uses event study methodology to measure the impact of Securities and Exchange Commission (SEC) regulations on the profitability and volatility of financial services firms that are listed on the stock exchange in the United States. She based her research upon a large database of the firms' share prices and the timing of 113 rules made by the SEC between 1997 and 2003 and finds evidence of a significant reduction in share price volatility but no effect on the level of stock price changes immediately after SEC rule adoption (cp. Oxera, 2006, p. 22). A similar approach was adopted in Dubow and Monteiro (2006), who examined share price movements ahead of regulatory announcements.

The event-study approach can also be applied to measure the impact of regulation on other market outcomes. Where, for example, regulation aims at reducing the price of investment products, measurement would concentrate on changes in prices, profits or margins of the products. These types of tools measuring changes in the market before and after an event (i.e., entry barriers created by regulation) are commonly employed by competition economists to empirically estimate the impact of the likely reduction in the number of market entrants on prices and quality. In cases where regulation allows (financial) firms to raise price above the competitive level, these approaches allow for an estimation of the resulting detriments in monetary terms by using data about the price level increase, the price elasticity of consumer demand and the size of the market measured by annual revenues (cp. Oxera, 2006, p. 16). Similar approaches are employed in Hausmann and Leonard (2002), who provide techniques to estimate the value of a new product or greater product variety.

A shortcoming of the event-study approach is that changes in market outcomes over the period of analysis are oftentimes influenced by other factors than the regulation. To avoid wrong inferences, a number of econometric techniques, such as regression analysis, can be applied to test for structural breaks before and after the implementation of regulation. In addition to the time-series data on the variable of interest (i.e. product prices), these techniques require data on all other variables (i.e., interest rate movements, change in distribution channels, etc.) that may bias product prices over the period of time and above regulatory intervention (Oxera, 2006, p. 17). However, in the majority of cases, these techniques require significant amount of data and research and, therefore, may not always be cost-effective to carry out in practice. In this regard, the feasibility of these techniques and the explanatory value of empirical models depend on the specific type of regulatory intervention under research and the available data and controls.

7.1.2 Ex-ante analysis

If an ex-ante measurement is needed to support policy decision-making, before-and-after comparisons are not effective. Therefore, in a first step of an ex-ante measurement the total (monetized) value of a market detriment that regulation seeks to address needs to be quantified. This maximum level of benefit would represent the upper limit of the benefit that regulation could be delivering theoretically (Oxera, 2006, p. 17). It would not provide quantification of the actual improvement resulting from regulation though. There are basically two types of ex-ante measurement techniques for the cost and benefit analysis of regulation, which will be closer examined: consumer surveys and benchmarking.

Consumer surveys can help to determine the value consumers would assign to the introduction of a specific regulation and their willingness to pay for the change. Furthermore, they could also be designed to estimate their willingness to accept certain compensation if the regulation were not introduced. A common empirical technique used in market research to derive such estimates is a conjoint analysis. It is based on the premise that each consumer's choice behavior is governed by utility trade-off values. By using stated-preference surveys, consumers choose between differing concepts of products and attribute the weight to various factors determining their decision, thus revealing utility trade-offs. An example of the practical application of conjoint analysis is the research on the regulation of the German energy market. A customer survey on the quality of supply was performed to enable analysis on consumers' choice behavior. The surveyed data provided the basis for a calculation of the relative importance of quality parameters as well as the willingness to pay for changes in quality (European Economic & Marketing Consultants, 2006). Depending on the benefits assessment under investigation, it is possible that a similar approach could be used to elicit consumers' willingness to pay for certain banking regulation.

Surveys could also be applied in ex-post analysis. Consumers' experience of searching for, being advised on or eventually buying a banking product or service could be tracked and compared to the changes in outcomes after a regulation is implemented. However, such an analysis is subject to detailed econometric analysis if data is available rather than to surveys.

While such measurement techniques have been applied successfully in various research projects to quantify consumers' benefits of regulation, their major weakness is subjectivity. Results may differ across countries and client groups, and their inability to fully foresee and quantify the effects of regulation cannot be ruled out. Furthermore, survey responses may not reflect consumers' actual decision-making when interacting with banks. A significant body of research shows that hypothetical willingness to pay based on survey responses may actually overstate an individual's willingness to pay or to accept certain compensation.[72] In order to eliminate potential bias in hypothetical valuation problems, different methods have been developed, such as the process of explaining the bias to individual interviewees prior to asking a valuation question.[73]

Surveys in general can only yield robust estimates of benefits of regulation aiming at mitigating detrimental market outcomes if consumers are well informed and knowledgeable about banking products, services or the quality of their bank in general. As long as they are not in the position to make a qualified judgment and to understand the size of a particular problem that gives rise for a regulatory action, survey techniques are unlikely to deliver good results.

On top of that, consumers often do not make use of financial information available and merely understand financial risk.[74] Depending on the complexity of certain banking products or services, they are also limited in their ability to make well-informed and rational decisions. The works of DeBondt and Thaler (1987) or McFadden (1998) may serve as an example for the existing academic literature on behavioral anomalies of consumers.

Some benefit measures can be derived from surveys, such as the reduction in search cost, for example. Other benefits may, i.e. those relating to the optimality of purchase decisions, be a lot more problematic. According to Oxera (2006, pp. 17-18), evidence of actual consumer decisions is required to provide reliable information about whether changes to regulation lead to optimal decisions. In cases where such information is required but not available, controlled experiments with samples of consumers can be conducted to assess the differences in decision-making behavior under the existing and the proposed regulatory environment. This, however, assumes that decisions are suitable, at least in principle, and that the assessor is capable to evaluate consumer needs and product characteristics.

The second type of ex-ante measurement techniques for the cost and benefit analysis of regulation is benchmarking. Pan-European regulatory intervention is, in particular, suitable to evaluate market outcomes by using international benchmarking, such as comparing market prices for certain retail banking products in Germany with those in other countries, which may have already implemented a similar regulation or have chosen to apply different regulatory approaches.

With this measurement technique, a conceptual distinction between the functional and the territorial dimension can be made. Benchmarking within a

---

72 See for example Harrison and Ruström (2008).

73 For different contingent valuation models, see for example, Cummings and Taylor (1999), and Lusk (2003) for "cheap talk" on consumers' willingness to pay.

74 See FSA (2003) and FSA and Conquest Research (2004).

country concentrates on one (domestic) market reflecting the functional view on regulation and may compare for example the market price of banking products subject to some form of regulation against products that are unregulated but otherwise similar in nature (Oxera, 2006, p. 19). International benchmarking as a measurement technique links to the territorial dimension of regulation, and the quality of inferences from an international comparison critically depends on the availability of suitable comparators. Taking EU directives as an example, the impact of the same, pan-European regulation may vary across countries because of differences in the national regulatory frameworks, institutional matrices and the macroeconomic environment. However, international comparisons may provide a high-level indication of the likely market outcomes following the implementation of the regulation, provided that a suitable comparator is available (i.e., a standardized product or contract), and that other, country-specific influencing factors can be controlled.

There are a number of academic studies that have adopted the international comparison approach to evaluate the benefits of regulations and laws. They mainly focus on assessing cross-country variations in the level of quality of the legal and regulatory frameworks using econometric techniques. Hail and Leuz (2005), for example, showed that countries with extensive securities regulation and strong enforcement of rules report a lower cost of equity than countries with weaker regulatory organizations, although country and other risk factors were taken into account. Their research work refers, among others, to the early work of LaPorta et al. (2003), who prove a relationship with stock market developments across different countries. However, none of these studies focuses on a specific rule, which is by far more difficult to measure than the overall quality of legal and regulatory frameworks applying the international benchmarking technique.

Both international and national benchmarking is subject to the existence of suitable benchmarks and the ability to control for other influencing factors. If the benchmarking exercise aims at evaluating relative performance of individual market players or general improvements in efficiency due to regulation and relevant data is available, a data envelopment analysis (DEA), occasionally also called frontier analysis, can be applied. Introduced by Charnes, Cooper and Rhodes (1978), this statistical tool has been applied over a wide range of cases to evaluate the relative performance or efficiency of comparable entities, for example a bank or a banking product. In DEA, these so-called Decision-Making Units (DMUs) are inefficient (efficiency < 1) if some other DMU, or some combination of DMUs, can produce at least the same amount of all outputs with less of some resource input and not more of any other resource. Hence, the relative efficiency of a DMU is defined in this model as the ratio of the total weighted output to the total weighted input.

In the context of banking, this tool allows estimations of the "efficiency frontiers" or individual DMU performance relative to the frontier, for example when assessing benefits that result from changes in capital adequacy regulation. DEA may be used to explore whether the new regulatory regime causes banks to reduce risks for the same return on equity, or whether it enables them to approach the efficiency frontier for the same level of risk to their ability to generate higher returns. Again, the suitability of benchmarking is dependent on the availability of data. With regard to European retail banking, efficiency benchmarks such as cost-income ratios or operating profit margins are disclosed publicly for individual banks, but mostly only on a cross-product, consolidated basis. Product bundling, a sales strategy characterizing the retail banking business, is, among others, a potential influencing factor on DMUs that deteriorates direct inferences of a the impact of new regulation on an individual product and is therefore difficult to control in a DEA approach.

7.2 The measurability of market outcome

The measurement instruments outlined before may be employed to market outcomes that regulation may be affecting both from an end-consumer and a supplier perspective. However, differences in the measurability of the relevant metrics make a direct measurement from a consumer perspective more difficult than from a supplier perspective Table 12 summarizes the relevant measures for each detrimental market outcome and provides examples of potential empirical approaches to quantify the impact of regulation.

From both the ex-ante and the ex-post viewpoint, judgments about the optimality of consumers' purchasing decisions at the time that the decision was made are required to be able to measure the benefits targeted at improving consumer choices (i.e., reducing product mis-buying or mis-selling). Otherwise, it would be difficult to understand whether an adjustment in consumer choices as a result of regulation had actually contributed to improving the fit between what consumers purchase and what they actually need. This can be illustrated by the example where despite the fact that consumers have been mis-sold a product that carries too high a risk ex-ante, from an ex-post perspective, they are actually better off if these products yield a higher return (Oxera, 2006).

Similar problems arise for the consumer detriment of financial exclusion and an ex-ante measurement of benefits for increased consumer access to domestic or international banking products. Likewise, quantification of benefits would generally require some judgment about the level of product and service provision consumers actually need. This also applies when measuring the benefits of enhanced choice in terms of increased product offerings and variety. The more options available to consumers, the better the allocation of capital (i.e., savings and credit products) will be, and the more efficient the settlement of economic transactions (i.e., payment products). Furthermore, other social objectives, such as the access to basic banking services like current accounts and home ownership through access to mortgage loans, can be achieved from an improved provision of retail banking products. With regards to measurability, the following distinction between the quantitative and the qualitative provision must be made. As far as the quantitative provision is concerned, provision with the same quantity of high-level products can be taken as indicative of advanced market integration (S. Schaefer, 2009, p. 8). In terms of banking products, this implies that, for deposits and credit products, the total amount and, for payments, the total transaction volume can be set in proportion to gross domestic products and the size of population, respectively.

Qualitative provision of retail banking products implies the differentiation of the product range across European countries. In an internal market, ideally the same, broad product range is available to all European citizens, and no or only minimal differences between the spectrums of products refer to a high level of integration. Even though it is difficult to quantify, the downside of measuring qualitative provision is that it takes the differentiation in the product range as its benchmark. In this respect, instead of focusing on the provision of a single product, the breadth of supply will be relevant, regardless of fact that the breadth could simply be established by enumerating the products on offer. This lack of clarity may deem a calculation of indices necessary to make quality of provisions in individual countries comparable. A prerequisite of such an approach is that detailed information on banks' product offerings is available. Each individual product variation must then be assigned a value and a weighting factor to calculate the index. The interpretation of the resulting figures must be treated with care, as cultural differences and path dependencies might exist. They could present fundamental differences in the demand for certain retail banking products as natural obstacles to establishing a harmonized range of products across all European countries. These cultural divergences exist in the attitude of EU citizens toward borrowing, which is unlikely to change even if all regulatory obstacles have been removed. Similarly, payment products such as card payments are determined by path dependencies, as high investments in payment systems and platforms are required to provide a certain range of products. Payment products are also characterized by network externalities, which may pose even greater barriers to integration than regulation (see Chapter E for an empirical analysis of this sub-market).

Another ex-post metric for direct measurement of market outcome is the change in market prices due to lower market power and transaction costs. Any observable price reductions or increases can be quantified in monetary terms by means of existing measurement techniques commonly adopted by economists. William Stanley Jevon's microeconomic law of one price (LOOP) can be used as an indicator for measuring integration. It is linked to the economic objective that in an integrated economic area the same kind of good is available to everyone everywhere in the market at a given point of time. However, price convergence as an improved market outcome driven by regulatory intervention can be difficult to measure even if required data is available for two reasons: first, banking products across European countries are not the same. They exhibit individual, national features, making it difficult to define classifications of similar products (see the earlier reference to product bundling as business strategy characterizing the retail banking business). Similarly, prices for loan products such as mortgages are determined by consumers' individual credit ratings and are therefore also difficult to compare (risk-adjusted returns). A second factor complicating the measurability of market integration by the reduction in market prices is bank charges. Besides an interest rate component, most retail banking products, including loans, have also a fee component. Unfortunately, the available data on these charges is insufficiently harmonized or even nonexistent for certain products, making an international comparison difficult.

Finally, there is the general issue of how far full application of the LOOP can be taken as the benchmark for regulatory integration attempts. Theoretically, harmonized pricing of same goods across different European countries is only achievable if there are no artificial or natural barriers hampering banks' and consumers' EU-wide activity. However, regulation can, at best, remove the artificial or regulatory obstacles to regulation, and natural barriers would still lead to price differences within the single market. On the one hand, one can try to examine the share of price differences arising from artificial obstacles to integration, which can then be narrowed down through regulatory measures. However, despite methodological difficulties, the significance of these barriers will also be difficult to quantify. Alternatively, Schaefer (2009, p. 7) proposes a relative rather than an absolute assessment of price differences in retail banking products. By this means, the extent and speed of price convergence rather than Europe-wide absolute price differences would be of interest (ibid.). However, interpretation of such an outcome is not clear and does not provide sufficient evidence of the effectiveness of regulatory interventions. Economic obstacles, for example, may gradually erode over time or continue to be the main reason for price divergence. As discussed earlier, end-consumers' national preferences for a choice of product could have a far more significant integration impediment effect than artificial barriers. In this respect, the law of one price concept may be a useful price metric to evaluate market outcome, but interpretation of the results may be difficult, depending on the type of product impacted by regulation.

Given the limitations of quantity- and price-based measurement of improved market outcome in terms of integration, it is important to measure benefits resulting from an increase of quality and a reduction of risk. As far as a Europe-wide alignment of service levels in retail banking is concerned, it can be assumed that the removal of artificial impediments to integration and the expected increase in competition will cause the quality of services in EU member states to rise to a largely harmonized level.

Measurement of service quality is made of two components: an objective and a subjective perception of quality. Objective service quality consists of factors such as branch density and can be measured and compared to a large extent directly if data is available. However, given the significant contrast in consumer preferences (i.e., for online banking usage compared to branch visits), measuring these objective service quality factors requires a broader methodological approach that caters for differences of this kind. Conversely, the subjective perception of service quality is reflected in customer satisfaction, usually identified through customer surveys. Alternatively, observing customer behavior could also help to understand customer satisfaction or dissatisfaction. The average duration of bank relationships is an example to measure the customers' willingness to switch banks. Such measurement may be suitable for an international benchmarking but may not be meaningful for inferring that a long duration is causally linked to a high level of customer satisfaction.

By their nature, most client satisfaction surveys bear several methodological problems, which make them less advisable to use in complex, macroeconomic research. These problems may range from the biased background of the organization conducting the survey (i.e., bank association, consumer protection organizations or governments), to the collection of comparable data from different EU member states, to the validity of answers given due to cultural differences. In cooperation with Eurostat survey, the EC regularly monitors the satisfaction levels of EU citizens with the quality of the services provided by their national banks.[75] Furthermore, in 2008, the Commission launched its *Consumer Markets Score Board* to systematically record the situation of consumers in the member states in collaboration with the competent national authorities. On a sector-specific basis, indicators on customer complaints and customer satisfaction feed into this scoreboard, which is constructed in such way to avoid the aforementioned problems of subjective service quality assessment. In the future, this integration policy tool may provide better a better measurement metrics of benefits resulting from improved access to higher quality services.

Finally, benefits resulting from risks can be measured directly, at least on an ex-post basis. The rate of operational failures, for example, can be compared before and after the implementation of a regulation and measured through price reductions, assuming the savings at the banks' level for reductions in operational losses. With regard to financial risk, improvements in market outcomes may also be directly measurable. However, this requires the availability of historical data to identify the impact of regulatory intervention on the reduction in banks'

75 See the *Financial Integration Monitors* of the European Commission (2004a; 2005c; 2006a; 2007a; 2008).

defaults and losses. The benefits resulting from lower risk of systemic failure are difficult to measure because likelihood and severity of systemic failures cannot be assessed properly ex-ante for an unregulated environment. Even ex-post, the absence of systemic failure does not represent benefits of regulation, as failures may not have occurred in an environment with new regulation.

Table 12: Direct measurement of market improvements for end-consumers

Obstacle type		Types of consumer detriment in the absence of regulation	Relevant measure of benefit	Potential measurement instruments	
				Ex-post	Ex-ante
Economy-related	Higher Costs	Operational risks	Value that consumers derive from reduction of losses and other costs associated with operational failure	• changes in operational failure rates and losses to consumers • changes in market prices	• international comparisons of failure/loss rates • consumer surveys (e.g., willingness to accept compensation for mis-sold products)
		Financial risks	Value that consumers derive from reduction of losses and other costs associated with financial failure	• changes in default rates and consumer funds lost • changes in market prices	• international comparisons of failure/loss rates • consumer surveys as above
		Systemic risks	Value that consumers derive from reduction of losses and other costs associated with systemic failure	• in principle, ex-post analysis as for financial risks, but including assessment of changes in employment, income lost by individual consumers, etc.	• international comparisons (e.g., drawing from costs incurred in countries where there have been widespread banking failures or bailouts)
	Reduced Choice	Sub-optimal choice	Value that consumers derive from better choice (i.e., more optimal fit between what they buy and what they in fact need)	• consumer surveys to establish willingness to pay to avoid mis-buying or willingness to accept compensation for mis-bought products and services • controlled experiments to establish what consumers purchase when faced with new regulations and external/independent evaluation of the suitability and value they derive from the more optimal choice	• before and after analysis of consumer decisions (e.g., using consumer surveys) to judge the actual increase in optimal purchases
		Limited choice	Value that consumers derive from increased choice (i.e., reduction in opportunity cost of not being able to buy what could be available)	• consumer surveys or controlled experiments as above	• econometric techniques to estimate the value of a new product
	Higher prices	From market power of firms	Value that consumers derive from reduction of excessive prices	• changes in market prices • econometric demand-modeling techniques to estimate resulting changes in consumer surplus	• international comparisons, benchmarking
		From transaction/ system inefficiencies	Value that consumers derive from reduction of transaction costs/prices arising from inefficiencies	• changes in market prices • changes in search costs to consumers	• international comparisons, benchmarking
Public policy-related	Restricted access	Financial exclusion	Value that consumers derive from improved access to financial services	c• hange in penetration of financial services (and valuation of the change in income distribution)	• international comparisons

Source: Author's illustration, adopted from Oxera (2006, p. 15).

7.3 Quantity-based indicators for cross-border retail banking activity

Along with price, service quality and risk measurement indicators, quantity-based indicators can be applied to measure cross-border activities on both the supply and the demand-sides. Such a measurement considers the territorial view on regulation, taking the cross-border retail banking transactions as an aspect of Europeanization into account. However, a more detailed analysis is necessary to be able to evaluate the measurability of integration and the extent to which banks and consumers see the entire EU as their home market.

Under a broader definition of cross-border banking, consumers purchase foreign retail banking products through domestic distribution channels, either through a foreign bank's proper distribution channels (online presence, branches, call centers, etc.) or through a local cooperation partner, such as another bank. In this context, cross-border transactions refer to consumers' usage of distribution channels in a foreign bank's home country to acquire retail banking products (online product purchase, border-crossing to visit a foreign branch or contacting a call center). Concisely, retail banking is cross-border if the respective product does not originate in a consumer's home country. Cross-border transactions are established when banks wish to offer their products outside their domestic markets and when there is a demand for these products beyond the borders of their national markets.

While the volume of cross-border transactions on the supply-side can be obtained through various types of data sources available, cross-border transaction data on consumers can only be identified through (customer) surveys. In order to answer the question on what actually impedes cross-border business on both the demand and the supply-side, and to understand the underlying reason for them in detail, the two sides need to be examined separately.

As far as the demand-side is concerned, it might stand to reason to compare the level of actual transaction volume of cross-border retail services to the level of potential business elicited in customer surveys, as illustrated in Table 11, for example. The proportion of customers willing to purchase retail banking products outweighs the proportion of customers who actually made the respective transaction in each product area. This may imply that the proportion may be a lot higher if artificial barriers did not exist. However, this interpretation may disguise methodological problems of surveys that may lead to far-reaching deductions from rather simple survey data on customers' actual willingness to eventually purchase services from foreign banks. Unless a more sophisticated approach is used that covers customers' cost-benefit consideration and risk preferences for making cross-border transactions, the validity of such data obtained is questionable and conclusions drawn upon the low volume or non-existence of cross-border transactions. Hence, the key challenge of quantity-based measurement is to identify the impediments to cross-border demand and supply and determine whether these barriers are of an artificial or natural character. As EU policy can only remove the latter, the barriers causing the detriment from the theoretically desirable state need to be analyzed in depth ex-ante, consequently evaluating the regulatory intervention necessary to remove these artificial barriers.

Regarding quantity-based indicators on the supply-side, the Europeanization of banking operations may provide practicable measurement techniques for integration. Currently, indicators are available on the number and size of cross-border mergers and acquisitions, especially of European retail banks, as well as the geographic composition of their assets and liabilities. However, the limitations of these indicators need to be realized and results interpreted with caution. While the assessment that low levels of activity are a sign for limited integration is generally correct, the absence of cross-border activity could itself signal that an integrated market has already been achieved. Kleimeier and Sander (2007, p. 3) refer to petrol prices as an example: "If prices are the same across Europe, no one will travel across the border anymore to fill their gas tank." Even though the recent wave of cross-border mergers in Europe is often interpreted as sign that market integration is progressing quickly, this wave may also simply reflect the fact that banks have discovered the benefits of cross-border activities in still highly fragmented markets such as retail banking. Strategic considerations such as exploiting returns to scale, utilizing comparative cost advantages of different locations within the EU or simply entering high growth markets or customer segments with a better product offering make cross-border activity attractive despite regulatory or natural barriers to integration. In this case, surveys help identify banks' motives for committing to Europe or for being frustrated by natural or regulatory barriers. The focus of regulatory intervention may then be to identify these detriments and a way of removing them.

Hence, quantity-based measures are difficult to interpret and need at least to be complemented by other indicators such as price and service quality measurement.

7.4 Measuring the removal of obstacles to integration

With reference to the initial definition, market integration is achieved when all obstacles to integration that prevent customers and banks from viewing the whole of the EU as their extended domestic market are removed. As pointed out earlier, natural obstacles will continue to exist in the EU simply because of the cultural heterogeneity. Artificial or regulatory barriers, however, must be removed by regulation policy.

Before assessing the progress on removing obstacles, the various types of hurdles that prevent either consumers or banks from considering the EU as their home market must be identified for each product segment. On the supply-side, banks must be able to realize economies of scale when operating their business across many European countries and can hardly afford developing different retail banking products adapted to up to 27 national legal systems. Different types of civil law and consumer protection legislation constitute problems for banks to conduct cross-border business. With regards to consumer protection, an objective that can be broadly related to most consumer detriments listed in Table 11, legal requirements may dictate advertising, information disclosure and right of withdrawal. These artificial barriers to integration represent entry barriers to banks intending to expand their business beyond national borders. For example, consumer lending, such as mortgages, is to a large extent computerized in banks and relies on a credit score of the borrower. Being part of a bank's overall business model and representing in some cases its competitive advantage, exporting its database to other EU markets where broadly the same profile of customers is found, without the necessity for major adjustments, is pre-requisite.

On the demand-side, the lack of confidence in the provision of services from foreign banks outside the consumers' home market can prohibit the acceptance of the single market. Similar to the supply-side, different legal frameworks provide disclarity to consumers with regard to contract cancellation or withdrawing possibilities, information disclosures or liability against quality defects. This lack of transparency of contractual relationships related risk with non-domestic banks (i.e., deposit protection) causes high transaction costs in terms of financial and non-financial expenses.

Benefits from regulation resulting from a removal of these artificial barriers to integration are difficult to measure, due to conflicting effects it can have on market outcome. On the one hand, it can smooth the path towards integration by removing conflicting behavioral patterns of banks and consumers. On the other hand, regulation may hinder integration when well-intentioned proposals to increase consumer confidence eventually reduce the incentives of banks to offer their products in other EU countries. In this respect, regulation needs to be designed in such a way that only those regulatory obstacles that impede a balanced market outcome for suppliers and consumers are removed. Thus banks are able to sell their products and services in other member states without incurring unreasonably high transaction costs on the one hand, and consumers feel confident about the level of transparency provided with these products.

A final assessment of whether all regulatory obstacles to integration have eventually been removed needs to be interpreted with caution; the removal of a barrier on the supply-side that deters banks from conducting business abroad may prevent consumers from taking up foreign banks' offers. Similarly, regulatory measures to promote cross-border demand may lead to new or increased costs for internationally operating banks. In this regard, it is very difficult to measure integration solely defined as the absence of artificial barriers (Kleimeier & Sander, 2003, 2007; S. Schaefer, 2009).

8. Summary

The overall conceptual model outlined in this chapter aims at providing a framework to assess the role and to measure benefits of regulation related to European retail banking market integration. Furthermore, this model aims to derive policy recommendations for the selection of the adequate instruments to correct detrimental market outcomes and overcoming barriers to integration. A first general conclusion of this work is the insight that there is no *silver bullet* for achieving integration, at least not for such a fragmented market as the European retail banking market. This model points out these complexities but seeks to advance measurement by systematically describing the benefits that should be measured and the different direct approaches currently available. It makes clear that the measurement of benefits is an even more complex assignment in practice than that of direct cost of regulation. The review of the latter shows that only by considering a wide variety of indicators in combination, valid conclusions can be drawn, serving as a starting point for regulatory action.

The structure of the conceptual model, briefly summarizing each step of analysis, is depicted below. Chapter E will illustrate the application of this framework to the EU regulation on cross-border payments and the resulting SEPA project.

(i) First, a wide-ranging, highly nuanced review of the status quo and the historical development of the market under consideration are required. Besides a description of market characteristics, market structure and the competitive environment, this may also include the underlying regulatory framework and current level of state intervention. The current degree of integration and potential detriments is determined, and the term integration in the given market is clarified.

(ii) In the next step, the requirements of potential regulation in terms of what are the expected benefits of regulation compared to the existing market outcome are analyzed. There are three possibilities in the context of integration: removing all regulatory barriers to the Europeanization of consumers' and banks' behavior, changing their attitude toward considering the entire EU as their home markets and finally, the occurrence of positive economic effects that can be theoretically related to market integration (i.e., price convergence at low levels).

(iii) Having defined the requirements, the market outcome dimensions that regulation may be improving are defined along the four key decision factors: market failure, government failure, coordination failures and a risk assessment. Concrete proposals for alternative types of regulatory intervention are developed subsequently. The direct measurement of improved market outcomes in terms of a higher degree of integration involves a systematic evaluation of the measurement techniques described in this model. Two fundamental limitations to direct measurement have been elaborated earlier and should be considered when establishing the degree of integration. First, the calculation of the indicators chosen must be possible and suitable data must be available. Second, the interpretation of the indicator values must be meaningful from an overall theoretical point of view and allow drawing conclusions on whether an EU retail (sub-) market is eventually fully, partially or not at all integrated.

(iv) Next, the analysis aims at validating the measurement results and their interpretation. Furthermore, it reveals unintended effects and the potential market outcome for the supply and the demand-side of the market under consideration. Special attention must be paid to cases where integration may have been achieved even though the chosen indicators do not indicate this. Conversely, indicators may denote high levels of integration while in reality markets are still fragmented. This again emphasizes that there is no single way of assessing retail banking market integration in the EU. Only a consideration of several indicators in parallel may reveal the weaknesses of single indicators and deliver clearer results to a concluding assessment of benefits of regulation.

This conceptual model for measuring benefits of regulation seeks to contribute to the broader discussion on the costs and benefits of regulation and its role in the promotion of market integration. In this regard, the results are finally reviewed from an Europeanization viewpoint to derive recommendations to EU policy formulation.

Analysis process step	Description
Review of status quo	■ Market characteristics, market structure, and competitive environment ■ Underlying regulatory framework and current level of state intervention ■ Current degree of integration and potential market and policy detriments
Assesssing market detriments and potential improvements through regulation	■ Expected benefits of regulation compared to the existing outcome ■ Three possibilities in the context of integration: (i) removal of all artificial obstacles, (ii) achieve change of attitude towards viewing Europe as a domestic market, (iii) materialize positive economic effects ■ Evaluation of market outcomes with regard to the four key decision factors: market failure, government failure, risk assessment and coordination failure. ■ Proposition of alternative types of regulatory intervention
Measurement of improvement through regulation	■ Systematic evaluation of measurement tools available ■ Measurement of cost and benefits for the type of regulation under consideration ■ Interpretation of results
Validation and conclusion	■ Validation of results and drawing conclusions from the degree of integration obstacle removal (effectiveness) and from the cost-benefit assessment of regulation (efficiency) ■ Infer recommendations for European policy formulation

Figure 10: Analysis process steps of proposed conceptual model
Source: Author's illustration, adopted from Oxera (2006).

Table 13: Summary Chapter D

Summary Chapter D – Conceptual model
• Based on the theoretical considerations on the role of regulation in creating a single market, this chapter develops a conceptual model that may support the assessment of effectiveness and efficiency of regulation in performing this role. • The model adopted in this study draws on elements of an existing impact assessment framework for regulation, developed by Oxera (2006) for the U.K. Financial Services Authority (FSA). The author refines the approach by incorporating territorial considerations of regulatory interventions that have an influence on policy- and decision-making. • From a European integration point of view, this model considers barriers to integration detrimental market outcomes that may require regulatory intervention to be improved (referred to as effectiveness). The associated costs and benefits with their removal through regulation refer to the efficiency of a regulatory measure. Prior to determining the potential costs and benefits of regulation, the actual existence of a failure that would justify regulation is analyzed along with four key decision-making factors: market failure, government failure, risk and incentive or coordination failure. • This chapter reviews academic research and discusses different ex-ante and ex-post measurement techniques and approaches to evaluate benefits of regulations with regard to a potential applicability to integration. The identified measurement includes both quantity- and quality-based indicators. • The chapter concludes that in due consideration of different kinds of obstacles and complexities on the supply- and the demand-side, a variety of measurements and indicators may be required for an empirical assessment of the effectiveness and efficiency of regulation to overcome barriers to integration. • A four-step analysis approach is proposed to conduct a structured assessment and to compare the market outcome before and after the regulation.

Source: Author's illustration.

E Harmonization of retail payments and the case of SEPA

1. Relevance for retail banking integration

This chapter provides an illustrative application of the conceptual model for assessing the benefits of EU banking regulation. It focuses on the European retail payment market, a submarket of the overall retail banking market, and on the Single Euro Payments Area (SEPA) initiative, which emerged as banking industry-led response to the EU price regulation in 2003. While the operation of payments systems has increasingly gained public and academic attention, the focus remained on systemic risk and efficiency issues of large-value, interbank payment systems.[76] Systemic risk arises because the insolvency of a major participant in a payment system may impose costs on other participants through a loss of liquidity or, in an extreme example, a collapse of the system itself. In this regard, the payment system's public good characteristics have been the basis of any case for public policy intervention in payment systems (Ganguly & Milne, 2002, p. 2). There is a very small amount of literature available on retail payment systems as a network industry, where in particular the competition-cooperation nexus and respective policy implications are analyzed (see, for example, Kemppainen, 2004a; McAndrews & Rob, 1996). However, even less academic attention has been paid to the economic and political justification of regulation and public policy intervention in order to create a single market for retail payments.

Recent developments in the European integration process have indicated that retail payment systems, especially on the cross-border level, are also a critical part of the financial integration process. The creation of a single market for financial services following the introduction of the euro currency will only be accepted by EU citizens and firms if benefits of a single currency materialize. Hence, intra-European trade and consumer spending require modern payment systems that allow for exploiting the new possibilities offered by a single market. Dissatisfactions with the development efforts by the banking sector and given the fact that two years after the euro introduction cross-border payments were charged several times higher than domestic payments (in euros), a debate started on potential regulatory intervention necessary to lower prices and increase service quality of cross-border payments (i.e., cycle times and value dating). Provoked by this poor progress, the European Parliament and the Council adopted *Regulation (EC) 2560/2001 on Cross-border payments in Euro (RPE)* in De-

76 Theoretical and empirical studies include, for example, Angelini (1998), BIS (2001), Lacker and Weinberg (2002) or Yu et al. (2002).

cember 2001. This regulation established the principle of equality of charges for payments up to EUR 12,500 within Member States (national) and between Member States (cross-border) and applied to ATM[77] cash withdrawals and payment card transactions since July 2002 and to credit transfers since July 2003.[78] This policy intervention was strongly criticized by the banking industry, which rather preferred a market-driven intervention in a first place.

The illustrative application of the conceptual model described in this chapter will set out the dimensions of market outcome that the pricing regulation may or may not improve. The illustration will differentiate between the immediate effects of the pricing regulation and the differed, long-term potential effects that can be expected from SEPA. Furthermore, it will depict the circumstances that have led to the sequencing of pricing regulation (Regulation 2560/2001) followed by self-regulation (SEPA) followed by an EU directive (Payment Services Directive, PSD). A quantification of the effectiveness of this process and its costs and benefits is conducted at a best effort basis, where relevant and suitable data is available. Where this may not be the case, the illustration will focus on the conditions that need to hold for there to be any benefits.

Costs of compliance to the EU directive are composed of, in general, operational costs and investments on both the supply and the demand-sides. Assuming that the largest amount of compliance costs is incurred by banks and payment service providers, economic logic implies that such costs will be born ultimately by the end-consumers of retail payment services, SMEs and corporations. In this regard, the level of these costs should therefore also be considered from a consumer viewpoint in order to assess whether the benefits of the EU directive actually exceed not only the direct compliance costs of compliance but also the indirect costs or negative market impacts the rule may cause.

The illustration presented in this section is structured to first provide a review of the situation before the regulation on cross-border payments was passed. It examines this specific rule and the circumstances of the underlying decision-making in more detail, including the reasons for the low level of integration and the associated European policy agenda. Following the conceptual model described in the previous chapter, this case study then explains the different types of detrimental market outcomes for consumers and banks and outlines the potential benefits that would come from the mitigation or elimination of these detriments. The key decision factors scrutinize the sources of detrimental market outcomes from a regulation theory perspective, determining the existence of market failure, government failure, risks or incentive misalignments (or coordination failure). However, some attributes of payment systems, such as network

77 Automated Teller Machine.

78 See: Regulation (EC) No 2560/2001 of the European Parliament and of the Council of 19 December 2001 on cross-border payments in euro (2003).

characteristics, may not be directly explainable by the theoretical framework provided in Chapter B and C. In this case, the study will derive the associated theoretical considerations form the relevant literature where necessary. After having explained the subject of measurement, the quantitative assessment of the costs and benefits of the payments regulation reviews statistic data available and measures the improvements in market outcome by means of changes of the transaction volume of cross-border, non-cash transactions, operational costs and investment expenses by consumers and banks, and the changes in product range and competition.

Finally, the actual post-intervention outcome (i.e., the establishment of SEPA) is compared to the market outcome without regulation to derive the net benefits of the payments regulation. Interdependent regulation, distribution and market infrastructure often reflect circumstances of past decades and exhibit path dependency of single markets. Fixed cost problems and network phenomena may preclude a fast adjustment of anachronistic structures to new circumstances. While the fragmentation of cross-border payment systems might have been acceptable (and efficient) in an era with a low frequency of cross-border transactions, European politicians and consumer interest groups considered this situation inappropriate after the introduction of the euro currency. In this particular case of the European retail market, the results of the market development process triggered by the payments regulation require a special examination of the way European regulation policy is shaped. SEPA was founded as a market-driven project resulting from the political pressure to harmonize prices for cross-border and domestic payments, aimed at developing an efficient and cross-European payment platform. While banks and payment service providers contribute with their industry and expert knowledge to its realization, regulators concentrated on their bystander role and defined the timeframe. To support the realization of SEPA and the development of a single market within the EU, harmonized rights and obligations were defined and published by the EU as the Payments Service Directive in December 2007. Similarly, the scope of PSD and its provisions was co-shaped by market participants and in particular by member state regulators. Therefore, not only the process of policy downloading but also the uploading of policy from a national to an EU level can be observed on this illustration.

Figure 11 provides an adaptation of the conceptual model from the previous chapter to the case of the retail payment market. Before each step of analysis is followed in more detail, the next section provides the necessary background of non-cash payment in Europe.

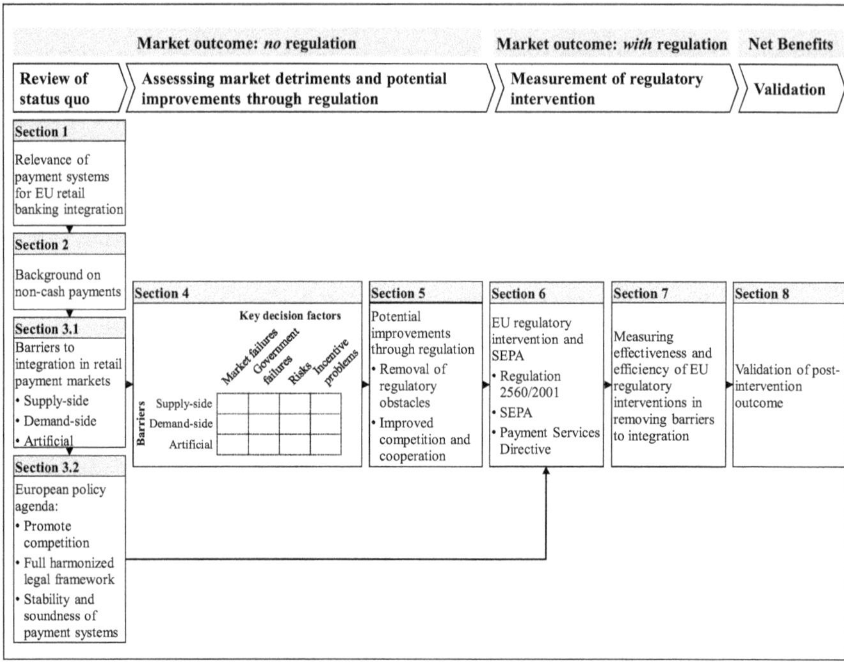

Figure 11: Illustrative application: retail payment market regulation
Source: Author's illustration.

2. Background on non-cash payments in Europe

Economic activities of enterprises and households are always accompanied by a payment. Payment systems, which are the subject of much recent discussion on market integration in Europe, are an indispensable part of the infrastructure that supports the entire economy (European Central Bank, 2006a, pp. 15, 50-51). They consist of legal frameworks, rules, institutions and technical mechanisms for the transfer of money. In the EU for example, with more than EUR 288 trillion, the total volume of all payment transactions in the EU is far larger than the EU GDP with 9.9 trillion in 2003 (European Commission, 2005f, p. 7). The ability to make payments at low cost and with moderate risk facilitates the exchange of goods and services. Largely, the efficiency of transactions in a market economy is determined by the efficiency of the payments system (Bank for International Settlements, 2000, p. 13). In the EU, however, to run their payments businesses, some countries focus on efficiency, while others rely on higher transaction fees.

2.1 Definition of payments services and payment arrangements

The ECB defines a payment as "the payer's transfer of a monetary claim on a party acceptable to the payee (beneficiary). Typically, claims take the form of banknotes or deposit balances held at a financial institution or at a central bank" (European Central Bank, 2009b). The ECB further distinguishes between two cashless types of payments: retail and large-value or commercial payments. "Large payments are payments, generally of very large amounts, which are mainly exchanged between banks or between participants in the financial markets and usually require urgent and timely settlement" (ibid.). Retail payment (or *mass payment*) is a very common, but rather vague term. It refers to payments that are processed via *retail payment systems*, i.e., systems that clear and settle high numbers of transactions every day. A retail payment is usually of low value and urgency, but there is no ceiling to the amount of a retail payment. Furthermore, high levels of standardization and efficiency characterize retail payments on a domestic level, whereas the level of automation on a cross-border level remains relatively low (see Figure 13). In the large-value payment segment, however, various (pan-) European payments systems needed to be in place before the introduction of the euro currency in 1999 for interbank transactions.

The following more differentiated characterization clearly reveals the complex and multi-faceted nature of retail payments in particular, which represent the focus of this chapter: "In the first place, retail payments are typically made in large numbers by large numbers of transactors and typically relate to purchases of goods and services in both the consumer and business sectors,[…]. Second, retail payments are made using a much wider range of payment instruments than large-value payments and in more varied contexts, including, for example, payments made in person at a point of sale as well as for remote consumer and commercial transactions. Third, retail payments markets are characterized by extensive use of private sector systems for the transaction process and for clearing" (European Central Bank, 1999).

As illustrated in Figure 12, a retail payment involves five different parties: the payer, the payee, two banks providing customers with transaction facilities and some kind of interbank payment arrangement (i.e., *payment systems*). Banks and other payment service providers have to have access to facilities to conclude the payment transaction (*payment arrangement*) in order to make payment services available to consumers.

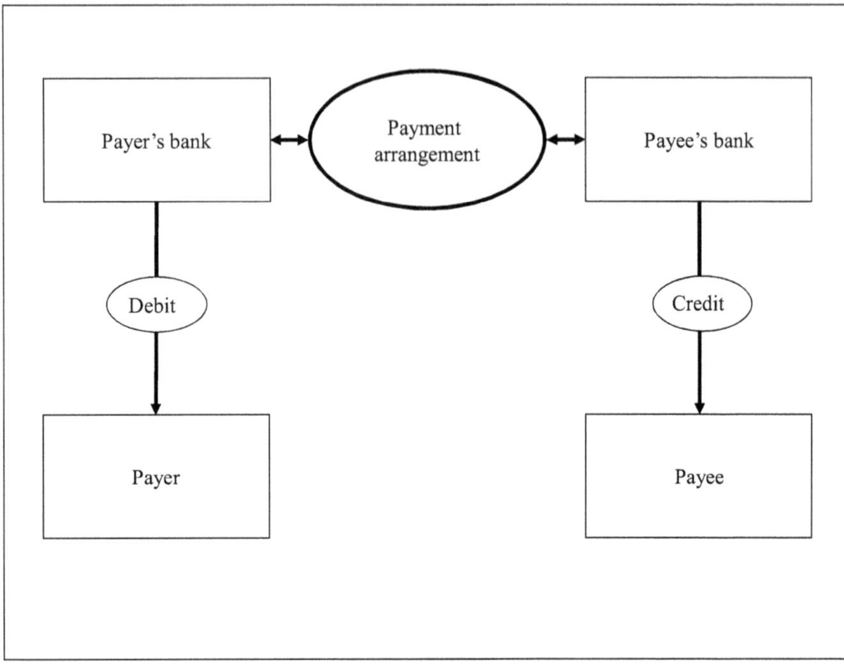

Figure 12: Simple model of cashless payment arrangements
Source: Author's illustration.

The way a payment is executed involves two main elements:

(i) Payment infrastructure: payment transmission, clearing and settlement of payments
(ii) Payment scheme: an arrangement to fix standards covering technical, operational and commercial aspects as well as financial aspects of the interbank relations

Based on these two elements, different kinds of arrangements to exchange information and calculate balances are possible. In *unilateral* arrangements, payer and payee have an account at the same bank, and payments are transferred within the institution (also referred to as *on us* payments). Transferring so-called *book money* implies debiting the account (deposit or credit line) of the payer and crediting the payee's account. Hence, any payment service provider who offers payment services to an end user (i.e., consumer, business and banks) needs to maintain an account for this user at the same time.

When payer and payee are customers of different banks, bilateral or multilateral arrangements are required. In a *bilateral* arrangement, the sorting and processing of payments takes place directly between two banks. In this regard, a common arrangement is when a third institution known as the "correspondent" provides payment arrangements to other banks according to contracts negotiated bilaterally (Mai, 2005, p. 18). *Multilateral* arrangements either can take the form of multilateral open arrangements or can be based on *clubs,* particular types of institutions. Frequently, these arrangements are organized in an automated clearing-house (ACH), where financial institutions exchange data and/or documents relating to funds transfer under a common set of rules. Other multilateral arrangements may be based on a clearing association, which organizes and facilitates bilateral clearing among institutions.[79]

Concerning cross-border credit transfers in the EU, some banks can make use of their own network of branches and subsidiaries as well as of their correspondent network to bypass external parties. Alternatively, banks can seek directly to participate in an ACH or other systems available in another EU member state. This option still seems to be the preferred arrangement for many European banks. A study conducted for the EC showed that 80% of cross-border bank-to-bank credit transfers are still made through correspondent arrangement or intra-bank transactions.

The choice of the payment arrangement depends on various economic and historical factors, the volume (i.e., the number) of payments to be cleared and the number of financial institutions involved determine the relative convenience of various types of clearing arrangements.

2.2 Domestic vs. cross-border payments in the euro area

Although the vast majority of payments in euros are already efficiently processed through domestic automated clearing houses, the processing of cross-border payments is still significantly less efficient. Before going into detail on some of the payment categories, at a high level, the current situation could be characterized as follows:

- Among the five main instruments fulfilling customer needs today,[80] cards dominate cross-border payments. Customer requirements in terms of cost, quality and time are clearly met at a domestic level, but performance is poor for cross-border transactions.

79 For more details see paper from BIS: "Clearing and Settlement Arrangements for Retail Payments in Selected Countries" (Bank for International Settlements, 2000).

80 The five main payment instruments used are credit transfer, direct debit, checks, cards and e-money (see Table 18).

- Domestic infrastructures are efficient but very different from each other. Until 2003, there was no real pan-European ACH infrastructure in place for mass retail payments.[81]
- Automation levels for each country are high due to well-developed standards and rules (as well as significant efforts to educate customers to their compliance), which again are very different from one country to another.
- Although several international standards are in place, cross-border automation levels remain low.
- Standards and infrastructures for cards are in place for seamless domestic and cross-border processing. However, significant price differences between domestic and cross-border transactions still exist. Overall, globalization is most advanced in cards, both in terms of business dynamics as in terms of governance structure.

Figure 13 provides an overview of the main differences between domestic and cross-border retail and large-value payments.

81 It should however be mentioned that TARGET is working efficiently for cross-border payments, but it does not target the mass low-value transactions as performed by consumers or small SMEs. Both, EURO1/STEP1 and STEP2 provide a first pan-European network to process low value (below EUR 12,500) cross-border payments. Their current market share for these types of payments is estimated at approximately 20%.

		Retail	Large-value
	Client segment:	Retail consumers, SMEs	Corporations, financial institutions
Domestic	Average execution time	0-2 Working days	Real time, same day
	Average value per transaction	Low	High
	Price	EUR 0.0-3.0	EUR 0.03-0.15[1)]
	No. of ACH clearing cystem	12 (one per country)	2 (TARGET,EBA)
	Level of automation:[2)]	67%	99%
Cross-border (Eurozone)	Average Execution Time	1-5 Working days	Real time, same day
	Average Value per Txn.	Low	High
	Price:	EUR 11.9-20.5	EUR 0.03-0.15[1)]
	No. of ACH Clearing System	Non available	2 (TARGET, EBA)
	Level of Automation:	17%	99%

Figure 13: Classification of payment types in the eurozone (status 2001)

Source: Author's illustration.

Note: 1) EBA STEP2 (committed volume per quarter of 640,000 transactions): EUR 0.36; RTGS+ and TARGET2: EUR 0.6 2) Weighted average (Electronic 99%, Paper 5%).

2.3 Domestic payments

The national payments market in the EU consists of all payment transactions carried out in EU member states. Thereof, the major share (98-99%) is domestic payments. In this context, domestic payments are euro-denominated money transfers debited and credited on accounts in a single country. In 2003, approximately 50bn transactions with a value of more than EUR 170 trillion were processed within the EU-25. In the past 20 years, these enormous volumes of payments have approved investments on the production side in technology and efficiency enhancements to achieve economies of scale in each EU member state. As a result, great efficiency and an exceptionally high level of automation could be achieved, allowing payments to be processed almost completely by machines (so-called Straight-Through Processing, STP) and payment instruments to be offered to the market at moderate prices. These payment instruments are adapted to different payment preferences in each country.

Today, domestic payment systems in almost every country in Europe operate at comparably high levels of efficiency within national borders, allowing a more or less low-cost, rapid and secure processing of domestic payments. The national systems are, however, all different and not interlinked, meaning that they cannot be used for processing cross-border or EU retail payments. Furthermore, payment instruments abide to national law and the respective legal framework for payments in each EU member state. A harmonization of national payment markets would lead to an integrated domestic payments area for national and cross-border payments in Europe (European Payment Council, 2002).

2.4 Cross-border payments

All payments sent out of a country or received from abroad are denoted cross-border payments. Furthermore, cross-border payments are subdivided into payments with non-EU countries and payments within the European Union. The latter include 13 member states of the EMU (the so-called *eurozone*),[82] 11 EU member states obligated to join the EMU,[83] and three countries participating in the European System of Central Banks (ESCB).[84] Since the introduction of euro banknotes and coins on 1 January 2002, citizens in the euro area have been able to make cash payments within and across all 12 countries[85] from a single purse, using the single currency, as easily as with the previous national notes and coins (European Central Bank, 2006c, p. 7). Yet what is now a reality for cash payments remains a vision for cashless payments.

In contrast to domestic payments, cross-border non-cash payments comprise of only 1-2% of all payments carried out in the EU (European Payment Council, 2002). The small share of total payments volume and the disproportionately low level of automation (STP) explain the high transaction costs and long cycle times of cross-border payments compared to domestic payments.

Payments are transaction-based services and require a certain settlement infrastructure. As explained earlier, in the EU these systems were originally created with the aim of meeting domestic requirements. They were rather diverse in nature and not necessarily suited to the needs of a single currency area. In the run up to and with the introduction of the euro, the financial infrastructure in the EU has undergone rapid changes, mainly driven through developments in technology. In addition, the emergence of the single currency has also accelerated

82 EMU member states: Austria, Belgium, Finland, France, Germany, Greece, Ireland, Italy, Luxembourg, Netherlands, Portugal, Slovenia and Spain.

83 Euro candidates: Bulgaria (2007), Cyprus, Estonia, Hungary, Latvia, Lithuania, Malta, Poland, Romania, Slovakia and Czech Republic.

84 Countries participating in the ESCB (besides 13 EMU countries): Denmark, Sweden and United Kingdom.

85 With Slovenia joining the EMU in January 2007, the EMU now includes 13 countries.

efforts to harmonize and consolidate payment settlement systems. However, cross-border retail payment systems and mechanisms available at present are far away from being efficient and meeting consumer' demand.

2.5 Retail payment systems

Compared to the high level of efficiency and harmonization characterizing cross-border high-value payment systems, each national retail market has remained isolated from other national payments markets, and the level of efficiency and service varies greatly from member state to member state. In contrast to fast and cost-effective national retail payment systems, retail cross-border payments still vary considerably by technical standards, national legislation and domestic customer preference for different payment instruments, impeding large-scale automation and resulting in higher costs per transaction. Although retail payment systems are important for the provision of payment services to the economy, most of them are *not* systemically important: their failure often does not trigger disruptions or transmit shocks across the financial system.

Looking now at retail payment systems, the distinction between domestic and cross-border payments systems is far more important than in large-value systems. Retail systems process large numbers of payments between different account-maintaining banks per day. In contrast to large-value payments, which are executed individually and immediately, retail payment instructions are bundled and processed in batches at given times in order to save costs. The data is transmitted and sorted between participating banks (clearing). Generally, the clearing of retail payments also includes a netting process, where only the calculated net positions are settled, i.e., each bank's account at the settlement agent is debited or credited respectively. It is common practice in most European countries that clearing and settlement of retail payments are executed by an ACH, which is usually affiliated to a private banking association. Alternatively, and this applies, for example, to most retail payments in Germany, payment batches can be cleared bilaterally or via a correspondent bank. Finally, settlement can also take place at an agent other than a central bank. The prerequisite therefore is that all banks involved in a payment transaction maintain an account with the settlement agent (Mai, 2005, p. 17).

Along with traditional correspondent bank relations, there are also several *club-type systems* to execute cross border payments. The most important ACH systems in Europe are listed in Figure 15, comparing transaction volumes, participation rules and ownership structure in different European retail payments systems. Transaction volume of retail payments is significantly higher than the volume of the respective large-value payment system in all European countries. In addition, national payment systems have developed proprietary standards to exchange payment information and transactions with participants to process retail payment volumes highly efficiently. This observation highlights the challenge ahead of payment service providers and regulators to develop an efficient and standardized payment system that could replace all different national payment systems.

2.6 Infrastructure

The strict distinction between domestic and cross-border payments, retail and commercial payments remains characteristic for the European payment system landscape (see Figure 14). The following comparison of large-value and retail payment systems highlights the differences of each system regarding technology, users and instruments. Furthermore, it is necessary to describe both systems in order to explain the higher policy and regulatory efforts of developing an efficient cross-border retail infrastructure.

		Domestic		Cross-border		
				Within EU		With non-EU countries
Type of payment	Payment instruments	*Retail*	*Commercial*	*Retail*	*Commercial*	*Individual/ Commercial*
Cash		☑	☑	☑	☑	N.A.
Cards	ATM Cash Withdrawals	☑	☑	☑	N:A.	☑
	Cards POS Transactions	☑	☑	☒	N:A:	☑
Electronic	Credit Transfers	☑	☑	☒	☑	☑
	Direct Debit	☑	☑	☒	☑	N:A.
	E-Money	☑	☑	☒	N.A.	N.A.
Paper-based	Checks	☑	☑	☑	☑	☑
Relative Transaction Volume (100% = 63,238 million transactions, 2001)		~98%		>2%		>0%

Caption: ☑ Payments processing systems in place ☒ Payments processing systems/infrastructure non-existent

Figure 14: Payment processing system availability in Europe in 2001
Source: Author's illustration.

Further to the distinction between domestic and cross-border, payments differ regarding the type of payments customers and the respective payment system. As explained earlier (Chapter A), there are two general types of customers with distinct payment behavior: retail and commercial customers. While commercial and inter-bank payments in connection with the necessary money market and foreign exchange business consist of individual euro or large-value payments, retail customers make virtually all small-value payments. In 1999, approximately 100 million domestic retail payments were processed daily in euro area countries, whereas the number of retail cross-border payments was very limited, probably only a few hundred thousand per day, most of which were card payments (European Central Bank, 2000, p. 7). As the establishment of large-value payments system was a prerequisite for the establishment of the ESCB and the adoption of the euro currency, cross-border individual euro and large-value payments could be executed just as quickly abroad as equivalent domestic payments. However, to date in Europe, a system for processing cross-border small-value payments (i.e., euro credit transfers or direct debits) in retail payments with a corresponding pan-European payment system infrastructure does not exist. This image of a disjointed, heterogeneous and – above all – decentralized payment system in Europe for cross-border retail payments is emphasized by the great variety of conventions, product definitions and standards as well as differing legal rules in the individual EU member states. The resulting patchwork of national systems and the lack of interoperability account for longer execution times and higher transaction fees for cross-border euro credit transfers within the 25 EU member states.

3. Retail payment markets prior to regulation

Retail banking market integration was primarily constrained by the disjointed European payments infrastructure, which was supposed to provide the platform for cross-border trade, consumer spending and economic growth within the EU. This section provides an overview of the European payment market and examines the market outcome before the EC passed the EC regulation 2560/2001 on cross-border payments in euros. Furthermore, it elaborates on the reasons for the fragmentation, which can be subsumed as economic (supply- and demand-sided) and artificial or regulatory obstacles to integration. Finally, given the territorial dimension of the problem under consideration, the situation in the payments market is put into the broader context of EU policy and single market creation. Therefore, the roles and policy targets of different political and regulatory organizations will be discussed conclusively.

3.1 Barriers to integration and market detriments

3.1.1 Supply-side barriers

In the euro area, national retail payment systems and their infrastructures have traditionally been developed for currency areas delineated by national borderlines and are largely very efficient. The third stage of the EMU has lead to dissociation between the new euro currency area and national boundaries. Since then, cross-border retail payments could still be processed throughout the entire euro area, however, processing was inefficient and required manual intervention by banks and expensive routing of low-value payments through the expensive interbank clearing systems. As the volume of such payments was very low compared to domestic payments and not STP-capable, cross-border payments were treated and charged as individual payments in the same way as large-value transactions. The resulting fees charged to end-consumers hence partially reflected the operational cost involved in processing. However, many multi-country banks with a large network of branch offices and subsidiaries and an efficient back-office in place were able to significantly reduce the operational costs involved in processing cross-border retail payments, increasing their profit margin. Given the attractive revenue stream generated with intra-Europe payments on the one hand and the high investment necessary to develop a new infrastructure for a small number of payments on the other hand, until 2002 the European banking industry had been reluctant to take the steps necessary to create an efficient infrastructure for cross-border retail payments. Besides the higher fees, the level of service for cross-border retail payments (i.e., execution time) differed significantly from that available for national payments. Typically, cross-border euro retail payments were executed more slowly than comparable national payments, providing additional interest income for banks from overnight deposits. In this regard, both domestic and multi-country banks did not want to make sizeable investments without being certain that other banks would also be willing to make similar investments so that the entire banking industry could reap the benefits. In addition to this lack of commercial interest of banks resulting from different processing chains for national and cross-border payments and the low volumes of the latter, the lack of use of agreed standards and low level of automation at the interbank and intrabank levels have hindered a market-sided development. Finally, the specific network characteristic of this industry requires that banks join their individual investments in the same infrastructure so that the critical mass for achieving economies of scale can develop (Kemppainen, 2004b).

Table 14 summarizes the supply-side obstacles to market integration and the bank or payment services provider detriments that may arise in the absence of regulation.

Table 14: Supply-side barriers to integration and detriments

Supply-side barriers	Type of detriment
Lack of commercial interest	Higher costs • High operating costs (processing, clearing and settlement) and low efficiency levels for cross-border retail payments • Significant supply-side investments required to develop a new infrastructure and payments scheme (cost of compliance, system development and migration) • Risk of cost duplications if domestic and cross-border retail payments are serviced by different infrastructure Lower Volume • Low volume of cross-border retail payments driven by higher operating costs and demand-side effects such as lack the of consumer confidence in the market, which renders the provision of cross-border payments unprofitable for most banks Fee revenue deterioration • Multi-country banks are able to efficiently process cross-border retail payments internally already and would lose the attractive profit margin on these transactions
Payment network competition issues	Ownership structures • Entry barriers faced by a potential new network: restrictions on access, poor transparency and anti-competitive pricing • Exclusion from membership of non-financial institutions such as processors or customers • Network cannot develop in ways that do not meet the needs of a significant group of users • Inability of clients to access clearing systems directly might increase their dependency on their current banking relationships Fees and fee structures • Existence of joining, transaction and interchange impedes competition between payment instruments and competition between banks
Lack of open and common industry standards	• No common core payment instruments and experiences • Lack of consistent standards to achieve interoperability • High complexity and low efficiency with cross-border transactions

Source: Author's illustration.

3.1.2 Demand-side barriers

In summary, the demand-side barriers impeding a harmonization of cross-border retail payments markets are strongly interlinked with the supply-side and the fragmented regulatory situation across the member states. Table 15 provides an overview of the demand-side obstacles to market integration and the bank or payment services provider detriments that may arise in the absence of regulation.

Unlike the supply-side, the consumers of retail banking products are usually less organized and therefore tend to have a more limited market power than the banking industry, especially on the European scale. However, consumer organizations have made complaints against the service providers on the price discrepancies that have continued to exist between domestic and cross-border payments, even after the introduction of the euro as the single currency in the area, and have been quite successful in lobbying at the political level. In this regard, the dominant political argument put forward to legitimize the price regulation on cross-border payments in euro was that the low volume of cross-border end-consumer financial transactions was solely attributed to the high costs of transaction. Hence, the regulation was declared to address the needs of European citizens to lower prices that, according to the political belief, impede retail banking customers from cross-border purchase and trade activities.

While systemic risk is inherent in all payments systems, it is beyond the scope of the retail payment market integration currently discussed. Most systemic risk concerns are raised in the context of large-value payment systems, where potential disruptive contagion effects may threaten overall system stability. To a lesser extent, this also applies to retail payment systems where the potential of system risk is also present, although not in such a prominent a way as in large-value payment systems. Therefore, the safety requirement for retail payment systems is well recognized, but as the present research work focuses on the barriers to integration, the following analysis assumes that safety requirements are fulfilled and concentrates then purely on the inferences about the benefits of regulation to facilitate market integration.

Table 15: Demand-side barriers to integration and detriments

Demand-side barriers	Type of detriment
Information asymmetries related to product offering and provider	Reduced Choice • Consumers' lack of access to and capability of processing relevant information • Product bundling disguises actual prices charged for single transactions
Information asymmetries related to transaction costs for cross-border payments	Sub-optimal choice • Complexity of products and their structuring may lead to misunderstanding of a product and hence to a mis-buying of a payment services • Price information provided to retail banking customers on their current account and on cross-border payments may be inadequate or complex, making it difficult to compare prices and choose between banks. Higher costs • Complexity forces customers to make a substantial investment of time in comparing product offerings from different suppliers, increasing search costs
Price-inelastic behavior of retail clients	• Low level of mobility of retail banking customers to change their banking relationship due to high switching costs • End-consumers do not forebear from purchasing products cross-border because of payment fees
Interdependence of demand and lack of public awareness	Higher prices from banks' market power • Chicken-and-egg problem: not sufficient demand for cross-border payment services and consequently restricted or highly-priced provisions and no *business case* for payment service providers Reduced Choice • The lack of public awareness of the situation relates to the comparably small number of cross-border payments users concerned. This has made it not worthwhile for banks to offer investments in the better product offering.
Historical national payment habits	Reduced Choice • Heterogeneity in demand for different payments instruments in different countries makes it difficult to deploy a truly compatible cross-border payment system due to differing national needs.

Source: Author's illustration.

3.1.3 Artificial barriers

While the liberalization of capital has facilitated cross-border money transfers within the EU, the Internal Market in particular for retail payments is still not as efficient as at national level. Legal barriers still prevent EU citizens, consumers, SMEs and payment services providers from reaping the full benefits of a truly integrated area for non-cash payments (European Commission, 2003a, p. 7). Major differences exist between national legislations and conventions with regard to payment services in the EU and provide hurdles that create an obstacle to the proper functioning of EU-wide payment infrastructures and systems and prevent either banks or consumers from considering the entire EU as their home market. Therefore, before cross-border standards and product specification can be aligned, a uniform regulatory framework needs to be in place first. The limiting factor for cross-border business is not a general end-user reluctance to purchase goods and services outside national border. Rather, lingering concerns about the legal certainty of the respective payment transaction prevent end-users from exploiting the opportunities of a single market.

Finally, national political obstacles have been a significant factor for the slow progress in developing cross-border retail payment instruments and services. Analogous to the lack of a uniform legal framework, a number of member states fall short in the basic tasks of transposition, coherent implementation and effective application of internal market legislation. The Kok Report points out that "member states persistently fail to transpose Internal Market rules correctly and on time" (Speyer, 2005, p. 3). Considering the various obstacles to integrated markets in the fields of tax, company law and consumer protection, there seems to be a tremendous lack of willingness of member states to transfer national sovereignty to the European level. Apparently, the integration of financial markets is not on top of the priority list of national governments, while the protection of national interests still seems to be ranked high by national policymakers (Speyer, 2005, p. 3).

Table 16 provides an overview of the legal barriers leading to market uncertainty, monetary or non-monetary expenses and hindering payment service providers and users from transacting without restraints.

Table 16: Artificial barriers to integration and detriments

Artificial barriers	Type of detriment
Consumer protection rules	Reduced or sub-optimal choice Differing requirement for product information hinder comparability, i.e., • possibility of withdrawing from a contract • cancellation possibilities • protection against quality defects • conclusion of the contract • utilization of the service during the term of the contract • termination of the contract
Disproportionate legal requirements	Higher transaction costs for banks and consumers • Market access requirements • Data protection requirements • Capital requirements • Requirements for the deployment of a payment instrument or innovative techniques • Requirements for legal provisions creating insufficient legal certainty • Reporting obligations
Political reluctance on national levels	Financial exclusion • Member states fall short in the basic tasks of transposition, coherent implementation and effective application of internal market legislation • National central banks' (pricing) sovereignty • Lack of willingness of member states to transfer national sovereignty to the European level

Source: Author's illustration.

3.2 European policy agenda

The analysis of the prudential organizations involved in European banking regulation performed in Chapter B showed that in the European context, there is a necessity to differentiate clearly the areas of regulation and supervision, although the two spheres and the allocation of competencies are inextricably linked. Defining regulation as the underlying legislative function (rule-making), the following regulatory bodies in the field of payment services in the EU/ euro area can be specified: the European Commission (EC), the European Central Bank (ECB)/the European system of Central Banks (ESCB) and other national/ European competition authorities. In the following, their respective roles will be discussed.

3.2.1 The European Commission

The EU Commission aims at creating a Single Payments Area in Europe to enable consumers and businesses to finally reap the full benefits of the single currency and to facilitate financial market integration. In its role in promoting the development of the single market, the EC has been arguing that high costs for cross-border payments are inhibiting market integration. In this context, the Commission has set the following objectives for the single payments area: first to generate more competition in payment markets by removing market entry barriers and guaranteeing fair market access, and second, to provide a simplified and fully harmonized set of rules with regard to the information requirements and the rights and obligations. In pursuing these goals, the commission has assumed a more active role in recent years and gave top priority to topics accelerating the creation of a single market. This explains the motive of adopting Regulation (EC) 2560/2001, which was seen as the ultimate tool to foster further development in the retail payments market, given the dissatisfactory progress made until 2001. Even though the regulation was an important step towards a Single Payment Area for non-cash payments in the Internal Market, further progress needed to be made. The existing legal framework for payments is largely based on national rules, which makes it difficult for payment services providers to deploy EU-wide infrastructures. Consequently, the EC has also decided to actively promote the development of a harmonized legal framework for payment services.[86]

3.2.2 European Central Bank/ European System of Central Banks

The ESCB applies to all EU member states and consists of the ECB and the national central banks. In order to differentiate between EU member states that have adopted the euro currency and those that have not to date, the name *Eurosystem* was coined. The smooth functioning of payment systems is of particular concern to central banks for three main reasons (European Central Bank, 2007):

- the stability of financial institutions and markets,
- the soundness and efficiency of payment systems and the confidence of users and the public in the currency and, ultimately,
- payment systems representing essential means for the implementation of monetary policy.

One way for central banks to promote the safe and efficient functioning of payment systems is to operate their own payment systems (BIS, 2003a, p. 83). The

86 See European Commission (2003c): *A New Legal Framework for Payments in the Internal Market.*

main operational role of the Eurosystem lies in the provision of the interbank payment system TARGET (European Central Bank, 2001a, p. 29). It is the real-time gross settlement system for the euro and not run by the central banks of the Eurosystem alone, but by all central banks of the ESCB (BIS, 2003a, p. 83). Beside the provision of facilities for settlement in central bank money, the ECB and NCBs also offer their settlement services to other payment and settlement systems – e.g., balances of large-value net settlement systems are settled at the central bank. In addition, some European NCBs also run retail payment systems (ibid.).

Besides the focus on providing safety standards to large-value payment systems, where potential for system risk is bigger than in retail payments, the Eurosystem has increasingly focused on providing efficiency to the euro retail payments market with the objective of facilitating the development of a single euro payment area. Its policy stance on retail payment harmonization has been communicated through various reports and studies. In September 1999, the ECB published the report "Improving Cross-Border Payment Services – the Eurosystem's View" (1999), in which it highlighted major inefficiencies and set first objectives regarding efficiency and pricing in cross-border retail payments. In the following year, several progress reports were published on a regular basis, in which the ECB reviewed the achievement of objectives, suggested ways to remove obstacles responsible for the high cost of cross-border payments and provided measures to improve the payment infrastructure. In this context, the following quotation underlines the earlier observation of the "network nature of payment systems" that have a strong effect on competition and the development of new standards: "The lack of competition among banks also explains the lack of progress with regard to the price level of cross-border credit transfers, whereas a lack of co-operation on standards and infrastructures explains the lack of progress in reducing the cost of processing cross-border transfers" (European Central Bank, 2001b, p. 4). In other words, two effects become apparent from this statement, which will be elaborated further in the later analysis: network and competition effects. Payment systems are networks that gain in value for their users the more users participate and are only attractive if reaching a critical mass of participants (*network effect*). Then again, each payment service provider in the system works hard to differentiate itself from rival participants to win business through innovation, value-added services and pricing (*competition effect*). Accordingly, the key challenge for policy-makers and regulators in this situation is to find measures that maximize social welfare in this type of environment.

This chapter has made clear that all the key parties involved in the development process of retail payment services are *doomed* to strengthen their cooperation in order to achieve the partly imposed, partly self-set objectives. On the regulatory side, the European Commission and the ECB/ESCB should also better coordinate their cooperation to avoid situations where too extensive and overlapping regulation impedes the development of an efficient system. In terms of *rule-making* on the national and the European level, the roles of competition authorities and other regulators (i.e., the ECB) in the creation process of a single market for retail payment services are not very clear. This is likely to require further cooperation efforts and needs to be resolved by the latest when harmonized governance and supervision structures for the internal market are established.

4. Sources of market detriments and potential benefits of regulatory intervention

The previous section has captured the barriers impeding the harmonization of the European payments landscape along the supply- and demand-side and with regard to artificial barriers. In addition, the types of detrimental market outcomes have been defined and explained, which will now be examined with regard to the key decision factors to analyze their sources and causes. Based on the theoretical assessment conducted in this section, the implications for potential regulatory interventions to overcome integration detriments are derived.

As discussed in an earlier chapter on an abstract level, the general argument is that regulation should compensate for the market failure that would prevail in a situation without regulation and supervision (Geiger & Klein, 2004, p. 38). Market forces alone will not necessarily achieve the objective of efficiency and safety sufficiently, as a market participant does not bear all the costs and risks arising. Furthermore, the times the business opportunity (profit) and the related risk (cost) materialize may differ (Bank for International Settlements, 2001). The other side of the story is the risk of government failure, or in the terminology of the new comparative economics, between disorder and dictatorship (Djankov, Glaeser, Lopez de Silanes, La Porta, & Shleifer, 2003, p. 3).

Following the argumentative logic of the conceptual model, the detriments are now analyzed with regard to the existence of market or government failure, risks and incentive or coordination problems. Prior to this, (cross-border) retail payment systems in the euro area are examined with reference to the characteristics of a network industry to facilitate the assessment of underlying market detriments of the research subject under consideration.

Retail payment instruments and systems show some inherent features that differentiate themselves from goods and services of traditional industries. The following part is an adapted list of features provided by Gangulny and Milne (2002).

(i) The presence of two final customers requires system compatibility (or at least interconnection) and affects the pricing conventions in retail payment business (allocation of payment charges to payer, payee, or shared).

(ii) Multiple payment service providers and the operation of an interbank payment system require cooperation among banks. This could lead to anticompetitive concerns if access conditions to the cooperatively operated system are limited.
(iii) The ownership structure of payment systems can play an important role in the access conditions to the system if some sort of exclusivity restrictions is applied. As retail payment systems are jointly owned by participating banks or are in public ownership (central banks), the ownership question and governance issues for a level playing field in payment service provisions is important.

Payment systems in general and the development of a pan-European retail payments system in particular have been recognized by the academic community and banking practioners[87] as a network industry. Networks play an integral part in financial markets, and network effects have certain implications for public policy and regulation, in particular when promoting market integration. In the following, the key attributes of retail payments systems such as a network industry are identified, and policy implications are derived. In addition, this section points out several other factors, such as the lack of a uniform legal framework or the existence of entry barriers, which draw the attention of regulators and policy-makers.

The theoretical framework provided in Chapter B concluded that the three types of economic failures diagnosed in the functional dimension of banking regulation, market, government and coordination failure require a case-by-case assessment of the degree of government intervention and the choice of instruments necessary to correct market detriments. Market and government failure differ diametrically, and their existence is therefore analyzed in the first instance, followed by a risk assessment and concluding with an analysis of existence of incentive misalignments and coordination failure.

4.1 Market failure

The preceding sections have identified a multitude of economic and artificial detriments that now have to be examined with regard to the assessment criteria of the normative theory on market failure: the reference to public goods, negative external effects, indivisibility and information asymmetries.

87 For a review of the main literature, see Ackerberg and Gowrisankaran (2004), Kemppainen (2004b), and McAndrews and Rob (1996).

4.1.1 Payment systems as public goods

Most goods and services that people or firms purchase or consume are *private goods* and have the characteristic that if one person consumes a unit of a good, no one else can consume that exact same unit (Weinberg, 1996, p. 17). As opposed to private goods, *public goods* are characterized by non-rivalry in consumption and non-excludability and are composed of the provision of, for example, social security or infrastructure as well as economic or price stability, fiscal or environmental sustainability, public education, lighthouses or public utilities, etc. Non-rivalry implies that one person's enjoyment does not reduce the amount available for others. The other characteristic of public goods is referred to as non-excludability and denotes that it is impossible to prevent any individual or firm from deriving benefits from a good that already has been produced. While pure public goods per definition consist of both properties, there are some goods that have one of the characteristics but not the other. Club goods are the most important and refer to goods that are non-rival but excludable such as networks.[88] They are non-rival in the context of individuals' utility of a large network, which does not diminish the amount of that benefit available for others. However, these benefits are excludable, and only those who choose or are allowed to join the network receive benefits. There are various aspects of payment networks that might be associated with public good characteristics. However, these aspects cannot necessarily be considered pure public goods. While benefits to utilizing a payment system accrue to the users of the system, individuals or firms can be left out from these benefits by being excluded from access to the payment system. In this respect, the importance of excludability does not mean that excluding banks or payment service providers from access is desirable but rather implies that access can be priced (Weinberg, 1996, p. 18). Unlike pure public goods, where access to a good or service is not priced because such pricing is impossible or because of public policy decisions (i.e., highway systems), access to payment networks can be priced, and users who are granted access are charged a membership or consumption fee. Furthermore, the non-rival characteristic of public goods may be apparent in payment system services, where, similar to other electronic networks, marginal costs of transferring a payment message is close enough to zero. However, given that material differences exist in processing electronic versus paper-based payments with regard to fixed costs, this public good property is likely to be more important to electronic payment systems. Further public good characteristics are in a broader, system-related view, where any enhancements made to the systems (for instance, improved security functionalities) feature no differentiation or discrimination among uses or

88 In the context of market failure theory, see Sander (2004)for a detailed elaboration on club goods representing other kinds of collective goods.

users of the system. A final aspect of payment systems as a public good worth mentioning in this respect is the establishment of commonly accepted standards, which may act as an important means for coordinating the actions of market participants. With benefits created by standards being non-rival, the fragmented European payments landscape composed of multiple national standards would, in particular, benefit from such coordination, enabling diverse market participants to take advantage of network effects. With regard to excludability, the adherence to standards provides the technical capability to payment network users to interact with other market participants. Depending on the extent access to a network can be priced, the benefits of the network's standards are excludable.

In summary, many non-rival characteristics of public goods can be attributed to aspects of payment systems in general and to cross-border retail payments in particular. With regard to the non-excludability property of pure public goods, it is uncertain that this is an important characteristic of payment networks. Instead, excludability is vital for thinking about the role of policy makers in providing non-rival goods. While the potential difficulties in the private provision of pure public goods are beyond question, club goods are in general more favorable to private arrangements, as excludability allows suppliers of club goods to decide upon the intended set of buyers and the access price to the payment system.

4.1.2 Network externalities in cross-border payment systems

There is an important difference between network externalities and other forms of externalities usually referred to in the context of market failure. A common textbook externality is pollution, where the economic activity of some individuals or market participants may emit pollutants that negatively affect a much broader group of people. Despite the fact that these individuals may choose whether to participate in the activity that generates pollution, they may have little or no choice as to whether to be affected by pollution (Weinberg, 1996, p. 5). Network goods or services are characterized by network externalities (also called *network effects*), which means that adding another customer or user increases the value to the customers/users of the existing network. Network externalities are more self-contained in the sense that market participants' decisions to join a network create external benefits for other joiners by increasing the size of the network (Ackerberg & Gowrisankaran, 2004). In this regard, the benefits of a network externality interact directly with the decisions that generate the externality, which has important consequences for the analysis of economic behavior in the presence of network externalities.

As a payment system shows explicit network characteristics, one can expect network externalities to be present. This applies to payments systems and instruments on the demand-side (demand-side externalities) as well as to the supply-side. The latter, so-called supply-side externalities, concern economies of scale in production of payment services that foster industry's willingness for co-operation through common standards or joint network ownership. There usually exists one major retail payment system at the national level, which ascribes to the existence of economies of scale and positive demand-side externalities on the one hand and reflects the historical developments of payment services by the banking community on the other hand. Both arguments do not necessarily imply a natural monopoly situation. In countries where two or more systems exist in parallel, these systems are often dedicated to different payment instruments.

In network markets, complementarities exist between users and products, which give rise to network externalities. They can be classified into two types of externalities: direct and indirect (Economides, 1996; Katz & Shapiro, 1985). For direct network externalities, the complementarities exist between users of the same product or service, and for indirect network externalities, the complementarities exist between products or services in different markets. In other words, direct network externalities arise from increasing the size of the network and are generated through the direct effects of the number of the agents consuming the same product, whereas indirect network externalities arise when additional network users spur the demand for complementary products (Bonello, Furstenberg, Kemppainen, & Salo, 2006, p. 65).

Complementarities in payment systems play an important role. Credit card systems are a straightforward example: Visa is more valuable to consumers the more merchants accept it; accepting Visa cards is more attractive to a merchant, the more consumers use them as a payment instrument. In order to exploit these complementarities, payment products or systems need to be compatible. Such a compatibility is crucial for the existence of network externalities and requires interaction channels, which operate on a compatible standard: "it is compatibility that makes complementarity actual" (Economides, 1996, p. 4). At a system level, compatibility is of crucial importance in enabling interoperability of systems, which is very clearly, for example, in ATM systems (Kemppainen, 2004a, p. 28). Still, technical compatibility does not necessarily mean that different systems can truly interact. Commercial compatibility is also necessary to provide rules or entry requirements (ibid., p. 29).

In order to achieve the compatibility that enables full network complementarity, establishing a process of setting standards for network components is crucial (McAndrews, 1997, p. 4). Standard setting can be done by markets, through cooperation of market participants or by authorities. In payment systems, this is achieved through agreements on common technical standards, infrastructural arrangements or interbank cooperation (*payment clubs*). The use of standards generally results in a positive network externality, in that the adoption of a standard in itself confers a benefit on others. By contrast, the benefits on the members of a network can also have a detrimental effect on competition by limiting entry by those that use different or competing standards (Pindyck, 2007, p.

21). On national levels, authorities and banking associations have set domestic standards in the past, whereas at a cross-border level, the distribution of responsibilities is less clear, and the enforcement of the adoption of new standards has been problematic with only few successful exceptions (i.e. SWIFT internationally with BIC, ECBS for Europe with IBAN). The European Payments Council (EPC) is likely to set and adopt common standards for Europe. However, authorities, such as the ECB have emphasized their role as the catalyst for the development of standardized processes in Europe (Tumpel-Gugerell, 2005b).

A consumption externality can be defined as creating a benefit (or disadvantage) for others owing to the way in which an individual consumes a product (Shy, 2001). Some authors, like Evans and Schmalensee (2005), have labeled this as *demand-side economies of scale*. In this context, if consumers expect a network system or a payment instrument to become popular, a "virtuous circle" will begin, and consumer's expectations will prove correct. The larger the network, the greater the number of users who would like to join it; in contrast, the smaller the network, the less attractive it will to new customers. Retail payment services clearly show the presence of these consumption externalities. To establish new payment systems or instruments, it is crucial to manage end-users' expectations of the future size and coverage of a payment network. However, the chances of achieving a critical mass of users to adopt new payments instruments tend to be limited in practice unless tangible benefits are provided. Currently, domestic payment systems operate on highly efficient level, covering approximately 98% of the overall payment traffic in Europe. Hence, consumptions externalities for establishing a smaller network for the remaining 2% of intra-European cross-border traffic are limited.

4.1.3 Competition and cooperation

Standard-setting

Given the network characteristics of payment systems, a competition analysis must refer on the market structure and antitrust issues within and between multilateral bank networks, which provide cross-border transactions for the designated payment services. This section considers economic features of payment systems (except for network externalities and public goods factors that have been considered above), transaction shares and volumes, product differentiation, ownership and governance, membership and subscription restrictions and innovation and standards. While focusing on the structure of payment services networks and competition within and between networks, a detailed analysis of incentives and individual firm behavior is conducted at a later stage. Given the limited availability of price and cost data, the focus is placed on identifying the conditions for competition based on the economic, technical and operational characteristics of the payment system industry in Europe, with a particular focus on credit transfers and direct debits.

As shown above, payment networks obtain benefits from the usage of externalities by maximizing the number of members who are able to receive and originate payments. In a network with a given number of members, any additional member increases the number of transactions that can potentially be transferred through the network. Assuming that the marginal cost of each network transaction is relatively lower than the cost of processing a transaction by means of other networks, existing members will benefit when new members subscribe to the network (European Commission, 2005f, p. 31).

In order to accept, process and exchange payment transactions through the network, standard setting is one of the most critical aspects of payment system design and operation. The BIS (2000) differentiates between technical, business and interoperability standards for payment networks that have significant impact on the competition and efficiency.

(i) Technical standards establish the common rules and features of payment instruments or systems, for example, rules with respect to message formats or communication protocols. They are important for both the domestic and in particular, the international levels, to enable a smooth functioning of all type of national and cross-border payments.
(ii) Business standards are agreements between providers of payment instruments and systems that specify the procedures, legal interpretations and technical standards to be adopted as common guidelines or legal contracts for interbank clearing and settlement transactions.
(iii) Interoperability standards are particularly important from a competition point of view, as they define the level of cooperation between different payment instruments. Providers of payment services may decide to cooperate beyond the level of applying the same business standards and to allow the shared use of payment instruments by means of agreements on interoperability.

In the context of defining cross-border payment instruments in Europe, agreements on the technical standards may lead to lower development costs for processing systems. Furthermore, they may facilitate the compatibility, which may enable consumers and providers to choose the best technology available, thereby favoring an optimal path of development (Kemppainen, 2004a, p. 39). Domestic retail payment systems in Europe have been using national payment standards for decades and deploy efficient technologies already. However, these domestic systems have been developed in their somewhat isolated and divergent domestic regulatory environments, and pan-European, cross-border retail payment standards that would be acceptable for all EU member states have been very difficult to achieve despite the single currency. Several factors have been impeding a shared development, mainly the standard setting process as such and the increased complexity of the international, European environment.

Despite the positive effects on efficiency and competition, standardization may also lead to negative market outcomes. One of the common problems of standard setting processes is that a premature adoption of a standard may lead to *locked-in effects* of technology because of the difficulty of switching to a new and more improved technology (Katz & Shapiro, 1985). Furthermore, it may lead to unnecessary delay in choosing a standard as alternative producers compete to become the market-leading standard. Finally, in some cases, agreements on standards may be used to limit competition in particular markets.

McAndrews (1997) differentiates between three ways standards may be defined: by the market-place, by the relevant industry forums for setting standards or by the government (regulator). While market participants and industry experts are likely to have the best market knowledge in this respect, standards set by the market tend to lead to the most efficient outcomes. In contrast, if regulators set standards, their lack of accurate information may be disadvantageous and lead to choosing standards that are inferior to a market chosen solution. On the other hand, required decisions on certain standards can be defined as binding rules a lot faster than a market-driven solution. Usually, they are characterized by a long-term bargaining process, involving a lot of different interest groups to be able to agree on the common standard. Furthermore, while regulation-driven standard setting can be enforced by legislation, any implementation of a market-driven solution may take a lot more time. If this is the case, or some type of market failure occurs, the enforcement of standards may require intervention by regulatory authorities. However, due to the market dynamics that are likely to lead rather than extreme market structures in the payment network industries, a judgment on whether the current problem is really a market failure or not is difficult.

On national levels, the formulation of standards to the payment service industry is usually carried out by standard-setting bodies, in which banks, banking associations and other payment service providers are represented. While these bodies have worked effectively on the national levels, similar structures were meant to be established on a pan-European level. Here, the European Committee on Banking Services (ECBS) was established to develop the standards of the International Bank Account Number (IBAN) and for the International Payment Instruction (IPI) (Kemppainen, 2004b, p. 29). Even though the IBAN could facilitate the execution process of cross-border payment in the euro area, one can bring forward the argument that the adoption of these standards has been rather slow due to the ineffective institutions: formal rules with a lack of enforcement power of the ECBS. The fact that only after the regulatory intervention by the EC (Regulation 2560/2001on Cross-Border Payments), the adoption process has gained momentum, providing some positive evidence on the effects of regulatory intervention by public authorities in facilitating implementation of common standards. This argument will be discussed further in the context of measuring the effectiveness of regulation in the next chapter.

The possibility that a set of standards will develop a dominant position in the market may cause an important threat to competition. This may, in particular, be the case where there is competition between sponsored standards, which can be used only by the holder of property rights to the standards (proprietary standards), and un-sponsored standards. Holders of property rights on sponsored standards tend to strive for obtaining a competitive advantage and will encourage and incentivize the adoption of that standard to establish market share. Unlike, un-sponsored standards, which are not incentivized by any means, short-term user incentives such as lower prices are used by holders of sponsored standards to make their standard more attractive relative to the equivalent un-sponsored standard. Hence, the existence of sponsored standards may create entry barriers as new entrants aiming for setting up a new network, as their potential members and users are locked in the sponsored standards and will face high switching costs (cp. Shapiro, 2000; Shapiro & Varian, 1999).

While in national clearing and settlement systems for credit transfer sponsored standards predominate, the key standards and protocols used in European cross-border payment networks are un-sponsored. They are created and maintained by the ECBS and now by the European Payments Council (EPC), SWIFT, and defined ISO and other standard-setting bodies (European Commission, 2005f, p. 39). These un-sponsored standards result in lower market entry barriers and allow all participants to operate under them freely and equally.

A cooperative approach, where market participants implicitly or explicitly communicate with each other in order to agree on standards and rules that will govern their production and consumption decisions (i.e., to make products compatible), assumes that economic decision makers will arrive at a set of rules that delivers an outcome that is in the “core” (Weinberg, 1996, p. 13). An outcome in the core (i.e., a basic technology for message transfers) would leave no incentive for market participants to deviate from the proposed outcome. Instead, it can be assumed that banks and payment service providers will jointly realize the benefits of coordinating on the superior core standard by, for example, a private standard-setting body. Agreeing on a standard may eliminate competition between (core) technologies but not competition in general. Instead, standard setting may channel competition into more conventional dimensions such as price, service and product features (Kemppainen, 2004a, p. 40) and will in this regard have also an impact on the locus of competition that banks and payment service providers will be facing in a cross-border payment network. Two ways of competition are possible in cooperative standard setting: incompatible systems compete *for* the market (inter-technology competition to become a standard), whereas compatible products compete *in* the market (intra-network competition with rivals) (Shapiro, 2000).

Another resemblance of payment systems and network industries, described by McAndrews (1997) and Kemppainen (2004a), is that network markets tend to get locked in to obsolete standards or technologies. This so-called *excess inertia* means that users are likely to stick with an established payment technology even when total surplus would be greater than adopting a new but incompatible technology (Katz & Shapiro, 1994). Furthermore, the opposite, the so-called *excess momentum,* could also be the case: the market may be biased in favor of a new, superior, but incompatible technology, leaving users stranded with their old technology and ignoring the cost they impose on yesterday's buyers. In retail payment service markets, both effects are possible, but as in many network markets, excess inertia is usually the dominant characteristic. Literature often refers to the slow development of e-money adoption as an example, where service providers have long waited for its startup but customers have been reluctant to start to use it.

Sunk costs and switching inertia in payment networks

From a competition point of view, there are a number of sunk costs associated with both developing and joining a payment network. These costs, irrevocable once incurred, can have an impact on competition and the viability of new networks in both contexts. For network providers, sunk costs of developing a network include the cost of creating the required commercial framework, operating rules and processing infrastructure and those associated with obtaining the members or partners to give the required geographic reach. For banks and payment service providers, sunk costs are associated with joining a network or switching between networks and include the network's joining fee (European Commission, 2005f, p. 38).

With regard to developing a network, technical barriers and related costs for creating a new multilateral bank network to compete with EBA[89] clearing such as STEP2 are limited. According to EBA, the central development cost for setting up STEP2 as pan-European Automated Clearing House (PEACH) amounted to EUR 1.78m, whereas the total costs, including those that incurred by the initial subscribers, were EUR 10m (Euro Banking Association, 2009). However, as mentioned above, the underlying commercial framework and the direct or indirect accessibility of all bank accounts in the EU is by far more difficult to create. A fundamental question for banks and payment network operators intending to create any new, multilateral bank networks is whether the size of such a network would grow to gain the necessary economies of scale, in particular in terms of transaction volume.

89 Euro Banking Association.

Assuming a new PEACH operator is able to reach critical mass to run the network profitably, its market entrance as such would result in greater competition in infrastructure provision and operations in Europe. The emergence of an additional network operator for cross-border retail payments may lead to lower wholesale prices for banks and eventually also to lower end-consumer prices. Furthermore, competition for the market may also improve the service and functionality provided to banks and indirectly to end-consumers. Based on the low level of sunk costs in creating a new network, it is unlikely that these costs have a significant impact on competition between payment networks or that they cause insurmountable obstacles to new market entries.

From a network subscriber point of view, namely for banks and payment services providers, sunk costs encompass two components: cost for joining a network or switching between networks (including the network's joining fee) and the costs associated with the changes to computer systems, communications facilities, business processes and procedures, marketing, product development and other functions (Katz & Shapiro, 1985). In order to be compliant with all the technical and operational specifications and standards defined by the network, a new member will be required to design and amend systems and processes.

The impact of sunk costs on network switching behavior is driven in particular by the level of network membership costs, the existence of sponsored or proprietary network standards or by the level of switching inertia. The latter refers to the benefit that banks gain from network membership in dependence on the number of other members the network has. Factoring out other considerations such as a network's functionality and service level capabilities, a subscriber would therefore only switch to another network if the member base of the new network is large and therefore attractive enough and if other participants the bank transacts with switch at the same time. If switching costs from one network to another are high enough, members can be locked in an existing system and encounter barriers, which may prevent customers from moving to competitors or to a superior technology (causing inefficiencies). Despite these theoretical obstacles, switching between networks can already be observed in the European cross-border retail banking market. The number of banks that are members of more than one multilateral cross-border payment network has steadily grown since 2003. While the EBA STEP2 network has gained strong market share since its inception in 2003, the influence of alternative networks Unicopay, IBOS or TIPANET has diminished constantly (European Commission, 2005f, p. 38).

In general, the impact of sunk costs on the feasibility of new network development is limited. However, switching behavior is constrained by sunk costs and switching inertia and can affect price competition in two opposite ways: locked-in users have to pay higher prices, and if not locked in, users are decoyed with low prices until they are locked in the technology later on (DaRin & Hellmann, 2002, p. 379).

Finally, payment systems are subject to economies of scale that take place if average production costs of a bank product declines as output of that product rises. Significant capital investments in infrastructure are needed to start the operation (large fixed costs) and marginal costs for services provided over the existing infrastructure are relatively low. Similar to other scale-driven industries, large production capacity to efficiently process the volume of retail payment transactions is required to establish a competitive system. In this business, which is characterized by a severe squeeze on margins, banks and payment service providers face significant investment needs to comply with regulatory requirements, such as embargo filtering or anti-money-laundering policies, to remain competitive. Being able to pool payment volumes from the market is a prerequisite for banks and clearing houses that see payments as a core business to achieving critical mass and optimal scale utilization. Therefore, to avoid sunk costs, especially smaller payment service providers tend to outsource this business to specialized payment service providers that are competing for payment volumes.

Market structure and related concentration issues

The European payments business involves, among others, transaction of money using cash, checks, credit cards, direct debits and transfers. Furthermore, integral instruments needed to make a transaction are also the transactional accounts that companies and consumers keep as well as the liquid balances – whether positive (deposits) or negative (overdrafts and credit card loans) – that payment users must hold in order to be able to transfer value. By this definition, Europe's payments business is a large industry in Europe. With total revenues amounting to EUR 125bn,[90] it is bigger in Europe than airlines, mobile telecommunications, or pharmaceuticals, and only slightly smaller than the chemicals industry (Ploey & Denecker, 2007).

From a profitability perspective, payments are below average compared to other banking services. Although they represent 25% of European banks' operating revenues, they also account for more than one-third of the banks' operating costs while generating less than 12% of their overall profits. Owing to this disproportion between cost and revenues, payments have a negative effect on banks' cost-to-income ratio of about 8%. This imbalance becomes even more evident when comparing costs and volumes of domestic and cross-border payments. In 2001, 98-99% of all payments within the EU were domestic payments, transferred within the borders of a single country. However, this low volume of

90 Including Germany, France, United Kingdom, Italy, Spain, Netherlands, Belgium, Sweden, and Poland.

payments transaction accounted for 28% of total credit transfer costs in 2001 (McKinsey & Company, 2003). More complex processing of cross-border payments in the eurozone, the lack of a consequent definition and use of agreed standards result in low interbank automation levels driving these costs. Until 2003, a system for processing cross-border euro credit transfers in retail payments with a corresponding pan-European payment system infrastructure did not exist. The slow development of interbank infrastructures and the use of clearing systems for cross-border credit transfers instead of correspondent banking alternatives remain an important cost factor.

As discussed in detail in the previous section, the provision of payments includes two main parties involved: payment service providers, i.e., financial and non-financial institutions, and clearing systems or ACHs. Both account for a different process step in the value chain of a payment transaction. Banks, for instance, provide the account for the payer and the payee and are responsible for the initiation and preparation of a transaction on the payer side and the final crediting to an account on the payee side. The execution and distribution of a payment is finally performed by a clearing system.[91]

This split of value performance is also reflected in market competition. The number of payment service providers strongly correlates with the total number of banks and financial institutions, reflecting the high fragmentation in the European banking market. With regard to clearing and ACH systems, the number of institutions providing respective systems is reduced to one per country, reflecting historical development and prevailing national standards from the time before introduction of the euro. A brief analysis of the competitive landscape of payment service providers and clearing systems for retail payments in Europe is provided in the course of this section.

According to the ECB, 6,261 institutions offered payment services in the eurozone in 2008. The number of institutions per domestic market is obviously smaller and varies from country to country (see Table 17). Nevertheless, customers are able to choose from a considerable number of payment service providers in the European market. The expected market consolidation following the introduction of a single currency has hardly taken place: between 2000 and 2008, the number of institutions in the euro area has decreased by only 2% on average.

91 The described procedure to a non-correspondent-banking scenario where banks hold bilateral accounts and execute a payment without using clearing systems.

Table 17: Number of credit institutions in the eurozone (2000-2008)

Country	2000	2001	2002	2003	2004	2005	2006	2007	2008	CAGR (2000-2008)
Austria	852	837	824	817	798	820	810	804	804	-1%
Belgium	120	114	113	110	106	106	107	112	107	-1%
Cyprus	47	410	412	414	410	398	343	223	171	18%
Germany	2.743	2.527	2.364	2.226	2.149	2.090	2.049	2.016	1.982	-4%
Spain	369	367	360	349	347	349	353	358	362	0%
Finland	342	370	370	367	364	368	362	361	358	1%
France	1.102	1.053	992	941	899	856	831	810	730	-5%
Greece	58	62	62	60	63	63	63	64	67	2%
Ireland	83	88	87	82	82	80	79	83	84	0%
Italy	872	857	835	815	800	807	824	837	837	-1%
Luxembourg	204	196	186	174	167	157	156	157	155	-3%
Malta	12	26	23	24	24	27	28	30	30	12%
Netherlands	447	599	566	514	492	430	371	374	332	-4%
Portugal	220	214	204	202	199	188	180	177	177	-3%
Slovenia	9	101	59	31	34	35	35	38	36	19%
Slovakia	2	25	24	24	24	26	27	29	29	40%
Euro area	**7.482**	**7.846**	**7.481**	**7.150**	**6.958**	**6.800**	**6.618**	**6.473**	**6.261**	**-2%**

Source: European Central Bank (2009).

Over the last years, banks and payment systems in the EU member states have been evolving largely independently of each other and within the scope of their national boundaries. While payment systems have selected and implemented their own technologies, formats and service levels, as well as governance models, banks have implemented those specific technologies and clearing practices on a per-country basis. In most countries, there is only one open clearing infrastructure for domestic retail payments. In countries, where there is more than one, such as in Greece, Ireland, Lithuania, Luxembourg, Malta or the United Kingdom, they are usually not in direct competition but complement one another instead. Figure 15 visualizes the resulting system landscape. For the purpose of this case study, ownership, membership and fees will be discussed in more detail.

Domestic system[2]	Retail system name	Transaction Volume (in mn) Retail[1]	Wholesale equivalent[1]	Membership Open membership for banks	Restricted membership (subject to criteria)	Ownership Banks	Central Banks	Domestic Communication Standard
Belgium	CEC	952	1.77	•		•5)	•5)	Yes
Denmark	DN Retail Clearing	1,120	0.11	•			•	Yes
France	SIT	11,868	4.32	•		•		Yes
Germany	EMZ/ RPS[4]	2,174	35.78	•			•	Yes
Greece	Diaz	29	1.4	•		•		Yes
Italy	Retail	1,895	10.38	•			•	Yes
Luxembourg	LIPSNet	14	0.52	•		•		-
Netherlands	Interpay	3,272	4.7	•		•		Yes
Portugal[3]	SICOI	1,519	1.03		•	•		Yes
Spain[3]	SNCE	1,277	6.76		•		•	Yes
Sweden	Bank Giro System	19	0.11	•		•		Yes
U.K.	BACS	5,134	5.06		•	•		Yes
Cross-border systems								
	EBA STEP 1[6]	3,11	N/A	•		•		-

Figure 15: Overview of ACH systems in Europe (2002)
Source: Adapted from European Payment Council (2002).
Notes: 1) Excluding Manual Clearing Houses; Wholesale equivalent includes the national TARGET component 2) Countries without ACH are not listed (i.e., Austria, Finland and Ireland) 3) Special ACHs supporting Real Time Transmission 4) This figure does not include the significantly higher number of transactions that are automatically processed, cleared and settled directly between Germany's biggest banks, who use the same technical standards and rules as EMZ/ RPS does. 5) Owner = banker; Manager = central bank 6) Controlled by a club of banks

In credit transfer systems, ownership and governance issues may constitute important determinants of the level of competition between networks. Usually, retail payment systems are jointly owned by the participating members, or they are publicly owned by national central banks (see Figure 15), which reflects the cooperative nature of payment provision services. This joint ownership structure leads to two aspects critical from a competition point of view. On the one hand, the existence of exclusivity rights may hamper the creation of an efficient level playing field for a cross-border payment landscape. On the other hand, safety concerns may arise when granting open access to a payment system, regardless of whether participants can actually fulfill their obligations as required. In this regard, central banks are obliged to maintain payment system oversight and to take necessary actions required to limit negative effect of system risk that is inherent in all payment systems, including cross-border retail systems (even though at a lower degree than in high-value, interbank clearing systems).

Besides the shortcomings of a joint ownership structure, cross-ownership and cross-membership between networks can further result in a conflict of interest for members and a reduced degree of competition among different networks. Banks may have no incentive to support a strategy of market growth and innovation through competition with other networks in which banks are also shareholders or members. The European Commission (2005f) conducted a market study on the competition for cross-border payments and investigated also the ownership and membership structure of respective credit transfer networks. Accordingly, the major cross-border transfer systems are owned by some or even collectively by all of their member banks. Several banks are shareholders of more than one network, and many banks have network shareholdings but also participate in other networks.[92]

An important issue to consider is the question of membership of payment systems. The same banks are often members of different payment systems, i.e., national or cross-border systems, which could result in conflicts of interest regarding inter-system competition on the one hand and joining restrictions on the other hand. Regarding conflicts of interest, a bank that is a member of one payment system may have less incentive to promote a strategy of intense competition with another network it participates in. For instance, a domestic clearing system does not yet seem to be considered a competitor to an international clearing system.

From a competition point of view, the classes of membership to clearing systems, their special requirements and the conditions under which potential and existing member institutions compete with each other appear even more relevant than the conflicts of interest mentioned earlier. The general distinction between direct and indirect members, in combination with a different participation in decision-making, requires further elaboration.

Firstly, a vertical structure is typical in retail payment markets. An indirect member will depend on the *goodwill* of a direct member with whom he will have to negotiate an agency contract, adding another layer of intermediation and

---

92 The EC report provides the following examples for cross-ownership and cross-membership in European payment networks (European Commission, 2005f, pp. 33-34):

- ING Bank of the Netherlands is a shareholder of both EBA Clearing and Eurogiro.
- Natexis Banques Populaires is one of the owners of both EBA Clearing and TIPANET.
- Most members of the UniCash Alliance are also owners of EBA Clearing and EURO1 participants.
- All but one of the owners of IBOS are also shareholders of EBA Clearing and EURO1 participants. Many STEP2 direct participants are also involved in other networks such as IBOS and UniCash.

leading to a total cost increase. On the other hand, such an arrangement is beneficial for smaller banks and niche players, who do not have to comply with the requirements linked to a direct membership. Secondly, indirect members are less involved than direct members in decision-making processes determining prices, deciding on membership application or any technical standards or rules. Finally, the access to business-sensitive data through direct members as *agents* of indirect members leads to one-sided information exchange. Indirect members are obliged to share their list of payments with principle members, which provides a competitive advantage to the information-collecting banks. In addition, the fact that these banks might also have voting rights on the scheme's board reinforces the concern that decisions might be taken that limit competition (European Commission, 2006b, p. 139).

Concerning the possibility of becoming a direct member, all systems require members to be regulated financial institutions; some presuppose the supervision by the National Central Bank or the physical presence in the member state. Furthermore, membership in a national retail ACH is open for banks in almost all euro countries except Portugal, Spain and the U.K. In these countries, membership criteria decide the acceptance of a bank. These criteria consist of legal, financial, volume and technical requirements (Kemppainen, 2004b, p. 19).[93] However, the fact that in Portugal and the United Kingdom, payment systems are owned by banks raises the question of accessibility to *club-like systems*. The exclusion of non-financial institutions like processors or some customers from a direct membership to a clearing system gives rise to two main concerns: firstly, being excluded from a network's decision-making process means that a network can develop in ways that do not meet the needs of a significant group of users. Secondly, the inability of corporate clients to access clearing systems directly might increase their dependency on their current banking relationships.

In summary, cross-membership or ownership of one network combined with the membership of another network may theoretically provide reasons for conflicts of interest. In most countries there is one clearing infrastructure, which is owned either by the National Central Bank or by a membership association controlled by the main banks in the country. On national levels, such an organization of payment arrangements could assume some kind of a *natural monopoly*, which might encompass competition and the existence of lower prices and a

93 These criteria contain in detail the following participation rules: *legal requirements*: legal status (i.e., banks, credit institutions and investment firms registered in the ACH country); *financial requirements*: solvency (minimum risk-asset ratio), ability to support engagement under predefined limits, holding an settlement account in wholesale systems or payment clubs; *volume requirements*: request to send and receive a certain percentage of volume annually exchanged in the system; *technical requirements*: capacity to send correctly formatted messages and information requests, existence of a database recording all transactions, ability to fall back on a remote backup.

greater range of services. However, this has not been the case in the past: economies of scale and network effects tend to give rise to strong conglomeration effects, where clearing and settlement of nation retail payments concentrate on one efficient system. Nevertheless, in such an arrangement, entry barriers faced by a potential new network are high and associated risks are numerous. The lack of innovation and adaptation to end-users' needs, possible anticompetitive restrictions on access, poor transparency and anti-competitive pricing are the most important to be named (European Commission, 2006b, p. 133). However, no empirical evidence is found that these conflicts of interest would lead to any anti-competitive behavior in the market due to this aspect of multilateral networks (European Commission, 2005f, p. 50).

4.1.4 Information asymmetries and pricing intransparency

There seem to be varying degrees of information asymmetries depending on the type of payment product. Unlike domestic retail payment, cross-border payment services are complex in nature, involving a lot more clearing and settlement process steps and related multilateral contracting. Complex products create information asymmetries, and banks or other suppliers of cross-border payment services have often not ensured that the customer fully understands the product being bought. This leads on the demand-side to reduced or suboptimal choice related to product offering and transaction costs for cross-border payment services. In the following, related market detriments are analyzed with respect to market failure problems.

Reduced or suboptimal choice

A potential source of market failure is asymmetric information, which may prevent the proper creation of a single market in Europe. Consumers and small enterprises may be unable to obtain *ex-ante* all relevant information from alternative banks to compare offers and make their choices. The lack of effective information provided by banks on their product offering, contractual terms and conditions, and the pricing of cross-border payment products does not only make consumers' choice difficult but also reduces the pressure on banks to compete aggressively on price and on quality of service. The economic literature (see, for example, Kay & Vickers, 1988) recognizes that the inability of end-consumers to evaluate properly the quality and benefits of a product can drive high-quality products or services out of the market or at least cause inefficiencies that inhibit demand from evolving and may therefore create a market failure. These inefficiencies may arise because the quality of a cross-border credit transfer is not recognized or valued properly by the end-consumers and reflected into prices (European Commission, 2006b, p. 22). This implies that high-quality payment service providers are discriminated and there are insufficient incentives for low-quality payment service providers to reduce information asymmetry at the domestic and EU levels and improve consumer education and confidence. This concretely translates into problems of access to relevant information, understanding the complex structures and related transaction costs of cross-border payments, and, finally, language problems that detain end-consumers from engaging in cross-border payment transactions.

Access to relevant information includes primarily details available to customers on the transparency of bank conditions as well as execution times and methods for cross-border credit transfers. The execution methods regulate the execution types and the cost allocation (i.e., all costs to be borne by the originator, divided between the originator and the beneficiary or all paid by the beneficiary). Differing disclosure rules for banks on the terms and conditions for payment services, charges, fees and exchange rates in European countries impede an informed choice and may discourage end-consumers from making cross-border payments.

An additional factor that nurtures intransparency is the complex structure of cross-border payment products offered by banks, which often do not ensure that the customer fully understands the product being sold. Complexity forces end-consumers to make a significant investment of time in searching for the best supplier in terms of price and quality for a cross-border payment transfer. It can be assumed that end-consumers would search for an alternative supplier only if the expected gain would compensate for the expected search costs. While most European citizens have no complex, multinational affairs and their economic activity concentrates on regional or national levels, these clients are generally assumed to be price-inelastic for products they use only sporadically (i.e., end-consumers are hardly going to restrain from purchasing a product from another EU member state only because of associated payment fees). Hence, their related level of mobility to change their banking relationship is assumed to be particularly low due to the high costs associated with switching to another banks.

There are three reasons for this price inelastic behavior, at least with regard to certain core retail banking products such as current accounts and related payment transactions (European Commission, 2006b, p. 98): firstly, current accounts are widely held and the most frequently used banking product in Europe. Secondly, current accounts are open ended and do not expire after a set time period like loans. Finally, current accounts play a gateway role and represent the basis for cross-selling other products to customers.

Intransparent product pricing and bundling structures

Cross-border price structures differ substantially across national boundaries. Figure 16 shows the development of the four main components of the annual price for banking products and services of a typical relationship in retail core banking over time.

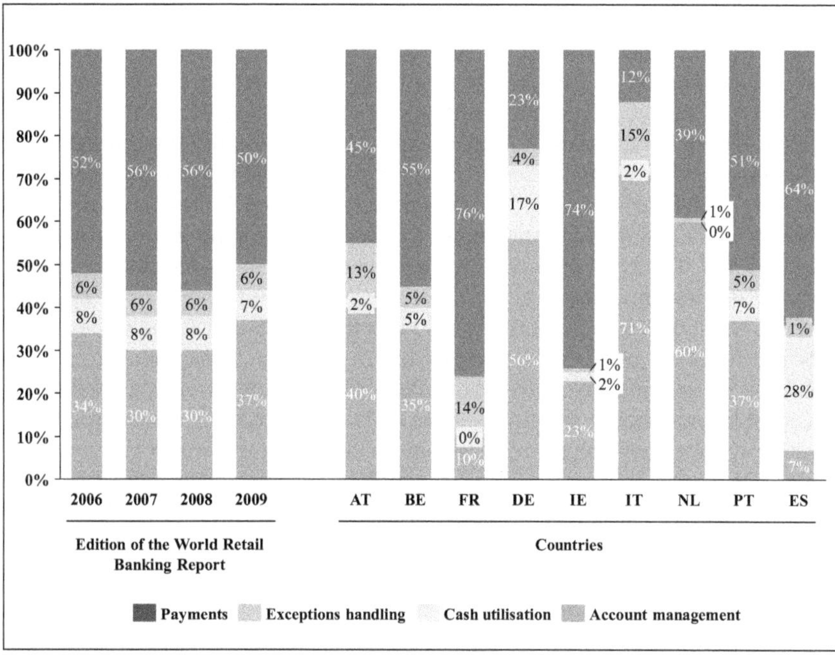

Figure 16: Sources of fees for core banking services in the eurozone

Source: World Retail Banking Report, Capgemini, EFMA and ING (2009, p. 16).

The weight of payments in the core banking activities has decreased from 2006-2009 (from 52% to 50%), and account management provided 37% of core banking fees in 2009. In a cross-country comparison, the weight of payment fees still varies significantly, from 76% in France to 12% in Italy. This shows that even if customers have a clear picture of their patterns of use of core retail banking services, these significant variations of price structures will hinder accurate price comparisons, particularly when considering cross-border banks or service providers.

Looking at domestic and cross-border retail payments as a product could sometimes be incomprehensible for end-users who never experience this service as a final product but as a bundle of other banking services, like deposits. Accordingly, the pricing remains intransparent to end-users, and payment services are often treated as the cross-subsidized loss-leader in this bundle of account-related services. As a result, the pricing of payment services does not reflect their actual cost. Instead, payment services are often offered free or for prices below production costs, but they are implicitly charged through low interest on current account balances.[94] Ploey et al. (2005) conducted a study of the pan-European payment service market and examined the activities of banks in the areas of current and credit card accounts and all their transactions, including cash. They discovered that every nation's payment business is distinctive, with different product and mixes of products and also differing pricing. Furthermore, their study evidenced that banks have been using their profitable payments products to subsidize other, loss-making products. Figure 17 illustrates the profit breakdown of EU payments and shows that exception handling for cross-border payments and the credit card business subsidize other account-related payment products and instruments. This could potentially lead to payment market inefficiencies, when production costs are not reflected in charges. If the price system does not function properly, the use of the most efficient payment instrument cannot be sufficiently promoted and influencing consumers choice through direct, cost-based pricing of payment services. Nevertheless, direct pricing of payment services has increasingly gained popularity in the recent years, so that also critics of this approach admit that guiding customers to use the most efficient payment instrument can increase efficiency of payment system. From a consumer point of view, a product-related, cost-based pricing for payment instruments has been irrelevant, as payments are not considered *real* products and are in most EU countries included in their regular account service fee. As will be shown later, the product cross-subsidization reveals a significant vulnerability in the present European banking system: if prices for cross-border payment transactions are being prescribed by regulation, cutting the profits from some of these profitable products, European banks could face further problems in operating payment services profitably.

94 See for example Tarkka (1995) for the theoretical analyses on the determination of deposit interest or service charges and Humphrey, Keppler and Montes-Negret (1997) for issues on cost recovery and pricing in payment services.

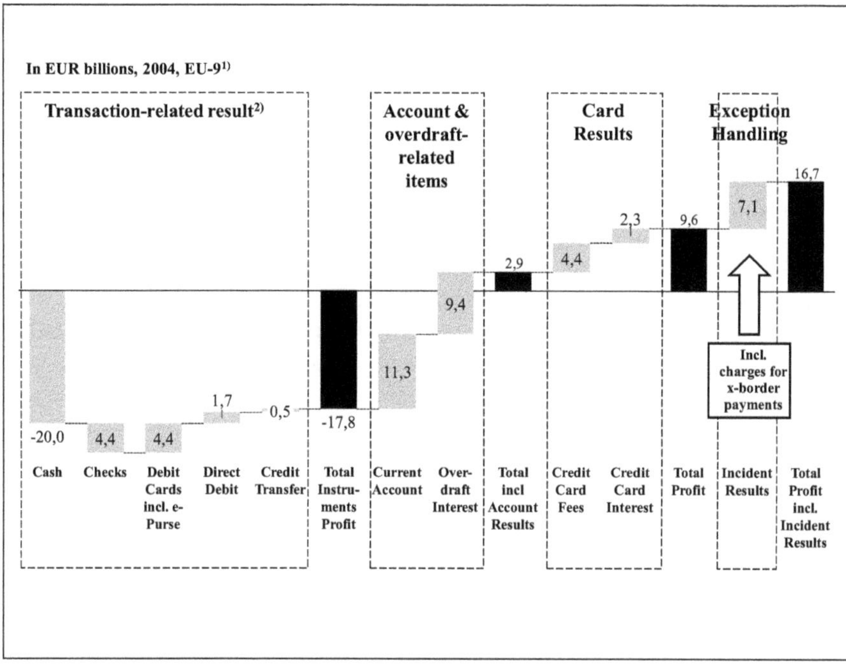

Figure 17: EU payments profit breakdown by product
Source: Author's illustration, adopted from Ploey (2005).
Note: 1) EU-9 covers GER, UK, F, I, E, NL, B, SE and PL; 2) Includes annual fees for debit cards.

Interdependence of demand

A final characteristic for the demand-side of retail payment in Europe is linked to the *chicken-and-egg* problem explained earlier. Due to the low volume of cross-border payments, less than 2% of all retail payment transactions are cross-border (European Payment Council, 2002). The insufficient demand for these services could not spark any commercial interest and consequently no *business case* for payment service providers to invest in these systems. Whether this volume will increase in the future naturally depends on customers' needs and payment behavior, but also on the willingness of banks to invest in cross-border retail payment infrastructure to execute these types of payments efficiently, reliably and cheaply. One can argue that the fact that the low volume of cross-border payments realistically reflects the banking patterns of European citizens who hardly make any cross-border transactions during the year, which is unlikely to change even if product offering improves or prices are lowered. On the other hand, European authorities and consumer associations claim that high prices are the main obstacles to activate and expand the demand for these services. This interdependence of demand will remain an obstacle until the innovation achieves critical mass, either in its own time or with authorities' help.

Historical national payment habits

National payment habits constitute so-called *natural* demand-side barriers, such as language, cultural preferences and the desire for (geographical) proximity (Diekmann, 2006, p. 5). The majority of retail banking customers in the EU have a strong, economic home base and tends to purchase their financial products through local distribution channels such as branches or national internet banking solutions offered by their banks. Accordingly, the number of cross-border transactions is relatively low compared to the domestic volume. Similarly, national preferences on the usage of payment instruments differ significantly. This section looks at the EU payment statistics on national payment habits and preferences, which reflect the current fragmented structure of retail methods and systems in the EU countries, clearly indicating the difficulty of achieving a harmonized market for payments in the future.

In 2008, it is estimated that 54.8 billion non-cash payments were made in the EMU.

Table 18 shows the number non-cash transactions per payment instrument. Looking at total transaction numbers illustrated in Figure 18, Germany, France, The Netherlands and Italy are by far the biggest cashless payment markets (82% of total eurozone transactions originate in these five countries). However, the composition of payment instruments applied varies significantly, not only across these three countries but also across all other EU member states.

Table 18: Payment and terminal transactions (2008)

in billion	Euro area[1)]	BE	DE	IE	GR	ES	FR	IT	CY[2)]	LU	MT[3)]	NL	AT	PT	SI[4)]	SK[5)]	FI
Total number of transactions	54,8	2,2	16,0	0,7	0,2	5,4	15,9	3,8	0,1	0,1	0,0	4,8	2,1	1,4	0,3	0,4	1,8
Credit transfers	1,5	0,9	5,6	0,2	0,0	0,8	2,7	1,1	0,0	0,1	0,0	0,1	1,0	0,1	0,2	0,2	0,7
Direct debits	16,6	0,2	8,0	0,1	0,0	2,3	3,0	0,6	0,0	0,0	0,0	1,2	0,8	0,2	0,0	0,1	0,1
Card payments[6)]	1,8	0,9	2,2	0,3	0,1	2,1	6,5	1,4	0,0	0,1	0,0	1,9	0,3	0,9	0,1	0,1	1,0
E-money purchase transactions	0,4	0,1	0,0		0,0	0,0	0,0	0,1		0,0		0,2	0,0				
Cheques	4,4	0,0	0,1	0,1	0,0	0,1	3,5	0,4	0,0	0,0	0,0		0,0	0,2	0,0	0,0	0,0
Other payment instruments	0,5	0,0			0,0	0,1	0,1	0,3	0,0				0,0	0,0			

Source: ECB (2009)

Notes: 1) The euro area total covers the EU Member States that had adopted the euro at the time to which the statistics relate, 2) Cypriot data are included in euro area aggregates as of 2008, 3) Maltese data are included in euro area aggregates as of 20008, 4) Slovenian data are included in euro area aggregates as of 2007, 5) Slovakian data are included in euro area aggregates as of January 2009, 6) Card payments, except with e-money cards (cards issued in the reporting country).

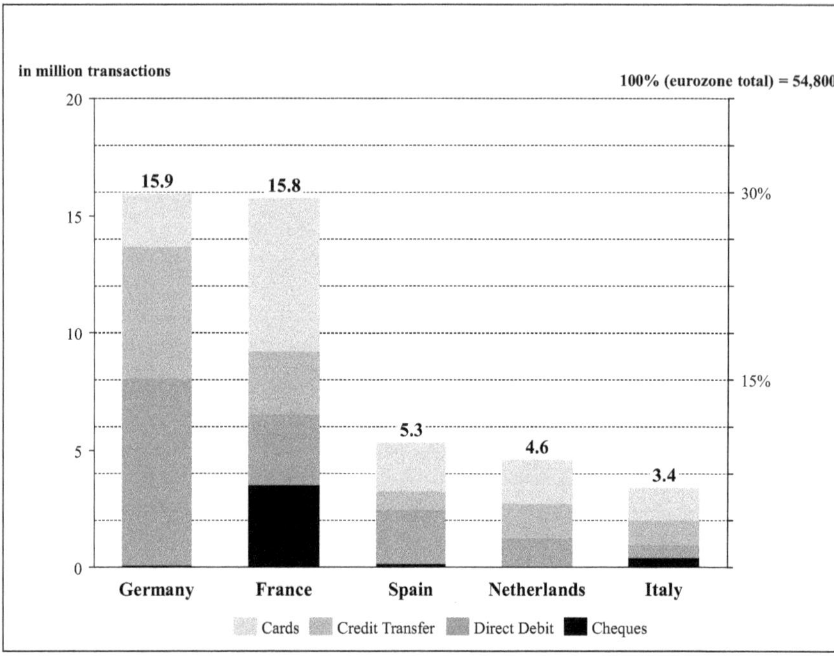

Figure 18: Use of cashless payments instruments in selected EU countries
Source: ECB (2008).

Naturally, differences in payment instruments used in different countries are reflected in the structure and organization of payment systems in these countries. Kemppainen (2004a, p. 13) notes that the degree of development of payment system infrastructure across EU member states is likely to have been influenced by some kind *path-dependency*. This phenomenon becomes apparent with regard to the structure of the service-providing sector, national payment practices developed in respective domestic markets and different payment legislation. As a result, each domestic payment system in Europe shows different access criteria, payment schemes and processes, as well as different product standards. Apart from these *hard factors* affecting the development of domestic retail payments systems, the importance of national payment habits, history and culture as *soft factors* is worth mentioning. This applies in particular to consumers, but to some extent, to corporations as well. One may, however, query whether and how these patterns would evolve if the principle of payments instruments competing for customer acceptance based on transparent pricing, and in a context of similar rules and consequences, was generally accepted and implemented (Karasu & Goralczyk, 2003, p. 3). The coming years will tell whether advances in payment transfer technology can accelerate financial market integration and if deepened financial linkages will change this picture.

Besides the fact that the EU consists of 30 different retail payment areas and that already some degree of convergence has taken place, these payment areas are characterized by such a level of heterogeneity that could potentially hinder the development of cross-border retail payments systems. More precisely, the heterogeneity in demand for different payments instruments in different countries makes it difficult to deploy a truly compatible cross-border payments system due to differing national needs. However, the debate on the formation of a single payments area in the EU implies that national payment habits and methods should not necessarily be entirely harmonized. Instead, the reliability and efficiency of European cross-border retail instruments and systems takes a center stage.

4.2 Government failure

As defined at an earlier stage, government failure is a common phenomenon in all areas of regulation where regulators become *captured* by the industry they regulate, meaning that they take on the objectives of management in the firms they regulate (Benink & Schmidt, 2004, p. 186). Regulators may thereby lose sight of the ultimate objectives of regulation. Regulatory capture is particularly severe in industries such as banking where there is a conflict of interest between the firms' objectives (to maximize profits) and the objectives of the regulation (to provide consumer protection and maintain systemic stability). Referring to Chapter B, government failure can be diagnosed when regulated markets include macro-economically inefficiently operating industries (due to market fragmentation) and a high cost of regulation (in each EU member state) that exceeds the costs of negative externalities. In this respect, this section examines whether the lack of integration of European retail payment market indicates symptoms that justify regulatory intervention.

4.2.1 Efficiency levels and regulation in retail payment markets

Assessing the efficiency levels of European payment systems requires a differentiation between the current domestic and the cross-border infrastructure. As the vast majority of payments are made within the member states, national payment service providers built efficient, automated and competitive payment systems at the domestic level and had no economic incentive to overhaul these highly efficient national systems to handle international transactions (Mai, 2005, p. 3).[95] From a macro-economic perspective, a fragmented payment system landscape in the single currency is highly inefficient and justifies understandably higher prices. Looking at the high regulatory intensity of the banking industry in

95 Chapter E elaborates on the different efficiency levels of domestic and cross-border payment systems available between 2001 and 2003.

general and the payment market in particular, the question of why a single retail payment market has not evolved through a market-driven process may require a more detailed examination of the artificial, policy-made barrier to integration.

Payments are traditionally made subject to consumer protection rules and various legal and contractual requirements defined by national regulation. Discrepancies in consumer protection regimes hinder product comparability for end-consumers on the one hand and prevent banks from designing pan-European retail payment products on the other hand. It is unclear to consumers who are willing to make cross-border payment transactions, what the terms and conditions in other EU member states are. These may include important aspects such as the possibility of withdrawing from a contract or cancellation possibilities, protection against quality defects, contract termination and conclusion conditions and requirements on the utilization of the service during the term of contract.

Banks and payment service providers, as well as corporations and retail customers, are facing partly intransparent national rights and obligations of payment services for cross-border transactions. For banks and payment service providers, national laws foresee different market access requirements, such as filing an application for a bank license for non-bank payment service providers, or requirements for the deployment of certain payment instruments, creating artificial market entry barriers. Further legal obligations include data protection or anti-money-laundering or financial reporting requirements. Similarly, some countries such as the United Kingdom require corporations or end-consumers to have a registered residence in the host country in order to open an account and to make a credit transfer. On the other hand, in Italy for example, in order to utilize a bank's direct debit service to make payment collections from Italian customers, corporations need to either be direct participants of Italy's BI-COMP payment system or have an account with a bank registered in Italy (OECD, 2006, p. 147).

Legal or regulatory provisions can obstruct market entry or impair competition between different types of institutions operating in the market (Bank for International Settlements, 2003, p. 30). However, in many cases these provisions may have a valid rationale, based, for example, on safety considerations. Outright restrictions on access are common on the settlement level for payment service providers. However, they occur also at the end-user level; for example, in some countries, legal or regulatory provisions restrict the banks' ability to issue payment instruments. Furthermore, there can also be less direct effects, such as the differences between the legal and regulatory regimes for banks and non-banks. These can impose different cost and risk burdens on participants, which may distort incentives to cooperate in network arrangements and compete efficiently in payment service markets.

As a result, it can be noted that individual national payment markets are operating very efficiently and that payment services are highly regulated by domestic law. From this, it follows that assuming there is a demand for cross-border payment services in the eurozone, the lack of market integration is less attributed to private sector resistance but more to lack of a harmonization of the individual regulatory frameworks on member state levels.

4.2.2 Regulatory capture by interest groups

One can argue that the fact that the retail banking market has not developed across national borders shortly after the introduction of the single currency was mainly the result of rigid, over-regulated member state markets that constrained banks to provide adequate products for the emerging demand that hindered competition for the benefits of lower prices and improved transparency for cross-border services. The reluctance on national levels reflects how particular interest groups seek to influence political decision makers to circumvent or at least delay the creation of a single market.

The complexity and diversity of European interest politics becomes apparent when examining the different channels and targets that private actors make use of to lobby in the EU multi-level system (Bouwen, 2002, p. 365). Bouwen (2002) developed a theoretical framework to explain the access of business interests to the organizations of the European Union through different forms of interest representation. The degree of access to these organizations is explained in terms of a theory of demand and supply of access goods.[96] EU organizations rely on the supply of these access goods because they provide information about encompassing and representative interests (so-called input legitimacy). As mentioned above, the single market integration process involves different interested parties that participate in the articulation of these interests. On the other hand, EU organizations depend on the industry's expert knowledge as an access good to have the necessary expertise to deal with their problems in an efficient way, legitimizing their decision-making (Bouwen, 2002, p. 371).

---

96 Bouwen (2002, pp. 369-370) defines access goods as "goods provided by private actors to the EU institutions in order to gain access. Each access good concerns a specific kind of information that is important in the EU decision-making process. The criticality of an access good for the functioning of an EU institution determines the degree of access that the institution will grant to the private interest representatives." Furthermore, Bouwen distinguishes between three access goods: expert knowledge (i.e., technical expertise), information about the European encompassing interest (i.e., information provided by the European Banking Federation on the needs and interests of its members) and information about the domestic encompassing interest (i.e., information provided by national banking associations).

Table 19: Organizational forms of interest representation in the EU

	Individual action	Collective action	Third part
National level	Individual national action	National association	National consultant
European level	Individual EU action	European association	Brussels consultant

Source: Bouwen (2002, p. 373).

Depending on the size, economic strategy and domestic institutional environment of the firm, business representation can rely on one or even all the different forms presented in Table 19. A large German international bank, for example, may have the following lobby portfolio: an individual action in Germany, individual action at the EU level through its liaison office in Brussels, a membership of the Bundesverband der Deutschen Banken in Germany and of the European Banking Federation. Furthermore, under certain circumstances, the bank might even use third-party representation at the national and European level. Hence, it is likely that firms seek several lobbying options to pursue their political strategies to influence the public authorities of the EU.

According to Bouwen (2002) the efficiency of provision and the quantity and quality of access goods are primarily impacted by two variables: (i) the number of organizational layers (individual, national association, European association), and (ii) the complexity of the internal decision-making process of the organizational form. As said by Schmitter and Schreek (1999, p. 76), the speed and flexibility of the supplied access goods depends primarily on the number of layers involved in their provision. Following this logic, the provision of access goods and representation of interests by individual firms is more advantageous than the one by national associations for example. While this may be the case in many situations, the more layers involved, the better the quality and the bundling of individual interest into an encompassing interest. Regarding the complexity, the more complicated the internal decision-making process in an organizational form, the slower and less efficient the provision of access goods. Salisbury (1984, pp. 67-68) evidenced in this respect that a hierarchically structured organizational form, such as a firm, is likely to be more efficient than a decentralized, democratically organized form like an association. However, in order to ensure proper quantity and quality of access goods, complex decision-making processes of bundling individual interests are unavoidable.

Besides the implications of the organizational form of interest representation on the provision of access goods, recent literature suggests that interest group influence varies considerably across issues and that influence is strongly shaped by the issue context. In this regard, one needs to further distinguish between two natures of interest, cause vs. sectional groups. According to Stewart (1958, p. 25) sectional groups represent a section of society, such as banks or payment service providers. Their task is to look after the specific interest of this particular section of society and their membership is usually limited to that section. The common interest of their members is specific and usually of primary material nature. By contrast, cause groups represent some belief or principle such as consumer protection, and their membership is not restricted. The common interest of cause group members is usually diffuse, and it is therefore hypothesized that cause groups are less influential since they cannot provide money, information or electoral power to decision-makers. Sectional groups, by contrast, represent well-defined homogenous constituencies with specific interests, which are of primary material concern to their members, so that they are willing to supply the interest group with the necessary financial and electoral support (Dür & Bièvre, 2007, p. 82). In the banking area, bank and firm associations on the national and European level represent sectional interest groups involved in lobbying activities on payment market topics. In the following, the author outlines the relevant interest groups, their positions and their influencing power on national governments and EU governmental bodies.

Consumer interest groups

Consumer interest groups are cause groups representing a rather diffuse objective of strengthening client confidence in financial transactions. Being organized on national levels, traditionally, their efforts focus on representing end-consumer interests on transparent product and service quality, data protection and pricing for the domestic home market, being binding for banks and financial institutions. In this respect, consumer interest groups do not relate to particular industry domains and narrow issues, according to historical attitudes and different cultural traditions in relation to financial institutions such as the single euro payment area initiative, but rather represent consumer interests on a broader basis. Consumer protection policies have been shaped by cultural considerations, traditions, and historical attitudes for regulatory structures and supervisory regimes in relation to financial institutions that prevail in the individual member states (Howell, 2004a, p. 109). In the multilevel, single currency environment of the European Union, national consumer protection associations are organized in umbrella organizations that are representing the interests of the affiliated national bodies on a consolidated European level, such as the BEUC97, seeking to in-

97 The Bureau Européen des Union Consommateurs (BEUC), the European Consumers' Organization, represents more than 40 independent, national consumer organizations from over 30 European countries (EU, EEA and applicant countries). BEUC defines its role as an "embassy" for these organizations, representing its members and defining the interests of all Europe's consumers. In addition to the pure lobbying activities, BEUC

fluence decision-making bodies of the European Union. Besides the traditional objectives of ensuring availability and accessibility of financial services and to decrease financial exclusion, the European umbrella organization for financial services, for example, aims at reinforcing consumer confidence in the Internal Market. In particular, they consider that access to a basic bank account is the initial step towards providing all EU consumers with basic banking services, and the Commission should remove all obstacles preventing these cross-border activities such as prohibitive discriminations based on residence and unfair commercial practices for all retail financial services (including accounts, payments, etc.) and tied and bundled products.

One can assume that the aggregation of national interests on a European level also bears certain conflicts of interest inherent in a system of multilevel representation. The conflicting agendas have become particularly apparent in payment services. From both the national and the BEUC perspectives, the primary objective for a single payment area is to improve efficiency, security and protection. This includes, among others, the avoidance of double-charges for cross-border credit transfers, contract cancellation fees or the establishment of standardized information on terms and conditions or mandatory execution times. However, consumer confidence will decrease if specific national consumer protection provisions are called into question, or if they do not apply to non-national providers (BEUC, 2009a). National consumer interest groups in the financial area have emphasized that consumers in their countries need to fully understand the level of protection they can depend on. Furthermore, unfamiliar legislation that provides less protection than consumers are offered under national law should be avoided. U.K. retail consumers, for example, might face liability limits before notification of theft or loss of their credit card of up to EUR 150, compared to only EUR 75 as they are charged now. Hence, maintaining consumer confidence is an important prerequisite for consumer interest groups for the development of cross-border payment activities, and national representations will by all means seek to avoid the pure application of the home country control principle,[98] which, from their point of view, would lead to regulatory arbitrage. A move toward the lowest common denominator of regulation and consumer protection should be avoided by sensible regulation (Banking Expert Group, 2004, p. 21).

The possibilities and benefits of a stable and integrated European financial market should be reflected in the daily transactions of consumers. They should

also formally represents consumers within the EU decision-making processes with a special focus on eight areas identified as priorities: Energy & Sustainability, Financial Services, Food, Health, Safety, Consumer Contracts, Digital Environment and Groups Actions (BEUC, 2009b)

98 See also Chapter C.

be able to enjoy advantages in terms of product quality and pricing as well as greater product variety. To this end, simple consumer protection rules are needed that will facilitate cross-border supply of financial services.

Interest groups representing corporations

According to the European Commission's impact assessment (carried out by Capgemini, 2007) medium-sized and multinational corporations, who operate across countries within the eurozone, will benefit most from a fully harmonized single payments area. Due to the current expense and complexity of cross-border payments operations, most corporations have to maintain multiple bank accounts, often one for each country (Skinner, 2008, p. 5). In the most optimistic scenario (the best fulfillment of the objectives of the Payment Services Directive and of SEPA) corporations may be able to run one treasury operation with one bank for the whole of Europe. Therefore, this interest group can expect significant transaction costs savings from SEPA, i.e., in terms of removing the need for multiple resources, currencies, languages, banks, and so forth. Furthermore, their ability to centralize treasury and working capital activities in Europe may allow them to consolidate their cash for investment purposes and to increase interest income. Against this background, multinational corporations in particular have articulated their support for SEPA. Two large associations consolidate and represent corporations' interests vis-á-vis the EU, the European Association of Corporate Treasurers (EACT) and the EuroCommerce. Unlike consumer clients, both types of corporate payment service users, multinational companies, as well as small- and medium-sized enterprises, are well-educated clients with regard to payments services. In a highly competitive market such as the payment market, corporations have a relatively strong negotiating position. With regard to legal protection, corporations' interest focuses on ensuring the freedom of contract rather than enforcing harmonized terms and conditions across Europe as demanded by consumer interest groups. Given the need for having the choice to agree on conditions that fit their business and client requirements, corporations favor the explicit right to agree on convenient terms individually with their bank or their payment service provider. Against this background, interest groups representing international corporations in Europe articulate their support for harmonized payments schemes on the one hand and tend to avoid standardization of legal requirements on the other (Mai, 2005, p. 13).

Banks and payment service providers

The banking sector has traditionally been the main payment service provider in Europe. On the public side, the Eurosystem actively operates Europe's largest interbank payment and settlement systems and plays, therefore, a special role in influencing political decision makers (see 4.2.3). In the private sector, there are a variety of banks and other firms or associations supplying services in the payment market: commercial, savings, and cooperative banks, and other institutions offering end-user payment services on the one hand, and companies providing network facilities on the other hand. These are, among others, SWIFT, clearing houses and processing firms offering back office operations for payment service providers, as well as specialized hardware and software providers (European Central Bank, 1999). However, banks and banking associations have traditionally dominated the field and have relied on well-organized forms of representation, both on the national and the European levels.

Considering the large number of banking and financial service associations in Europe, the level of business interest representation and lobbying activity of political actors is preeminent. There are approximately 27 banking associations in Europe representing the interests of private, cooperative and savings banks on a national level. Each association is represented on the European level with a European association for the respect sectional group:

(i) The European Banking Federation (EBF)
(ii) European Savings Banks Group (ESBG)
(iii) European Association of Co-operative Banks (EACB)
(iv) The European Association of Public Banks (EAPB)

Hence, due to this multi-layer organizational form of representations and the bottom-up aggregation of individual interest of sectional groups for private, savings and cooperative banks, the banking industry is recognized to undertake collective actions rather than individual third-party lobbying. Investigation on the politico-strategic agendas of these European banking associations for the purpose of this study notices that the information disclosed on their web sites is limited to a formal presentation of the organization, for example, place of registration, foundation details, and member and employee numbers. Information on the fiscal objectives, the characteristics and structure of the domestic associations that are being represented, the way European association seeks to influence political EU or national organization and, finally, the effectiveness of their work actually being reflected in concrete rules and decision-making is limited.

However, if considering the geographic footprint, business characteristics and client profile of their members, general inferences on position and assumed politico-strategic agenda of the bank association represents their interests regarding market integration in general and cross-border euro payments in particular. Nevertheless, their strategic position is not only determined by the characteristics of their business, but sometimes also articulated jointly on specific issues (i.e., supervisory or reporting requirements), reflected in comments to the EU consultation process. As part of the CESR in the Lamfalussy law-making process, banking associations provide expert knowledge as in access good to the political organization in an institutionalized way.

The resulting position towards opening domestic payment markets and actively lobbying for the creation of a single market of cross-border payment is presented in Table 20.

Table 20: European associations 'position on payment market integration

Bank association	Geographic footprint	Business characteristic	Client profile	Perceived position towards a single market for payments	Lobbying activity level / visibility
The European Banking Federation (EBF)	Global Regional Municipal	Interbank Wholesale Retail	Financial organizations Corporations Retail	Supportive	High
European Savings Banks Group (ESBG)	Regional Municipal	Non-profit oriented lending and savings Financing	Small- and mid-sized Corporations Retail	Neutral/ resistant	High
European Association of Co-operative Banks (EACB)	Regional Municipal	Industry specific, non-profit oriented lending and savings Financing	Small- and mid-sized Corporations Retail	Neutral	High
European Association of Public Banks (EAPB)	Regional Municipal	Public/ municipal financing	Federal and municipal organizations	Neutral/ supportive	Medium

Source: Author's illustration.

Eventually it can be observed that with an increasing shifting of law-making to the EU level, European umbrella bank associations become more and more important. Furthermore, the diverging interests between different banking groups seem to move as well from the national to the European level.

4.2.3 The interest of national central banks and governments

Central banks

Since the creation of the ESCB, national central banks have had a double identity: on the one hand, it has been deeply rooted in national traditions and sovereignty, which reflects specific national tasks and responsibilities. On the other hand, it is part of the system of central banks and therefore responsible for all tasks related to the fully supra-nationalized monetary policy. The fact that government-owned, national central banks (NCBs) also own and manage national retail payment systems, having even a *natural monopoly* in some countries, may lead to competition issues. The question arises whether central bank services are provided transparently and are keeping pace appropriately with changing patterns of market demand and whether access to central bank services is arranged in a way that innovation and competition is facilitated, while containing moral hazard and credit risk (BIS, 2003b, p. 33). Hence, a conflict of interest may arise if central banks are obliged to ensure transparency in the provision of services, for example over pricing and access while acting as a market player with a dominant position in many countries, competing with private banks and payment service providers and potentially hindering the emergence of new, innovative payment networks. For example, the Spanish NCB, Banco de Espana, maintains a price control on all retail payments processed through its network with the argument of contributing to business continuity and price stability (Sydbank, 2008, p. 6).

Hence, NCBs can be assigned to the sectional interest groups in their role as a supplier of retail payment services. However, as they are government owned, NCBs are not involved in lobbying but tend to influence decision makers on certain issues in an informative, consultative manner.

National governments

Artificial obstacles to integration of retail payment markets on member state levels represent the major symptoms for government failure. These regulatory and fiscal determinants are national competences and therefore account for differences across member states. Examples of these institutional determinants include consumer protection rules, regulation related to the remuneration of deposits and tax treatment of income from deposits (European Commission, 2006b, p. 167). Overcoming these barriers is, therefore, strongly dependent on the responsiveness of member states' public authorities to agree on a harmonized legal framework. Naturally, the critical positions of some member states towards the Europeanization trend elaborated earlier in this book also apply to the integration of retail banking markets. However, the promotion of retail financial services on a cross-border basis will only be successful if customers become more confident about the legal and regulatory framework for these transactions (Diekmann, 2006, p. 4). In other words, the limiting factor for cross-border business is not a general reluctance to purchase financial services from other member states (online or by branch visit) but rather persistent concerns about the legal framework applicable.

On a different note, even if a harmonized legal framework was agreed, national resistance may result in a deficient transposition and implementation of internal market legislation at a later stage, by which member states may delay the removal of artificial obstacles to protect national interests. The Kok Report (European Commission, 2005b, p. 12) points out that one of the most important obstacles that reduces the benefits of market integration is the failure of member states to act on the commitments they make in the Council within the agreed time limit. In view of the various obstacles to integrated markets in the fields of tax, company law and consumer protection numerous member states seem to be highly reluctant to transfer national sovereignty to the European level. Because of this lack of willingness, one can draw the conclusion that unlike for the EU organizations, the integration of payments markets is not of top priority for national governments, and the protection of national interests still seems to be ranked high by national policymakers.

Besides monitoring market power problems, regulatory intervention in network industries may sometimes be motivated by distributional concerns (Weinberg, 1996, p. 23). In these industries discrimination of users was traditionally counteracted by price regulations, aiming at lessening the impact of differences among users in the real costs of connecting to a network. In payment systems across Europe, such differences mainly relate to user characteristics (banks, non-bank financial organizations or corporations) and their geographic location (home country). However, the main difference is between a large number of low-volume users and a small number of high-volume users who might enjoy cost advantages if costs of using the payment network are dominated by the fixed cost connecting to the network. As the majority of users with a low volume have a cost disadvantage, they represent an attractive target group for politicians and bureaucrats to use regulation as a means to reduce inequalities. According to Peltzman (1989), this political concern for distribution has significantly influenced the public sector intervention in network industries. Similarly, these types of distributional concerns seem to be articulated by small, remote banks and payment service providers in discussions of payment system access policy.

In this context it can be noted that public sector intervention may not be necessary for a pricing that favors or at least does not discriminate against small users. In privately owned networks with an equal status of all members, pricing arrangements that are made of a small fixed fee and a variable, volume-driven component are already being applied.

Table 21 provides an overview of the individual interest groups and their articulated (or perceived) position towards an integrated payments market in Europe. This comparison reveals that interest groups' positions may vary significantly across different viewpoints. Besides the inherent discrepancy between the view of the market and the view of the regulator, conflicts of interests also arise between member states and the EU level. Furthermore, formally aligned positions on the national level (i.e., the interests of banks) seem to oppose on the European level, where interest groups representing particular market segments are taking up different stances.

As shown below, each position of an interest group has certain implications for EU regulation. The degrees to which one or the other articulated interest will find an attentive ear among EU policy-makers largely depends on the influencing power of the respective interest group.

Table 21: Interest groups' positions and implications for regulation

Interest group	Perceived/articulated interest	Implications for regulation
Consumer interest groups	• Reinforcing confidence in the Internal Market through transparent and binding banking product and service quality, pricing and data protection • Avoiding discrimination of national consumer protection through an EU legal framework (expand , not replace domestic regulation)	• Cultural and historical path dependency of national consumer protection policies make a harmonization to the lowest common denominator politically difficult • An expansion of national consumer protection by additional EU requirements however would not remove but stabilize regulatory barriers to integration
Interest groups representing corporations	• Supportive of a Europe-wide standardization of payment schemes and instruments • Skeptical towards obligatory EU legal framework that may limit freedom of contract between corporations and banks/payment service providers	• Removal of country-specific legal requirements that hinder the consistent application of the new SEPA payment schemes across Europe • Provision of consistent legal requirements and implementation timelines binding for all member states and market participants to allow for better planning reliability
Banks and payment service providers	• Mixed position of banking industry towards a single payment market due to diverging geographic footprints, business characteristic and client profile • For most banks, harmonization will lead to further revenue loss and margin squeeze driven by an increased competition • International banks favor a swift implementation of new payment schemes and lobby for a harmonized legal framework	• The banking industry owns the technical expert knowledge and the market experience to design and implement pan-European payment instruments and schemes, which is critical for legitimizing EU policy-making • In order to enforce the EU's vision of a harmonized payment market, policy makers should focus more on a the removal legal barriers to integration and to leave the development of the underlying infrastructure to the knowledgeable experts in the banking industry
Central banks	• Potential conflict of interest towards further driving consolidation of payment systems in the EU • In some member states the NCBs own the retail payment system and supervises the financial market at the same time	• EU policy-makers must consider potential conflicts of interest inherent with the harmonization of payments markets in Europe, as is associated with an increasing delegation of national roles and responsibilities into the market (by selling the payment system) or to the European level (for supervising all payments systems)
National governments	• Limited ability of politicians to use the single market project effectively on the public due to low number of citizens that would currently benefit from SEPA • Reluctance to engage in a European project that will lead to further transfer of national sovereignty to the EU level	

Source: Author's illustration.

4.3 Risks

Traditionally, clearing infrastructures were created on a non-profit basis for the domestic market, often with the involvement of national central banks. The ownership and management of the system by central banks had the statutory objective of fostering financial stability and promoting the soundness of payments and settlement systems to protect the economy from systemic risk. Sudden liquidity and solvency problems caused by one or more participants in the settlement process may result in *domino effects* on netting systems, causing serious liquidity shortfall problems for other participants. Furthermore, participants also face operational and legal risks when providing payment services to their customers. In view of these inherent risks of payment systems, any disruption in a major payment system may directly impact the citizens' confidence in non-cash payment transactions, the economy and financial stability. For this reason, the ECB has defined quantitative characteristics of a systematically important retail payment system. Once this is classified as systemically important, a payment system has to fulfill clearly defined requirements to mitigate risks.[99]

Due to the systemic importance of certain payment networks, access requirements for all participants must be well defined, objective and publicly disclosed. As the majority of payment systems are self-regulated, there may be the risk of protectionist behavior by incumbents. Decisions on the conditions for access must hence be transparent to potential new entrants, and any denial of access must subject to comprehensive reasons. However, for risk reasons, access by law to a certain payment system to any participant may not be desirable either: "[I]mposing restrictions on access may be warranted in order to protect participants against undue risks resulting from the participation of other parties" (European Central Bank, 2003b, p. 6). Hence, payment systems are systemic important networks that are only as reliable as their weakest participants.

In addition to the systemic risk that needs to be mitigated to maintain public confidence in the banking sector, operational risks, money laundering and deposit protection comprise further important risk-related aspects for payment service provisions. Potential systems outages or human errors can be grouped under the umbrella term of *operational risks*. Under Basel II regulation, banks are required to back up these risks by capital, similar to financial risk capital requirement. Tight anti-money-laundering rules bar the banking industry from engaging in money transactions related to criminal activities such as terrorism or economic embargos. As the implementation of these rules requires significant investments in IT and legal infrastructure and leads to a significant increase of opera-

99 The retail standards to be fulfilled as defined by the ECB are based on the BIS core principles for systemically important payment systems (BIS, 2001).

tional costs to monitor and enforce these rules for all payment service providers, it is for the reasons of fair competition that rules on mitigating anti-money-laundering and operational risks must apply equally to all payment service providers. Finally, payment service providers are obliged to ensure sufficient protection of consumer funds when executing payments against a deposit instead of a credit line. In this regard, payment service providers must be incentivized to refrain from risky or illiquid investments or to register as credit institution, which would allow them to receive deposits or other repayable funds from the public and to grant credits for their own account.[100] In return, the regulatory status of a credit institution obligates payment service providers to fulfill solvency criteria, requirements for participation in deposit insurance schemes, risk management standards, etc., to mitigate the risk involved in their business.

However, unlike high-value, interbank payment settlement systems where systemic risk of sudden liquidity and solvency problems and resulting *domino effects* on netting systems and the financial industry is inherent, retail payments are less crucial for economic stability. As explained earlier, the low value per transaction and uncritical settlement times of retail payments is not system critical and, therefore, regulatory intervention is not required.

4.4 Incentive and coordination problems

As learned from the theoretical discussion in Chapter B, a firm's production and investment decisions in the upstream and downstream parts of the industry are interdependent with not only general economic conditions (e.g., the macroeconomic environment or the legal system), but also with the actions of other firms, regulation, infrastructure and other public goods. The problem in the payment services industry is that due to economies of scale, network effects, externalities and other problems of club-like goods, the provision of these inputs and services is plagued with market outcome (Rodriguez-Clare, 2005, p. 5). According to Rosenstein-Rodan (1943), the investment of one firm could have a positive effect on the profitability of investment by other firms. Murphy, Shleifer and Vishny (1989) further showed that higher investment gives rise to an increase in aggregated demand, which, under economies of scale, increases the profitability of investment elsewhere in the economy, often giving rise to a multiplicity of equilibria, a low- and a high-investment equilibrium. Although all stakeholders would benefit from the high-investment equilibrium, there is no market force that would take the economy from the low- to the high-investment equilibrium. In this regard, the theoretical framework concluded that some kind of coordination is necessary to facilitate or complement the move from a bad equilibrium of

100 See: Directive EU Directive 2000/12/EC of the European Parliament and the Council of the European Union (2000).

a coordination failure to a good equilibrium. The theory of coordination failure recommends governments to resolve these coordination problems with incentive setting if market forces are held up from providing an optimal resource allocation. According to Rodrik (1996, p. 2), the necessary conditions prevailing for coordination failure are (i) the existence of some scale economies and (ii) imperfect tradability across national borders of some of the goods or services. The questions of whether coordination failure can be diagnosed and whether government policy is able to facilitate or complement private-sector coordination using private-sector institutions to promote the integration of European retail payment markets are examined in this section.

Critical mass and economies of scale in the payment industry

The assessment of network economies conducted in the preceding section implied already that a critical mass of a payment instruments is needed to utilize economies of scale. While it was concluded that they might cause some kind of market failure, economies of scale can also lead to coordination failure.

First, the critical mass plays a crucial role in the start-up and growth of a network. On the supply-side, for banks or payment system providers to invest, it is necessary that they believe a critical mass of other firms will also invest simultaneously. The critical mass is then defined as the smallest number of users necessary such that investing is the only (equilibrium) strategy for all other firms (Economides, 1996). A bank will only invest in a new, more efficient payment system if the bank expects to recover its losses, which can only occur when enough customers are attracted to validate the existence of a new system. On the demand-side, consumers are not interested in purchasing a payment product or becoming a member of a new network because the installed base is too small, and the installed base is too small because an insufficiently small number of consumers have purchased the good (Bonello et al., 2006, p. 68). These start-up problems are often referred to as the chicken-and-egg or catch-22 problem (Osterberg & Thomson, 1998). Accordingly, the potential problem for the payment system development is that a new, more efficient payment system may not attract enough customers to validate its existence.

Second, the existing literature often argued that payment systems are subject to economies of scale because significant investment in infrastructure is required to initiate the operation (large fixed costs) and a relatively small marginal cost for services produced incurred over the existing infrastructure.[101] As in the case of traditional industries, the presence of economies of scale in the production supports the existence of large production units. Hence, this argument is of rele-

101 Most famous in this context are the works of Kemppainen (2004a; 2004b; 2005), McAndrews and Rob (1996), McAndrews (1997), and McAndrews and Strahan (2002).

vance for electronic credit transfers processed by banks or payment service providers where a sufficiently large volume of payments is a prerequisite for the establishment of an automated clearing house.

The problem with this view is that payment systems are already operating scale-efficiently in most member states, benefiting from a high degree of specialization. While this indicates that a production equilibrium exists with the existing domestic infrastructure in individual countries, this may not be the case anymore on a European level and cross-border payments.

With regard to the second necessary condition for coordination failure to exist, the nontradability of services, one can argue that payment infrastructure is a nontradable good. According to Murphy, Shleifer and Vishny (1989), there are two types of market failure related to investments in infrastructure in general that could be applied to the situation of cross-border payment in particular. First, they refer to the classic problem of the monopolist that introduces a good to the economy but cannot appropriate the entire consumer and producer surplus generated. This would imply that although being optimal from a welfare point of view to introduce the good – or in the case of cross-border payments to develop appropriate instruments – banks or payment service providers do not make adequate profits to compensate the initial investment and fixed costs. As evidenced earlier, the low volume of cross-border payments in the euro area reflecting the marginal end-consumer demand and regulatory obstacles has not justified the development of large-scale pan-European payment systems until 2003. Second, it can be assumed that once the infrastructure project (i.e., the cross-border payment system) is built, there will be multiple equilibriums: a bad equilibrium characterized by low demand for the new pan-European payment system and a good equilibrium with a high demand for the infrastructure project. Some conditions (for example the inability of overcoming artificial barriers to integration in terms of providing a harmonized legal framework) would generate negative profits from undertaking any investments in such a system if the bad equilibrium prevails, and positive if otherwise. From a bank's or payment provider's perspective, a cautious approach would be to choose not to invest, although it would be macro-economically optimal for the investment to take place. Hence, coordination through government policy or incentive setting would be beneficial to take the economy to the good equilibrium.

This assessment shows that coordination failure happens in the case of the European retail payment sector. While economies of scale in production of payment services foster industry's willingness for cooperation (common standards, joint network ownership) in providing these services, heavy investments in infrastructure are necessary, and the outlook to increase aggregate demand and making such investments profitable is uncertain and subject to conditions not controllable by free markets.

The experience curve[102] in Figure 19 illustrates the relationship between cross-border payment volume and average processing unit costs as result of the combined effect of specialization, investment and scale. Scale effects lead to decreasing processing unit costs with a growth of transaction volume. The current state of the market is reflected in curve I_0. Besides the severe margin squeeze charactering the payment industry (see section 0 for the profitability of payment services), banks and payment service providers face significant investment needs to remain competitive in the payment business. Irrespective of the current single market development for financial services, European banks are expected to invest significantly in voluntary projects to achieve greater efficiency. Examples include improved reporting standards, implementation of electronic billing and invoicing solutions, new technologies such as mobile payments, back office investments to provide higher levels of standardization and the consolidation and decommissioning of legacy systems (Viner, Rutsstein, Storz, & Sarma, 2004, p. 25). Because of these investments (reflected by the scale curve I_1) unit costs for payment transactions will increase on average assuming constant transaction volume. Hence, if banks want to maintain their current profitability levels in terms of average processing unit costs, they will therefore have to either increase volume or improve efficiency to return to their original production equilibrium.[103]

102 Developed by Bruce Henderson of the Boston Consulting Group (BCG) in the late 1960s, the experience curve is a measure of the potential effect of specialization and investment (Stern & Deimler, 2006). The curve states that the more often the production of any good or service task is performed; the lower will be the cost of doing it. Each time cumulative volume doubles, unit costs decrease by a constant and predictable percentage.

103 Viner et al. (2004) estimated that these investments would increase unit costs by about 10 percent per year on average. Consequently, European banks would have to increase their absolute payments volumes by 40-45% (compared to realistically projected growth rates of 6-9%) and improve efficiency by 10% per year (compared to traditional net efficiency improvements of 1.5-3.5% per year).

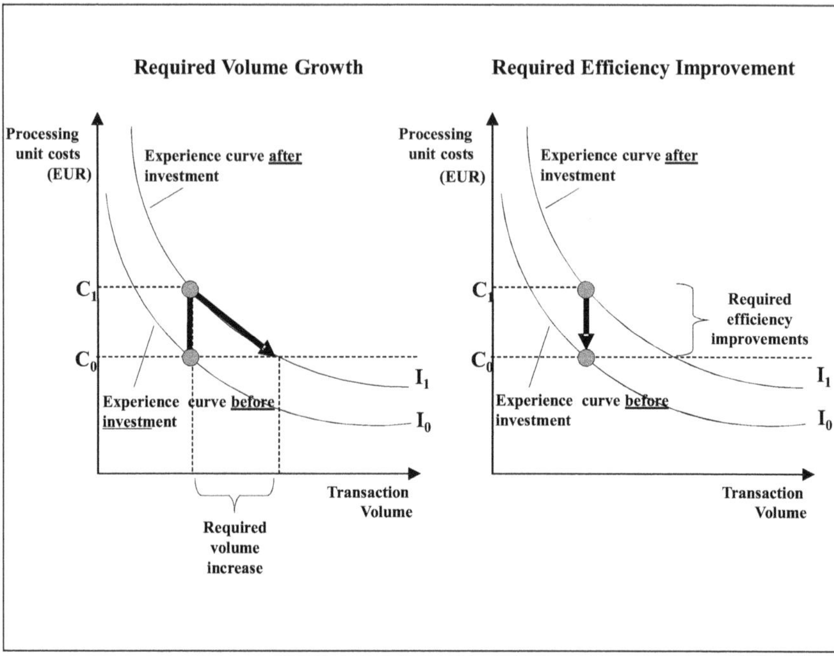

Figure 19: Offsetting SEPA investments by volume growth and efficiency
Source: Viner et al. (2004).

Nonexcludability and specialization

Coordination failure usually exists in a model with a multiplicity of equilibria, where one equilibrium Pareto-dominates the others (Rodriguez-Clare, 2005, p. 6). Hence, if the European retail payment market fails to coordinate expectations to achieve the best equilibrium, one may argue that it suffers from a coordination failure (ibid.). However, coordination failure may also exist in cases where there are no multiple equilibria, for example when banks provide activities that are never profitable. For banks, for example, retail payments are not profitable on a stand-alone basis and are often subsidized by other account-related products sold as bundles to end-consumers. In this context, literature traditionally refers to the nonexcludability characteristic of public goods, which traditionally is given as a justification for coordination action by government. However, the previous discussion on the public goods aspects of payment systems concluded that they are club goods rather than public goods, as they are non-rival but excludable (compared to public goods that are non-rival and nonexludable). With payment system being a club good, the benefits and the costs of providing these services are accrued to and allocated among those who make use of the system.

Hence, this clearly shows that there is a market equilibrium that does not require governmental coordination actions.

Considering the explanatory power of TCE, the provision of payment services is determined by the level of transaction costs. Lower transaction costs mean greater specialization and higher level of economies of scale. While both specialization and economies of scale have reached their natural limits on a national level where transaction costs are already low, with a European payment market emerging, the payment industry can expand into a new market where there is room for further specialization among banks and payment service providers on the European level, which will lead to higher productivity in the overall industry. Besides the heterogeneity of individual market regarding payment instrument preferences and standards, the most important precondition for this development is again the elimination of regulatory barriers, which artificially keep transaction costs high for retail banking activities on a pan-European level.

Table 22 summarizes the result of the key decision-making assessment:

Table 22: Summary of theoretical assessment

Type of barrier	Barrier to integration	Detriment	Applicability of key decision factor: Market failure	Government failure	Risk	Incentive and coordination problem
Supply-side	*Lack of commercial interest*	High investment and operating costs Low transaction volume of cross-border payments Fee revenue deterioration	• Existence of network externalities • Competition problems of standard setting on a European level • Payment systems for club goods rather than public goods • High market concentration on national levels • Potential entry barriers for new networks	• High efficiency levels in domestic payment systems are seen alongside inefficient or non-existent cross-border systems • Potential threat of regulatory capture by interest group	• Safe and efficient retail payment systems and instruments are in the public and bank interest • Systemic risk threatening the stability and effectiveness of the financial system • Lower risk criticality level for retail payment systems than in interbank clearing and settlement systems	• Critical mass crucial to achieve to start up and grow a cross-border retail payment network (*chicken-and-egg* problem immanent) • Cautious investors are reluctant to setup a system where the likelihood of failing to attract necessary transaction volume to operate profitably is high
	Payment network competition issues	Ownership structures Exclusion from membership Fees and fee structure				
	Lack of open and common standards	Lack of cross-border standards enabling interoperability				
Demand-side	*Information asymmetries*	Reduced / sub optimal choice and higher costs related to product offering and transaction costs	• Inability of consumers to obtain and process required information to assess quality of a product • Complexity induced product intransparency • Intransparent product pricing and bundling structures • Path dependency on national preferences	• Potential threat of regulatory capture by consumer interest group	• Increased risk of fraud (i.e., money laundering)	• The existence of regulatory, artificial obstacles increases transaction costs
	Price-inelastic behavior	Low level of mobility and high switching costs				
	Interdependence of demand	Higher prices from suppliers' market power Reduced choice				
	Historical payment habits	Reduced choice				
Artificial	*Consumer protection rules*	Reduced choice Lack of cross-country comparability	N/A	• Highly regulated national legal frameworks with divergent consumer protection and civil laws • Transposition issues • Potential threat of regulatory capture by national, euro-skeptic authority interest group	N/A	• The existence of regulatory, artificial obstacles increase transaction costs, and lower the likelihood of specialization and economies of scale to develop on a European cross-border level
	Disproportionate legal requirements	Higher transaction costs for banks and consumers				
	Political reluctance on national levels	Financial exclusion				

Source: Author's illustration

4.5 Conclusion

This section has analyzed the barriers to integration of the European retail banking market by means of the key decision factors derived from both the theoretical framework and traditional banking regulation. The economic theories on market, government and coordination failure applied in this chapter have provided relevant evaluation criteria to examine the economic and regulatory detriments and the role of regulation from different argumentative angles. A high degree of cooperation, network externalities, information asymmetries, a low price elasticity of demand and fragmented markets throughout Europe have been investigated with regard to potential competition concerns and consumer harms in view of market integration. It is quite evident that certain common forms of market behavior may fail to produce efficient outcomes in the market and impede integration with these features. The lack of cooperation on the exploitation of network externalities, common standards or joint network makes this point. However, it is not clear why market organizations like banks, payment service providers and end-consumers and their behavior cannot adapt to a form that yields efficient outcomes without regulatory intervention. The cooperative characteristic of payment services, which has been working well on the national levels, reflects the reasonable doubt of regulation being able to produce a better outcome than the institutions of the market on the pan-European level. In addition, as network externalities are contained within the group of market participants that purchase network services, the analysis provides reasons to believe that appropriate market organizations can adequately allocate these services. Similarly, the club's good characteristic of payment systems, non-rival but excludable, are more conducive to private arrangements. The non-rivalry underlines the cooperative characteristic of the network, for example, in terms of standard setting for the single European market. Excludability allows the owners of the network to determine the intended set of buyers and price access to payment services. Hence, these characteristics by themselves do not imply a necessary role for public regulation. Concerning the risk of entry barriers resulting from market structures and conduct of participants, one has to distinguish between regulatory and behavior barriers. Whereas the latter are the result of inherent economies of scale of payment system networks, access to these networks may also be hindered by means of artificial barriers, such as regulatory provisions or legal restrictions on the forms of contracts into which private parties may enter. These impediments to the adaptation of market participants and their behavior may lead to pricing rules that cannot support an efficient network. If there are restrictions on a network owner's ability to offer general, discriminating pricing arrangements, payment networks may be too small to fully take advantage of network externalities, failing to achieve a critical mass necessary to operate profitably. If such legal restriction, in particular on the national level, could not be removed, then it could, theoretically, be possible for regulatory intervention on the EU level to improve the performance of the industry (Weinberg, 1996). One further qualification to this argument arises if there are impediments to market integration in the form of frictions that limit the speed with which market participants might take advantage of profit opportunities. This may be the case if the benefits of a large pan-European network lead to a concentrated industry and the existence of legal or technological entry barriers. In this respect, the payment market may be subject to the exploitation of market power by incumbent payment network owners, where the monitoring of such market power would be the inherent activity of the ECB or European competition authorities.

With regard to information asymmetries between the suppliers of payment services and end-consumers for cross-border euro payments, market inefficiencies exist on both the provision of relevant information to assess the quality for a cross-border payment transaction and the high level of intransparency on the pricing of payment services. Payment services are often treated as loss leaders as part of a banking service package and are offered free or underpriced through cross-border subsidization with other account-related services. This aspect is of special relevance, because direct pricing, which has been gaining popularity in recent years, may be used to influence end-consumers' choice to use the most efficient payment instruments (D. Humphrey, Moshe, & Vale, 2001; Kemppainen, 2004a). While regulatory intervention to force banks and service providers to disclose relevant information on cross-border payments may be desired from an end-consumer point of view, it remains questionable that ex-ante transparency by itself would facilitate the creation of further demand for these services. The problem of incomparability of payment services on a cross-border level is mainly attributed to national legal differences and contract law. Furthermore, language barriers and the limited number of European citizens that actually make cross-border payments on a regular basis and are thus interested in the provision of relevant information will continue to make a cross-border product comparison difficult. On the contrary, legal provisions to provide transparency on pricing may, in fact, not necessarily spur demand, but may signal the actual costs of payment processing to the market, resulting in better comparability and competition. Hence, information asymmetries of retail cross-border payments are an important market inefficiency that regulation may cure.

Regarding the assessment of government failure, the high degree of national regulation and the threat of regulatory capture by interest groups on the European level have raised and stabilized artificial barriers to integration, on both the supply and the demand-sides of the payment market. As pointed out in the analysis of traditional banking regulation, due to the importance of the banking industry for the stability and efficiency of the economy, it is one of the most regulated industries in general. Considering the existence of 27 legal systems in the

EU, most aforementioned problems of attested market failure are directly or indirectly linked to the national regulatory framework in which payment systems have historically developed. Most of these national payment systems operate highly efficiently and all market participants, national central banks, commercial banks, payment service providers and end-consumers have arranged themselves within this framework. In an emerging single market, these self-contained regulatory systems now cause problems on a cross-border transaction basis with consumer protection rules, legal requirements for foreign firms to fulfill if intending to engage in cross-border trade, or banks and payment service providers to entering foreign markets. Given the low volume of demand for cross-border services and the significant changes required for the business model of retail banks to offer these services efficiently, whose principle markets are municipal, regional or national, the resistance of respective interest groups on the supply-side articulated in the lobbying of EU organizations present further artificial barriers to integration. Hence, unless these obstacles and the political reluctance on national levels shift responsibilities of law making to the European level, the markets on their own will not be able to advance payment market integration.

The preceding detailed analysis on coordination failure and incentive misalignment evidenced that the integration of payment market in Europe is subject to hold-up or *chicken-and-egg* problems. This implies that as long as the supply-side of the payment market expects an investment in a pan-European payment network not to pay off due to the lack of critical mass of payment volume to achieve economies of scale, there will be no market-driven initiative. This market inefficiency could then be corrected by the catalytic effect of regulatory intervention that would set incentives for markets to develop a European standard and payment system. Due to the large investments required, authorities could, for example, reward first movers with cost-re-imbursements or subsidies. However, the correction of coordination failure requires the removal of regulatory and artificial obstacles first, which hinder transaction costs to decrease and suppliers of payment services to invest in setting up cross-border retail systems.

Finally, regarding the risk aspect in cross-border payment systems, from the public authorities' point of view, a smooth operation of financial markets is necessary to maximize social welfare. Payment systems have to be both safe and efficient: the safety requirement to mitigate systemic risk of payment systems must be fulfilled first, and only thereafter the efficiency requirement steps in. Accordingly, the safety aspect for retail payment systems is well recognized; however, as the present analysis focuses on the obstacles to integration and as any incumbent or new payment system is subject to control by the ESCB, this analysis assumes that safety requirements are fulfilled.

In summary, the theoretical assessment of different kinds of failure and the market characteristics of retail payments, as well as significant country differences do not permit easy policy implementation. While payment systems bear an analogy to network industries, the provision of payment services has many special characteristics where the application of regulatory tools used in many other network industries cannot be applied directly. However, when comparing findings from the four decision factors, supply-side barriers to integration are subject to a tense relationship of cooperation and competition. According to Kemppainen (2004a, p. 56), cooperation is desired to achieve compatibility as the key requirement for payment system efficiency to make the payment system market in Europe contestable, leading to increased competition, and as a further consequence, enhanced choice and lower transaction costs on the demand-side (the so-called *competition-cooperation-nexus*). Regulation constitutes the third element in this trilemma. The interaction of these three elements characterizing European cross-border retail payment systems is important to understand in order to derive policy recommendations, which could not be drawn from lessons in other industries.

First, the network nature of payment systems has strong effects on cooperation. Banks and service providers need to cooperate to establish standards and infrastructures in order to have a customer base that is large enough to facilitate the creation of economies of scale and to avoid overlapping investments and unnecessary duplication of networks. End-consumers benefit from this cooperation through improved access and destination points in the system. Hence, a certain degree of cooperation among operators in the provision of payment services is highly desirable or even prerequisite if the system is to function efficiently. Moreover, the compatibility of competing systems, or at least the existence of common standards, can also contribute to the efficiency in retail payment markets (Kemppainen, 2004b, p. 27).

Second, competition between payment service providers on services or infrastructures may lead to both, benefits for consumers and increases in efficiency in the market as whole. However, such benefits may only evolve if potential competition concerns are effectively resolved by European competition policy. The analysis of market failures identified the potential risks of coordinated behavior regarding pricing of standardized products such as credit transfers, non-price conditions, raising or stabilizing market entry barriers through access conditions, or fee structures. This behavior further determines the level of information asymmetry for end-consumers, who are then unable to assess the price of certain products (in particular those tied to product bundles).

Regulation is the third element characterizing payment service network, both with regard to representing a major barrier to integration and also being the means to overcome these barriers and to provide a level playing field for payment system competition, under which safety and efficiency are ensured and innovation incentives to develop new products and services are not hindered (Kemppainen, 2004a, p. 45).

Based on these assessments of this chapter, potential regulatory tools are developed that may be applied to correct the issues raised earlier. Furthermore, the role of regulators in retail payment systems is elaborated.

5. Potential improvements through regulation

The previous chapter analyzed the economic (demand- and supply-side) and artificial barriers to integration by applying the key decision-making factors that determine the source of detrimental market outcome. Based on the framework of regulation theory and the assessment of market failure, government failure, risks and coordination failure, this section will derive implications for regulatory policy and tools.

There are several general policy implications that can be drawn from the presented evidence and applied to the case of payment service market integration by means of regulatory tools. In general, it is important that EU regulators take into account the natural limits to the integration of the retail payment market in order to avoid counterproductive over-harmonization, which may cause damage to the efficiently working national markets (Barros et al., 2005). Having said that, the next steps with the highest priority for EU policy makers are to reduce artificial and political barriers to entry and thus to integration first. Second, a balance between competition and cooperation in payment networks needs to be allowed by EU competition law. In the following, areas where competition can improve detrimental market outcome and facilitate market integration will be elaborated further.

5.1 Removal of regulatory obstacles

According to the Treaty Establishing the European Community (European Community, 1957, Article 4), the single market for payments will be an important element of the internal market for goods and services. Hence, any industry or legislative action must be based on the principle of an *open market economy with free competition* as stipulated in the treaty. Furthermore, legislation must be in line with the principles of market economy and balance the provision of legal certainty and leaving decisions up to citizens and companies as much as possible so that innovation and development can evolve. Only fair competition and a level playing field enable market selection mechanisms to function so that the best service providers prevail at the expense of less efficient providers. Hence, any regulation regarding payment services must apply to all payment service providers in Europe according to the principle of "same risks, same regulation" (Mai, 2005, p. 4).

While a lot of legislative action towards the creation of a single market for financial services in the EU has concentrated on the wholesale markets, the legal harmonization of the fragmented retail banking market and abolishing artificial competitive distortions in retail markets should be one of the EC's main priorities for the next years. Critics to retail market integration often argue that regulatory action to facilitate the creation of a single market is undesirable for two reasons: first, no significant level of retail cross-border business can be expected, and second, further regulatory intervention may only create costs rather than any tangible benefits to suppliers and end-consumers of payment systems (Diekmann, 2006, p. 6). Still, these opponents disregard that market liberalization is about the creation of trade opportunities rather than trade itself and that even the threat of new market entrants may already raise the level of effective competition and in the same way lower the prices. Accordingly, market liberalization must not be made dependent upon forecasted trade volumes but must instead create the scope of market participants to exploit market opportunities (ibid.).

Deriving from the theoretical assessment of the key decision-making factors, the main regulatory or artificial objectives are consumer protection rules and legal requirements for banks and service providers. Their removal or at least a harmonization on a European level should be approached first.

5.1.1 Consumer protection

While there is always the threat that EU regulation may become *too* consumer focused, incoherent or counterproductive, there is a clear need for having a targeted harmonization of key aspects of consumer protection for payments that will ensure client confidence on the one hand, reflected in the daily transactions of consumers, and at the same time, allow the profitable exploitation of the emerging potential of cross-border business in Europe. Hence, harmonization on a pan-European level of the different member state consumer protection laws should primarily enable consumers in the euro area to enjoy noticeable advantages in terms of product quality (including transparency), pricing and greater variety. To this end, simple consumer protection rules are needed that will facilitate the creation of a single market where consumers do not experience any more difference between a national and a cross-border payment.

In order to reduce fragmentation of legal frameworks for consumers and the resulting loss of welfare, the following regulatory interventions on the EU level would be necessary to remove these severe detriments to payment market integration, covering in particular credit transfers and direct debits.

(i) Harmonization of rights and obligations of payment users and providers with respect to execution timeframes, fees and valued dating.
(ii) Mandatory information requirements: retail clients need to be informed ex-ante on pricing and conditions of payment services and ex-post about the transaction details, such as the amount, fees, exchange rate and the date to receipt of the payment order.

5.1.2 Legal requirements for payment service providers

Other legal barriers towards the establishment of a single payments area are composed of market access requirements for non-bank payment providers, conflicting legal provisions on both the national and the EU and differing core legal provisions. The most critical points that need to be addressed by regulation to provide consistent rules for all payment service providers in the EU are outlined in the following.

(i) Harmonization of legal definitions. A legal framework underlying the retail cross-border payment market requires a clear legal definition of the geographic and currency scope (all EU or EMU countries only), the scope of payments instruments, the distinction between corporate clients and end-consumers and the definition of the payment service provider (only banks or also non-banks).
(ii) Harmonization of liability. Credit transfers are financial transactions with obligations on both parties and an inherent risk of fault that needs to be regulated through a legal contract. The exact level of liability between a payment service provider and a payment service user differs across member' states and thus needs to be harmonized to reduce information asymmetries on both sides.
(iii) Harmonize balance of payments reporting. National legislators traditionally obligate banks to report the cross-border payments of their clients that exceed a certain amount to the national central banks. These reporting requirements had the objective to collect data for the national balance of payment statistics and mainly created cost to banks, also increasing prices for cross-border payments. As these reporting duties differ from one member state to another in the EU, it is important that this reporting hurdle is either removed or chosen high enough to exclude retail payments.

Ultimately, as national differences in contract law, consumer and data protection and taxation play a greater role in retail than in wholesale banking, these will have to be tackled head-on in the broader context of retail banking integration. Whereas gradual full harmonization in the payment area would be best, these other legal detriments may require also, on a case-by-case basis, an intelligent mixture of minimum harmonization and mutual recognition to set retail market integration in motion. Full harmonization, followed by a uniform body of contractual law culminating in a body that does not complement but replaces national legal provisions.[104]

104 The establishment of a common framework for contract and private with shared rules on the European level is disregarded for the scope of this analysis.

All in all, the European commission must take ownership in harmonizing the fragmented legal landscape in the field of payments in order to facilitate the single market development. In this respect, a legal framework is required that consistently replaces the current ruling in each member state. While undertaking the legal harmonization through regulatory intervention would be an inherent responsibility of European law-makers, such a top-down method is likely to encounter political resistance from the member states. However, if a single market for retail payment services in particular and retail banking services in general should be achieved, a consequent downloading and transposition of harmonization policy from the EU to the national level (and consistent transposition and enforcement) is required.

5.2 Competition and cooperation

Regulation should promote competition and prevent market abuse as well as account for the particular network characteristics and resulting cooperation requirements in the payment industry. Joint ventures and shared ownership are inherently important in payment networks, as they help to achieve the critical mass required to establish the network and to utilize the potential economies of scale in production. In this regard, banks' costs of a network decrease with any additional participant joining the network, and the related transaction volume increase allows for a better utilization of economies of scale in production. While these arguments would support the existence of joint ventures and shared networks without any significant regulatory intervention, the case of retail payment systems is, in practice, more complicated than this simplified description. According to McAndrews and Rob (1996), as payment service providers have an inherent incentive to cooperate in order to establish an efficient payment network, the problem of monopoly pricing in such form of ownership and the resulting potential danger of abusing market powers is clearly present and complicates the decision-making of regulatory authorities significantly. On the other hand, if regulators aim at limiting cooperation by, for example, limiting the size of a network in order to eliminate market abuse, positive network externalities related to efficiency gains cannot be exploited (i.e., compatibility or common standards). Hence regulatory decision-making on joint ventures depends on the preference of EU regulatory authorities to facilitate either intersystem cooperation (competition *for* the market) or intrasystem cooperation (competition *in* the market) (Kemppainen, 2004a, p. 42). Whereas the goal of antitrust legislation is to maximize the benefits society obtained from competition, the fact that in payment system networks competing firms must cooperate to provide the service renders a simple policy recommendation inadequate (Carlton & Frankel, 1995, p. 53). The EU competition law reflects well this ambivalence between cooperation and competition in payment networks and provides policy guidelines that have been summarized by Vesala (2000) as follows:

(i) Competition law distinguishes between interbank and bank-client relationships and tolerates cooperation in the former as long as no adverse impact on the bank-client relationship is assessed.
(ii) The EC regards attempts to block entry to shared payment networks and to protect participants from outside competition as violations of the EU antitrust law.
(iii) Discriminatory entry conditions, such as the excessive entry charges and unit compensations for the services provided by the host network that exceed the cost of operating the network also violate antitrust rules, even if the system were open.

In conclusion, due to the potential economies of scale and increased cost efficiency of joint payment network systems, EU authorities should be tolerating such ownership structures if the development of cross-border payment networks is desired. On the other hand, regulation is necessary to ensure that "fair and open" access to systems is granted to potential participants (CEPS, 1994). However, the principal problem in this regard refers to two basic questions of definition. First, how is "fair and open" access defined, and second, who are the relevant authorities that will determine regulatory intervention (i.e., competition authorities as general competition regulators or central banks), as overseers of payment systems in Europe? This second question is similar to the question raised in the discussion in the field of banking stability extensively analyzed in Chapter C, where the relative roles of competition and supervisory authorities in the EU is discussed. While some countries give a stronger role to prudential supervisors than to competition authorities, other member states take the opposite approach. Based on the above, one can conclude that a wide variety of approaches exists in the EU member states, and the roles of central banks and competition authorities are not yet fully defined for the field of payment systems. However, their goal is the same, which is increasing efficiency by ensuring a level playing field and contestable markets (Kemppainen, 2004a, p. 50).

As far as the potential role of regulators and EU authorities in facilitating the development of a single market for payments is concerned, much progress in the development of geographically integrated large-value payment systems has been made in the last decade, which was in particular attributed to the operational involvement of central banks. Among others, the development was largely driven by arguments of safeguarding the transmission channel of monetary policy, limiting systemic risk and facilitating the integration of financial markets in the EU (European Central Bank, 2001a). Unlike in large-value payment systems, retail cross-border payment systems have made little progress in developing an efficient infrastructure in the EU. As extensively surveyed in the previous chapters, the reasons for this are multifaceted, and various obstacles on the supply and on the demand-sides of the market have been identified.

The phenomenon of coordination failure and network externalities in retail payment markets is reflected in the chicken-and-egg problem, where the interdependence of demand for cross-border payment services and the expectation of the supply-side to achieve the critical mass required to pay off initial investment cost and achieve economies of scale to operate a payment network profitably remains the most important obstacle to market integration. According to the theory of coordination failure, there are two potential scenarios possible to correct this market inefficiency, in which regulators need to take certain actions.

First, assuming that regulatory obstacles are removed in a first instance, a market-driven integration process would develop by itself. The regulatory prerequisite here would be to tolerate the formation of joint ventures and shared networks, and at the same time, ensure a level playing field and contestable markets by different antitrust measures such as monitoring discriminating access conditions or pricing. In such a scenario, banks would compete with their products in the entire euro area for retail clients, irrespective of the geographic location of both the bank and the end-consumer. Those banks with the most innovative or best-priced product offering would succeed in the market, crowding out inefficient competitors and their products.

In a second scenario, regulatory obstacles in terms of harmonized consumer protection and legal requirements for payment service providers remain or are abolished rather gradually, making a market-driven process difficult. In this case, EU authorities can correct this market inefficiency in different ways and with different regulatory intensity. First, regulators may promote competition by tolerating stronger cooperation of payment service providers (including mergers) and the creation of oligopolistic market structures in the field of euro cross-border payments and by allowing for competing payment clubs. Second, EU authorities incentivize first movers in the industry who decide to make the initial investment in a cross-border retail payment network. These investment incentives may be composed of financial subsidies such as bearing a portion of the investment costs or tax advantages. Third, provided that expert knowledge and input legitimacy exists on the regulators' level (i.e., the central banks), authorities can act as a catalyst or facilitator for an efficient development. Similar to the development of infrastructure and standards for large-value payment systems in the EU, public authorities may participate in the design and enforcement of standards in the European banking industry, mediating between differing interests of member states and bank associations. Fourth, as a stronger regulatory intervention, authorities may draw on a specific ruling to consciously produce a favorable market development. The EU regulation on cross-border payments, for example, was such a measure that was imposed on the banking industry to oblige them to reduce prices. Finally, public authorities may become operationally involved in the integration process by establishing their own payment systems to provide cross-border retail payment services. Such a measure may only come into consideration if authorities deem the market incapable of establishing reliable and efficient payment systems.[105] However, the above findings show that from a market economic perspective, the fact that cross-border retail payment networks are club goods rather than public goods, no universal service obligation can be derived as a supporting argument for the operational involvement of public authorities without further ado.

The adequate role of regulators in retail payment systems has also been under discussion among the relevant European authorities. The BIS (2000) and the ECB (2001b), for example, do not see the necessity for becoming operationally active and tend to rely more on indirect ways to improve efficiency in the field of retail payment systems in Europe. They prefer not to intervene operationally or through regulation and to leave the design and development process to the banking industry, which has the best practical, technical and market knowledge of the field. Instead, and this has also been derived in this chapter, they see the main task for the regulator to provide a level playing field and a harmonized legal framework.

In summary, this assessment concluded that given the ambivalence of cooperation and competition prevailing in the European payment network and the necessity of regulators to intervene in a certain way to remove artificial barriers to integration and to overcome coordination failure, it is of great importance that authorities act as promoters and facilitators for a market-driven development of efficient cross-border payment systems. Their role should focus on the immediate harmonization of consumer protection laws and legal requirements for payment service providers. Creating such a supportive regulatory environment demands strict and disciplined downloading of harmonization policies and affects transposition in the respective EU member states. Given the significant lobbying from various interest groups on the EU level and the unpopular political nature of required legislative changes on the member state level, constraining further their decision- and law-making sovereignty, the midterm chances of success are relatively low. Other types of involvement, such as setting investment incentives for first movers to establish a pan-European payment infrastructure, are justifiable from an NIE perspective to overcome coordination failure. Stronger regulatory intervention, however, such as an involvement of authorities on the opera-

105 With regard to the management of clearing infrastructures by the National Central Banks, the European Central Bank recognized the problem of possible competition and published a policy statement regarding central banks' provision of retail payment services in euros to credit institutions in August 2005. This statement documented the importance of avoiding competitive distortions or crowding out of market initiatives when NCBs provide retail payment services to credit institutions (European Central Bank, 2003b).

tional level or the use of price regulation, is from a market efficiency and welfare point of view questionable and would need to be assessed on a case-by-case basis.

6. Regulatory intervention in the European retail payments market

One of the key components of the FSAP and the Lisbon Agenda in March 2000 was to create a single payments area in Europe, which would provide a level playing field for payments in the retail and commercial banking markets of Europe, including single infrastructures, charging and fee rates across Europe. A subordinate objective was to reduce bank costs, increase bank and corporate efficiency and eradicate wasteful country practices. Above all, it was a political objective to promote the benefits of a single currency and a single economic area to the citizens of Europe, especially to the large number of retail clients.

The historic starting position was extensively surveyed in the previous chapter. It was explained that the development of a single market in the retail payment system area cannot take place overnight and that harmonization efforts will remain constrained by natural barriers such as path dependencies and national payment habits. Furthermore, even though many national payment systems are already highly efficient, the fact that there was no well-functioning and efficient cross-border retail payment infrastructure was regarded as highly inefficient from a European economy and integration point of view. In particular, the high bank fees deducted from cross-border payments at that time were heavily criticized by consumer interest groups and drew EU politicians' attention to this subject, not least because members of the European parliament themselves have been mainly affected by these charges when transferring their money to their home country on a monthly basis. Despite numerous early attempts by the regulators (see for example European Central Bank, 1999, 2000; European Commission, 1990) to persuade the European banking industry to develop a cross-border payment infrastructure also for retail transactions, these early signs have been ignored by banks for a long time. Instead of taking ownership for the requirements at an early stage and making minor concessions in designing a concept with regulators and consumer interest groups, the industry remained relatively defensive, provoking a strong regulatory action and triggering the European Commission and Parliament to adopt regulation EC No. 2560/2001 on cross-border payments in euros (RPE) in December 2001. Later, the European Commission adopted the Payment Service Directive (PSD) as regulation 2007/64/EC to provide the necessary legal foundation to make a single market for euro payments possible, reinforcing the rights and protection of all users of payment service. Both directives and their objectives are presented in more detail below.

6.1 The cross-border payments regulation and the SEPA initiative

The "Regulation 2560/2001 on Cross-border payments in Euros" (in the following referred to as *RPE* or *Regulation 2560/2001*) came into force over a period of time, obliging banks to reduce charges for cross-border payments of up to EUR 12,500 as of 2003 and to EUR 50,000 as of 2006 to the level of those of corresponding domestic payments.[106] Furthermore, the regulation applies to card payments and cash withdrawals as from July 1, 2002, and to cross-border credit transfers as from July 1, 2003 (2006 for the higher threshold). The regulation also introduced major changes to bank systems, as it mandated that banks change national sort codes and account numbers to new standards, using International Bank Account Numbers (IBANs) and Bank Identification Codes (BICs). Hence, this regulation was heavily criticized by the payment service industry for not only dictating prices but also demanding radical changes in most banks' IT systems and operations to handle these new code structures. In view of these regulatory provisions, a bank response came out of a meeting in Brussels in April 2002, when 42 of the major European banks, along with representatives from the key bank associations, jointly discussed how to avoid losses from such intra-EU payments and how to implement the demands for the new standards and the EU the price regulation. First, they mandated that corporate customers' cross-border euro transactions must conform to IBAN and BIC data formats; otherwise punitive fees would be charged. Second, the Credeuro interbank transfer service scheme was created to manage the requirements of low-value credit transfer. Finally, the participants formed the European Payments Council (EPC) as a governing body to join forces and to guide the creation of the payment infrastructures to create the Single Euro Payments Area (SEPA) to make the euro-area payments similar to domestic ones (European Payment Council, 2002). The importance of the EPC is that they have created the critical frameworks and technical rulebooks to enable SEPA, due to economic and technical reasons, to transact in euro payments only. As a result, the EPC released two important rulebooks in 2007, the SEPA Credit Transfer (SCT) and the SEPA Direct Debit scheme. While the former replaces the Credeuro Convention of 2002 and enables payment service providers to offer a core credit transfer service for individual, bulk and repetitive payments as of January 2008, with no value limits or deductions from the payment principle and a maximum execution time of three days, the SDD scheme aims at replacing existing domestic direct debit scheme by 2010, offering a pan-European direct debit euro service (Skinner, 2008, pp. 7-8). Both the SCT and SDD scheme create infrastructure for pan-European

106 Regulation (EC) No 2560/2001 of the European Parliament and of the Council on 19 December 2001 on cross-border payments in euro.

clearing and settlement of credit transfers and direct debits and require the establishment of new systems and technologies. In addition, the EPC has also created schemes that address the harmonization of policies, processes and procedures around cards and cash: the SEPA Cards Framework (SCF) and the SEPA Euro Cash Area Framework (SECA).

Besides the harmonization of payment instruments, the EPC has also signaled the willingness of the payment service industry to also move forward the necessary harmonization of payment systems as much as possible driven by the market. According to the EPC (2002), legislation and regulation should only be used if harmonization cannot be achieved by market economic means. In this respect, the European banking sector has been advocating the establishment of a pan-European ACH as quickly as possible in order to facilitate the smooth adaptation of the RPE. Hence, the Euro Banking Association's STEP2 system was established to focus primarily upon retail cross-border bulk payments as classified by the RPE. Given the findings from the theory of coordination failure and the existence of network externalities, the viability of such a system requires a sufficient number of participants and of payments processed through it to reach the critical mass. As the volume of pure European cross-border payment transactions is estimated to be only 2% of Europe's total non-cash payments, the EPC was keen to rationalize and endorse the EBA STEP2 systems as the first real pan-European ACH that would be able to process also part of the national/domestic volume of retail payments in a highly automated and efficient way, provided that the new SEPA schemes, SCT and SDD have been implemented in the member states. Figure 20 shows the critical milestones for the SEPA project, with a SEPA launch in January 2008. This is seen as an interim step towards a real single market with the ultimate objective to replace national payment infrastructures after a period of co-existence. Originally, decommissioning of any non-SEPA compliant national scheme was envisaged for the end of 2010. However, this end date for a migration has been modified and postponed several times; hence, the critical mass for the new payment schemes, SCT and SDD, has not yet been reached.

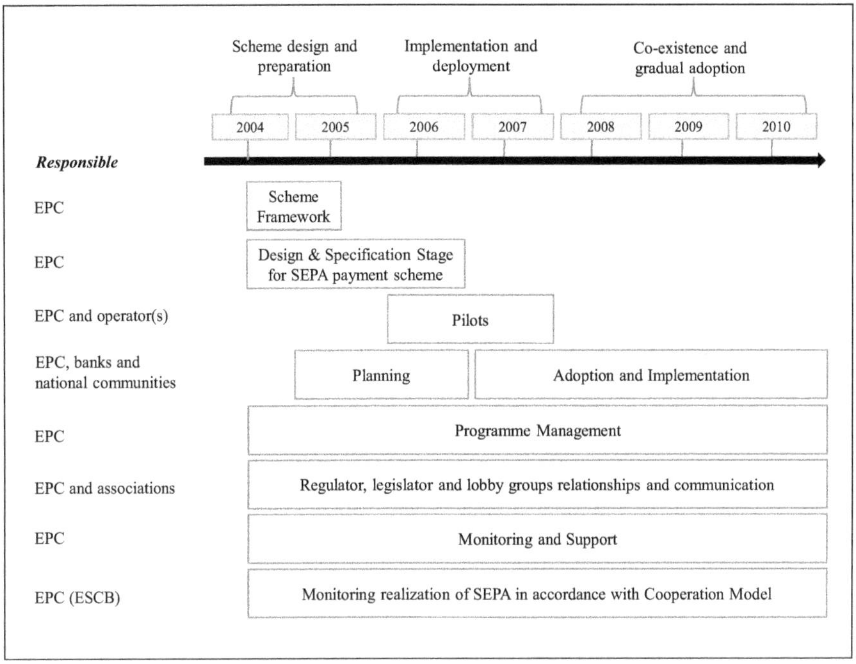

Figure 20: The SEPA timeline
Source: European Payments Council (2007, p. 12).

6.2 The Payment Services Directive

In a parallel development to the technical frameworks and rulebooks of SEPA, the European Commission has proposed a legal framework (initially called *New Legal Framework*, today referred to as the *PSD*) in order to harmonize the legal basis for the EU payment market. This legal framework is designed "to make cashless payments – such as card transactions, bank transfers and direct debits – simpler and cheaper, paving the way for a single Euro payment area,"[107] and stipulated the rights, obligations, liabilities and information requirements for payment service providers and end-consumers.

It was adopted in April 2007 as a result of a wide-ranging consultations period with all payment market participants after its first publication in December 2005. Although it was originally targeted for transposition in member state laws

107 Directive 2007/64/EC of the European Parliament and of the Council of 13 November 2007 on payment services in the internal market amending Directives 97/7/EC, 2002/65/EC, 2005/60/EC and 2006/48/EC and repealing Directive 97/5/EC Text with EEA relevance

by November 1, 2007, to enable a replacement of national retail clearing and settlement systems (see original timeframe of the SEPA initiative above), the Directive was finally transposed two years later, by November 1, 2009.[108]

However, the final text of the Directive agreed upon in 2007 was mainly a compromise between the European member states. There were major arguments over the details of the text, and over 600 amendments were submitted by key members of the European Parliament (MEPs) to the proposal of the Economic and Monetary Affairs committee (ECON). These amendments, mostly of a high level of technical detail, related to capital requirements for payment institutions, amendments to consumer protection and payment cycle time. According to Sharon Bowles (MEP, 2008), the controversial discussion related in particular to allowing a new category of market players – *payment institutions* – to compete with banks and their capital requirements. It divided the Parliament's political groups along national lines, reflecting the diametrically opposed political directions in the EU of free market economics and *principle-based regulation* of northern Europe and the *rule-based*, protectionist preference of the south of Europe. With regard to payments cycles, there was also a major divide over shortening the payments execution to the end of the next business day (D+1), followed by a continuous discussion on whether all countries would be able to evolve infrastructures from processing cycles of up to five days for certain products and instruments, in particular in the short time frames of five years.

Finally, the PSD attempts to harmonize consumer protection rights in the field of payment services and to introduce greater competition in the provision of these services in a single European market. Despite its focus on harmonization, the PSD also acknowledges the local dimension of retail payment services and allows member states to waive for 23 of the provisions of the European text (ESBG, 2009, p. 143). Having reflected the predominantly local dimension of retail banking in the Directive, EU legislators conceded that local customers continue to enjoy protection and convenience provided by local regulators. The transparency provided through PSD brings benefits to both local retail clients who have made the choice for a local provider and those who seek to make use of services outside of national borders.

All in all, the PSD seeks to strengthen competition in European payments markets by removing artificial, national barriers to market entry, allowing *passporting* of authorization in one member state to another and setting a legal framework applicable over the entire EU for new types of payment service providers (*payment institutions*), such as mobile phone operators (Sharon Bowles,

108 Although this Directive was supposed to be implemented in all 27 EU member state, in the Extended Economic Area (EEA), Iceland, Norway and Liechtenstein, and in Switzerland by November 1, 2009, only 14 out of the 32 countries have actually met that deadline.

2008, p. 67). Furthermore, the harmonized set of rules concerning the information requirements and the rights and obligations related to cross-border retail payments services is intended to facilitate cross-border transactions for both individual consumers and businesses. However, already during the elaboration phase of the PSD, significant concerns were articulated that the intended harmonization target would be missed due to translation, transposition and conflict of law issues. The following two tables summarize the structure and the scope of RPE, SEPA and PSD

Table 23: Comparison of Regulation 2560/2001, SEPA and PSD

Feature	Regulation 2560/2001	SEPA	PSD
Currency	Euro	Euro	All EU member state currencies
Legal nature	Regulation	Self-regulatory initiative	Directive
Geographical scope	Eurozone	EU, EEA and Switzerland	EU and EEA
Scope	Cross-border payments in euros	Domestic and cross-border payments in euros within the SEPA area	Intra-EU payment in member state currencies
Timing	July 2003 (for payments up to EUR 12,500), July 2006 (for payments up to EUR 50,000)	Various – starting with January 2008 for launch of SCT and initial SCF deliverables, November 2009 for SDD	By November 2009

Source: Author's illustration, adapted from Cap Gemini (2008).

Table 24: Proposed instruments to measure impact of the RPE and PSD

Type of barrier	Barrier to integration	Detriment	Addressed by RPE	Addressed by PSD	Measurement instrument
Supply-side	*Lack of commercial interest*	High investment and operating costs	Yes	No	• Total cost of compliance for the banking industry • Profitability development for payment services
		Low transaction volume of cross-border payments	Yes	No	• Change in volume of cross-border retail payments in euro
		Fee revenue deterioration	Yes	Yes	• Net margin development
	Payment network competition issues	Ownership structures	No	Yes	• Changes in market structure of pan-European ACHs • Consolidation in payment systems
		Exclusion from membership	No	Yes	• N/A
		Fees and fee structure	Yes	Yes	• N/A
	Lack of open and common standards	Lack of cross-border standards enabling interoperability	Yes	No	• Development of common schemes and standards
Demand-side	*Information asymmetries*	Reduced / Sub optimal choice and higher costs related to product offering and transaction costs	No	Yes	• Perceived level of transparency
	Price-inelastic behavior	Low level of mobility and high switching costs	No	Yes	• Consumer account mobility (churn)
	Interdependence of demand	Higher prices from suppliers' market power	Yes	Yes	• Consumer Price Indices development
		Reduced choice	Yes	Yes	
	Historical payment habits	Reduced choice	Yes	Yes	• Change of national payment habits
Artificial	*Consumer protection rules*	Reduced Choice	Yes	Yes	• Qualitative assessment
		Lack of cross-country comparability	Yes	Yes	• Qualitative assessment
	Disproportionate legal requirements	Higher transaction costs for banks and consumers	Yes	Yes	• Qualitative assessment
	Political reluctance on national levels	Financial exclusion	No	Yes	• Qualitative assessment • Number of countries transposing regulation on time

Source: Author's illustration

7. Measuring the improvements in market outcome through regulation

Following the logic of the conceptual model, and having defined the market outcomes that regulation may be improving, this section seeks to identify the measurements to assess the level of retail market integration achieved through the RPE and PSD. Both regulatory interventions aim to establish the principle of equality of charges for payments within member states (national) and between member states (cross-border) (European Commission, 2005g, p. 1). This principle comprises the non-discrimination between national and cross-border payments services in euro based on price and requirements on cross-border payment service providers. Being more of a rule than a principle-based approach, the impact of these regulations can be along the dimensions of efficiency and effectiveness, but also with regard to resulting market development over time. With regard to effectiveness, this section seeks to measure the extent to which barriers to retail payment market integration can be overcome. The efficiency measurement assesses the costs and benefits of these regulatory interventions in terms of welfare effects. Finally, given the limited amount of consistent data and information available throughout the member states, the current developments of the self-regulatory SEPA initiatives, triggered by the RPE, are included in the assessment. The following assessment is based on a comprehensive research on industry and academic impact studies and reports, and includes quantitative and qualitative indicators and analysis. Before the impact on each single barrier is examined, the next section provides an overview of recently published studies that seek to assess the potential costs and benefits that may arise with the creation of a SEPA over time and discusses the differences among the various methodologies proposed.

7.1 Supply-side barriers

The preceding analysis identified three main barriers to integration from a bank's perspective:

- lack of commercial interest;
- payment network competition issues; and
- the lack of common and open standards.

Thus, the impact of Regulation 2560/2001, SEPA and the PSD is assessed based on quantitative and qualitative data available.[109]

109 Most organizations that operate cross-border payment networks do not provide data on the joining, membership, transaction-based fees and other fees they charge to their members and other network participants. They stated that such information was com-

7.1.1 Lack of commercial interest

The lack of commercial interest for banks and payment service providers to invest in cross-border payment infrastructure, to achieve economies of scale and to compete in the entire European internal market for retail customers strongly correlates with the lack of demand arising from higher prices and lack of transparency. While the latter will be examined in the course of this chapter, the immediate effects of the price regulation on the development of cross-border payment volumes and prices and the mid-term effect on national prices are significant. Table 25 shows that before regulation RPE and SEPA, the profitability of payments (all domestic and cross-border) differed across European countries. Some countries, such as France, Italy and Spain make solid profits while most other EU countries, such as Poland, are break-even or make substantial loss.

Table 25: Total operating profit of payments in selected EU countries (2002)

Country	Total profit	Direct profit from fees	Interest-related profit
All amounts given in EUR bn			
Italy	3.9	1	2.9
France	2.1	-0.9	3
Spain	1.5	-0.7	2.2
Sweden	0.8	0.3	0.5
Belgium	0.2	-0.1	0.3
Germany	-0.1	-1.5	1.4
Netherlands	-0.1	-0.7	0.6
Poland	-0.7	-0.8	0.1

Source: Ploey et al. (2005, p. 3)

With the differences between countries, operating cost and revenue structures, the convergence forced by the price regulation will have an immediate and long-term effect on the profitability of this business.

Immediate effect of the RPE

The immediate effect is reflected in the required convergence of prices for cross-border payments in euro to the level of domestic payments and occurs with the payment regulation RPE coming into force in 2001 and 2003. Most multinational banks, who were already operating their payment business across European borders profitably (with average costs per cross-border transaction being below the price charged to end-consumers), experienced a significant loss of revenue from incident charges.[110] Other, mostly national or regional, banks that had a limited cross-border engagement of both their clients' and their own business

mercially sensitive and thus confidential to their members and potential new members (European Commission, 2005f, p. 16).

110 See the profit breakdown of the EU payment business illustrated in Figure 17.

activity were negatively impacted on their overall profitability. Their operating costs for cross-border payment transactions were much higher than those of multinational banks. The lack of a proper, efficient processing infrastructure for these kinds of payments and their dependence on other banks that were handling these transactions on their behalf leads to a negative profit margin per average cross-border transaction as a direct consequence of the payments directive.

In 2001, the EC mandated a survey on the costs, timing and information provision of retail-cross-border payments. The results of this transfer exercise confirmed that despite earlier regulatory appeals, charges for a transfer of EUR 100 within Europe amounted to approximately EUR 24 in average.[111] These results affirmed the judgment of EU regulators that without a price regulation only little progress in the harmonization of retail payment services in the single market can be expected. In 2005, initiated by the discussion that banks have raised charges on domestic payments in the aftermath of Regulation 2560/2001, the EC mandated the preparation of an impact study to assess the change of bank charges for domestic payments in selected euro member states.[112] Table 26 reflects the result of both studies and shows the evolution of fee charges for credit transfers for both cross-border and domestic payments, differentiated between the Straight-Though Processed (STP) payments and non-STP payments that consist of paper-based or manually processed transactions. Furthermore, to quantify the concurrent financial impact, bank revenues are calculated by means of transaction volume and assumptions on underlying automation levels for Germany, France, Italy and Spain. While charges of cross-border STP payments (scope of Regulation 2560/2001) have decreased to the required level of national euro-denominated credit transfers in all four countries under investigation, charges for the less cost-effective non-STP payments in euro remained at pre-regulation levels. Despite being an attractive source of income for those payment service providers that can process most of these payments efficiently (for example, by using intelligent scanning software for paper-based payments or artificial intelligence software to automatically repair repetitive transaction detail errors), the relative high charges for these kind of payments reflect the high operating costs of most market participants. Hence, the high charges also reflect the differentiated pricing introduced by banks to encourage customers to correctly apply IBAN and BIC codes and to use more cost-efficient service delivery channels, such as the Internet. Furthermore, the EC-study on bank charges for national payments (European Commission, 2005g, p. 8) has found some, albeit limited, evidence suggesting that Regulation 2560/2001 may have impacted on the increases for

111 See "*Study on the Verification of a Common and Coherent Application of Directive 97/5/EC on Cross-Border Credit*", (European Commission, 2001c).

112 See "*Study of the impact of regulation 2560/2001 on bank charges for national payments*", (European Commission, 2005g).

domestic payments in Italy and Spain. Whether there is a causal link between the introduction of the Regulation in July 2003 as the only contributing factor and the increase on domestic bank charges, is difficult to empirically evidence. The main difficulties of isolating the influence of the Regulation relate to significantly differing national pricing structures and to the tendency of banks to sell payments in account product bundles to retail clients, hindering an unbiased cross-country and cross-industry comparison. The latter can be encountered in countries like Germany, in particular, where the basic fixed account package fee includes a limited number of free transactions after which a charge is levied (European Commission, 2005g, p. 14). Hence, domestic payment charges are assumed to be zero both before and after the Regulation. While in France, Italy and Spain prices for domestic payments both STP and non-STP increased between 2002 and 2005, the increase may not necessarily be exclusively attributed to the impact of Regulation 2560/2001. The introduction of new pricing structures by banks, wishing to incentivize end-consumers to switch from manual transactions to an increased usage of cost-efficient direct service channels provides a further explanation. Nevertheless, the fact that the price increase coincides with the introduction of the Regulation provides some evidence that there has also been an impact on national payments. Again, there exists no empirical evidence that would allow to clearly assign the relative weights to each of the two influencing factors and to quantify the impact of one versus the other.

Table 26: Evolution of average transaction fees and payments revenues

		Average fee per transaction		Estimated revenues in EUR mn	
Country	**Transaction**	**2002**	**2005**	**2002**	**2005**
Germany	Cross-border STP	11.93	0.00	284,178	0
	Cross-border Non-STP	11.93	11.93	576,967	497,663
	Domestic STP	0.00	0.00	0	0
	Domestic Non-STP	2.00	2.00	109,607	121,813
France	Cross-border STP	18.10	2.85	199,109	46,225
	Cross-border Non-STP	18.10	18.10	404,252	318,031
	Domestic STP	2.30	2.85	576,282	7,238,381
	Domestic Non-STP	3.50	3.90	8,858	100,052
Italy	Cross-border STP	13.70	2.00	58,133	13,083
	Cross-border Non-STP	13.70	13.70	118,028	97,084
	Domestic STP	0.25	2.00	241,623	2,048,621
	Domestic Non-STP	4.00	5.00	39,050	51,733
Spain	Cross-border STP	20.50	3.18	36,022	14,238
	Cross-border Non-STP	20.50	20.50	73,136	99,436
	Domestic STP	2.52	3.18	1,008,586	2,229,568
	Domestic Non-STP	28.10	29.10	113,601	206,087

Source: European Commission (2001c; European Commission, 2005g), EPC (2002) and author's analysis.

Another indicator that can be considered to evaluate the immediate impact of Regulation 2560/2001 is the overall transaction volume development in the euro area. illustrates the evolution of payment volumes between 2000 and 2008, increasing on average by 6% year-on-year. Given the relatively small share of cross-border retail payments denominated in euros included in these volume figures, no significant increase of the total volume in the year of the introduction of the Regulation can be observed. Furthermore, various other factors influence the volume development of payments in Europe, among others the GDP growth in each country, population growth and the transaction per capita growth, which cannot be factored out effectively.

Looking at the share of credit transfers in overall non-cash payments volume, a shift from credit transfer instruments to card and direct debit payments can be observed. While this reflects a change of consumer preferences rather than the impact of the price increase related to the payment Regulation in 2003, the fact that banks have changed their pricing instruments to encourage the usage of more cost effective payment instruments provides some explanations for the shift in proportions.

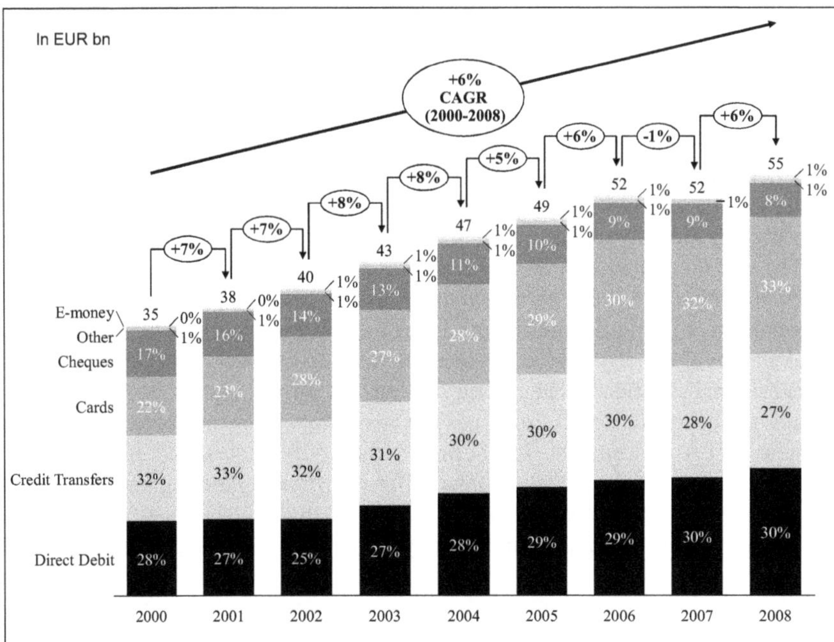

Figure 21: Non-cash payment volumes per instrument (2000-2008)
Source: ECB statistics (2009).

Creating a SEPA – the long-term impact of Regulation 2560/2001

The long-term effect of Regulation 2560/2001 is reflected in the SEPA project that emerged from the necessity of banks to counteract to the price convergence by creating harmonized euro payment instruments and standards domestic and cross-border payments in the euro area. To operate profitably, the pan-European payment standards are developed in ways that not only provide an efficient processing of cross-border transactions but are an ultimate replacement of all domestic systems and standards. As the payment business is characterized by economies of scale, only the joint volume of both domestic and cross-border euro payments will enable the industry to operate payment systems efficiently in Europe and allow for ultimately decreasing average costs of transactions and the absorption of the negative effects of the price regulation.

There is almost no academic literature available that investigates barriers to integration in the retail payment market from a theoretical viewpoint, and the attempt to assess the economic impact of SEPA has also been picked out as a central theme of research only in a limited number of the industry and consultancy studies. While the existing studies differ in several aspects, they all seek to quantify the impact of SEPA for different stakeholders and to develop recommended action. This section reviews the most recent studies with regard to measurement methodology and results and comments on a potential relevance for this research project.

While most of these studies were either commissioned or conducted by independent consultancy or policy advisory firms and were based on qualitative findings from surveys and interviews, results are subject to many uncertainties and vary significantly in some parts.

The study conducted by Ploey et al. (2005) from McKinsey & Company analyzes the impact of SEPA on the payment industry with regard to strategy, pricing structure, costs and benefits, product mix and processing. The analysis undertaken develops hypothetical scenarios to derive likely consequences for banks and market effects. Their main findings reveal that significant investments in back-office systems and processes are necessary to enable banks to process the new SEPA instruments. Furthermore, the study shows that SEPA-related changes in business revenues of banks differ significantly among payment products. Finally, corporate customers will have to change the way they initiate their European cross-border and domestic payments for banks or payments service providers. Ploey et al. (2005) conclude that a move from labor-intensive cash and-checks-related instruments to electronic payment transfers is required in order to reduce costs. A prerequisite, therefore, would be a suspension of subsidies for cash in all markets and a compensation for the use of electronic payments instead, as the majority of all direct payment costs are related to the physical handling of cash. The cost-saving potential of a substitution of cash by electronic payment instruments is estimated by the authors with up to 25% in some European countries.[113] According to Ploey et al. (2005), a fee level convergence due to SEPA resulting at a European average price may cause market distortions. While banks in countries with high fees, such as Spain and Italy, would lose a share of their revenues, banks in countries where domestic payments are processed already in a cost-efficient way, would benefit from an average EU-wide transaction fee. However, this study concludes that an increased competitive pressure on corporations may partly lead to increased costs for end-consumers. This is explained with the heavy cross-subsidization of profitable with unprofitable payment products within European banks. While such business models are vulnerable to changes in regulation, specialized competition may break up existing cross-subsidization practices and take over the profitable parts of the market by offering better products.

The Boston Consulting Group (in Viner, Creyghton, Rutstein, & Storz, 2006) examines the potential economic impact of SEPA and analyzes the challenges and difficulties that exist for banks and corporations. While the study acknowledges the macroeconomic and political rationale behind the payments regulation and the SEPA project, the report concludes that there is a large discrepancy between investments that will be required to be compliant with the SEPA requirements and the related benefits for banks and corporations. The study calculates the investments necessary to achieve compliance with SEPA for banks and payment service providers by 2008 at approximately EUR 500m. The largest part of these costs is estimated to be borne by European banks for adapting their payment processing infrastructure. According to the authors of this study, the full migration to SEPA in 2010 will require up to EUR 5bn of investments to align IT architecture, products and contracts with SEPA standards. Against these investment needs and together with the increased pressure on margins, European banks will be forced to further reduce costs along the transaction value chain, in particular in the labor-intensive areas of payment initiation and customer service.

Capgemini, ABN Amro and the European Financial Management and Marketing Association (EFMA) have been publishing a report on the worldwide payment business development with a particular focus on the changes in the European market related to SEPA on an annual basis. In their 2006 report, they attempt to quantify the impact of SEPA on EU-12 banks' fees and commission income revenues for payment services. Even though the study concludes that SEPA will lead to price convergence for payment services in Europe, it falls short on elaborating whether banks are able and willing to accept pricing levels

113 These findings are further supported by a another report of McKinsey & Company (2006) on the Dutch payment service market, acknowledging that payments services is a loss-making business and that only further substitution of cash and paper transfers by electronic payments can increase cost-efficiency.

that prevent them from recuperating their investments in the mid- to long term. However, a *race to the bottom scenario* for the prices of payment services seems to be neither likely nor sustainable.

According to this report, the total impact on European bank's revenues differs significantly across countries, and there is no clear trend in revenues observable on the consumer and corporate business. Payment revenues are estimated to increase in the euro area countries from EUR 31bn to EUR 47bn between 2004 and 2010. However, after 2010, annual revenues are expected to decline significantly (between EUR 18-29bn) mainly caused by price erosion resulting from competition on float and interchange fees. However, EFMA estimates that in case banks develop adopt policies aimed at substituting further cash with non-cash transactions, a revenue potential of EUR 8bn could be untapped by 2010. While these additional revenues will mainly be driven by increased volumes in credit transfers and debit cards, the authors conclude that it is unlikely that these additional revenues are able to offset the downward pressure on revenues due to increased competition within SEPA. In order to minimize revenue losses, the study suggests a number of measures that mostly aim at replacing cash payments with non-cash means and recommends banks rethink their cash pricing strategies by encouraging the use of non-cash payments instead. Currently, banks' pricing practices do not accurately reflect their internal structure and, therefore, fail to provide adequate incentives to use cost-efficient payment systems. In conclusion, the EFMA study disregards the costs and benefits of SEPA besides the initial investments related to achieve SEPA compliance. Benefits such as modernization, consolidation in the longer run, improved efficiency and achievement of economies of scale and scope are factored out.

An interview-based study conducted by Accenture (2006) and PSE Consulting (2006) surveyed the views with respect to SEPA among 75 senior European bankers and payment system executives to derive predictions on the future payment industry landscape in Europe. According to that, the actual implementation costs of SEPA for Europe's major large and medium-sized banks are expected to amount to EUR 3-8bn until 2011, exceeding earlier estimations of Tower Group (2005) by far. The majority of banks interviewed by Accenture/PSE refer to in- and out-sourcing strategies and joint venture solutions as key response strategies to SEPA. While many survey participants pointed out the opportunity costs related to IT investments in achieving SEPA compliance instead of developing new products and businesses as disadvantage, they, however, shared the view that SEPA represents an opportunity for modernization and for developing European-wide payment standards, providing the basis for consolidation of national payment systems. The study estimates that only seven of the existing 15 automated clearing houses in Europe are likely to survive beyond 2010.

I-flex solutions/Financial Insights (2006) surveyed the views of banks and financial organizations across the EU-25 countries on the impact of SEPA on payment operations and business strategy. The majority (79%) of the respondents takes a positive view of the SEPA project and considers that SEPA will create new business opportunities. On the revenue side, these positive effects refer in particular to business expansion, new geographic reach, improved management of the financial supply chain for corporate customers and additional business from value-added customers. With regard to cost savings within SEPA, most of the surveyed banks hope to improve cost efficiencies and achieve greater *straight-through processing*. Depending on their starting position, the authors of this study expect early SEPA movers to be better positioned and to benefit most from an integrated, harmonized and open pan-European payments market. According to I-flex solutions/Financial Insights, initial investments for banks to become SEPA compliant amount to EUR 5.4bn by 2010.

In 2007, the Fédération Bancaire Francaise (2007) investigated the economic impact of SEPA on payment services stakeholders. In essence, they concluded that the size of the economic impact is directly related to the transition period, when national legacy payment systems and SEPA systems run in parallel. Furthermore, they estimate initial investment costs borne by banks and payment systems to range between EUR 9.1-11.9bn, with a prospective payoff period as of 2013.

Besides these consultancy papers, a number of other empirical contributions examine additional aspects of the potential impact of SEPA and address further payment-related issues in the harmonization process of the European payment landscape. Bolt (2006), for example, provides empirical evidence that harmonization and standardization of retail payment instruments across the euro area are expected to result in economies of scale on the payment service industry. He concludes that potential benefits and scale effects, such as the change in processing volumes that may help debit cards to cost effectively replace smaller value cash-transactions, are likely to result from the realization of SEPA and greater cross-border consolidation. Similarly, the findings of Beijnen and Bolt (2007) empirically support the existence of substantial economies of scale in the European payment processing industry. The authors reveal that a doubling of payment volume may lead to an incremental cost increase of only 22% in a SEPA environment. They conclude that a resulting decrease of average costs may support further consolidation in the European payment services market in the future.[114]

A SEPA impact analysis undertaken by the ECB (in Schmiedel, 2007) represents an attempt to quantify the average impact on payment-related cost and

114 In a current study, Beijnen and Bolt (2009) found evidence for the existence of significant economies of scale in the European payment processing industry. The analysis also reveals that ownership structure is an important factor to explain cost differences across European processing centers.

revenues for the European banking sector, differentiated by three different scenarios and by payment instrument. The author concludes that banks expect their revenues to decline by between 3-10%, depending on the SEPA scenario under consideration[115] resulting in a cost increase of about 5% in the SEPA coexistence scenario. However, these initial investments are likely to be paid off in an ideal SEPA and e-SEPA world, when harmonized and standardized payment schemes and products are implemented and a full migration to one pan-European payment IT platform completed. Cost savings in both scenarios are expected at 1% and 7% respectively. Interestingly, the net effect compared to the baseline scenarios remains negative in all scenarios. The aggregated effect of revenue and cost decline is estimated at -9% for the coexistence scenario and between -1.5 to 3% in the long-term e-SEPA scenario.

The European Commission mandated Capgemini (2007) to conduct a study on the impact of SEPA on the market, the resulting issues and potential remedies for successfully attaining the single payments area in Europe. Similar to the ECB study, Capgemini deployed an impact analysis based on different scenarios. Their research methodology aims at quantifying the effects on stakeholders on the demand and the supply-side over time. Overall, Capgemini found out that SEPA holds a market potential of up to EUR 123bn in benefits in the most optimistic *SEPA Big Time* scenario (cumulative over 6 years) with a significant upside for all demand-side stakeholders. In this net effect, a loss on the supply-side (including investments to achieve SEPA compliance, operational costs and decreasing banking fees) compared to the baseline is outweighed largely by a gain on the demand-side, where consumers in particular benefit from SEPA. This study estimates a resulting positive market outcome per country of 0.2% of GDP on average, which differs between countries and the most and the least aggressive scenarios.

Several other papers have been published that investigate the impact of SEPA on the product offering and on prices. Guibourg and Segendorf (2004), for example, provide evidence from the Swedish payment market. Consumers lack sufficient price incentives in their choice of payment instrument to change their behavior and to shift away from paper-based payment instruments to direct debit and electronic credit transfers. Furthermore, the authors find evidence of significant cross-subsidization between different payment services, especially from acquiring card payments to cash distribution to the public. Swartz et al

115 The questionnaire developed by the ECB (in Schmiedel, 2007) aims at obtaining a view of the potential cost and revenue impacts of SEPA under four different scenarios: (1) "Baseline," which is an extrapolation of the status quo, (2) "Coexistence of payment schemes", which assumes that no consolidation of IT platforms can be achieved, (3) "Ideal SEPA world", which builds on the first two scenarios but taking the full advantage of SEPA schemes into consideration, and (4), *e-SEPA*, which aims at going beyond SEPA and considering fewer cash-payments in the euro area.

(2004) empirically prove that the shift away from cash and check payments may improve welfare. This idea is further supported by the evidence found for the Dutch market, where Brits and Winder (2005) argue that purchases above EUR 11.63 are economically more cost-effective using a debit card than for example cash or e-purse payments. Hence, cash payments would continue to be an important payment instruments and an entirely cashless society is unlikely to be established, at least not in the medium term. Finally, DeGrauwe et al. (2006) ascertain that the introduction of a cost-based pricing strategy would reduce costs of EUR 150-200m in the Belgium and Dutch market, which would lead to cost reductions of 0.14% of GDP if extrapolated to the European level.

Table 27 provides an overview of the economic impact estimated of SEPA as available in the reviewed literature. In particular, the one-off investment costs required to achieve SEPA compliance can be aggregated and compared on a European level. On average, these SEPA-related investments for the banking industry range between EUR 5.2-7.7bn. However, these findings should be compared and interpreted with care because of the differing underlying approaches, methodologies, model assumptions and the number of countries and products in scope of the studies.

In conclusion, from a microeconomic perspective, the RPE has had an immediate negative effect on the profitability of the payments industry in Europe. Despite the low volume of cross-border payments in euro, profit margins used to be positive (or break even) on average for most banks before the price regulation. Since 2003, when the EU prohibited banks from charging differently for domestic and cross-border retail payments, operating cost could not be decreased by the equal amount given the fragmented payment infrastructure landscape existent at that time, resulting in (further) loss of profitability. However, there is also a positive effect arising from the situation that was caused by the Regulation 2560/2001, which will materialize in the long-term view. By confronting the market with a fait accompli, banks in Europe joined forces (under the lead of the EPC) and developed payment instruments and schemes that allow for increasing efficiency of payment services in the EU and for advancing European financial integration. The SEPA initiative, however, requires high investments by the banking industry. Whether these costs pay-off through future operating cost savings or even additional revenues from accessing the entire European internal market, depends on the pace that domestic payment standards and systems are replaced by the new SEPA standards, providing the required critical mass, on the one hand and the willingness of payment users to adopt to these new standards on the other hand. Only then the RPE and SEPA will yield a positive net impact for the industry, hence removing the *lack of commercial interest* barrier to market integration.

Table 27: Overview of selected SEPA impact studies

Study / research paper	Estimated SEPA investments in EUR bn Low	High	Impact of SEPA on payment service providers	Other economic impacts
McKinsey & Company (2005)	N/A	N/A	• Fee levels to converge around the present European average would affect European countries differently • Overall cost savings of EUR 8.9bn through product standardization, scale, cross-border consolidation and sharing of best practices	• Up to 25% cost savings from improved cash handling would increase banks' profits by EUR 5.3bn overall • Convergence of consumer behavior across the EU affects instrument mix • Entry of new competitors who aim for the profitable parts of the market
The Boston Consulting Group (2006)	0.5	5	• Increased margin pressure for banks. • Cost-saving potential along the transaction value chain, in particular in the labor-intensive areas of payment initiation and customer service	N/A
Capgemini, ABN Amro EFMA (2006)	N/A	N/A	• Annual revenues to decline significantly (between EU 18-29bn) after 2010 when SEPA Direct Debit is implemented • Total impact differs significantly across European countries	• Additional revenue potential of EUR 8bn by 2010, provided that banks develop and adopt policies aimed at substituting cash • Variation across countries in the potential revenue increase
Accenture/ PSE Consulting (2006)	3	>8	• The scale and complexity of change around SEPA is overloading banks' and processors' IT departments and restricting investment in new product innovation • SEPA delivers to banks a greater reach, enabling sales to new customers in the EU • Larger banks will aggressively leverage both scale and geographic reach • SEPA's common standards will enable smaller banks to deliver competing services to their national market customers	• Banks also perceive SEPA as an opportunity to further displace cash by innovative products such as contactless cards, pre-paid cards and unattended payments. • SEPA will help to facilitate cross-border M&A: banks may leverage a single platform more effectively and drive greater cost-benefits from acquisitions
I-flex solutions / Financial Insights (2005)	5.4	5.4	• New business opportunities for banks •Standardization will lead to economies of scale for multinational banks and to substantial cost saving potential over time	N/A
FBF (2007)	9.1	12	• Size of the economic impact is directly related to the transition period	N/A
Towergroup (2005)	8	8	• Substantial net decrease in revenue and margins earned for processing payments • Banks that have the scale to benefit are likely to seize the advantage from smaller banks that lack resources or foresight to develop compliant payment platforms	N/A
Capgemini (2007)	N/A	N/A	• SEPA market potential: up to EUR 123bn in cumulated benefits over six years Directly related positive market outcome per country of 0.2% • Highest Net benefits from SEPA for corporations and lowest for consumers	N/A
ECB (2007)	N/A	N/A	• Revenues to decline by between 3-10% for banks and payment service providers • Cost increase of about 5% if SEPA and legacy infrastructure continue to co-exist	N/A
Average	**5.2**	**>7.7**		

Source: Compiled by author, adapted from ECB (in Schmiedel, 2007).

7.1.2 Payment network competition

In 2005, the EC conducted a study to assess the effects of Regulation 2560/2001 on the competition for cross-border payment service in Europe.[116] Furthermore, the study evaluated the changes to the infrastructure of cross-border payments and the conditions of competition in the provision of these services. Given the focus of retail payments processed by ACHs, this section compares the market and ownership structure as well as the access requirements before and after the Regulation.

Consolidation in the European ACH market

Between the early 2000s and 2006, all EU member states had at least one national ACH system per country, owned either by the National Central Banks or by joint ventures of banking groups, providing only national coverage due to technical and legal barriers. In some countries, such as France or The Netherlands, one dominant ACH exists, while others, e.g., the U.K. and Spain, have several clearinghouses for different payments or subsystems of a central ACH like in Italy. In Germany, however, only a minor share of all the payment transactions is actually cleared through an ACH; around 85% of the total volume is cleared bilaterally between the banks or banking groups. Given the historical path-dependent development of each national clearing system, the market structure in terms of number of payment system providers has not changed materially in the aftermath of Regulation 2560/2001 except for the emergence of an additional, multilateral cross-border payment transfer network, EBA STEP1 and STEP2. The latter was the first real PEACH that could handle a high volume of cross-border euro payments compliant to the IBAN and BIC format requirements for payments below EUR 12,500, achieving a reachability[117] to cover all eurozone, EU and European Economic Area (EEA) countries. However, accompanied by the progress of the SEPA initiative in developing pan-European retail payment schemes, and with the increasing concern from market participants that EBA would capture a major market share for being the first real PEACH established in Europe, a consolidation process in the retail clearing market began in 2006. In fact, a number of Europe's national ACHs or their operating companies have been preparing themselves to maintain their position in the future payments market. However, even before SEPA has been fully implemented and the differences between domestic and cross-border retail payments in euros start to van-

116 See "*The Study of Competition for Cross-Border Payment Service*" by the European Commission (2005f).

117 The term *reachability* often used by the banking community in relationship to SEPA. It implies that al financial institutions must be able to provide credit transfers from any domestic account to any receiving account with the participating countries (Skinner, 2008, p. 15).

ish, some banks are offering other banks throughout Europe insourcing of SEPA payments, attempting to secure sufficient volumes in the market through consolidation. According to market expert estimations (i.e., Mai, 2009, p. 17), an annual payment transaction volume of 10 billion is required to achieve the critical mass necessary to operate profitably with the new SEPA payment instruments and unit costs comparable to the level currently achieved in national ACHs. Considering the current volume of around 55 billion payment transactions in the eurozone, the European retail payment market can be shared between five pan-European ACHs in the future. Hence, a number of clearing service providers have started to invest in new ACH operations to increase their market share via insourcing and mergers. In France, for example, the current ACH, Système Interbancaire de Télécompensation (SIT), created a new company, Systèmes Technologiques d'Echange et de Traitement (STET), in 2004. This system supports full SEPA functionalities and replaced SIT in 2007. The U.K. bank-owned ACH, Bankers Automated Clearing System (BACS), was spun-off into a commercial payments provider and merged with the ATM operator to become VocaLink Ltd in 2007. Since then, VocaLink operates not only the U.K. retail clearing houses BACS and Faster Payments but also the Swedish clearing house Bankgirocentralen BGC AB. Similarly, the Dutch Interpay clearing house merged with the German cooperative banks' processor Transaktionsinstitut in 2006, and further expanded their reachability through a merger with the Italian clearing house, Seceti S.p.A., to become Equens S.E. In Germany, PAYCE, the payment and clearing system of the saving banks, is offering other banks the insourcing of SEPA payments.

The SEPA rulebook for Clearing and Settlement Mechanisms (CSM) also foresees alternative clearing and settlement methods for credit transfer than those of the PEACH, which is currently the only provider through EBA's STEP2 system. To extend their reachability and to be able to offer their clients proper clearing channels in addition to the link to EBA STEP2, the major European ACHs (VocaLink, Equens, Iberpay, Seceti, and STET) have created the European ACH Association (EACHA) and established bilateral interoperability for the exchange of SEPA payments from January 2008 onwards (Skinner, 2008, p. 16). The combined group processed over 25 billion transaction (direct debit and credit transfers) in 2007 (see Figure 22). Besides centralized third-party clearing and settlement, the bilateral clearing of SEPA payments represents an alternative for particularly big European banks. By forming a joint processing entity for retail payments, a relatively small number of participants would cover a considerable market share of European retail payments, hence competing directly with the emerging pan-European ACHs such as Equens, VocaLink or EBA.

Finally, with the introduction of the Payment Service Directive (PSD) in November 2009, the competition for payment services in the European market will be further spurred. While to date, only banks have had direct contact with the end-users of payment services due to their privilege of being the only account-holding organizations for consumers, corporations and public authorities, PSD now licenses companies, such as ACHs and insourcers of payment processing and back-office services for banks, as so-called *payment institutions*. Being allowed to maintain end-consumers' accounts themselves, they are granted access to the clearing service market and can provide their services directly, without using banks as intermediaries.

The final outcome of the competition between different institutional settings for the low-value retail payments space is still unclear and it is only once national restrictions disappear (i.e., when SEPA has eventually been fully implemented) that it will prove which clearing routes and providers will establish themselves in the single European market by merging with other entities or poaching clients from competitors (Mai, 2009, p. 18).

Regardless which business model will survive in a single European payments market in the future, achieving economies of scale and lower unit costs through generating additional payment volumes will be crucial for European competition to prevail. According to the SEPA impact studies investigated earlier, margin squeeze and reduced bank profits will further drive market consolidation, decreasing the number of clearing and processing firms for retail payments in the single European market below the level before Regulation 2560/2001.

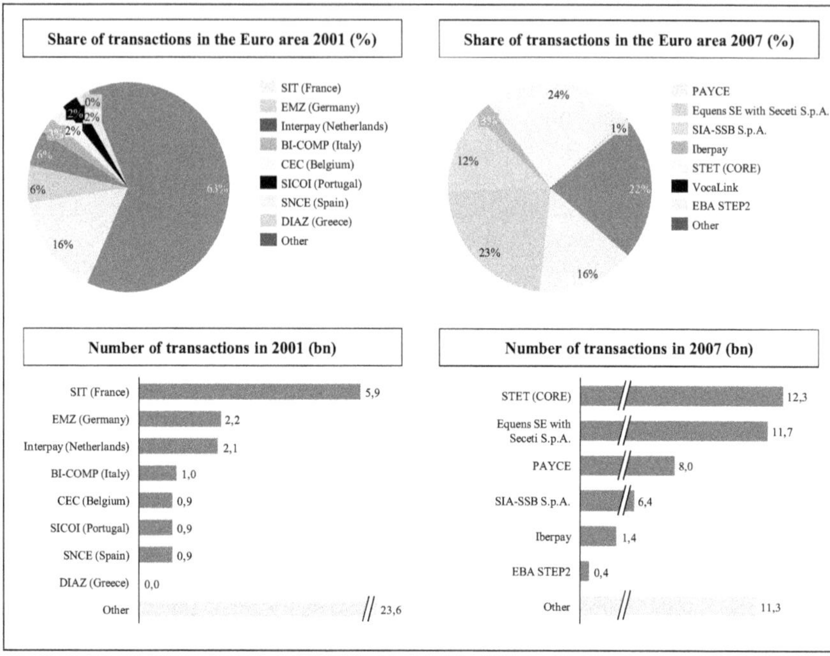

Figure 22: ACH market structure in Europe (2001 vs. 2007)
Source: ECB Payments Statistics, company data, DB Research, EPC (2002).

Access and membership restrictions

All cross-border payment networks impose certain restrictions on existing and potential new members. As examined earlier, memberships to retail payment networks can be either direct/indirect or full/associated, and the dual status of some banks being both network shareholders and members may on the one hand impose unreasonable rules and access criteria for potential members and on the other be reasonable from a financial security and systemic risk point of view. Nevertheless, one common requirement, which has not changed directly in the aftermath of Regulation 2560/2001 in 2003 but will only change with the implementation of the PSD in 2009, is that all networks require their members to be regulated financial institutions, hence excluding corporations and other stakeholders from membership (European Commission, 2005f, p. 51). These restrictions are inconvenient and costly for corporations, as they are obliged to send their payments via their commercial bank instead of accessing networks directly or even becoming members of the network and thus involved in the decision making and investment processes. Such a denial of access and membership to corporations limits the entry of new market entrants on the one hand but ensures network stability on the other. The trade-off between the two objectives is difficult to quantify, making a single edge recommendation difficult. Hybrid forms of access for corporations, such as non-settlement categories, represent promising alternatives that mitigate the systemic risk but do not address the need for non-regulated firms to be represented in the governance of networks. While the PSD aims to create a new type of non-bank payment service provider, called *payment institutions*, which entitles non-regulated firms to engage directly in clearing and settlement services, a positive impact on the European payments market through the market entry of formally excluded corporations from payment has to be awaited.

Besides the clear benefits of gaining more influence on the governance of networks the cooperation between banks and corporations in defining the requirements for SEPA-compliant payment instruments and infrastructures may also prove beneficial for both sides. Nevertheless, given that even after the implementation of Regulation 2560/2001 and the earlier stage of SEPA hardly any cooperation took place between banks and corporations, banks have preferred to remain with the traditional bank-client or principle-agent arrangement rather than allowing corporations to compete for retail clients payment clearing and settlement without the involvement of a commercial bank as an intermediary. On the one hand, corporations may bear the blame for not having consistently formulated the requirements for corporations among all EU member states. Whilst on the other, the lack of an authoritative association representing the interest of corporations towards the banking industry has led to an infrequent and only informal contribution of the corporations' views in the cross-border payments and overall SEPA development process.

While further cooperation between banks and corporations would be desirable, i.e. by providing formal mechanisms to obtain the views and comments of corporates, consumers, national ACHs and possibly other organizations, two premises have fallen short in the SEPA creation process. First, payment networks are club-goods (non-rival but excludable) and bear an intrinsic systemic and financial stability risk reflected by membership restrictions of allowing direct access to regulated financial institutions only. Allowing non-regulated corporations to access payment networks may indeed foster competition but, at the same time, raises questions about the risk control and capital requirements for such firms. Second, information exchange between banks and their customers (corporations, end-consumers or other banks) has taken place already. While only few formal mechanisms and processes exist, by which banks or payment network providers are established to obtain corporations' views, it is the nature of bank-client relationships to understand client requirements and to adequately translate these into products and payment systems. Any further regulated cooperation process would literally deny banks' competency to understand their business.

Lack of open and common standards

The greatest achievement of consequence deriving from Regulation 2560/2001was that it created a necessity for the banking industry to join forces with the European Payments Council (EPC) as a coordination body to realize the creation of a harmonized, open and interoperable European domestic payment market. The objective to deliver the technical basis that SEPA will build on, including commonly applicable payment schemes and standards, has been achieved through industry self-regulation. Considering that the EPC now consists of more than 70 members, composed of banks and bank associations from the entire European market, representing all sizes and sectors of banks and financial services providers, who only joined because of the necessity of meeting regulator's expectations to develop efficient European domestic payment schemes and standards, one becomes aware that the market itself could have hardly created a more efficient market outcome for standard setting than the Regulation did. As an immediate result of this process, the European banking industry has defined *rulebooks* of each new SEPA payment scheme as definitive sources of information, specifying the related rules and obligations, for all payments in euros.

Table 28 provides an overview of the two new payment schemes for credit transfers (SEPA Credit Transfers, SCT) and direct debits (SEPA Direct Debit, SDD) that are used for cross-border payment transfers as of their adoption date and that are meant to gradually replace domestic payment schemes in the future.

Table 28: Key characteristics of the SEPA schemes and rulebooks

SEPA Credit Transfers (SCT)	SEPA Direct Debit (SDD)
• Adoption date: January 2008 • Bulk payments (non-urgent) in euro • Maximum execution time of one banking day (max. of three banking days until 2012) • The full amount credited to the beneficiary account with no deductions • No cap on the value of the payment • IBAN and BIC instead of national account number and bank sort code • Full remittance information transmitted (max. 4 x 35 characters) • Dedicated field for originator reference, if supplied by the originator • Dedicated field to indicate *on-behalf-of* payments	• Adoption date: November 2009 • Cross-border direct debits made possible for the first time • Submission two banking days before due date (debtor's debit date) for recurring direct debits and 5 days for first time or one-off direct debits • Debtor can return the direct debit up to 8 weeks after the payment has been debited from his account • Returns by the debtor bank must be effected no later than 5 days after the due date • International Bank Account Number (IBAN) and Bank Identification Code (BIC) instead of national account number and bank sort code • Direct debit mandate: debtor gives a signed mandate to the creditor; when the direct debit is submitted the transaction data includes the mandate in digital form; the digital mandate data is forwarded by the clearing organization to the debtor bank; the mandate expires 18 months after the last initiated direct debit • New end-to-end data elements that simplify electronic processing by users' accounting departments: mandate number, creditor identifier • Originator reference and remittance information (if supplied by creditor) • Dedicated field to indicate *on-behalf-of* payments

Source: Mai (2009) and EPC (2009).

All banks and payment service providers that process cross-border credit transfers or direct debit payments through the euro area must have formally adhered to the schemes and the resulting rulebooks. However, any domestic credit transfers or direct debit transactions may still be processed through domestic payment schemes. For a certain period, SEPA and domestic payments schemes will co-exist to allow the market to adapt to the new schemes and to make required investments in infrastructure and payment processing systems. As the banking industry has not fixed the end-date for the final replacement of domestic payment schemes by SEPA schemes, and as there is no legal obligation to do so, a highly inefficient parallel operation of domestic and SEPA schemes will exist for an unnecessarily long period. While those banks and payment service providers that have invested early in their systems and infrastructure to ensure SEPA compliance at an early stage, mostly multinational banks or banks with respective international client needs, have already moved to the new standards. Other banks (mostly regional or municipal) and their predominately regionally oriented clients, have been far more hesitant to invest in their infrastructure to become SEPA-compliant. Such a situation is consequently also characterized by incentive misalignments and a similar hold-up problem as encountered before Regulation 2560/2001. Even worse, operating costs are even higher than before as some banks and their customers must operate their payment business on two systems and schemes, without being able to capture the cost savings for end-users and synergies of payment service providers. This situation has sparked a fierce debate about setting an end-date for the old schemes and dividing the market into two groups. The European Associations of Corporate Treasurers (EACT), representing the interests of corporations, strongly supports a fixed end-date for national schemes to be replaced by the new SEPA schemes and favors a smooth but consequent decommissioning of national legacy systems (EACT, 2008). Due to their high transaction volumes, these payment users are the ones who will benefit most from a clear timetable for a migration to harmonized European standards, which would permit reliable planning for investments and implementation of required measures for a changeover to SEPA schemes. Multinational banks and payment service providers that have already been servicing international corporations and have made investments in achieving SEPA compliance at an early stage share this view. In contrast, other market participants, both users and providers of payment services in the eurozone, have articulated reservations about committing to an end-date fixed by the industry and would like to continue using national schemes alongside SEPA for cross-border payments. These concerns are mainly attributed to their business being either focused on the national market or their business practices being based on traditional national systems.

On the regulatory side both the ECB and the EU unequivocally demand that SEPA be implemented and advocate a realistic, but ambitious end-date for the co-existence of national schemes and SEPA. Against this background, the EC has initiated a public consultation process on a possible end-date for a full migration to the new SEPA schemes in mid-2009 (European Commission, 2009a). All relevant stakeholders of SEPA were invited to give their opinion on potential end-dates and to articulate their preferences for either a self-regulated or legislation based implementation. The result of this consultation was that the majority of respondents were in favor of the idea of setting some end-date(s) to stimulate the migration to SEPA, and a large majority preferred to have the end-date established by regulation to a self-regulated fixing (European Commission,

2009b). The summary of the survey results indicate several reasons for this preference (ibid., pp. 9-10) which are outlined below.

(i) An end-date established by regulation is more in line with the political vision of the single market for payments in Europe, giving a clear signal to market participants that SEPA is irreversible
(ii) Regulation would have the advantage of being enforceable within the whole area, which may be necessary to force stakeholders to migrate to SEPA. Furthermore, it may be seen as necessary to avoid competition issues that such migration may raise if implemented only by market participants.
(iii) While EU legislation is favored by almost all respondents, a few mentioned ECB regulation as being one of the possible tools that could be used to complement EU legislation.
(iv) Many respondents emphasized the importance of involving all stakeholders in the decision-making process in case a regulated end-date is established.
(v) A few respondents on the supply-side suggested following a regulatory approach on the EU level but keeping the option open to set earlier end-dates through balanced solutions between regulation and self-regulation on member state levels.
(vi) A few respondents on the demand-side of the market indicated their preference for an end-date set by the market, given that SEPA was considered a project of the market, which should therefore also decide when to migrate.
(vii) Finally, a few respondents mainly on the demand-side, suggested a balanced solution, whereby self-regulation could be accompanied by some regulatory support to either accelerate market growth or to be put forward in case a pure self-regulated process failed.

Whether set by regulation or established through a self-regulated process, an end-date should be agreed and come into force on an EU-wide basis to ensure fair competition conditions. Otherwise, a regulatory arbitrage between national markets with an immediate and others with a distant end-date could lead to the creation of protective market entry barriers for the national banking industry. Considering the experience of Regulation 2560/2001, the EC has a strong case to favor an end-date set through legislation, however, this will have to be agreed in consensus with both the demand and the supply-side of the European retail payment service market. It is expected that a decision-making process involving the view of such a large number of stakeholders may again not yield satisfactory results from a single European market point of view. Considering that Regulation 2560/2001 and PSD were originally enacted using the pretext to make the single currency and the European market more attractive for retail clients, the BEUC has lately criticized that SEPA has been conducted as a pure *banking project* with no real involvement of end-users in the analysis and design of the new payment schemes and instruments (BEUC, 2009a). The lack of transparency in the objective setting of Regulation 2560/2001 and the misjudgment of the political assumptions is now taking its toll when having to decide upon the end-date for SEPA migration. From a normative point of view, standard setting and design are key competencies of the supply-side of the market. Denying banks the ability to make a sound judgment on the superior technical solution based on their expert knowledge and experience would imply that the banking industry does not know the needs of its customers.

The EC has placed itself in a situation where it will be difficult to remain passive and to leave it to the market's devices to decide on the end-date for migration. Hence, unless EU regulators intervene again to fix a target-date for the decommissioning of national legacy payment schemes, those market participants, who are reluctant to switch to new standards, will delay the adoption of SEPA standards and respective investments for as long as possible.

Similar to all other technical standards, achieving a critical mass of SEPA-compliant transactions at an early point in time will attract followers in the market. However, as explained earlier, this would require an irreversible suspension of old schemes with new SEPA standards and, ultimately, the discontinuation of the national systems as well as the current volume of SEPA credit transfers. As shown in Figure 23, the share of SEPA credit transfers (SCT) has increased to 4.5% of the overall payment volume in the euro zone within two years of its launch. Nevertheless, the majority of payments are still being processed via national ACH systems and standards, indicating that a co-existence of SEPA and domestic standards will hardly provide the critical mass required to operate cost-efficiently. Therefore, SEPA payment processors have demanded that the public sector, which is responsible for some 20% of all payments in the euro area (Mai, 2009, p. 13), should migrate onto the SEPA standards in the first place to give a clear signal of support to SEPA from the public to the private sector. To date, many public administrations have been hesitant to adopt the new schemes for their credit transfers. Despite the political determination on the EU level to integrate the European payment markets, even the public sector hesitates about a migration and puts required investments off as long as no clear end-date is fixed. In this regard, the above-mentioned difficulties imply the existence of a coordination problem, which requires EU policy to set proper incentives, in particular, to eventually see the expected efficiency gains and economies of scale materialize.

Looking at the evolution of the share of euro payments since the introduction of Regulation 2560/2001, it took the industry almost five years to develop and implement the harmonized SCT payment scheme, gradually replacing the interim-solution of STEP2 cross-border credit transfers (XCT) and absorbing the market share of non-regulated payments and domestic ACH payments. While the decrease of non-regulated payments is largely attributed to the enhanced levels of automation as well as to the consistent application of IBAN and BIC, the SCT could gain relatively low market share from the domestic ACHs.[118]

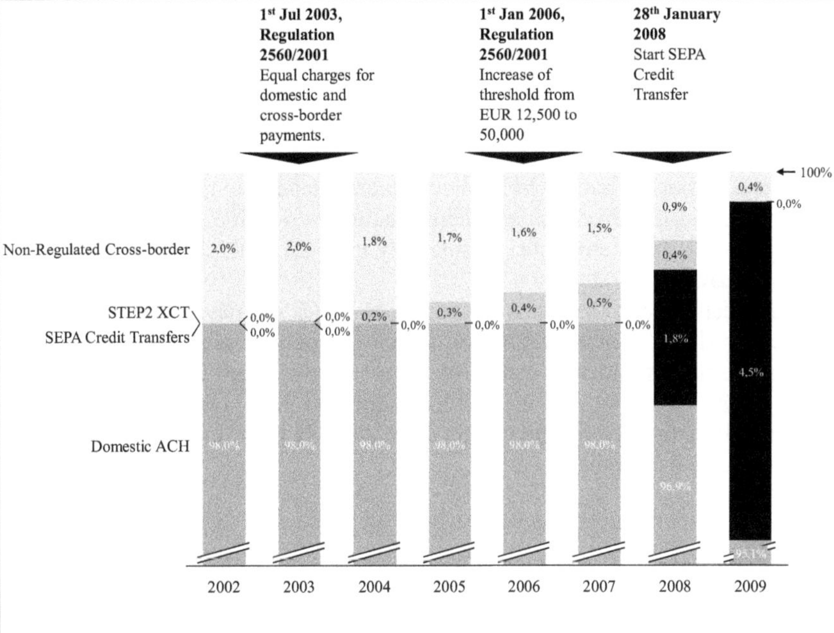

Figure 23: Schematic evolution of payment standard's market share

Source: Author's estimation based on EBA (2009), EPC (2003), BDV (2009) and expert interviews.

In summary, the positive effect of RPE was that it united the European banking industry to design SEPA payment schemes and standards on a self-regulated basis, which may not have been achieved more quickly and efficiently in a market without a price regulation as a catalyst for development. However, the adaption process in the market has been costly and cumbersome for early adopters and a large part of the market remains hesitant about fully migrating their domestic ACH payment volume to the SEPA standard. Unless a definite target date for all countries is provided by the EC, both schemes will continue to co-exist and harmonization will, if at all, take place at different speeds across Europe.

118 Until mid 2009, only Luxembourg has migrated its domestic retail payment business entirely to the new SEPA credit transfer schemes.

7.2 Demand-side barriers

Besides improving market efficiency, Regulation 2560/2001 also aimed to establish the principle of equality charges and ex-ante information provided for payments within and between member states. The base principle of non-discrimination between domestic and cross-border payments laid down in the Regulation aimed at removing demand-side barriers to integration for retail end-consumers in Europe in two respects directly: price and information. Furthermore, as a higher aspiration, EU policy makers intended to create an opportunity for the demand for cross-border credit transfers to develop, which was, following regulators' argumentations, withheld by unequal bank charges and poor ex-ante information provided.

This section seeks to assess the degree to which the payment directive actually removed the identified barriers. Given the poor availability of consistent data for the period under investigation, direct measurement cannot be applied in some cases. Therefore, an indirect measurement with complementary proxy metrics will be applied for the impact assessment in price-inelastic behavior and interdependence of demand.

7.2.1 Information asymmetries and price-inelastic behavior

The existence of information asymmetries and inelastic behavior in the European retail banking business is reflected in the lack of clarity of information on cross-border payment-related services. Especially there, it is difficult for consumers to understand the final price they will pay for the payment-related services they need. Therefore, the clearer and more user-friendly information is provided ex-ante, the better customers are able to compare tariffs of different banks, and consequently, the more mobile they will potentially become.

Due to the complexity of cross-border payments and the involvement of counterparts across national borders, ex-ante information asymmetry is more existent in this product than in domestic payments. While, ex-ante, the individual price for a national credit transfer may not be transparent to customers, it is part of an account-centric bundle of different products and services, sold at an ex-ante agreed price.

Against this background, information transparency can be measured with regard to the ex-ante provision of price information and of information on the description of services. The first includes information on the charge characters of services, incomplete or insufficient provision of price details or inconsistent pricing for the same service. The description of cross-border payment services includes a sufficient and coherent wording across all client related documentation (i.e. information brochures, websites, contracts, etc.) and the consistent and unambiguous presentation of information leaving little room for misinterpretations.

For Regulation 2560/2001 to have a positive effect on the fit between the costs quoted by banks for cross-border payment services prior to making a transaction and the actual costs consumers are charged afterwards, several conditions need to hold:

- all providers of cross-border payments provide the information on transaction and service fees to the end-consumer prior to the transaction;
- the consumer reads and understands the content of the information provided;
- after having received the information, consumers may change their decision if not satisfied with the terms and conditions which would reflect a more optimal choice.

Whether all these conditions hold under the information disclosure requirements of the RPE is difficult to measure. Hence, all three conditions would have to be assessed and measured individually.

With regard to the first condition, banks' provision of the key facts on price and service would need to be assessed prior to, and sometime after, the regulation to measure the improved provision of information. As various price studies and progress reports by the EC and the ECB have shown, bank charges and charging principles differ significantly among banks and member states even after Regulation 2560/2001 took effect.[119] The ECB and the NCBs have received a number of customer complaints regarding banks' charging principles for cross-border credit transfers, evidencing that not all banks yet apply the Regulation correctly (European Central Bank, 2004b, p. 24). Nevertheless, due to the lack of a euro-wide database for retail payment services fed by national levels that would be accessible by the public and managed according to an agreed methodology, a comparison of the disclosure of bank prices and services before and after the Regulation is hardly feasible.

However, the results of two surveys conducted on behalf of the European Commission provide at least an empirical indication of the degree that ex-ante information provision for payment services has taken place after the Regulation. An EU study performed in 2001 evaluated the actual situation in the provision of retail banking services in each EU member state. Besides assessing the fees charged for cross-border payments and the time taken for such transfers to occur, the study also empirically assessed the availability and transparency of information about conditions and charges to customers (European Commission, 2001c). While several interim progress reports have been published by the EU in the following years, the lack of regularly performed retail consumer surveys on the payment service provision with a consistent methodology caused the Direc-

119 See, for example, the progress reports of the European Central Bank (2000; 2004b; 2006c) or of the European Commission (2003d; 2004a; 2004b; 2005c; 2005g; 2006b; 2007a; 2008).

torate-General Health and Consumer Affairs to publish a comprehensive report on payment services and prices in the various European countries. This provides a benchmark for future reports monitoring the impact of SEPA and the PSD on consumers (Directorate General Consumer Protection, 2008). The results of both studies with respect to the provision of services are summarized in Table 29.

Table 29: Provision of information prior to credit transfer (2001 vs. 2008)

	2001	2008
Objective	• Evaluation of the full transposition if the provisions of Directive 97/5/EC have been fully transposed into national laws by adequate national legislative measures of the 15 member states. • Evaluation of the actual situation in each member state by presenting the results of an exercise whereby transfers were made throughout the EU.	• Assessment, measurement and evaluation of the impact of SEPA payment-related services on the prices paid by consumers. • Data collection on the prices of payment-related services before the introduction of SEPA at the end of January 2008 as a source of comparison with similar data collected at later stages.
Scope	• Fifteen EU member states (Austria, Belgium, Denmark, France, Finland, Germany, Greece, Ireland, Italy, Luxembourg, The Netherlands, Portugal, Spain, Sweden and the UK). • Banks were selected according to criteria defined by the EC: size of each bank in terms of balance sheet, public and private ownership, retail banking and Internet presence). • Single product: cross-border credit transfers..	• One hundred and six financial institutions (FIs) from the eurozone countries (including Malta and Cyprus) as well as the United Kingdom and Sweden were selected. • Eight payment-related services that may be directly or indirectly affected by the implementation of SEPA, i.e. packages, accounts, credit transfers, direct debits, debit cards, credit or delayed debit cards, ATM cash withdrawals and Internet banking.
Research methodology	• Transfer with a total of 1,480 cross-border payments of EUR 100 to all but the banks in their own country. • Measurement of time, documentation and charges.	• Data collection on prices of payment-related services • Exploratory interviews • Documentary review • Development and testing of the comparison tool; • Analysis of the data collected
Results (related to ex-ante information provision)	• Sixteen out of the 40 senders in the transfer exercise were provided with a brochure/printed material of any sort prior to the transfer. • Quality of information on costs receives the highest rating, between adequate and good. • Brochure information on timing, exchange rates and value date was generally poor, and information on complaints and redress procedures was considered nearer useless than poor.	• Availability of tariffs on the FIs' websites was satisfactory for two thirds of the FIs since they showed their tariffs on one single web page or document. • Only 31% of the FIs provided sufficient explanations of prices, for 69% contacts with the relevant institutions were required to get further explanations.

Source: European Commission (2001c) and Directorate General Consumer Protection (2008).

Acknowledging the different sets of data and research methodologies applied in both studies, the results indicate that there seem to be some kind of improvement of both the quantity and the quality of information provided over time. While the information disclosure requirements of Regulation 2560/2001 may have a significant impact on the improved provision on credit transfers, other factors, such as the further development of web-based information and the resulting improved capability of consumers to obtain and understand information may have also contributed to the indicated improvement.

Provided that: (i) information asymmetries are abolished; (ii) consumers receive the required information to make a more optimal choice, i.e., choosing another bank's services instead; and (iii) no other switching costs exist, consumer mobility can be used as a proxy to measure the effect of the payment regulation on the retail consumer behavior over time. Given the practice in retail banking business to bundle account-related products, such as current accounts and all related transactions, it is a prerequisite in most banks to have a current account with the respective bank before being able to execute a (cross-border or domestic) credit transfer. Hence, if customers choose to change their bank relationship on the pretext of dissatisfactory price and service levels for cross-border payments, increased customer account mobility would be expected to follow when Regulation 2560/2001 became effective in 2003. However, as illustrated in Table 30, no significant increase of churn could be observed between 2002 and 2005 in the selected countries under investigation. Given the negligible share of cross-border retail payments in these countries (<2%) and high account-related switching costs associated with high administrative burdens), it can be concludes that the demand-side barrier to integration, price-inelastic behavior in the retail segment, could hardly be abolished through the payment regulation, at least in pre-SEPA time. With the PSD coming into force in November 2009, the harmonized legal framework aims at overcoming legal uncertainties related to payment services for retail clients and corporations. New payment schemes, such as pan European direct debit instrument (SDD) decrease the need for internationally active retail clients to maintain more than one account in the euro area, hence further reducing the need to change the bank account.

Table 30: Customer mobility (churn), weighted average (2002-2005)

	2002	2003	2004	2005	Average
France	7.35%	7.41%	7.67%	7.75%	7.58%
Germany	9.16%	10.83%	8.38%	9.73%	9.51%
Italy	9.36%	9.74%	9.41%	8.45%	9.16%
Netherlands	5.32%	4.26%	4.28%	4.30%	4.54%
Spain	14.98%	13.78%	13.49%	13.93%	14.02%
EU-15 Average	9.04%	9.18%	8.85%	8.72%	8.91%

Source: European Commission, (European Commission, 2006b).

7.2.2 Historical payment habits

As explained earlier, the main reasons for the fragmentation of retail banking markets in Europe and, at the same time, also the major obstacles to integration are country differences related to customer behavior and habits or historical reasons.

Figure 24 compares the payment instrument usage in selected eurozone countries between 2003 and 2008. On a first sight, major differences still exist among the selected European countries, indicating that local habits still shape the relative preference for payment instruments by country (Capgemini, EFMA, & ING, 2008, p. 19). However, three key trends hold true for the selected countries, which represent more than 80% of the overall euro payment market.

(i) The usage of checks has been declining in all countries, mainly due to cost-inefficient processing, which has been reflected in higher charges to end-consumers, encouraging the usage of other more cost-efficient instruments.
(ii) The number of card transactions has grown significantly in all countries between 2003 and 2008 and now represents a relative share of around 40% in France, Spain and Italy.
(iii) The usage of direct debit payments has been growing in all four countries, with Germany being the leading country in terms of preference for direct debits as a payment instrument (50% in 2008).

Overall, differences among EU member states with regard to payment instrument preferences will persist, helping to delay the day when users across Europe all prefer the same relative mix of non-cash payment instruments. Since the period under investigation focuses around the mid-term impact of Regulation 2560/2001, the long-term impact of SEPA and PSD on payments behavior is not yet known and would need to be taken into account by further research in the coming years.

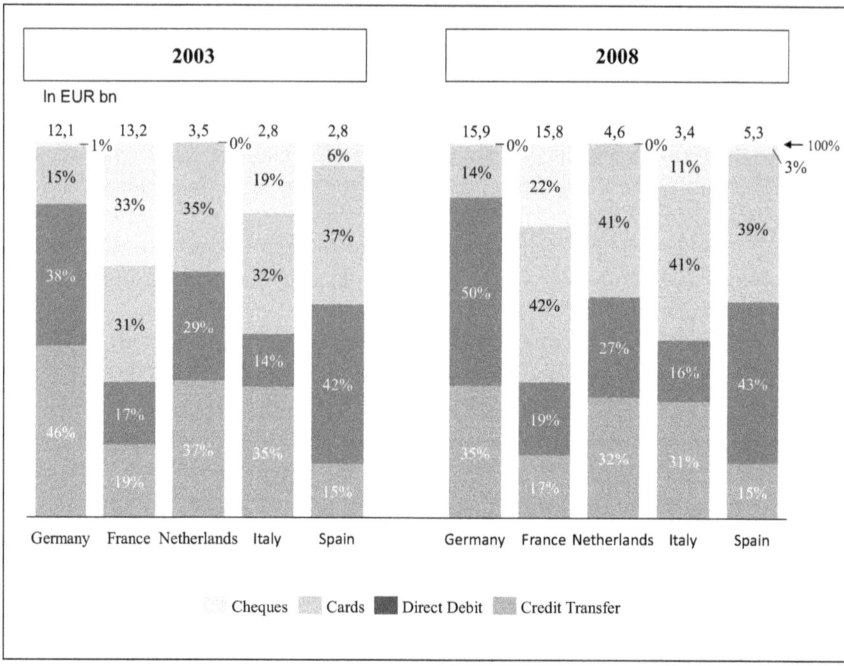

Figure 24: Non-cash payment instrument mix per country
Source: ECB (2009).

7.2.3 Interdependence of demand

Referring to the theoretical explanations in the earlier chapters, EU regulators have argued that the discriminatory prices for euro cross-border payments compared to the domestic payments have constituted the main reason for retail clients not to make use of the single currency from a non-cash point of view. The supply-side analysis showed that with the dictated price convergence the transaction volume of the affected payments has barely increased between 2003 and 2008 (only analog to the overall payment volume growth of approximately 6% on average). Conversely, the demand for cross-border retail payment systems is insignificantly related to the price for these payments. This fact is conclusive considering that a typical EU citizen makes on average between 1–2 cross-border transactions per year. Looking at the impact the Regulation had on domestic payments (see previous section), and considering that the requirement of RPE urged for cross-border and domestic payment prices to converge, banks in several EU member states have increased charges for domestic payments instead. In the following, the evolution of consumer price indices between 1996 and 2008 are examined to provide further indicative evidence for this observation.

The Harmonized Indices of Consumer Prices (HICP) are economic indicators constructed to measure the changes over time in the prices of consumer goods and services. Since 1996, and with an indexation in 2005, the indices have been produced by each EU member state using a common system of calculation developed by European price statisticians led by Eurostat. While the overall HICP provides comparable measures of inflation in the eurozone, the HICP Financial Services is a sub-index that includes charges for common banking services provided by banks, the Post Office and other financial institutions. Among others, the index consists of all account related products and services, such as current accounts, transaction charges for payment services, annual charges for credit cards, Internet banking, safety deposit boxes, brokerage fees, investment advisory and so on. As there is no uniform basket for the HICP due to the different consumption patterns in each member state, all countries are obliged to use a representative basket that reflects the national household final monetary consumption expenditure for financial services. Hence, not only the composition but also the weighting of credit transfers in general and cross-border payments in particular may vary significantly (see evolution of national payment habits discussed earlier). The index excludes however expenses related to intermediary services, Financial Intermediation Services Indirectly Measured (FISIM), such as banking charges paid through interest rate differentials, for example with credit and charge cards (European Commission, 2005g, p. 19).

Figure 25 shows that the HICP for financial services has grown at a higher rate than the overall HICP (see trend line for both indicators). Between 1996 and 2001, costs for banking services increased faster than the overall consumer price index. Already in the initiation phase of Regulation 2560/2001 and prior to its final issuance in December 2001, average prices for banking services decreased until the adoption of the directive for cross-border payments in euros in July 2003. Within one year, the price index for banking services again reached its pre-Regulation level and, since then, has increased with the same growth rate as the overall HICP until 2007. In this year, the final agreements on the wording of law for the PSD between the industry and the EC took place, leading to the issuance of the Directive in December 2007. During this year, a faster growth of the HICP for the financial services index compared to the overall HICP could be observed.

Particular high price inflation for financial service could be observed in the Benelux countries (see representative chart for The Netherlands) relative to the overall consumer price index. However, countries such as Germany and Italy also experienced a faster price index growth for financial services until 2003, followed by a similar growth rate thereafter. In France, meanwhile, hardly any abnormal price development of the HICP for financial services could be registered compared to the overall HICP. The price index in Spain dropped heavily prior to the adoption of Regulation 2560/2001 and increased immediately in the months afterwards. Besides the analogies in price indices development patterns, differences in pricing structures across member states make international comparisons subject to considerable uncertainty (European Commission, 2005g, p. 19).

Drawing direct conclusions from the above date should be handled with care. First, the financial services price index is not sufficiently granular to isolate the price development for domestic and cross-border credit transfers, ATM cash withdrawals or card transactions, making a direct comparison of national price indices and charges for certain payment transactions unfeasible. Second, according to a study performed on behalf of the EC (2005g, p. 19) banks have increased charges on manual teller services to encourage customers to shift to more cost-efficient services such as Internet banking, which may explain the dramatic increase in the index prior to the adoption of the Regulation (European Commission, 2005g, p. 12). Furthermore, the empirical findings of the EC study, which was quoted earlier in the chapter on the measurement of supply-side obstacles to integration, have highlighted several country cases where banks alleged that they increased charges on non-STP, paper-based domestic payments, while reducing or maintaining charges for Internet banking transactions. However, due to the fact that Internet services and teller services are treated as different products, the price index does not reflect any potential gain from product substitution for the end-consumer.

Finally, despite the empirical shortcomings of the EC study, comparing these results with the Eurostat's price index evolution, it is conceivable that Regulation 2560/2001 impacted the pricing of different financial services significantly and has contributed to driving up prices in many EU countries. It is also noticeable that countries, which used to have comparatively low charges for payment and account-related services (such as The Netherlands), have changed their pricing schemes significantly since the initiation of the payment regulation at the expense of the people in the member state.

Without anticipating the long-term effect of SEPA and the benefits arising from the harmonized legal framework provided by SEPA, Regulation 2560/2001 has not yielded the expected benefits for retail clients as promised. In contrast, while prices for affected payments have converged at the required level of domestic payments, overall prices for banking services have increase on average faster than all other consumer prices.

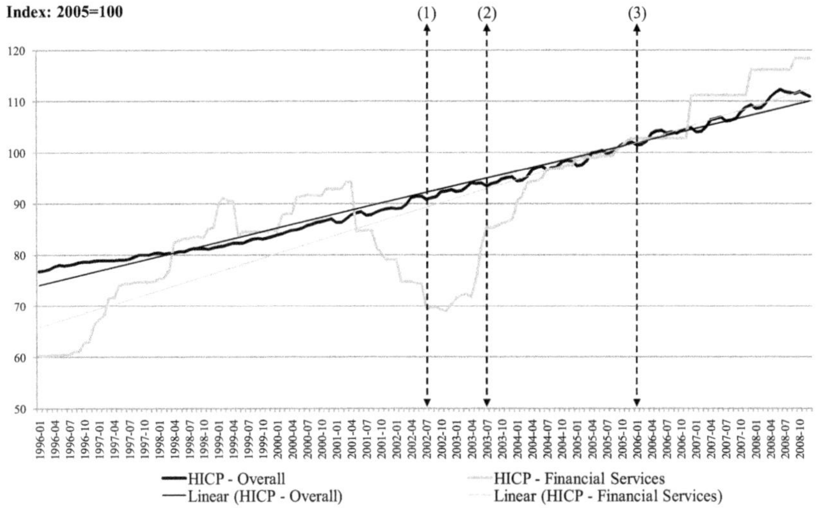

Regulation milestones

(1) 1st Jul 2002, Regulation 2560/2001: Equal charges for domestic and cross-border cash withdrawals and cards
(2) 1st Jul 2003, Regulation 2560/2001: Equal charges for domestic and cross-border payments.
(3) 1st Jan 2006, Regulation 2560/2001: Increase of threshold from EUR 12,500 to 50,000

Figure 25: Consumer price index for financial services in the eurozone
Source: Eurostat (2009).

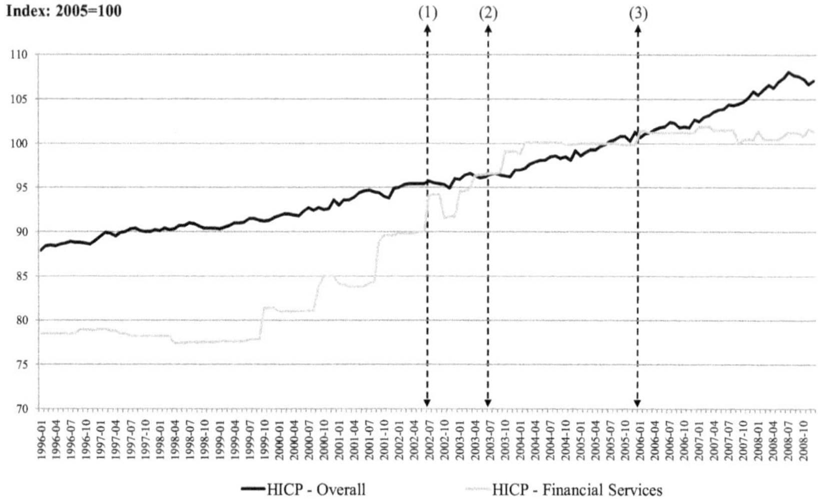

Regulation milestones

(1) 1st Jul 2002, Regulation 2560/2001: Equal charges for domestic and cross-border cash withdrawals and cards

(2) 1st Jul 2003, Regulation 2560/2001: Equal charges for domestic and cross-border payments.

(3) 1st Jan 2006, Regulation 2560/2001: Increase of threshold from EUR 12,500 to 50,000

Figure 26: Consumer price index for financial services in Germany
Source: Eurostat (2009).

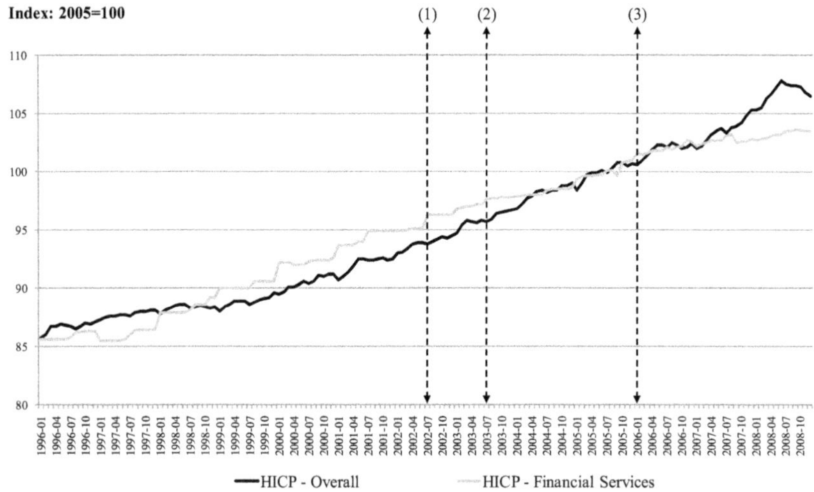

Regulation milestones

(1) 1st Jul 2002, Regulation 2560/2001: Equal charges for domestic and cross-border cash withdrawals and cards
(2) 1st Jul 2003, Regulation 2560/2001: Equal charges for domestic and cross-border payments.
(3) 1st Jan 2006, Regulation 2560/2001: Increase of threshold from EUR 12,500 to 50,000

Figure 27: Consumer price index for financial services in France
Source: Eurostat (2009).

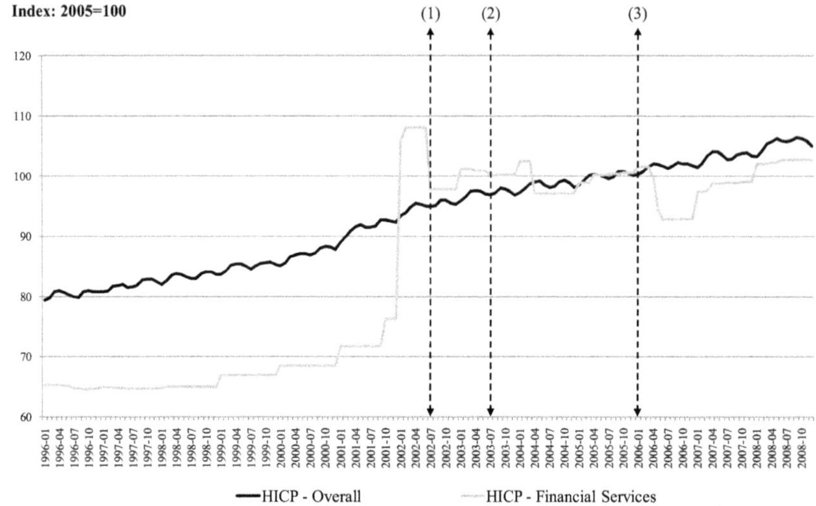

Regulation milestones

(1) 1st Jul 2002, Regulation 2560/2001: Equal charges for domestic and cross-border cash withdrawals and cards
(2) 1st Jul 2003, Regulation 2560/2001: Equal charges for domestic and cross-border payments.
(3) 1st Jan 2006, Regulation 2560/2001: Increase of threshold from EUR 12,500 to 50,000

Figure 28: Consumer price index for financial services in The Netherlands
Source: Eurostat (2009).

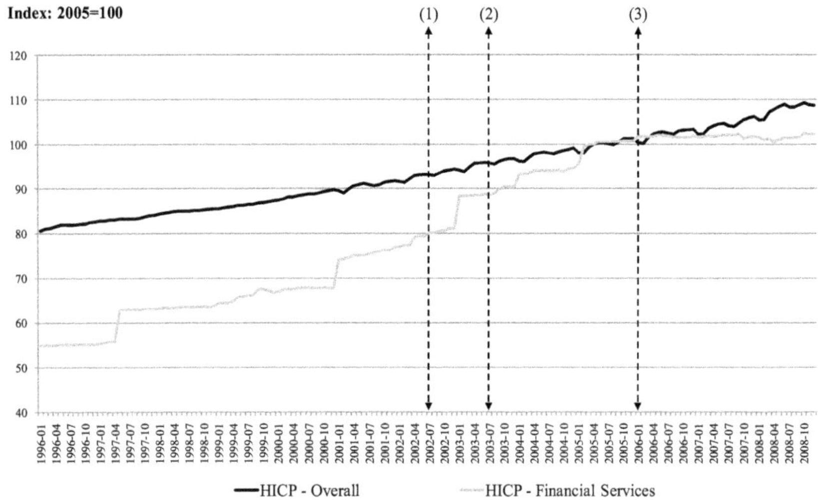

Regulation milestones

(1) 1st Jul 2002, Regulation 2560/2001: Equal charges for domestic and cross-border cash withdrawals and cards

(2) 1st Jul 2003, Regulation 2560/2001: Equal charges for domestic and cross-border payments.

(3) 1st Jan 2006, Regulation 2560/2001: Increase of threshold from EUR 12,500 to 50,000

Figure 29: Consumer price index for financial services in Italy
Source: Eurostat (2009).

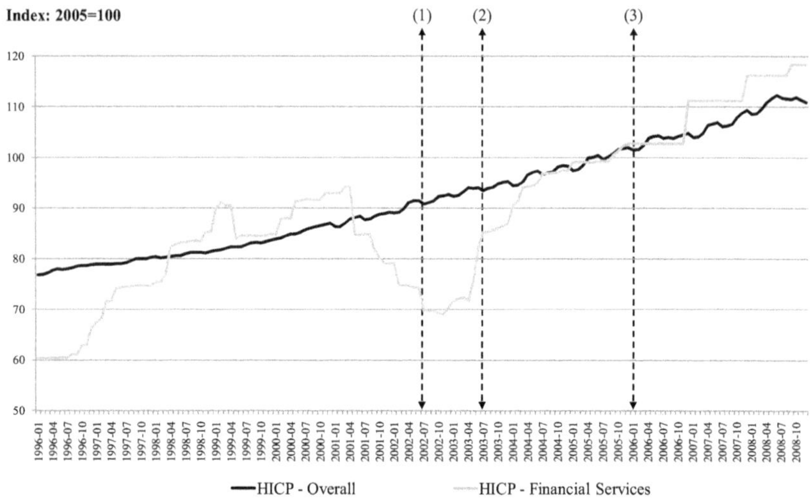

Regulation milestones

(1) 1st Jul 2002, Regulation 2560/2001: Equal charges for domestic and cross-border cash withdrawals and cards
(2) 1st Jul 2003, Regulation 2560/2001: Equal charges for domestic and cross-border payments.
(3) 1st Jan 2006, Regulation 2560/2001: Increase of threshold from EUR 12,500 to 50,000

Figure 30: Consumer price index for financial services in Spain
Source: Eurostat (2009).

7.3 Artificial barriers

Having assessed the impact of Regulation 2560/2001 on the economic obstacles to integration, this section will discuss the capacity of government intervention to remove the artificial, regulatory obstacles to integration.

Again, given that there has been a two-phased impact of the Regulation (mid-term from 2003–2008 and a long-term impact with the launch of the first SEPA credit transfer scheme), this analysis will draw upon the findings from the supply- and demand-side analysis and differentiate between the immediate and the long-term effects.

7.3.1 Consumer protection rules and other legal requirements

While the RPE aimed at removing price discrimination between domestic and cross-border payments in euro, the PSD began as an attempt to provide the required legal framework for the realization of SEPA. However, the EC eventually decided to extend the scope towards a more far-reaching legal framework that would standardize the information requirements, rights and obligations of payment users and service providers. In addition, the PSD is an attempt to spur competition in the provision of these services by allowing a new category of market players (the *payment institutions*), to compete with banks and existing ACHs. In order to ensure that this new category of payment service providers obeys to the same customer protection and transparency requirements as credit institutions, PSD introduces a prudential framework to capture their operations by regulation. Against this background, PSD is considered to be the most comprehensive piece of EU financial services legislation related to payments ever seen to date. With regard to consumer protection, PSD sets common standards for terms and conditions, focusing on a high level of transparency and on minimizing execution time for payments, and shifts liability between consumers and providers in the interests of the end-consumer. Finally, with a view to SEPA, PSD seeks to encourage the adoption of more cost efficient payment types such as SCT and SDD.

While the payment service directive targets the right obstacles to integration to be removed for a single market for payments to develop, significant concerns were expressed by the industry and many stakeholders during the elaboration and also the during the transposition and implementation phase of PSD. In particular the fact that PSD comprises a broad set of objective, consumer protections, transparency, competition, efficiency, consolidation and integration, as some of these objectives conflict with each other in the practical implementation process, leading to disclarity of requirements, interpretation leeway and irregularities in the transposition into national law in member states.

Taking the objective to harmonize consumer protection as an example, it has been clear at an early stage of consultation that PSD will conflict with national law in many member states. Hence, under the influence of the BEUC and national consumer interest groups, EU policy makers acknowledged the local dimension of payments services, and allowed member states to waive no less than 23 of the provisions of the European text in favor of choices made at national level (ESBG, 2009, p. 143). This implies that local retail customers will continue to have the benefit of consumer protection and convenience provided by local legislators and payment service providers, but will, in addition, be able to have access to services under better known conditions outside their place of residence. While progress has been made with regard to the provision of cross-border transactions, the initial objective to harmonize the fragmented legal landscape is not achieved with this Directive. Instead of replacing 33 different regimes by one European regime, a 34th regime is created, co-existing with the national frameworks.

Similar complications occur with the interpretation of the geographic scope of PSD or with the fact that a number of member states derogate from the PSD requirements, which results in gold plating of regulation and will eventually lead to a further fragmentation of EU legislation (contrary to the initial objective).

7.3.2 Political reluctance on national levels

Even though most countries have initially confirmed 1 November 2009 as the target date for PSD to become effective, only 16 out of 30 countries actually complied with the term. Given this inconsistent transposition of PSD across EU member states, the realization of SEPA the creation of a single payment market, which relies on the legal framework provided through PSD, will be further delayed.

While it is inevitable that there will be potential variations in the way PSD is implemented in different countries, these should have been known before and actively negotiated in the legal text of the Directive. Currently, despite a protracted policy consultation process that involved all stakeholders in the industry, and the lengthy negotiation process between the EC, Parliament and Council, a significant number of member states have still either derogated from the agreed text or postponed the transposition of PSD to a later date. To ensure a proper transposition and implementation of the Directive across the EU, the Commission set up a Transposition Working Group consisting of representatives from all member states to discuss and agree proper interpretations on key open issues (Capgemini et al., 2008).

In summary, the artificial and regulatory obstacles to integration could not be fully removed through the PSD. This was, however, less attributed to incorrect objective setting or to the policy development process. The fact that the transposition of the Directive, i.e. the enforcement of the rules, fell behind expectations, can be ascribed to ineffective institutional settings. Instead of a rule-based regulation, where the Directive is considered an imperfect contract between the EC (principal) and the member states (agents), involving high transaction costs but with a dissatisfactory result, a principle-based regulation, defining the necessary overarching framework, may be deemed more effective.

7.4 Summary of findings

The objective of this chapter was to assess the effectiveness of two interrelated payment market directives, RPE or Regulation 2560/2001 and the PSD, in overcoming the defined obstacles to integration as detrimental market outcomes on the one hand and the associated costs and benefits as an efficiency measure on the other.

During the analysis, it has become apparent that both regulatory interventions had an immediate and deferred market effect on both the supply- and the demand-side of the retail banking market. One can define the immediate impact phase as the time between the initiation of Regulation 2560/2001 and its full adoption in 2003. The deferred impact phase begins with the self-regulated development of SEPA initiated by the EPC in 2003, includes the adoption of PSD in 2009 and will end with the ultimate replacement of all national payment infrastructures and schemes. Therefore, a comprehensive measurement of the overall benefit of both payment services regulations cannot be provided within this research project but would require a final assessment once the envisaged single market is fully accomplished. However, this analysis exemplifies how policy intervention may lead to improved market outcomes under certain preconditions. The case of the retail payment market indicates two types of failures. First, the existence of a hold-up or coordination problem in the market, where market forces on their own fail at driving market integration due to lack of commercial interest and the interdependence of demand. Second, the existence of a government failure with respect to an inconsistently adopted legal framework across the EU leads to insufficient legal certainty for markets participants to engage further in cross-border activities. However, the case of the payment market provides evidence for regulatory priorities to remove these obstacles being set wrongly. Not the price discrimination of cross-border retail payments but the regulatory differences in each member states have hindered cross-border competition beyond national borders to emerge. Therefore, EU regulators should have taken measures to harmonize legal frameworks first (i.e., before Regulation 2560/2001), before intervening in the price mechanism of the market.

The results of this chapter are summarized as illustrated in Table 31.

Table 31: Summary of impact assessment

Type of barrier	Barrier to integration	Summary of findings	Immediate impact of RPE and PSD: Removal accomplished	Immediate impact of RPE and PSD: Net-welfare effect	Deferred impact due to SEPA: Removal accomplished	Deferred impact due to SEPA: Net-welfare effect
Supply-side	*Lack of commercial interest*	• Price increase for domestic payments coincides with the introduction of the Regulation • Investment cost to achieve compliance of EUR 5.2–7.7m • Long-term positive net-effect only under best-case migration scenario	No	Negative	Potentially	Potentially positive
	Payment network competition issues	• Further consolidation in the payment services market • Improved market access for new entrants	Yes	Neutral	Yes	Positive
	Lack of open and common standards	• Development of harmonized payment schemes and standards	Yes	Positive	Yes	Positive
Demand-side	*Information asymmetries*	• Improved ex-ante information transparency • Improved quality of information	Yes	Neutral	Yes	Neutral
	Price-inelastic behavior	• No increase of customer mobility registered • PSD will reduce necessity to change bank accounts	No	Neutral	Yes	Positive
	Interdependence of demand	• HICP for financial services fell first and then increased faster than the HICP overall between the 2000-2008 • Increase of domestic pricing schemes in countries with traditionally low charges	No	Negative	Potentially	Potentially positive
	Historical payment habits	• Differences between payment habits continue to exist • Similar key trends observable across major euro countries	No	Neutral	Potentially	Positive
Artificial	*Consumer protection rules*	• No harmonization of consumer protection law achieved due to numerous waivers for many member states • Gold plating of regulation in some countries	No	Neutral	Potentially	Positive
	Disproportionate legal requirements	• Standardized information requirements • Introduction of new category of market players	Yes	Positive	Yes	Positive
	Political reluctance on national levels	• By November 1, 2009, only 16 out of 30 countries transposed PSD as required by the EC • Further delay expected	No	Negative	Potentially	Potentially positive

Source: Author's illustration.

8. Validation and conclusion

This section critically validates the measurement results and their interpretation. First, for measuring the benefits of regulation in overcoming the obstacles to integration a number of different indicators need to be considered. Both quantity- and quality-based measurements have been applied in this case study. The combination of formal observations and the use of a variety of sources of evidence in case studies has been a well-proven approach in the fields of case study research (Yin, 2002, p. 93). Therefore, this research project reviewed all sources available and analyzed these together with the observational evidence of the payment regulation since its coming into effect in 2003. As mentioned several times throughout the work, the lack of consistent data series on cross-border retail banking payment pricing, information provision and market competition has not allowed for a purely empirical research. Hence, the explanation has occurred mostly in narrative or descriptive form, acknowledging that such studies cannot be precise, but they reflect well the theoretical significant propositions. The causal links established in the conceptual framework between the existence of barriers to integration, the level of market integration and the impact of Regulation 2560/2001 and PSD reflect critical insights into the EU's public policy process and regulation theory. While the EU public policy propositions will lead to recommendations of future policy actions, regulation theory propositions of this work may contribute to regulation theory building. By considering several indicators on the supply-side and on the demand-side in parallel, the weakness of single indicators could be revealed. The extensive review of existing literature, in particular of EU progress reports for the retrospective analysis and industry studies on the future, deferred impact of SEPA, provided further evidence for the choice of indicators applied to measure the effectiveness and efficiency of regulation in overcoming barriers to integration in the European retail payment market.

Comparing the overall findings in terms of removal of barriers to integration with the objectives of Regulation 2560/2001, SEPA and PSD, it can be concluded that only four out of six barriers to integration could be removed and that market, government or coordination failures could be corrected as an immediate effect. Only the removal of two barriers to integration has eventually had a positive market impact, whereas the impact of the pricing regulation and the payment directive have been neutral or negative in all other cases. Looking at the deferred, long-term impact of SEPA as a result of the pricing regulation, many more questions exist about the final economic impact. SEPA's success depends heavily on the successful incorporation of PSD into national law in order to provide legal and contractual clarity. At the end of 2009, no consistent transposition of law has taken place so far. Furthermore, given the need for payment service providers to achieve a critical mass and efficiency levels of SEPA payments on domestic levels, further involvement by the regulators is required. Government agencies must be obligated to make changes to the new standards first. In addition, European policy makers must admit that SEPA is public policy-driven and, finally, set a mandatory end-date for the migration from national payment schemes to SEPA.

In this respect, the concept of regulating prices as a function that is originally performed by market players (i.e., the provision and pricing of payment services) expresses clearly that the future European retail payments landscape is first and foremost shaped by political vision and legislation, rather than by end-consumer requirements. However, the euro notes and coins were introduced also with support of legislation, which avoided dual circulation of legacy currencies, very high operating costs and an overall acceptance for the new currency. Considering the long-term impact on the overall payment market and on the European single economic area, SEPA is a much bigger change. The hold-up problem in the market and the need for EU legislation to intervene again with regulation that demands a fixed end-date for a national migration to SEPA has meanwhile galvanized key stakeholders and EU politicians. By taking the European payment market as an example, this case study showed that if regulation is based on wrong economic assumptions or is motivated by wrong political objectives, policy-making and market development enter into a vicious circle, which requires additional regulation to be broken. Hence, regulation may act as a catalyst, but only if an initial assessment of the type of failures impeding integration is performed. Finally, the choice of regulatory intervention should concentrate on the removal of regulatory and legal barriers.

Table 32: Summary Chapter E

Summary Chapter E – Harmonization of retail payments and the case of SEPA
• The European retail payment markets is an important sub-market of the overall retail market. Payments are a key product in this business and are characterized by a high level of fragmentation with regard to systems, instruments, standards and user preferences. Therefore, like no other retail banking product, payments represent a relevant area for research on overall market integration. Similar to the introduction of the euro currency, SEPA, which emerged from the pricing regulation, will lead to a fundamental change in the European financial market.
• This chapter applies the conceptual model to assess the impact of Regulation 2560/2001 (RPE) and the Payment Service Directive (PSD) on payment market integration. Their capacity to remove barriers to integration is evaluated theoretically and the extent, to which an improved market outcome through regulation can be assessed, is measured empirically by means of quantity- and quality-based indicators.
• On the supply-side, the characteristics of payment services (i.e., network externalities, cooperative-competitive relationships and payments considered a club rather than a public good) do not imply a necessary role for public regulation. Therefore, the immediate effect of the RPE on the profitability of the payments industry in Europe has been negative, mainly driven by revenue loss and investment needs. Increased transaction volumes and higher charges on domestic payments cannot compensate for the negative effect. In the long-term, the SEPA initiative may improve the profitability of the business if the critical mass on the new standards is achieved.
• End-consumers overall have not yet experienced the proclaimed benefits from the RPE and the evolving SEPA standards. Information asymmetries will be improved with the transposition of the PSD into national law. Clients' price-inelastic behavior and their mobility have not improved over the period of investigation, which is mainly attributed to the common practice in the industry to bundle and cross-subsidize banking product bundling. Natural barriers such as language and cultural preferences in each member state continue to persist.
• Artificial barriers to integration could not be fully removed through the PSD. Complications occurred primarily in the design of the directive (too much room for interpretation) but also in the transposition into member state law.
• In summary, the price regulation has not accomplished the envisaged economic effects. This was partly due to deficiencies in the consultation process with the private sector but can also be attributed to the political character of the regulation. Nevertheless, a promising self-regulated initiative (SEPA) emerged in the market, which would otherwise be held-up in a coordination failure. In combination with the PSD, the course is set for an internal payment market. However, further regulation is required to set a binding end-date for migration.

Source: Author's illustration.

F Implications for the territorial dimension of banking regulations

The previous chapters have provided the conceptual framework to assess the role of regulations in creating a single market for retail banking in Europe and illustrated the assessment using Regulation 2560/2001 and PSD as an example. Besides this functional view on regulations and the examination of whether regulatory interventions yield a better market outcome than a market driven solution, questions on the design of both policy-making processes and the governance structures of the European retail banking market, and on potential functional and institutional spillover on other industries arise. By drawing on the developments in the European retail payment market and the creation of a SEPA, this chapter seeks to derive implications for the territorial dimension of banking regulations for integration.

1. Europeanization impacts on policy making processes

1.1 Policy uploading and downloading within the FSAP process

Given the economic rational of an integrated financial services sector in the EU and the savings potential in terms of financing and transaction costs, the EU and the member states have stepped up their activities in the pursuit of a single market with the adoption of the Financial Services Action Plan (FSAP) in May 1999 (European Commission, 1999). The goal of the FSAP was to create an adequate framework for a single European market in financial services, consisting of three overarching objectives: a single wholesale market, an open and secure retail market and adequate prudential rules and supervision. The full implementation of the FSAP legislation as a package of 42 measures to achieve the overarching objectives was politically demanded by the Heads of States and Government of member states by 2005.

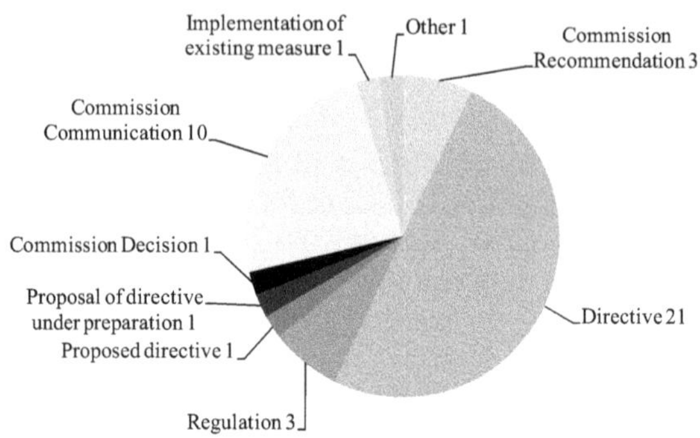

Figure 31: FSAP measures by type
Source: Author's illustration, adopted from European Commission (2005d, p. 23)

Of the 42 FSAP measures, 24 were of a legislative nature (21 directives and 3 regulations), with the remaining 18 being mostly Commission Communications or non-binding recommendations to the member states. While the original action plan included two regulations,[120] Regulation 2560/2001 on cross-border payments in euros was added at a later stage, underlying the extraordinary position of this regulation in the original action plan. While with EU *directives*, member states are freer to reconcile EU rules with national particularities, EU *regulations*, as a binding legislative instrument, demand that the provisions contained therein were applied in exactly the same way in each member state. However, compared to the other two regulations that clearly aimed at providing a level playing field for financial services in Europe and harmonizing legislations, Regulation 2560/2001 intervened with full rigidity in the market's price setting. In terms of Europeanization theory, both policy instruments, regulations and directives, characterize the process of policy downloading from the EU to the member state level. However, they differ with regard to the antecedent uploading of member state preferences and belief structures to the EU level. While regulations demand complete uniformity, directives allow member states to implement different interpretations of EU policy and will result in a diversity of regulatory structures and institutional forms. The extent, to which the financial market integration envisaged by the FSAP is shaped by the processes of policy up- and downloading and the choice of a regulation over directive as legislative instruments, depends on economic but moreover on political considerations. While a clear differentiation between the two motivations and the resulting choice of leg-

120 The Regulation on the European Company Statute (EC) 2157/2001 and the Regulation on International Accounting Standards (EC) 1606/2002.

islative instruments is not always conceivable, there seem to be some indication on the nature of a situation that, assuming the cause and effect can be clearly identified, dominates one process over the other. The empirical study of Howell (2004a; 2004b) on the Europeanization and European integration of financial services and the in-depth analysis of the FSAP process illustrated the difficulties in identifying the cause and effect without methodological simplifications. In this context, Howell showed that European integration involves policy up- and downloading in the formulation of directives and the market place (Howell, 2004a, p. 178). Therefore, the FSAP consists of macro uploading of member states' regulatory preferences, micro uploading of the financial services sector's requirements and an expert view in the consultation processes, formulated into directives that are further downloaded by EU policy to all member states. These directives are then implemented at an EU member state level with different interpretations, leaving room for cultural diversity.

Considering that there are several economic and regulatory barriers to integration identified in the earlier chapters, some kind of policy intervention by the EU is necessary to harmonize fragmented markets such as the European retail banking market. However, the regulatory means required to overcome these impediments (directive versus regulation versus recommendation for self-regulation) depend on a prior assessment of the sources of market detriments (market failure, government failure or coordination failure). Identifying and understanding the economic and regulatory causes that establish a barrier to integration may enable EU policy makers to differentiate better between policy-making processes that are solely driven by downloading through regulation or by a process of both up- and downloading, ensuring the extension of mutual recognition between member states' preferences and the EU level over harmonization and uniformity.

Chapter C outlined that the Lamfalussy Process (the only *Commission Decision* of the FSAP) was introduced in response to the call for an integrated approach to supervision and regulation, which involves EU member states more closely in the legislative process and seeks to provide more comfort and awareness of the ongoing adoption of European rules. Indicating the necessity to link policy uploading and downloading, the Lamfalussy Process aimed at improving the co-operation among regulators and at facilitating the consistent transposition of EU directives into national law. Given the overall positive response received from parties involved, mentioning in particular the enhanced quality and shortened adoption process of legislation,[121] in 2005 the EC extended the Lamfalussy Process to other areas of banking services, such as investment funds, insurance and banking.

121 See EC's "*FSAP Evaluation Report*" (2005d, pp. 10-13) and its subsequent "*Greenpaper on Financial Services Policy (2005-2010)*" (2005e).

Despite the overriding objectives of the original FSAP to establish the single market in financial services, more use of regulations as a legislative instrument has not been made between 2000 and 2005 (European Commission, 2005d, p. 23). This pattern, however, changes when the level-1 policy proposals for directives are passed on to the institutions responsible for level-2 measures in the Lamfalussy Process. At this step of the legislative process technical implementing measures are adopted by the Commission on the advice of the relevant advisory committee and after a binding vote of the competent regulatory committee representing the member states. By 2005, two level-2 regulations had been adopted; the Commission Regulation (EC) 809/2004 of 29 April 2004 (*Prospectus Directive*) and the Commission Regulation (EC) 2273/2003 of 22 December 2003 (*Market Abuse Directive*). The Inter-Institutional Monitoring Group's Third Report Monitoring the Lamfalussy Process (2004, p. 22) concluded:

> "The Group attaches much weight to the significant threat which Member States' non-compliance with the obligation to transpose Directives on time may have for the whole Lamfalussy Process. […] (T)he need for a level playing field (uniformity) is better served by Level 2 Regulations than by Level 2 Directives, which require timely transposition in the laws of the Member States."

Considering that the Lamfalussy Process has been extended to the area of investment funds, banking and insurance, the use of level-2 measures and therefore also of regulations as a legislative instrument, becomes more common. While this needs to be assessed on a case-by-case basis, it can be concluded that in areas where artificial obstacles impede market integration, EU regulations should be used over directives to ensure the establishment of a level playing field in financial services and to avoid member states *goldplating* EU directives by adding extra measures on the national level.

The EU's recognition of the necessity to link member states and industry experts closer to the policy making process is reflected in the establishment of consultation processes. In one of the early directives of the FSAP, the Prospectus Directive, banking industry participants and the public at large were not formally consulted on the proposals drawn up by the Commission. As a result, the European Parliament, the Council and the banking markets had serious objections to the content of the text. The Commission had to consider these concerns and amended the proposal that was eventually adopted by the legislative bodies of the EU on 4 November 2003. In the directive that followed thereafter, the Commission were keen on ensuring the formal pre-consultation with expert groups and the European Parliament in order to avoid the difficulties experienced with the Prospectus Directive. Where formal or informal consultation took place, the general reaction was that it had an "overwhelming positive influence on the resulting legislative texts" (European Commission, 2005d, p. 16). Therefore, public authorities and the banking market had to undergo a learning process to steadily advance the consultation process in the elaboration of legislative proposals on the directives of the FSAP. This shows that a long-term discovery procedure for the most efficient institutional arrangement between the member states and the EU level is required to develop an effective standardized approach to the preparation of financial services regulation. Consultation before and during the introduction of new EU legislation should therefore continue to follow the Commission's principle of *good regulation* policy and to take practical constraints, such as timetables and drawing up feedback statements, into account. Against this background, valuable insights on the further development of the policy-making process can also be derived from Regulation 2560/2001 on cross-border payments and form Directive EC 64/2007 (PSD).

1.2 Lessons learned from Regulation 2560/2001, SEPA and PSD

Despite the evidence provided in the previous chapter that the RPE did not yield net benefits for the European market economy to date, the policy-making process itself showed several shortcomings, making Regulation 2560/2001 a negative example to derive recommendations from for future improvements.

Regulation 2560/2001 was not included in the original FSAP as it was intertwined with a previous measure, the existing cross-border transfers Directive (97/5/EC), which came into force in August 1999. This Directive outlawed double charging and requires banks to systematically provide information prior to a transaction. Despite repeated appeals from the Commission to the banking sector for them to reduce charges, banks continued to ignore these early soft signs of EU regulation and remained defensive when being publically confronted with the results of a study mandated by the EC on bank charges of cross-border payments. Furthermore, the support of member states to enforce the Directive by transposing it into national law fell short of expectations and hardly any measures were taken to enforce the Directive's requirements. When the discussion at the EU level started to involve consumer interest groups, representing in particular the interest of border-zone areas of the Benelux countries with historically strong cross-border work, trade and therefore payment habits, the political pressure on the European banking industry increased. While fragmented markets in the EU were considered inefficient from a macro-economic point of view and a harmonized retail payment market was desirable, a substantiated impact assessment on the required costs and benefits and the prioritization of the timing harmonization after the introduction of the euro currency was not performed at that time. Instead, the political motivation for a single market became apparent when Regulation 2560/2001 was introduced under the (mistaken) political assumption that high costs for retail cross-border transactions impede cross-border trade, consumption and competition. On the pretext of providing clear benefit for all EU citizens (hence the retail banking clients), such as lower charges for payment transactions and the freedom of choice for a better payment environment, prices for cross-border payments were fixed at domestic payment levels. Beyond doubt the frustration of the EC with the member states for not enforcing the previous Directive sufficiently and the banking industry for not becoming actively involved, has contributed to the decision.

In the aftermath of the payment regulation, SEPA evolved as a self-regulated process by the European banking industry to cope with the constraints set by the regulators. While new standards and payment schemes have been developed and the industry has invested heavily in its infrastructure to become compliant with these new standards, national retail banking fragmentation remains. Furthermore, in contrast to the original objective of the Regulation to provide benefit for end-consumers, it increasingly becomes obvious that retail banking markets are local because their clients' needs are local, and that in particular multinational corporations and multi-country banks, who have a broad geographic footprint in the euro area will benefit almost exclusively from SEPA.

Several lessons learned can be derived from this case study. First, whether a new legislative proposal will be introduced as a directive with room for interpretation on member state-level or whether it is a regulation, demanding uniform transposition across all member states, clear objectives must be defined and a consistent message must be conveyed in the market. Secondly, and this refers to the previous analysis of barriers to integration, EU legislation should utilize its power to focus on the removal of artificial, regulatory barriers to integration first, before intervening and tackling obvious other market or coordination failures with regulation. In the case of RPE, the EC took the line of least resistance and blamed the unwillingness of the banking industry to reduce charges. Instead of imposing political pressure on member states and their government agencies to harmonize national legal frameworks, and to remove artificial barriers to integration first, the EC gave in to consumer interest group pressure to further regulate the banking industry. Finally, an impact assessment or a macro-economic business plan should be prepared and flow into the policy-making process, trying to quantify the expected economic welfare effects for the targeted recipients. Such a cohesive business plan would also incentivize market participants to be supportive of the legislation and to be willing to follow the road and accept some cost in the short term as they can plan for investments to pay off in the mid-term.

In 2001, EU legislators had the option not to intervene by further market regulation, even though the cross-border transfers Directive (97/5/EC) failed to achieve its objective, being largely ignored by member states regarding transposition and enforcement in the banking industry. A prior assessment of the obstacles to integration would have evidenced that the removal of legal barriers was the most important impediment to the evolution of a single market on the one hand and an inherent responsibility of a supranational regulatory body such as the EC on the other. Today, there is an industry-wide consensus that if an earlier harmonization of regulatory requirements towards banks and payment service providers, such as consumer protection, warranties or return conditions on the consumer side and contract law or insolvency rights on the corporation side had taken place, a market-driven integration process from the demand-side would have emerged. Considering direct debits as an example, multinational corporations, such as utility and telecommunication firms with branches or subsidiaries across the eurozone have to collect payments from their retail clients on a regular basis. Given that these payment collection processes differ significantly among the euro member states, i.e. there is a regulatory requirement for foreign European banks to have a banking license in Italy before being able to collect payments from Italian retail clients, the demand for cross-border direct debits could not evolve prior to the cross-border payment directive, SEPA and PSD. Therefore, if legal requirements had been harmonized in the first instance through EU regulation, taking into account the massive resistance from the member states but ensuring cross-European uniform application, banks would have availed themselves of the opportunity of serving an inherent demand of corporate clients to consolidate their bank accounts in Europe to a single account to save costs by developing products that exactly fit client requirements. Competition detriments would be dissolved over time through the market entry of new competitors that aim at expanding their home market into Europe and that invest into pan-European payment processing and services platforms. Given the admittedly high progress achieved with the transposition and implementation of the PSD, further competition from outside of domestic borders can only be achieved if legal frameworks are uniformly harmonized and the demand for certain payment services evolves by itself.

With regard to information asymmetries, more transparency on payment product characteristics would be expected through an increase in competition and a more distinct product differentiation of banks and payment service providers provided that no regulatory obstacles to integration and no antitrust threats exist in the payment market. However, with regard to price transparency, no improvements would be expected in this regard. First, similar to mobile phone tariffs, account-related services such as payments will always be sold in product bundles to end-consumers as it is part of each bank's individual sales strategy. Second, and this can also be referred to the mobile phone industry, payments and related services are complex products. End-consumers' search costs for a tariff that is incrementally better than their current tariff and the associated switching cost to change to another bank outweighs the expected cost savings.

This case study showed that regulation can represent a distinctive form of governance provided that it is underpinned by a single normative justification (i.e., the correction of market failures or coordination failure) that can be derive from science and theory. By this means, economic efficiency can be ensured. If regulation and EU policy-making becomes an arbitrary whim or political discretion in order to prioritize social efficiency (i.e., the political motivation to create a single market to make Europe more attractive to its citizens or to blame certain stakeholders for delaying the integration process), no theoretical position would be required (Armstrong & Bulmer, 1998, pp. 260-261). While regulation may correct market failure, such as the inefficient allocation of goods and services as a result of restrictive agreements and the abuse of market power, considering the results of the previous analysis of different barriers to integration, it becomes apparent that EU regulation does not possess a single normative justification of the correction of market failure. Moreover, the concept of market failure relates to the control of a market that appears to presuppose being integrated, which is obviously not the case of the European retail banking market. Looking at the internal market and revisiting Majone's arguments of the regulatory state (1994b), EU regulation is less concerned with correcting market failure than with overcoming the barriers arising from divergent national regulation. Therefore, one can further develop this argument that EU regulation is correcting the failure of the market in national public goods, such as national regulation. However, the functional assessment of the role of regulation performed in the previous chapter showed the fragmented regulatory landscape in Europe is more a governmental than a market failure and EU regulations exist because of the historical lack of market or other mechanisms by which national regulations were exposed to one another. In order to correct market, government or coordination failures, the primary policy instrument at the EU's disposal is control through legal rules. Its capacity to effectively remove barriers to market integration depends on how well the rules elaborated through the process of policy up- and downloading (including expert consultation at an early stage) are enforced on the member state level, that is, the quality of EU institutions.

1.3 Transposition and enforcement problems

Referring to the term *governance* as defined in the first chapter, stating that governance focuses on rule structures or institutions influencing the behavior of actors, mediating the claims of affected interests and, in the context of integration, seeking to overcome barriers to integration, this chapter will draw on the observations from the case study of the payment market regulation. Furthermore, this section will also refer to the key feature of EU governance: the exercise of regulation beyond the national state in the form of the transfers of power to the EU institutions. The problem of transposition of the EU payment directives and difficulties in enforcing these rules plays a dominate role.

The analysis of the European retail payment market integration has several general implications on the governance of the internal market. First, Regulation 2560/2001 could have been avoided if markets had taken previous informal indications or formal directives seriously and taken self-regulatory actions to satisfy the comparably moderate information and charging requirements. Realizing that market harmonization in a multi-level EU can merely be done through informal rules or formal rules without corresponding measures of reinforcement could be evidenced in this case. Furthermore, the governance structure and the policy-making process in the EU still show institutional disadvantages of being driven by national interests, even more than five years after the introduction of the Lamfalussy Process and improved consultation processes. On both the supply- and the demand-side of the market, national associations or interest groups are consolidated on a European level, where the umbrella organization on top represents the merged interest of a particular group, such as the European Savings Banks Group (ESBG) for saving banks or the BEUC for consumer interests. An uploading of particular, in many cases national, interests, may diverge diametrically with the interest of a European market as it may imply a material worsening of the current national status. In addition, those individuals heading the European representations of a particular interest group are not appointed to this office for their capability to drive harmonization and to implement the European ideal of a harmonized market, but for their political finesse to lobby for the interest of their clients towards regulators.

With the establishment of improved consultation processes for market participants and member states to provide their opinion on envisaged EU legislation, all kinds of stakeholders are now able to join the process under the pretext of delivering better regulation through early involvement in the market. In the case of the payment market, it could be observed that European governance boards have successively enlarged with representatives from all areas, becoming more *debate clubs* – dictating the banking business – than an industry expert group that can legitimize EU rulemaking through their product knowledge. Considering that banks would have obviously failed in their business if not knowing best how to serve their clients' needs, and being able to design the technical properties of their products accordingly, the current involvement of payment user interest groups and politicians seems to reflect the regulators' intention to shift the blame for the lack of harmonization progress to market participants. Instead of challenging the existing old product, infrastructure and legal structures that interest groups in member states seek to conserve, the industry's resistance to invest in SEPA compliant systems is often referred to as the main reason why the desired positive economic impact has not yet materialized.[122]

122 Resistance to implement SEPA and the SCT and SDD payment schemes also comes from many corporations, in particular insurance companies. As part of the required formal declaration of consent that needs to be provided by every retail client, corporations with a large number of *dormant* clients who, either deliberately or by nescience, have an existent direct debit contract or transfer an amount on a regular basis, might notice this mistake and cancel the contract.

Drawing on the lessons learned from the theoretical considerations and the practical implications of the case study, the question of how different national regulation traditions and policy approaches can be arranged to suit the uniformity requirements of a single market, can be answered with reference to the following recommended principles for EU regulation.

- Tighter deadlines: Regulation 2560/2001 has forced the banking industry to comply with the rule by 1 July 2003 whereas the transposition of the PSD was envisaged for 1 November 2009 and a third of member states have delayed the timeline recommended by the EC. Given that a second hold-up problem or coordination failure is appearing with no final end-date for the decommissioning of domestic payment systems and full migration to SEPA being set, means EU policy makers will need to set an end date by rule in order to avoid the failure of the SEPA idea.
- Utilization of expertise: Banks and payment service providers should be in the lead of the development of harmonized European payment products and standards due to their best market, product, and process expertise. If legal obstacles are removed through regulation, national payment products will have to withstand the competition with SEPA or other products that will compete in their home market. Those products that have a strong competitive advantage will be surviving competition.
- Design and elaboration of directives: Consultations before and after the introduction of new legislative proposals between expert groups and committees and the Commission should continue to legitimate rulemaking. However, the process must be kept efficient in terms of stakeholders involved and consultation timelines set. The author suggests a similar consultation approach as used in the G8 or G20 summits, where the most important economic market participants determine the strategic direction to take and have the political power to implement decisions consistently.
- Implementation and enforcement: Particular improvement is required on the transposition and rule enforcement process. Regulators may apply a conceptual framework similar to the one adopted in this study to assess the type of failure to correct and choose an adequate regulatory intervention (i.e., regulation, directive, recommendation etc.) that will most effectively tackle the cause of market detriment. Depending on the choice of legislative instruments, either the desired full harmonization or an interpretation into national law can be expected.

2. Consequences for the multilevel governance structure

The functional and the territorial dimensions of banking regulation are reflected in the process of policy-making (policy uploading and downloading in European integration) and in the multilevel governance structure of the EU. Putnam (1988) has described international regime formation as a two-level game, where the result is determined by the cooperation of governments involved and the domestic policy interaction. However, considering the observations of the payment market integration, but also in the European financial market in general, the developing governance structure in the EU may be better described as a complex, multilayered game with changing alliances. For example, the line of bargaining positions may be drawn

- between governments on the one hand and the European financial services industry as a whole on the other;
- between member states' governments allied with their domestic financial services industries versus other member states and their respective national industries; and
- between multinational banks or financial organizations with or without governments (the wholesale and investment banking market) versus a financial industry focusing on national or regional markets (retail banking markets).

The participation of the financial services industry in the design of European governance structures has two main causes: the financial services industry has self-interest to exercise influence on EU policy-making on the one hand, and public norm and standard setting requires the banking industry to participate on the other. Considering the definitions of negative vs. positive integration made initially (see Chapter A), EU interventions and European banking regulation have recently been focusing on positive integration, that is, the development and implementation of effective supranational policies to correct market failures and to ensure social protection. In this area, the banking industry regulation is strongly interlinked with other rules and standards, such as company, tax or trade law. All developments in these areas toward deeper integration have a direct impact on the competitiveness of the national and the profitability of the overall European banking industry. Furthermore, the wider the gap between the private and the public economic area the higher the transaction costs for operating in different institutional frameworks. Therefore, the point can be made that the exertion of influence of the banking industry on the policy-making process in financial services and the design of a multilevel governance structure is in the interest of both the industry and the regulator. The involvement of expert and market knowledge and regulation *with* the market instead of a regulation *of* the market will increase the effectiveness of a regulatory intervention (Walter & Speyer, 2005, p. 19) or even make regulation superfluous in favor of self-regulation or *soft-law*.

The overview of national and EU supervisory structures provided in Chapter C already indicated the promising developments toward more cooperation and consultation on regulatory topics between the banking industry, national supervisory authorities and the ESCB. While considerable progress has been made with the Financial Services Action Plan, the case of retail payments market integration shows that further work needs to be done to facilitate an effective coordination of the banking industry's expertise and the decision-making power of supervisory agencies and the central banks.

Besides a stronger involvement of the private sector, a multilevel governance structure requires closer alignment of roles and responsibilities between the central banks on the national and the European levels. Today, most cooperation among authorities takes place informally or is mainly subject-driven, but formal arrangements to develop supervisory cooperation are starting to emerge. In 2005, the European Financial Services Roundtable (EFR) presented a concept of a lead supervisor, designed to reduce the duplication of supervisory activities to the greatest extent possible under the confines of existing EU legislation (Speyer, 2005, p. 12). The proposal foresees to establish a lead supervisor or supra-agency to act as the single point of contact for pan-European financial institutions within the prudential supervisory framework.

This study refrains from elaborating the pros and cons of a European lead supervisor as this topic has been extensively discussed in relevant literature.[123] However, this discussion has important implications for the creation of a single market for financial services. A lead supervisory agency, which would be empowered to strike down regulations of member state agencies, would change the balance of regulatory influence in favor of such a hypothetical central agency and at the expense of individual, national regulatory agencies. Therefore, member states will attempt to protect national supervision agencies and underlying national financial industries. In order to ensure that the vision of an internal market for Europe is continuously incorporated in the integration policy-making process and enforced on member state levels, a robust mandate must assigned to such central supervision function (Cowen, 1998, p. 26).

123 See, for example, Barth et al. (2004), Das, Quintyn and Chenard (2004), European Banking Federation (2007), European Central Bank (2003a), European Commission (2005e), Kern (2003) or Schoenmaker (2005).

Table 33: Summary Chapter F

Summary Chapter F – Implications for the territorial dimension of banking regulation
• The case study on the developments in the European retail payment market provides extensive insights on the Europeanization and European integration process. Referred to as the territorial dimension of banking regulation this chapter embeds the findings into a broader picture of the policy-making process and governance structure of the European financial market. • The Financial Services Action Plan (FSAP) consisted of a legislation package to create an adequate framework for a single European market in financial services. The retail payment market represents a focus area in this action plan. • The research of Howell (2004a; 2004b) explains Europeanization by means of uploading and downloading between the member states and the EU level, using the FSAP process as an example. The findings from the retail payment market refine Howell's observations by examining what went wrong in the process of regulated market creation that has led to the current situation. • The overall lessons learned derived from the retail payment market concern the initial objective-setting of regulation, but moreover to the process of policy-making, choice of regulatory instruments and the governance structure of the market. • The EC as a political promoter of the development of a single market and the ESCB as a facilitator and overseer need to set the political agenda and the objectives for integration. These objectives must be enshrined in the vision for a true single market in Europe. At the same time, their economically rational and transparent formulation and communication to all stakeholders is critical. In the payment market, a large part of legislation was originally made under the pretext of serving all EU citizens and retail clients. Looked at the findings in this study, it turns out that multinational banks and corporations will benefit most. • The process of elaborating EU regulation to create a single market must include a prior assessment of potential improvements to the market outcome, similar to the conceptual model proposed in this study. Furthermore, an effective consultation process with relevant stakeholders ensures that expert knowledge is considered to legitimize the resulting state intervention. • The choice of regulatory instruments should reflect the results of the initial impact assessment and the overall policy objectives. In areas where uniformity is necessary among all member states, such as the legal framework, regulation is preferred over directives and recommendations. • Formal arrangements to develop supervisory cooperation are necessary to ensure a consistent transposition, enforcement and control of EU legislation among the member states.

Source: Author's illustration.

G Conclusion

This study investigated the role of European regulation in facilitating the creation of a single retail banking market. The choice of policy measures to overcome barriers to integration persistent in the retail banking integration process took a center stage in the analysis. This study initially hypothesized that in highly fragmented, heterogeneous markets, market forces on their own may fail to develop a single market, so that the intervention of regulation is required. With respect to the role of EU-regulation in promoting market integration this study raised the research question about the key decision factors influencing the choice for regulation compared to a market solution and how can policy interventions be measured with regard to their effectiveness and efficiency. To answer the research question and to fill the identified research gap in regulation theory, this study developed a theoretical-conceptual framework that allows both theorists and practitioners to systematically examine the barriers to integration in a market, to identify the underlying market, government or coordination failures justifying policy intervention, and to finally derive efficient and effective policy measures.

Due to the general thematic focus on banking regulation and the high complexity of the European banking markets, regulation was analyzed by a conceptual-empirical approach, following an analytical and empirical research strategy. The conceptual model was directly tied to the economic theories on European integration and banking regulation. It assessed the efficiency and effectiveness of regulation, encompassing a comparative institutional approach to regulation and combining the functional and territorial view on regulation. The explanatory case study on the European retail payment market in Chapter E illustrated the application of the framework. A single case study design was selected, as there are no comparable cases known in the financial service industry that would be more exposed to market fragmentation and heterogeneity.

The overall findings of the case study may be of a major relevance for the research on European integration and for EU policy makers in the internal market. The results from both the theoretical as well as the empirical analysis concluded that there is not one single type of failure impeding the creation of a single market for retail payments in Europe. Instead, all three can be diagnosed but with a varying degree of value: market, government and coordination failure. While traditional banking regulation has a functional focus on preserving system stability and resilience, the integration of a fragmented European retail banking landscape demands a different assessment of the factors that determine and justify regulatory intervention.

With regard to the location of regulation, a shift of regulatory intervention to correct market failures from the EU member state to an EU level is taking place.

The institutional change process under way has implications on the design of policymaking processes and on the resulting governance structure of the EU. However, there is no economic theory available that would model the transformation of fragmented markets, such as retail banking, into a single market. Furthermore, there is no single model available that can be applied by EU regulators to assess the effectiveness and efficiency of their regulatory means in overcoming obstacles to integration.

Based on theoretical considerations of regulation theory with a focus on banking and Europeanization theory, a four-step analysis process was developed that builds on existing regulation impact assessments, broadened and deepened by incorporating the territorial dimension to reflect the multilayered policymaking process. The conceptual framework identified four generic key decision-making factors that imply certain potential regulatory interventions to correct indicated market detriments. Whether barriers to integration always relate to a market, government or coordination failure or to risk is established on a case-by-case basis. Furthermore, the territorial dimension of regulation is incorporated in the model through the policy objectives set by the EU. The way regulatory intervention is eventually shaped depends on the decision-making process of uploading and downloading between member states and their industries to the EU level, and vice versa.

Potential improvements in the market through regulation should be made measurable. In this regard, the developing of the conceptual framework included a discussion on the current state in academic literature on how to make integration measurable ex-ante and ex-post, through quantity-, price- and quality-based indicators. However, the lack of comprehensive data and data granularity in retail banking makes a precise empirical assessment of regulation difficult.

Applied to the retail payment market, this research study explained how EU intervention may fail to accomplish its original goals and how regulators are required to mend decisions made on wrong assumptions, selling a political vision as an economic necessity. In this respect, EC Regulation 2560/2001 on cross-border payments in euros has not provided a positive net welfare effect, at least not as an immediate impact. However, the self-regulated SEPA initiative and the consolidation process of payment service providers that resulted from the regulation indicate that a positive net welfare effect can be achieved with SEPA in the long- to mid-term. This, however, depends on the role of public authorities to swiftly adapt to the new standards and the EC to demand a fixed end-date for the migration of all domestic standards to SEPA.

A thorough analysis of the background of the EU policy-making process that led to the adoption of Regulation 2560/2001 and of the PSD has shown that the price regulation was not necessary from an ordoliberal point of view. The EU policy-making process lacked formal consultations with the private sector and other member states and has therefore led to law transposition and enforcement problems of EU directives. In addition, the exploitation of room for interpretation and discretion given to national legislative bodies has also led to inconsistencies. In situations like this, the use of regulation as the ultimate means of EU intervention may be required to ensure uniformity in Europe. However, as evidenced with the development of SEPA, the risk remains that political motivation for creating a single market will prevail over economic sensibility. The rigidity with which the EC has intervened in the pricing sovereignty of the market and the lack of this rigidity when it came to harmonizing legal frameworks in the EU confirms this assessment. The author recommended that EU legislators should consider applying the mutual recognition principle for those aspects of a service in retail payments that have not been deemed necessary to be fully harmonized.

With respect to overall theoretical implications, traditional explanations for banking regulation fall short in justifying regulatory intervention by the EU to create a single market. Therefore, this study sought to establish a theoretical link between the functional and the territorial dimensions of regulation to examine the specific research questions on the role of regulation in integrating highly fragmented European (banking) markets. With reference to the existing academic literature on cost-benefit assessment models applied to traditional banking regulation topics, the respective decision-making criteria derived from the comparative institutional analysis were conceptualized into a framework of analysis, which can be further applied to other areas of regulation beyond the financial market. Furthermore, the findings of this analysis also attempt to contribute to an enhanced understanding of European policy-making in terms of uploading and downloading and to the design of an effective governance structure. Finally, the case of European integration showed that institutions matter, but good rules require an effective enforcement, which is not always the case when applying EU directives to harmonize the financial market. Finally, the theoretical implications stress the importance of effective governance as the capacity of the EU's institutional matrix to implement and enforce public policies and to improve private sector coordination (Ahrens, 2002, pp. 128-129).

For market practitioners and EU policy makers, the overall findings may be relevant for their future decision-making. The fact that a single market in retail banking has not yet evolved is less a sign for market or coordination failure than of government failures: artificial and regulatory barriers need to be removed in a first instance to provide a level playing field for banks and payment service providers on the one hand and a safe and trustworthy legal environment for consumers on the other. Here, the legislative bodies of the EU should focus on their core competency as regulators to achieve harmonization in these areas first, even if political resistance from the EU member states will be very high.

Depending on the outcome of a prior theoretical assessment, the elaboration of EU legislation requires the consultation of relevant stakeholders that can provide the legitimacy for EU policy-making. Relevance in this context relates to a thorough selection of parties to involve for taking advice. The focus should less be made on the political or popular considerations and more on the sources of detriments, understanding economic causes and effects.

This study has shown that informal consultations hardly lead to an overall positive market result, because they favor those particular interest groups that already exert a strong influence on the EU decision makers. Therefore, the consultation processes should be further formalized to empower the EU level and to establish transparency. In this regard, the Lamfalussy Process represents a significant intermediary step toward a harmonized banking regulation and supervision system and has rightly been extended to the insurance and banking sector as well.

In the mid-to long-term, as a result of an increasingly formalized EU policy-making process, the creation of an efficient and effective structure for financial supervision in Europe is required. With reference to the territorial dimension of regulation, an Europeanization of financial supervision may be required. Comparable to the ESCB, the establishment of a European System of Financial Supervisory Authorities (ESFSA) will be necessary to ensure proper transposition and enforcement of EU rules.

In the aftermath of the worldwide banking crisis and the need for the EU to develop harmonized rules to ensure financial market stability in order to avoid a *regulatory race to the-bottom* or an arbitrage among member states, a centrally led supervisory agency is deemed necessary. However, this may be implemented only at the expense of national supervisory agencies that will have to hand over responsibility and sovereignty to the EU level. A strong political determination, supported by all heads of government and inspired by the European idea is critical to establish a single market with a central supervisory agency.

The limitation of this conceptual-analytical study is twofold. On the one hand, the explanatory case study of SEPA may be a unique and extreme case and a critical test of regulation theory. However, further comparable cases in other sectors, such as in the mobile phone industry and in the utility sector, need to be investigated to provide further empirical proof. Second, the fragmentation of the retail banking market in Europe is reflected in the inconsistencies of quantity- and price-related data for retail banking products in general and payment services in particular. Therefore, a significant amount of empirical data used in this work is based either on secondary sources or on price indices such as the HICP for financial services, which lacks granularity to apply econometric analysis. Therefore, the analytical-conceptual nature and qualitative approach of this dissertation reflects the eminent of available data. Furthermore, a major limitation of this dissertation is the lack of external validity and generalizability. Yet, this dissertation provides an initial study base for subsequent quantitative and qualitative research:

- As more data on the impact of SEPA becomes available, for example, through the data collection project initiated by the Directorate General Consumer Protection (2008), future research should aim to quantitatively test impact of Regulation 2560/2001 and PSD on prices, volumes and characteristics of payments instruments in Europe.
- Furthermore, the investigation into the question whether the conceptual model presented in this study on measuring the effectiveness and efficiency of regulation in the multilayered European governance structure can also be applied in policy areas other than the financial industry.

Reference list

Accenture. (2006). *The European Payments Revolution*: Accenture European Survey 2006.

Achleitner, A.-K. (2001). *Handbuch Investment Banking* (2nd ed.). Wiesbaden: Gabler.

Ackerberg, D. A., & Gowrisankaran, G. (2004). *Quantifying Equilibrium Network Externalities in the ACH Banking Industry.* University Arizona.

Adam, K., Jappelli, T., Menichini, A., Padula, M., & Pagano, M. (2002). *Analyse, compare and apply alternative indicators and monitoring methodologies to measure the evolution of capital market integration in the European Union.* Solerno: Department of Economics and Statistics at the University of Salerno.

Adshead, M. (2002). Conceptualising Europeanisation: Policy Networks and Cross-National Comparison. *Public Policy and Administration, 17*(2), 25-42.

Ahrens, J. (2002). *Governance and Economic Development.* Cheltenham, UK; Northampton. MA, USA: Edward Elgar Publishing Limited.

Akerlof, G. A. (1970). The Market for "Lemons": Quality Uncertainty and the Market Mechanism *The Quarterly Journal of Economics, 84*(3), 488-500.

Alchian, A. A. (1977). Some Economics of Property Rights. In A. A. Alchian (Ed.), *Economic Forces at Work* (pp. 127-149). Indianapolis: Liberty Press.

Alchian, A. A., & Demsetz, H. (1972). Production, Information Costs, and Economic Organization. *American Economic Review, 62*(5), 777-795.

Aldridge, I. E. (2005). *Do Financial Companies Benefit from SEC Regulation?* , University of Totonto, April 23.

Andenas, M., & Gebhardt, I. (2001). Financial Market Regulation in Europe - Some Institutional Aspects. In D. Hummel & R.-E. Breuer (Eds.), *Handbuch Europäischer Kapitalmarkt* (1 ed., pp. 151-174). Wiesbaden: Gabler.

Angelini, P. (1998). An analysis of competitive externalities in gross settlement systems. *Journal of Banking & Finance, 22*(1), 1-18.

Angelini, P., Maresca, G., & Russo, D. (1996). Systemic risk in the netting system *Journal of Banking & Finance, 20*(5), 853-868.

Aoki, M., Murdock, K., & Okuno-Fujiwara, M. (1998). Beyond The East Asian Miracle: Introducing the Market-Enhancing View. In M. Aoki, K. Murdock & M. Okuno-Fujiwara (Eds.), *The Role of Government in East Asian Economic Development* (pp. 1-37). Oxford: Clarendon Press.

Apolte, T., Bender, D., Berg, H., Cassel, D., Erlei, M., Grossekettler, H., et al. (Eds.). (2003). *Vahlens Kompendium der Wirtschaftstheorie und Wirtschaftspolitik* (8 ed. Vol. 2). München: Verlag Franz Vahlen.

Armstrong, K., & Bulmer, S. (1998). *The governance of the Single European Market*. Manchester: Manchester University Press.

Baele, L., Ferrando, A., Hördahl, P., Krylova, E., & Monnet, C. (2004). *Measuring financial integration in the Euro area*. Frankfurt: European Central Bank.

Bank for International Settlements. (2000). *Clearing and Settlement Arrangements for Retail Payments in Selected Countries* Basel: Bank for International Settlement.

Bank for International Settlements. (2001). *Core Principles for Systemically Important Payment Systems* Basel: Bank for International Settlements.

Bank for International Settlements. (2003). *Policy issues for central banks in retail payments* Basel: Bank for International Settlements.

Banking Expert Group. (2004). *Financial Services Action Plan: Progress and Prospects* Brussels: European Commission.

Barros, P. P., Berglöf, E., Fulghieri, P., Gual, J., Mayer, C., & Vives, X. (2005). Integration of European banking: the way forward. In Centre of Economic Policy Research (CEPR) (Ed.), *Monitoring European Deregulation* (Vol. 3, pp. 13-103).

Barth, J. R., Caprio, G., & Levine, R. (2004). Bank regulation and supervision: what works best? *Journal of Financial Intermediation, 13*(2), 205-248

Barth, J. R., Caprio, G., & Levine, R. (2006). *Rethinking Bank Regulation: Till Angels Govern*. Cambridge: Cambridge University Press

Baumol, W. J. (1982). *Contestable Markets and the Theory of Industry Structure*. New York: Harcourt College Pub

Begg, I. (1996). Introduction: Regulation in the European Union. *Journal of European Public Policy, 3*(4), 525-535.

Beijnen, C., & Bolt, W. (2007). *Size matters: economies of scale in European payments processing*: Netherlands Central Bank, Research Department.

Beijnen, C., & Bolt, W. (2009). Size matters: Economies of scale in European payments processing. *Journal of Banking & Finance, 33*(2), 203-210.

Beitz, C. (1979). *Political Theory and International Relations* Princeton: Princeton University Press.

Benham, A., & Benham, L. (2004). *The Costs of Exchange: An Approach to Measuring Transaction Costs*.Unpublished manuscript, St. Louis.

Benink, H. A., & Schmidt, R. H. (2004). Europe's single market for financial services: views by the European Shadow Financial Regulatory Committee. *Journal of Financial Stability, 1*(2), 157-198.

Benston, G., & Kaufmann, G. (1996). The Appropriate Role of Bank Regulation. *Economic Journal*(106), 688-697.

Bernstein, M. H. (1955). *Regulating Business by Independent Commission*. Princeton: Princeton University Press.

BEUC. (2009a). Commission's consultation on possible end date(s) for SEPA migration - BEUC's Response, *BEUC, the European Consumers' Organisation* (pp. 1-8). Brussels.

BEUC. (2009b). Financial Services Retrieved 29 December 2009, from www.beuc.org/

Bieling, H.-J., & Deppe, F. (1996). Internationalisierung, Integration und politische Regulierung. In M. Jachtenfuchs & B. Kohler-Koch (Eds.), *Europäische Integration* (pp. 481-511). Opladen.

BIS. (2000). *Clearing and Settlement Arrangements for Retail Payments in Selected Countries*. Basel: BIS.

BIS. (2001). *Core Principles for Systemically Important Payment Systems* Basel: Bank for International Settlements.

BIS. (2003a). *Payment systems in the euro area*: Bank Of International Settlement.

BIS. (2003b). *Policy issues for central banks in retail payments* Basel: Bank for International Settlements.

Blum, J., & Hellwig, M. (1995). The macroeconomic implications of capital adequacy requirements for banks *European Economic Review, 39*(3-4), 739-749.

Blundell, J., & Robinson, C. (1999). Regulation without the state. *Occasional paper / Institute of Economic Affairs, 109*.

Bolt, W. (2006). *Payment Scale Economies and the Replacement of Cash and Stored Value Cards*: Netherlands Central Bank, Research Department.

Bonello, M. C., Furstenberg, G. M. v., Kemppainen, K., & Salo, S. (2006). *The Adoption of the Euro, Choice of Currency Regime, and Integration of Payments Systems*. Vienna: SUERF.

Bouwen, P. (2002). Corporate lobbying in the European Union: the logic of access. *Journal of European Public Policy, 9*(3), 365–390.

Bowles, S. (2008). Creating the Payment Service Directive for SEPA. In C. Skinner (Ed.), *The future of finance after SEPA* (pp. 65-67). London: John Wiley & Sons.

Bowles, S., Durlauf, S. N., & Hoff., K. (2006). Introduction. In S. Bowles (Ed.), *Poverty Traps* (pp. 1-14). Princeton, N.J.: Princeton University Press.

Brander, J. (2005). *Government Policy Toward Business*. Toronto, Ontario: Wiley.

Breyer, S. (1982). *Regulation and Its Reform*. Cambridge/ Massachussets.

Brinker, B. (1998). Strategische Herausforderungen im Investment-Banking: Integration von Wholesale und Retail Banking. Wiesbaden: European Business School.

Brits, H., & Winder, C. (2005). Payments are no free lunch. *De Nederlandsche Bank Occasional Studies, 3*(2), 122.

Buchenrieder, G. (2002). *Sequencing of institution building in the transition process of central and eastern Europe's financial systems*. Frankfurt am Main.

Bulmer, S. J. (1998). New institutionalism and the governance of the Single European Market. *Journal of European Public Policy, 5*(3), 365 - 386.

Calcagnini, G., Farabullini, F., & Hester, D. D. (2002). *Financial convergence in the European Monetary Union?* Paper presented at the Launching Workshop of the ECB-CFS Research Network on "Capital Markets and Financial Integration in Europe".

Calomiris, C. W., & Kahn, C. M. (1991). The Role of Demandable Debt in Structuring Optimal Banking Arrangements. *American Economic Review, 81*(3), 497-513.

Canalis, J. (1999). Scale Versus Specialization: Banking Strategies After the Euro. *European Management Journal, 17*(6), 567-575.

Cap Gemini, ABN Amro, & EFMA. (2008). *World Payments Report 2008*. Amsterdam.

Cap Gemini, EFMA, & ING. (2009). *World Retail Banking Report 2009*. Amsterdam.

Capgemini. (2007). *SEPA: potential benefits at stake - Researching the impact of SEPA on the payments market and its stakeholder*: Capgemini Consulting.

Capgemini, EFMA, & ING. (2008). *World Retail Banking Report 2008*. Amsterdam.

Caporaso, J. A., Cowles, M. G., & Risse, T. (1998). *Europeanization and Domestic Change: Introduction*. Paper presented at the Europeanization and Domestic Change.

Carlton, D. W., & Frankel, A. S. (1995). Antitrust and Payment Technologies. *Federal Reserve Bank of St. Louis Review*, 41-54.

CEPS. (1994). *European Payment Systems and EMU* (No. 11): Centre of European Policy Studies.

Cezanne, W., & Mayer, A. (1998). Neue Institutionenökonomik – Ein Überblick. *WISU, 11*, 1345-1353.

Charnes, A., Cooper, W., & Rhoades, E. (1978). Measuring the efficiency of decision making units. *European Journal of Operation Research, 2*, 429-444.

Coase, R. H. (1937). The Nature of the Firm. *Economica, 4*, 386-405.

Coase, R. H. (1960). The Problem of Social Cost. *Journal of Law and Economics, 140*, 229-231.

Coase, R. H. (1984). Transaction Costs, Institutions and Economic History. *Journal of Institutional Theoretical Economics, 140*, 7-17.

Cohen, B. H., & Crockett, A. D. (2001). Finanzmärkte uns Systemrisiko in Europa. In D. Hummel & R.-E. Breuer (Eds.), *Handbuch Europäischer Kapitalmarkt* (1st ed., pp. 33-51). Wiesbaden: Gabler.

Corbey, D. (1995). Dialectic Functionalism: Stagnation as a booster of European Integration. *International Organization, 49*(2), 253-284.

Cowen, T. (1998). *Using Cost-Benefit Analysis to Review Regulation*. Paper presented at the New Zealand Business Roundtable.

Cummings, R. G., & Taylor, L. O. (1999). Unbiased Value Estimates for Environmental Goods: A Cheap Talk Design for the Contingent Valuation Method *The American Economic Review, 89*(3), 649-665

DaRin, M., & Hellmann, T. (2002). Banks as Catalysts for Industrialization *Journal of Financial Intermediation 11*(4), 366-397.

Das, U. S., Quintyn, M., & Chenard, K. (2004). *Does Regulatory Governance Matter for Financial System Stability? An Empirical Analysis* (Working Paper): International Monetary Fund.

daSilva, L. C. (2006). *A framwork for assessing the benefits of financial regulation*. Oxford, Brussels: Oxera.

DeBondt, W. F. M., & Thaler, R. H. (1987). Further Evidence on Investor Overreaction and Stock Market Seasonality. *Journal of Finance, 42*(3), 557-581.

DeGrauwe, P., Rinaldi, L., & VanCayseele, P. (2006). *Issues of Efficiency in the Use of Cash and Cards*: University of Leuven Discussion Paper.

Dehousse, R. (1997). Regulation by networks in the European Community: the role of European agencies. *Journal of European Public Policy, 4*, 246-261.

Deloitte. (2006). *The Cost of Regulation Study*: Study commissioned by the Financial Services Authority and the Financial Services Practitioner Panel.

Demirgüc-Kunt, A., & Maksimovic, V. (1998). Law, Finance and Firm Growth. *Journal of Finance, 53*(6), 2107-2137.

Demsetz, H. (1968). Why Regulate Utilities? *Journal of Law and Economics, 11*(1), 55-65.

Demsetz, H. (1969). Information and Efficiency: Another Viewpoint. *Journal of Law & Economics, 12*(1), 1-22.

Dermine, J. (2002). *European Banking, Past, Present and Future*. Paper presented at the Second Central Banking Conference. from http://ssrn.com/paper=357500

Devereux, S. (2001). Sen's Entitlement Approach. *Oxford Development Studies, 29*(3), 245-263.

Diekmann, R. (2006). *EU retail banking: Drivers for the emergence of cross-border business*. Frankfurt: Deutsche Bank Research.

Directorate General Consumer Protection. (2008). *Preparing the Monitoring of the Impact of the Single Euro Payment Area (SEPA) on Consumers*. Brussels: European Commission.

Dixit, A. K. (1996). *The Making of Economic Policy. A Transaction-Cost Perspective*. Cambridge: MIT Press.

Djankov, S., Glaeser, E. L., Lopez de Silanes, F., La Porta, R., & Shleifer, A. (2003). The New Comparative Economics [Electronic Version] from http://ssrn.com/paper=392995

Dowd, K. (1996). The Case of Financial Laissez-Faire. *Economic Journal, 106*(436), 679-687.

Dubow, B., & Monteiro, N. B. (2006). Measuring Market Cleanliness. *SSRN eLibrary*.

Dür, A. d., & Bièvre, D. (2007). Inclusion without influence? NGOs in European Trade Policy. *Journal of Public Policy, 27*(1), 79-101.

Dyson, K., & Goetz, K. (Eds.). (2004). *Germany, Europe, and the Politics of Constraint*. New York: Oxford University Press.

EACT. (2008). Single Euro Payments Area: EACT favours setting an end date for SEPA Credit Transfer, *Press Release*: European Association of Corporate Treasurers (EACT).

Eberlein, B., & Grande, E. (2000). Regulation and infrastructure management. German regulatory regimes and the EU framework. *German Policy Studies/Politikfeldanalyse, 1*(1), 39-66.

Eberlein, B., & Grande, E. (2005). Beyond delegation: transnational regulatory regimes and the EU regulatory state. *Journal of European Public Policy, 12*(1), 89-112.

Economides, N. (1996). The Economics of Networks. *International Journal of Industrial Organisation, 14*(6), 673-499.

Eggertsson, T. (1990). *Economic Behavior and Institutions: Principles of Neoinstitutional Economics* Cambridge: Cambridge University Press.

Eichner, V. (2000). *Das Entscheidungssystem der Europäischen Union - Institutionelle Analyse und demokratietheoretische Bewertung*. Opladen: Leske + Buderich.

Eickhof, N. (1993). Zur Legitimation ordnungspolitischer Ausnahmeregelungen. In *ORDO - Jahrbuch für die Ordnung von Wirtschaft und Gesellschaft* (Vol. 44, pp. 202-222).

Eickhof, N. (1997). Staatliche Regulierung und kartellrechtliche Branchenfreistellungen. *Wirtschaftswissenschaftliches Studium, 26*, 562 – 567.

Erlei, M., Leschke, M., & Sauerland, D. (1999). *Neue Institutionenökonomik*. Stuttgart: Schäffer-Poeschel.

ESBG. (2009). *Retail Banking in Europe - The Way Forward*. Brussels: European Savings Banks Group (ESBG).

Euro Banking Association. (2009). EBA General Anual Meeting Report 2002. Retrieved 29 December 2009, 2009, from http://www.abe-eba.eu/

Eurofi. (2006). 26th Regime - Making the 26th regime, an attractive option. Pensions as a case study [Electronic Version]. *eurofi.net*, 1-8. Retrieved February 16, 2008 from http://www.eurofi.net/pdf/26th_Regime_en.pdf.

European Banking Federation. (2007). *Report on Integration of European Financial Services Markets*. Brussels: European Banking Federation.

European Central Bank. (1992). *Statute of the European System of Central Banks and of the European Central Bank*. Retrieved. from.

European Central Bank. (1999). *Improving cross-border retail payment services in the euro area - the Eurosystem's view*. Frankfurt: ECB.

European Central Bank. (2000). *Improving cross-border retail payments systems - Progress Report*. Frankfurt: ECB.

European Central Bank. (2001a). *Payment and securities settlement systems in the European Union*. Frankfurt: ECB.

European Central Bank. (2001b). *Towards an integrated infrastructure for credit transfers in Euro* (Report). Frankfurt: ECB.

European Central Bank. (2003a). *Developments in national supervisory structures*.

European Central Bank. (2003b). *Oversight Standards for Euro Retail Payment Systems*. Frankfurt: ECB.

European Central Bank. (2004a). *Auf dem Weg zu einem einheitlichen Euro Zahlungsverkehrsraum - Fortschrittsbericht*. Frankfurt: ECB.

European Central Bank. (2004b). *Towards a Single Euro Payments Areas - Third Progress Report*. Frankfurt: ECB.

European Central Bank. (2006a). *Payment and securities settlement systems in the European Union and in the acceding countries*. Frankfurt: ECB.

European Central Bank. (2006b). *The Single Euro Payments Area (SEPA) - An integrated retail payments market* (Brochure). Frankfurt: ECB.

European Central Bank. (2006c). *Towards a Single Euro Payment Area - Objectives and Deadlines (4th Progress Report)*. Frankfurt: ECB.

European Central Bank. (2007). *Financial Integration in Europe*. Frankfurt: ECB.

European Central Bank. (2009a). *EU Banks' Funding Structures and Policies*: ECB.

European Central Bank. (2009b). Glossary (Publication no. http://www.ecb.int /home/glossary/html/glossp.en.html). Retrieved 29 December 2009:

European Commission. (1985). *Completing the Internal Market - White Paper from the Commission to the European Council* Retrieved. from.

European Commission. (1988). *European economy: The economics of 1992* (No. 35). Brussels.

European Commission. (1990). *Making payments in the internal market*. Retrieved. from http://aei.pitt.edu/4685/.

Commission Communication of 11 May 1999 entitled "Implementing the framework for financial markets: action plan" COM/99/0232 C.F.R. (1999).

European Commission. (2001a). *European Governance - A White Paper* (No. 428). Brussels: European Commission.

European Commission. (2001b). Realising the European Union's potential: consolidating and extending the Lisbon strategy [Electronic Version]. Retrieved February 15, 2008 from http://eur-lex.europa.eu/LexUriServ/ LexUriServ.do?uri=CELEX:52001DC0079:EN:NOT.

European Commission. (2001c). *Study on the Verification of a Common and Coherent Application of Directive 97/5/EC on Cross-Border Credit Transfers in the 15 Member States*. London: European Commission.

European Commission. (2002). *A Possible Legal Framework for the Single Payments Area in the Internal Market*: Internal Market DG, Financial Institutions.

European Commission. (2003a). *Communication from the Commission to the Council and the European Parliament concerning a New Legal Framework for Payments in the Internal Market (Consultative Document)*. Retrieved. from http://www.europarl.europa.eu/meetdocs/committees/econ/20040315/com(2003)0718_en.pdf.

European Commission Recommendation of 6 May 2003 concerning the definition of micro, small and medium-sized enterprises, 1422 C.F.R. (2003b).

European Commission. (2003c). *A New Legal Framework for Payments in the Internal Market*. Retrieved. from http://ec.europa.eu/internal_market /payments/framework/index_en.htm.

European Commission. (2003d). *Public Opinion in Europe: Financial Services Report* (No. B). Brussels: EU.

European Commission. (2004a). *Financial Integration Monitor 2004*. Brussels: DG Internal Market.

European Commission. (2004b). *Public Opinion in Europe: Financial Services Report* (No. B). Brussels: EU.

European Commission. (2005a). *Annex to the Proposal for a Directive of the European Parliament and of the Council on Payment Services in the Internal Market, Impact Assessment*: Commission Staff Working Document.

European Commission. (2005b). *Communication from the Commission to the Council, the European Parlaiment, the European Economic and Social Committee and the Committee of the Region* (Report No. 2nd). Brussels: European Commission.

European Commission. (2005c). *Financial Integration Monitor 2005*. Brussels: DG Internal Market.

European Commission. (2005d). *FSAP Evaluation - Part I: Process and implementation*. Brussels: European Union.

European Commission. (2005e). *Green Paper on Financial Services Policy (2005 - 2010)*. Brussels: European Commission.

European Commission. (2005f). *Regulation 2560/2001 Study of Competition for Cross-Border Payment Services*. London.

European Commission. (2005g). *Study of the impact of regulation 2560/2001 on bank charges for national payments*. London.

European Commission. (2006a). *Financial Integration Monitor 2006*. Brussels: DG Internal Market.

European Commission. (2006b). *Interim Report - Current Accounts and Related Services*. Brussels: European Commission.

European Commission. (2007a). *European Financial Integration Report 2007 (EFIR),* . Brussels: DG Internal Market.

European Commission. (2007b). *Report on the retail banking sector inquiry*. Brussels: Europen Commission.

European Commission. (2008). *European Financial Integration Report 2008 (EFIR),* . Brussels: DG Internal Market.

European Commission. (2009a). Commission launches consultation on possible end-date for Single Euro Payments Area (SEPA) migration, *Press Release*: European Commission,.

European Commission. (2009b). *Feedback on the public consultation on possible end-date(s) for SEPA migration*. Brussels: Internal Market and Services DG.

European Community. (1957). *Consolidated Version of the Treaty Establishing the European Community*. Retrieved. from http://www.hrea.org/erc/ Library/hrdocs/eu/Amsterdam-treaty.pdf.

European Economic & Marketing Consultants. (2006). *The new German regulatory approach: incentive based regulation in energy markets* (No. 17/2006): Bundesnetzagentur.

European Payment Council. (2002, May 2002). *"Euroland: Our Single Payment Area!"* Paper presented at the EPC Workshop, Brussels.

European Payment Council. (2007). *Making SEPA a Reality*. Brussels: European Payments Council

Evans, D. S., & Schmalensee, R. (2005). *The Economics of Interchange Fees and Their Regulation*. Boston: MIT.

Federal Reserve Deposite Insurance Corporations. (1999). *Managing the crisis*. Washington: FDIC.

Fédération Bancaire Francaise. (2007). *Economic impacts of the SEPA project*: February 2007.

Franks, J. R., Schaefer, S. M., & Staunton, M. D. (1998). The direct and compliance costs of financial regulation *Journal of Banking & Finance, 21*(11-12), 1547-1572.

Fritsch, M., Wein, T., & Ewers, H.-J. (1999). *Marktversagen und Wirtschaftspolitik* (3rd ed.). München.

FSA. (2003). *The development of more effective product disclosure*. London: Financial Services Authority.

FSA, & Conquest Research. (2004). *Consumer Understanding of Financial Risk*. London: Financial Services Authority.

Furubotn, E. G., & Pejovich, S. (1972). Property Rights and Economic Theory. A Survey of Recent Literature. *Journal of Economic Literature, 10*(4), 1137-1162.

Furubotn, E. G., & Pejovich, S. (1974). Introduction: The New Property Rights. Literature. In E. G. Furubotn & S. Pejovich (Eds.), *The Economics of Property Rights* (pp. 1-9). Cambridge, MA: Ballinger Publishing Co.

Galati, G., & Tsatsaronis, K. (2001). The Impact of the Euro on Europe's Financial Markets. *BIS Working Paper, 10*.

Ganguly, B., & Milne, A. (2002). *Do we need public policy intervention in UK retail payment systems and if so how?* , City University Business School, London.

Geiger, H., & Klein, F. (2004). Payment systems and regulation. *Journal of Financial Transformation, 12*, 31-38.

Genschel, P. (1998). Markt und Staat in Europa. *Politische Vierteljahresschrift, 39*, 55-79.

Glavan, B. (2008). Coordination Economics, Poverty Traps, and the Market Process: A New Case for Industrial Policy? *Independent Review, 13*(2), 225-243.

Goldberg, V. P. (1976). Regulation and Administered Contracts. *Bell Journal of Economics, 7*(2), 426-448.

Goodhart, C. A. E., Hartmann, P., Llewellyn, D., & Rojas-Suarez, L. (1998). *Financial Regulation: Why, How and Where Now?* New York: Routledge.

Gortsos, C. (2007). *Integration of European Financial Services Markets*. Athens: Hellenic Bank Association.

Grande, E. (1993a). Entlastung des Staates durch Liberalisierung und Privatisierung? Zum Funktionswandel des Staates im Telekommunikationssektor. In R. Voigt (Ed.), *Abschied vom Staat - Rückkehr zum Staat?* (pp. 371-392). Baden-Baden.

Grande, E. (1994a). *Vom Nationalstaat zur europäischen Politikverflechtung. Expansion und Transformation moderner Staatlichkeit - untersucht am Beispiel der Forschungs- und Technologiepolitik*. Universität Konstanz.

Grande, E. (1997c). Vom produzierenden zum regulierenden Staat: Möglichkeiten und Grenzen von Regulierung bei Privatisierung. In K. König & A. Benz (Eds.), *Privatisierung und staatliche Regulierung. Bahn, Post und Telekommunikation, Rundfunk* (pp. 576-591). Baden-Baden.

Grande, E. (2000). Multi-Level Governance: Institutionelle Besonderheiten und Funktionbedingungen des Europäischen Mehrebenensystems. In E. Grande & M. Jachtenfuchs (Eds.), *Wie problemlösungsfähig ist die EU? Regieren im europä-*

ischen Mehrebenensystem (Vol. 4, pp. 11-33). Baden-Baden: Nomos Verlagsgesellschaft.

Grande, E. (2005, September 15-16, 2005). *De-Regulation and Re-Regulation of Public Utilities: The Regulatory State in the European System of Multi-Level Governance.* Paper presented at the Transformation of the Modern State: From State Provision to State-Regulated Markets in European Old-Age Security, Berlin.

Grochla, E., & Wittmann, W. (Eds.). (1976). *Enzyclopädie der Betriebswirtschaft* (4 ed. Vol. 1). Stuttgart: Poeschel

Gross, N., Bernstein, M., & Giacquinta, J. B. (1971). *Implementing Organizational Innovations: A Sociological Analysis of Planned Educational Change* New York: Basic Books.

Guibourg, G., & Segendorf, B. (2004). *Do Prices Reflect Costs? A study of the price- and cost structure of retail payment services in the Swedish banking sector 2002*: Sveriges Riksbank (Central Bank of Sweden) Working Paper Series.

Haas, E. B. (1958). *The Uniting of Europe*. Stanford, CA: Stanford University Press.

Haas, E. B. (1976). Turbulent Fields and the Theory of Regional Integration. *International Organization, 30*(2), 173-211.

Hail, L., & Leuz, C. (2005). International Differences in the Cost of Equity Capital: Do Legal Institutions and Securities Regulation Matter? *SSRN eLibrary*.

Harrison, G. W., & Rutström, E. E. (2008). Experimental Evidence on the Existence of Hypothetical Bias in Value Elicitation Methods. In C. R. Plott & V. L. Smith (Eds.), *Handbook of Experimental Economics Results* (pp. 751-767): Elsevier.

Hausman, J. A., & Leonard, G. K. (2002). The Competitive Effects of a New Product Introduction: A Case Study. *Journal of Industrial Economics, 50*, 237-263.

Hayek, F. A. (1972). Die Theorie komplexer Phänomene. In Ders. (Ed.), *Die Anmaßung von Wissen - Neue Freiburger Studien* (pp. 281-306). Tübingen.

Heinemann, F., Schröder, M., Schüler, M., Stirböck, C., & Westerheide, P. (2003). *Towards a Single European Market in Asset Management*. Mannheim: Zentrum für Europäische Wirtschaftsforschung.

Héritier, A. (1996). The accomodation of diversity in European policy-making and its outcomes: regulatory policy as a patchwork. *Journal of European Public Policy, 3*, 146-167.

Howell, K. E. (2004a). *Europeanization, European Integration and Financial Services: Developing Theoretical Frameworks and Synthesising Methodological Approaches*. New York: Palgrave MacMillan.

Howell, K. E. (2004b). Uploading, downloading and European integration: Assessing the Europeanization of UK financial services regulation. *Journal of International Banking Regulation, 6*(1), 53-68.

Hummel, D. (1999). Neoinstitutionalismus in der Finanzierungs- und Banktheorie - Entwicklungsaspekte und Anwendungsfehler der New Institutional Economics.

In T. Edeling, W. Jann & D. Wagner (Eds.), *Institutionenökonomie und Neuer Institutionalismus* (1st ed.). Opladen: Leske + Budrich Verlag.

Humphrey, D., Moshe, K., & Vale, B. (2001). Realizing the Gains from Electronic Payments:Costs, Pricing, and Payment Choice. *Journal of Money, Credit, and Banking, 33*(2), 216-234.

Humphrey, D. B., Keppler, R. H., & Montes-Negret, F. (1997). *Cost recovery and pricing of payment services*. Washington D.C.: Policy Research Working Paper Series from the World Bank.

I-flex solutions/Financial Insights. (2006). *Big Revenue Opportunities Seen for Early SEPA Adopters*: White Paper October 2006.

IIMG. (2004). *Third Report monitoring the Lamfalussy Process*. Brussels: Inter-institutional Monitoring Group.

Inter-Institutional Monitoring Group. (2003). *First Interim Report: Monitoring the New Process for Regulating Securities Markets in Europe (The Lamfalussy Process)*. Brussels.

Jackson, H. E. (1999). Regulation in a Multi-Sectored Financial Services Industry: An Exploratory Essay. *Harvard Law School Discussion Paper, 258*, 1-117.

Jayaratne, J., & Strahan, P. E. (1996). The Finance-Growth Nexus: Evidence from Bank Branch Deregulation. *The Quarterly Journal of Economics, 111*(3), 639-670.

Jensen, M. C., & Meckling, W. H. (1976). Theory of the Firm: Managerial Behavior, Agency Costs and Ownership Structure. *The Journal Of Financial Economics, 3*(4), 305-360.

Kahn, A. (1971). *The Economics of Regulation: Principles and Institutions*. New York.

Karasu, I., & Goralczyk, A. (2003). *Towards a Single Euro Payments Area*. Frankfurt: Deutsche Bank AG,.

Katz, M. L., & Shapiro, C. (1985). Network Externalities, Competition, and Compatibility. *American Economic Review, 75*(3), 424-440.

Katz, M. L., & Shapiro, C. (1994). Systems Competition and Network Effects *The Journal of Economic Perspectives, 8*(2), 93-115.

Kay, J., & Vickers, J. (1988). Regulatory Reform in Britain. *Economic Policy, 8*, 285-351

Kemppainen, K. (2004a). *Competition and regulation in European retail payment systems*. Helsinki: Bank of Finland.

Kemppainen, K. (2004b, September 2, 2004). *Regulating Cross-border Retail Payment Systems – A Network Industry Problem.* Paper presented at the The Structure of Financial Regulation, Helsinki.

Kemppainen, K. (2005). *Assessing Effects of Price Regulation in Retail Payment Systems*: SSRN.

Keohane, R. O., & Hoffman, S. (1990). Community Politics and Institutional Change. In W. Wallace (Ed.), *The Dynamics of European Integration*. London: The Royal Institute of International Affairs / Pinter.

Kern, S. (2003). *Reform of EU regulatory and supervisory structures: progress report*. Frankfurt: Deutsche Bank AG.

Khemani, R. S., & Shapiro, D. M. (Eds.). (1993) Glossary of Industrial Organisation Economics and Competition Law. OECD.

Kleimeier, S., & Sander, H. (2003). *Towards a single European Banking Market? New Evidence from Euroland on the Role of the Euro*. Melbourne: Contemporary Europe Research Centre.

Kleimeier, S., & Sander, H. (2007). *Integrating Europe's Retail Banking Market: Where Do We Stand?* Brussels.

Knorr, A. (1999). Staatliche Bankenaufsicht – eine effiziente Institution? *ORDO, 50*, 345-369.

Kohler-Koch, B. (1996). Catching up with change: The transformation of governance in the European Union. *Journal of European Public Policy, 3*(3), 359 - 380.

König, K., & Benz, A. (1997b). Zusammenhänge von Privatisierung und Regulierung. In K. König & A. Benz (Eds.), *Privatisierung und staatliche Regulierung. Bahn, Post und Telekommunikation, Rundfunk* (pp. 13-79). Baden-Baden.

Krahnen, J. P. (1993). Finanzwirtschaftslehre zwischen Markt und Institution: Ein Essay (The Changing Role of Markets and Institutions in the Theory of Finance: An Essay). *Die Betriebswirtschaft, 53*(6), 793-805

Lacker, J. M., & Weinberg, J. A. (2002). Payment economics: studying the mechanics of exchange. *Journal of Monetary Economics, 50*(2), 381-387.

Lannoo, K. (2008). *Concrete Steps towards More Integrated Financial Oversight: The EU's Policy Response to the Crisis*. Brussels: Centre of European Policy Studies.

LaPorta, R., Lopez-de-Silane, F., & Shleifer, A. (2003). What Works in Securities Law? *National Bureau of Economic Research Working Paper Series, No. 9882*.

Levine, R. (1997). Financial Development and Economic Growth: Views and Agenda *Journal of Economic Literature, 35*(2), 688-726.

Lindberg, L. N. (1963). *The Political Dynamics of European Integration*. Stanford: Stanford University Press.

Llewellen, D. (1995). *Costs and benefits of regulation in retail investment services*. Paper presented at the AUTIF Annual Conference.

London Economics. (2002). *Quantification of the Macro-Economic Impact of Integration of EU Financial Markets*. London: Final Report to The European Commission - Directorate-General for the Internal Market.

Lusk, J. L. (2003). Effects of Cheap Talk on Consumer Willingness-to-Pay for Golden Rice *American Journal of Agricultural Economics, 85*(4), 840-856.

Mai, H. (2005). *Payments in Europe: Getting it right* (Internal Report). Frankfurt: Deutsche Bank Research.

Mai, H. (2009). *SEPA: Changing times for payments*. Frankfurt: Deutsche Bank AG.

Majone, G. (1990). *Deregulation or Re-Regulation? Regulatory Reform in Europe and the United States*. London.

Majone, G. (1996). *Regulating Europe (European Public Policy)*. London.

Majone, G. (1997b). The Agency Model: The Growth of Regulation and Regulatory Institutions in the European Union. *Revue de l'Institut européen d'administration publique, 3*, 9-14.

Majone, G. (2005). *Dilemmas of European Integration: The Ambiguities and Pitfalls of Integration by Stealth*. Oxford: Oxford University Press.

Majone, G. (Ed.). (1994b). *The Rise of the Regulatory State in Europe*. Ilford.

Matsuyama, K. (1997). Economic Development as Coordination Problems. In M. Aoki, H. Kim & M. Okuno-Fujiwara (Eds.), *The Role of Government in East Asian Development: A Comparative Institutional Analysis* (pp. 134-162). New York: Oxford University Press.

McAndrews, J. (1997). *Network Issues and Payment Systems*: Federal Reserve Bank of Philadelphia.

McAndrews, J., & Rob, R. (1996). Shared ownership and pricing in a network switch. *International Journal of Industrial Organization, 14*, 727-745.

McAndrews, J., & Strahan, P. E. (2002). Deregulation, Correspondent Banking, and the Role of the Federal Reserve. *Journal of Financial Intermediation, 11*(3), 320-343.

McFadden, D. (1998). Rationality for Economics. *Journal of Risk and Uncertainty, 19*, 73-105.

McGowan, F., & Wallace, H. (1996). Towards a European Regulatory State. *Journal of European Public Policy, 3*, 560-576.

McKinsey & Company. (2003). Initiative Finanzstandort Deutschland - Arbeitsgruppe Gestaltung Euro-Zahlungsverkehrsraum - Dokumentation. Unpublished Presentation.

McKinsey & Company. (2006). *Payment Services in The Netherlands: an analysis of revenues and costs for banks*.

Mendizabal, H. R., & Perez-Quiros, G. (2001). *The daily market for funds in Europe: has something changed with the EMU?* Frankfurt: European Central Bank.

Merton, R. C. (1993). Operations and Regulation in Financial Intermediation, A Functional Perspective. In P. Englund (Ed.), *Operation and Regulation of Financial Markets*. Stockholm: The Economic Council.

Merton, R. C., & Bodie, Z. (1993). Deposit Insurance Reform, A Functional Approach. In A. Meltzer & C. Plosser (Eds.), *Carnegie-Rochester Conference Series on Public Policy* (Vol. 38).

Mishan, E. J. (1969). *Welfare Economics: An Assessment* Amsterdam, London: North Holland Publishing Company.

Mitrany, D. (1970). The Functional Approach to World Organizations. In C. A. Cosgrave & K. Twitchett (Eds.), *New International Actors: The United Nations and the EEC* (pp. 65-75). London: Macmillan.

Mitrany, D. (1975a). *The Functional Theory of Politics*. London: St. Martin's Press.

Mitrany, D. (1975b). Functionalism: Theory and Practice in International Relations. In P. Groom & A. Taylor (Eds.), *Functionalism*. London: University of London Press.

Mitrany, D. (1975c). A Political Theory for a New Society. In P. Groom & A. Taylor (Eds.), *Functionalism*. London: University of London Press.

Monnet, J. (1943). Inauguration Speech at the French National Liberation Committee Algier.

Moravcsik, A. (1993). Preferences and Power in the European Community: a liberal Intergovernmentalist Approach. *Journal of Common Market Studies, 31*, 473-524.

Moravcsik, A. (1997). Negotiating the Single European Act. In R. O. Keohane & S. Hoffman (Eds.), *The New European Community: Decision making and Institutional Change*. USA: Westview Publishers.

Moravcsik, A. (1998). *The Choice of Europe: Social Purpose and State Power from Messina to Maastricht* USA: Cornell University Press.

Mosca, M. (2006). *On the Origins of the Concept of Natural Monopoly*: SSRN.

Motta, M. (2004). *Competition Policy. Theory and Practice.* Cambridge: Cambridge University Press.

Müller, W. C., & Wright, V. (1994). *The State in Western Europe: Retreat or Redefinition*. Ilford: Frank Cass.

Murphy, K. M., Shleifer, A., & Vishny, R. W. (1989). Industrialization and the Big Push. *Journal of Political Economy, 97*(5), 1003-1026.

Noll, R. (Ed.). (1985). *Government Regulatory Behaviour. A Multidisciplinary Survey and Synthesis*. Berkeley.

Noll, R. (Ed.). (1989). *Economic Perspectives on the Politics of Regulation* (Vol. 2). Amsterdam.

North, D. C. (1990). *Institutions, Institutional Change, and Economic Performance* (2002 ed.). Cambridge.

Noyer, C. (2006, June 2006). *Recent developments and policy challenges affecting large-value and retail payment systems in Europe*. Paper presented at the High-Level International Conference on Central Banks in the 21st Century, Madrid.

OECD. (1997). Co-operative Approaches to Regulation *Public Management Occasional Papers*.

OECD. (2006). *Competition and Regulation in Retail Banking*: OECD.

Ogus, A. (2004). W(h)ither the economic theory of regulation? What economic theory of regulation? In J. Jordana & D. Levi-Faur (Eds.), *The Politics of Regulation* (pp. 31-44). Cheltenham (UK), Northampton (US): Edward Elgar.

OPTEM. (2003). *Qualitative study among cross-border buyers of financial services in the European Union*.

Osterberg, W. P., & Thomson, J. B. (1998). Network externalities: the catch-22 of retail payments innovations. *Economic Commentary*.

Ostrom, E. (1990). *Governing the Commons - The evolution of institutions for collective action*. Cambridge: Cambridge University Press.

Osugi, K. (1990). Japan's experience of financial deregulation since 1984 in an international perspective. *BIS Economic Papers*.

Oxera. (2003). *Assessing Profitability in Competition Policy Analysis* Office of Fair Trading Economic Research Papers.

Oxera. (2006). *A framwork for assessing the benefits of financial regulation*. Oxford, Brussels: Oxera.

Panetta, F., Faeh, T., Grande, G., Ho, C., King, M., Levy, A., et al. (2009). An assessment of financial sector rescue programmes. *BIS Papers, 48*, 1-77.

Paul, S. (2000). "Qualitative" Bankenaufsicht -"Königsweg" der Regulierung? *Perspektiven der Wirtschaftspolitik, 1*(3), 281-299.

Pedersen, T. (1992). Political Change in the European Community: The Single European Act as a Case of System Transformation. *Co-operation and Conflict 27*(1), 7-44.

Peek, J., & Rosengreen, E. S. (1997). How well capitalized are well-capitalized banks? *New England Economic Review*, 41-50.

Pejovich, S. (1974). Economic Development and Property Rights. In D. Collier (Ed.), *Accelerated Development in Southern Africa*: Macmillan Interactive Publishing

Peltzman, S. (1976). Toward a More General Theory of Regulation. *Journal of Law and Economics, 19*(2), 211-240.

Peltzman, S. (1989). Comments on "The Control and Performance of State-Owned Enterprises". In P. McAvoy, W. T. Stanbury, G. Yarrow & R. Zeckhauser (Eds.), *Privatization and State-Owned Enterprises*. Boston: Kluwer Academic Publishers.

Pigou, A. C. (1938). *The Economics of Welfare* (4 ed.). London: MacMillan & Co.

Pindyck, R. S. (2007). Governance, Issuance Restrictions, and the Competition in Payment Card Networks. In J. Kwoka & L. White (Eds.), *The Antitrust Revolution* (Vol. 5, pp. 1-21). Oxford: Oxford Press.

Ploey, W. D., & Denecker, O. (2007). Payments in Europe: a Tower of Babel with Construction Problems. *gtnews.com on SEPA* Retrieved 03 July 2007, 2007, from http://www.gtnews.com/article/6816.cfm

Ploey, W. D., Denecker, O., & Kehrmann, T. (2005). *European Payment Profit Pool Analysis: Casting Light in Murkey Water*. New York.

Polski, M. (2000, Sept 2000). *Measuring Transaction Costs and Institutional Change in the U.S. Commercial Banking Industry*. Paper presented at the International Society for New Institutional Economics, Tübingen.

PSE Consulting. (2006). *SEPA - One year on*: PSE Consulting.

Putnam, R. (1988). Diplomacy and Domestic Policies: The Logic of Two-level Games. *International Organization, 42*(3), 427-460.

Rajan, R. G., & Zingales, L. (1995). What Do We Know About Capital Structure? Some Evidence from International Data. *Journal of Finance, 50*, 1421-1460.

Reinhart, C. M., & Rogoff, K. S. (2008). Is the 2007 US Sub-Prime Financial Crisis So Different? An International Historical Comparison. *American Economic Review, 98*(2), 339-344.

Richardson, J. (Ed.). (1996). *European Union. Power and Policy Making*. London: Routledge.

Richter, R. (1991). Bankenregulierung aus Sicht der Neuen Institutionenökonomik. In J. Siebke (Ed.), *Finanzintermediation, Bankenregulierung und Finanzmarktintegration* (Vol. 204, pp. 323-355). Berlin: Schriften des Vereins für Socialpolitik.

Richter, R. (1996). Neue Institutionenökonomik, Ideen und Möglichkeiten. *Zeitschrift für Wirtschafts-und Sozialwissenschaften, 6*, 323-355.

Richter, R., & Furubotn, E. G. (1996). *Neue Institutionenökonomik: eine Einführung und kritische Würdigung*. Tübingen: Mohr.

Rodriguez-Clare, A. (2005). Coordination Failures, Clusters, and Microeconomic Interventions. *Inter-American Development Bank Working Paper, 544*.

Rodrik, D. (1996). Coordination failures and government policy: A model with applications to East Asia and Eastern Europe. *Journal of International Economics, 40*(1-2), 1-22.

Rodrik, D. (2004). *Industrial Policy for the Twenty-First Century (Faculty Research Working Papers Series)*. Cambridge, Mass.: Harvard University.

Rosenstein-Rodan, P. (1943). Problems of Industrialization of Eastern and South-Eastern Europe. *Economic Journal, 53*, 202-211.

Salisbury, R. H. (1984). Interest representation: the dominance of institutions. *American Political Science Review, 78*(1), 65-76.

Samuelson, P. A., & Nordhaus, W. D. (1987). *Volkwirtschaftlehre 2 - Grundlagen der Makro- und Mikroökonomik* (J. Frenzel, Trans. 8 ed. Vol. 2). Köln: Bund-Verlag.

Sander, T. (2004). *Global Collective Action.* Retrieved January 5, 2010, from http://common.books24x7.com/book/id_15482/book.asp.

Sandholtz, W. (1993). Choosing Union: Monetary Politics and Maastricht. *International Organization, 47*, 1-39.

Santos, J. A. C. (2001). Bank Capital Regulation in Contemporary Banking Theory: A Review of the Literature. *Financial Markets, Institutions & Instruments, 10*(2), 41-84.

Schaefer, G. (2008). An Economic Analysis of the Single Euro Payments Area (SEPA). *FIW – Working Paper, 11.*

Schaefer, S. (2009). *EU retail banking: Measuring integration* Frankfurt: Deutsche Bank Research.

Scharpf, F. W. (1996). Politische Optionen im vollendeten Binnenmarkt. In M. Jachtenfuchs & B. Kohler-Koch (Eds.), *Europäische Integration* (pp. 109-140). Opladen.

Schich, S. (2009). Expanded Guarantees for Banks: Benefits,Costs and Exit Issues. *OECD Journal: Financial Market Trends, 2009*(2), 1-37.

Schierenbeck, H. (2006). Bankbetriebslehre. In R. Köhler, H.-U. Küpper & A. Pfingsten (Eds.), *Handwörterbuch der Betriebswirtschaft* (6. ed., pp. 240-258). Stuttgart.

Schmidt, S. K. (1997). *Die wettbewerbsrechtliche Handlungsfähigkeit der Europäischen Kommission in staatsnahen Sektoren.* Universität Hamburg, Hamburg.

Schmiedel, H. (2007). The economic impact of the Single Euro Payments Area. *European Central Bank Occasional Paper Series, 71*, 3-23.

Schmitter, P. C. (1971). A Revised Theory of Regional Integration. In L. N. Lindberg & S. A. Scheingold (Eds.), *Regional Integration: Theory and Research* (pp. 232-264). Cambridge, MA: Harvard University Press.

Schmitter, P. C., & Streeck, W. (1999). The organization of business interests: studying the associative action of business in advanced industrial societies. *Max-Planck-Institut Für Gesellschaftsforschung Discussion Paper, 99*(1).

Schoenmaker, D. (2005). Central banks and financial authorities in Europe: What prospects? In D. Masciandaro (Ed.), *Handbook of Central Banking and Financial Authorities in Europe - New Architectures in the Supervision of Financial Markets* (pp. 398-457). Cheltenham: Edward Elgar Publishing.

Schuppert, G. F. (1997). Vom produzierenden zum gewährleistenden Staat: Privatisierung als Veränderung staatlicher Handlungsformen. In K. König & A. Benz (Eds.), *Privatisierung und staatliche Regulierung. Bahn, Post und Telekommunikation, Rundfunk* (pp. 539-575). Baden-Baden.

Selznick, P. (Ed.). (1985). *Focusing Organizational Research on Regulation*. Berkeley.

Sen, A. (1984). *Resources, Values and Development*. Oxford, Basil: Blackwell.

Shapiro, C. (2000). Competition Policy in the Information Economy. In E. Hope (Ed.), *Competition Policy Analysis*: Routledge Studies in the Modern World Economy.

Shapiro, C., & Varian, H. R. (1999). *Information Rules: A Strategic Guide to the Network Economy*. Retrieved 24. February 2007, from http://www.books24x7.com/book/id_2411/toc.asp?bookid=2411.

Shepsle, K. A., & Weingast, B. R. (1987). The Institutional Foundations of Committee Power. *American Political Science Review, 81*(1), 85-104.

Shirreff, D. (2007). *European retail banking: Will there ever be a single market?* Brussels: Centre for European Reform.

Shleifer, A. (2005). *Understanding Regulation*: SSRN.

Shleifer, A., & Vishny, R. W. (1998). *The Grabbing Hand: Government Pathologies and Their Cures* Cambridge: Harvard University Press.

Shy, O. (2001). *The Economics of Network Industries*. (Cambridge University Press ed.). Cambridge: Cambridge University Press.

Skinner, C. (2008). An Introduction to SEPA. In C. Skinner (Ed.), *The future of finance after SEPA*. London: John Wiley & Sons.

Speyer, B. (2005). *Post–FSAP agenda: Window of opportunity to complete financial market integration* (No. 24). Frankfurt a.M.: Deutsche Bank AG.

Steden, P. (2002). *Marktorientierte Bankenregulierung: eine ökonomische Analyse unter besonderer Berücksichtigung der Einlagensicherheit* (Vol. 2). Potsdam: Verlag Wissenschaft und Praxis.

Stern, C. W., & Deimler, M. S. (2006). Part Two - The Development of Business Strategy. In C. W. Stern & M. S. Deimler (Eds.), *The Boston Consulting Group on Strategy*: John Wiley & Sons.

Stewart, J. D. (1958). *British Pressure Groups: Their role in relation to the House of Commons*. Oxford: Clarendon Press.

Stigler, G. J. (1971). The Theory of Economic Regulation. *Journal of Economics and Management Science, 2*, 1-21.

Stiglitz, J. (1988). *Economics of the Public Sector* (3 ed.). New York: W W Norton & Co.

Swartz, D., Hahn, R., & Layne-Farrar, A. (2004). The economics of a cashless society: An analysis of the costs and benefits of payment instruments. *AEI Brookings Joint Center for Regulatory Studies*, 4-24.

Sydbank. (2008). *Spain - Country Background.*

Sydow, J. (1999). Quo Vadis Transaktionskostentheorie? - Wege, Irrwege, Auswege. In T. Edeling, W. Jann & D. Wagner (Eds.), *Institutionenökonomie und Neuer Institutionalismus* (1st ed.). Opladen: Leske + Budrich Verlag.

Tarkka, J. (1995). *Approaches to Deposit Pricing: a Study in the Determination of Deposits Interest and Bank Service Charges* (Vol. E:2): Bank of Finland Studies.

The Economist. (2001, January 20). Sweeter Basle. *The Economist,* p. 16.

Regulation (EC) No 77/780/EEC of the European Parliament and the Council of 12 December 1977 on on the coordination of the laws, regulations and administrative provisions relating to the taking up and pursuit of the business of credit institutions, 77/780/EEC C.F.R. § L344 (1997).

Directive 2000/12/EC of the European Parliament of 20 March 2000 relating to the taking up and pursuit of the business of credit institutions, L 126/1 C.F.R. (2000).

Regulation (EC) No 2560/2001 of the European Parliament and of the Council of 19 December 2001 on cross-border payments in euro L 344 C.F.R. (2003).

Tower Group. (2005). *The European Payments Market: Working to Make Fragmentation Look like Unity*: press release dated 23 May 2005.

Tranholme-Mikkelson, J. (1991). Neo-functionalism Obstinate v Obsolete. *Millennium: Journal of International Studies, 20*, 1-22.

Tumpel-Gugerell, G. (2005a). Regulation, Competition and Integration in EU banking: What Drives Performance? - Revisiting Freiburg *Speech by Gertrude Tumpel-Gugerell, Member of the Executive Board of the ECB Albert-Ludwigs University of Freiburg, Faculty of Economics and Behavioural Sciences, Opening of the Integrated Master Programmes of the academic year 2005/2006*: European Central Bank.

Tumpel-Gugerell, G. (2005b). SEPA: making the dream become a reality, *Speech by Gertrude Tumpel-Gugerell, Member of the Executive Board of the ECB First EU/US Retail Banking Forum in Brussels*: European Central Bank.

Unknown Author. (1996, February 17). State and Market. *The Economist,* p. 66.

Vesala, J. (2000). *Technological Transformation and Retail Banking Competition: Implications and Measurement.*

Viner, N., Creyghton, A., Rutstein, C., & Storz, N. (2006). *Navigating to Win: Global Payments 2006* (Unpublished Report). Boston: Boston Consulting Group.

Viner, N., Rutsstein, C., Storz, N., & Sarma, S. (2004). *Preparing for the Endgame.* Boston: Boston Consulting Group.

Vogel, S. K. (1996). *Freer Markets, More Rules: Regulatory Reform in Advanced Industrial Countries.* Ithaca: Cornell University Press.

Walkner, C., & Raes, J. P. (2005). Integration and consolidation in EU banking - An unfinished business. *European Economy, 226*, 1-48.

Wallis, J. J., & North., D. C. (1986). Measuring the transaction sector in the American economy, 1870-1970. In S. L. Engerman & R. E. Gallman (Eds.), *In Long-Term Factors in American Economic Growth*. Chicago: University of Chicago Press.

Walter, N., & Speyer, B. (2005). Zwischen Governance und Polymorphie. *WeltTrends, 46*(13), 12-25.

Webb, C. (1983). Theoretical perspectives and problems in Policy Making. In H. Wallace, W. Wallace & C. Wallace (Eds.), *The European Community*. London: John Wiley & Son.

Weinberg, J. A. (1996). *Network Externalities and Public Goods in Payment Systems* (Research Paper). Richmond: Federal Reserve Bank of Richmond.

Weingast, B. R. (1984). The congressional-bureaucratic system: a principal agent perspective (with applications to the SEC). *Public Choice, 44*(1), 147-191.

Weingast, B. R. (1995). The Economic Role of Political Institutions: Market Preserving Federalism and Economic Development. *Journal of Law, Economics, and Organization 11*(4), 1-31.

Williamson, O. E. (1975). *Markets and Hierarchies*. New York: Free Press.

Williamson, O. E. (1985). *The economic institutions of capitalism: Firms, markets, relational contracting*. New York, London: Free Press

Williamson, O. E. (1996). *The Mechanisms of Governance*. Cambridge: Oxford University Press.

Wilson, J. Q. (1980). The Politics of Regulation. In J. Q. Wilson (Ed.), *The Politics of Regulation* (pp. 357-394). New York.

Wolz, A., Blass, G., Namerova, I., & Buchta, S. (1998). *Agricultural Transformation in Slovakia: The Change of Institutions and Organisations*. Saarbrücken: Verlag für Entwicklungspolitik.

World Savings Bank Institute, & European Savings Bank Group. (2006). *A Comparative Analysis of the US and EU Retail Banking Markets*. Brussels: WSBI/ESBG.

Yin, R. K. (2002). *Case Study Research - Design and Methods* (3 ed. Vol. 5). Thousand Oaks, London, New Delhi: Sage Publications.

Yu, H.-C., Hsi, K.-H., & Kuo, P.-J. (2002). Electronic payment systems: an analysis and comparison of types. *Technology in Society 24*(3), 331-347.

Zimmer, K. (1993). *Bankenregulierung: Zur Begründung und Ausgestaltung der Einlagensicherung: Eine ordnungstheoretische Analyse auf der Grundlage der Modernen Institutionenökonomie* Baden-Baden: Nomos.

Corporate Finance and Governance

Herausgegeben von Dirk Schiereck

Band 1 Sebastian Michael Gläsner: Return Patterns of German Open-End Real Estate Funds. An Empirical Explanation of Smooth Fund Returns. 2010.

Band 2 Patrick Ams: Directors' Dealings and Insider Trading in Germany. An Empirical Analysis. 2010.

Band 3 Joachim Vogt: Value Creation within the Construction Industry. A Study of Strategic Takeovers. 2011.

Band 4 Fabian Braemisch: Underpricing, Long-Run Performance, and Valuation of Initial Public Offerings. 2011.

Band 5 Matthäus Markus Sielecki: Creating and Governing an Integrated Market for Retail Banking Services in Europe. A Conceptual-Empirical Study of the Role of Regulation in Promoting a Single Euro Payments Area. 2011.

www.peterlang.de

www.ingramcontent.com/pod-product-compliance
Ingram Content Group UK Ltd.
Pitfield, Milton Keynes, MK11 3LW, UK
UKHW020834290926
15470UKWH00004B/1339

9 783631 608340